The
CAPTIVE
WHITE WOMAN
of
GIPPS LAND

The
CAPTIVE
WHITE WOMAN
of
GIPPS LAND

In Pursuit of the Legend

Julie E. Carr

MELBOURNE UNIVERSITY PRESS

MELBOURNE UNIVERSITY PRESS
PO Box 278, Carlton South, Victoria 3053, Australia
info@mup.unimelb.edu.au
www.mup.com.au

First published 2001

Designed by Pages in Action
Typeset by Syarikat Seng Teik Sdn. Bhd., Malaysia in Adobe Garamond 11 point
Printed in Australia by the Australian Print Group

National Library of Australia Cataloguing-in-Publication entry
Carr, Julie, 1948– .
    The captive white woman of Gipps Land: in pursuit of the legend.
    Bibliography.
    Includes index.
    ISBN 0 522 84930 X.

    1. Legends—Victoria. 2. Rumor—Victoria—History—19th century.
    3. Gippsland (Vic.)—History—19th century. 4. Victoria—Race
    relations—History—19th century. I. Title.
994.502

The publication of this book was made possible with a generous subsidy from the La Trobe
University Publications Committee.

For my sisters—
Paula and Noela

Contents

Illustrations

Maps

Preface

The William Cuthill manuscript, held in the La Trobe Collection at the State Library of Victoria, has typescript copies of most of the primary source material relating to the White Woman legend. This manuscript material includes newspaper reports, official correspondence, literary and historical accounts up until the mid-1970s and represents a substantial archive for researchers.[1] Extensive material not included in the Cuthill collection has also been uncovered in the course of researching this book.

Other principal sources for my research include the newspapers and journals from Port Phillip, Sydney and London from 1838 to 1847, and other contemporary newspapers. These grounded the White Woman story in the broader context of contemporary debates in Port Phillip and Sydney and related it to the social, cultural, political and economic issues of the day. I have consulted published histories of Gipps Land, Melbourne, Port Phillip, New South Wales and Australia, biographies, settlers' journals and explorers' reports, Australian, English and Scottish cultural and literary texts, material on Aboriginal ethnography, history and culture, revisionist historical and fictional works by Aboriginal and non-Aboriginal writers, American captivity narratives and stories about Europeans—fictional and actual—who lived with Australian Aborigines in the colonial period.

Significant to my understanding of the story within its geographical locale were visits to key locations in the story—the Heart, Corner Inlet, Bushy Park, Eagle Point, Lake King, Lake Wellington, the Ninety Mile Beach, and Port Albert, and other Gippsland sites. Many more primary and secondary historical materials pertaining to early Gippsland, the people mentioned in the White Woman accounts, and the story itself were also uncovered during these visits.

Acknowledgements

My first acknowledgment must go to Mary Reilly, who brought the White Woman story to my attention and thus set me on the path which has resulted in this book. I am indebted to Dr Susan K. Martin, Professor Lucy Frost and Dr Suvendrini Perera, who supervised the PhD thesis from which the book is drawn, for their encouragement and guidance. I would also like to acknowledge the help of Professor Robert Dixon, Dr Terry Goldie, and Dr Kerryn Goldsworthy, who provided positive suggestions for turning the thesis into a book. La Trobe University, Faculty of Humanities, provided several small research grants which allowed me to copy archival material, attend conferences and pursue research in the U.K. In particular, I wish to thank the La Trobe University Publications Committee for providing a generous subsidy towards publication of the book.

At Melbourne University Press I have been fortunate to have received the support of Teresa Pitt, Commissioning Editor; the editorial expertise of Caroline Williamson, Senior Editor; and the helpful assistance of Gabby Lhuede, Production Controller; and Melissa Mackey, Publishing Co-ordinator. Chandra Jayasuriya ably assisted with the preparation of maps.

Along the way, numerous people have generously aided the project. Alwynne Buntine provided the greatest thrill by allowing me to see the original White Woman handkerchief—a precious family 'relic' surviving from the 1846 searches. William Cuthill talked to me about the Cuthill manuscript collection. Stephen Russell, Louise Bowers and other members of the extended Russell and Poynder families helped in the labyrinthine task of tracing copyright for Robert Russell's 1849 unpublished manuscript 'The Heart'.

For permission to reproduce Sidney Nolan's 'Gippsland Incident' as the cover illustration, I should like to thank Lady Nolan, Wales, and the Art Gallery of South Australia. Permission to reproduce illustrations and manuscript material has also kindly been provided by A. C. Black Publishers, Heather Freedman, Thelma Rawlings, Genevieve Rees [Melrose], Ian Russell, Merilyn Grey (Editor of *The Victorian Naturalist*), the State Library of Victoria, Museum Victoria and the National Library, Canberra. For permission to reproduce excerpts from *The White Woman* I am grateful to the author, Liam Davison, and the University of Queensland Press. An extract from *Ghosting William Buckley* is reproduced by kind permission of the author Barry Hill and publisher William Heinemann. Articles which appeared in the *Journal and the Record* in 1959–61 have been extensively cited with the kind permission of Lyn Smith, editor of the *Morwell Express*.

I particularly wish to thank Sandra Burt, Manuscripts Librarian, Australian Manuscripts Collection, State Library of Victoria, for her generous and expert assistance, as well as Dianne Reilly, Des Cowley, Michael Galimany and Jane Nicholas. Thanks also must go to the librarians, archivists, museum staff and members of historical societies in Australia and Britain (many of whom remain unnamed) who have provided information and expertise, including: Margot Hyslop, Eve Fish and the reference librarians at the Borchardt Library, La Trobe University; Graeme Powell, Manuscripts Librarian, and Julia Sutherland, Information Services Section, National Library of Australia; Melanie Raberts, Head, Indigenous Collections Department, Leah Breninger, Collections Manager, and Elizabeth Willis, Curator, Social History Department, Museum Victoria; Megan Goulding, Acting Historical Archaeologist, Aboriginal Affairs Victoria; Francesca Hardcastle, Librarian, School of Scottish Studies, Edinburgh University Library; Michelle Murray, Serials Librarian, Macquarie Library; Port Albert Maritime Museum—Dee Nicol, Secretary, and museum members Margaret Smallbone, Gwen Fraser, Fred Hobson, Gwen Hobson and Nance Fordham; Richard Overell, Monash University Library; Vicki Ritchie, Chief Librarian, *Herald and Weekly Times*, Melbourne; Margaret Sharp, Assistant Director (Libraries), Edinburgh City Library; Inga Simpson, Client Access,

National Film & Sound Archive, Canberra; Naomi Tarrant, Curator of Costume and Textiles, Museum of Edinburgh; and the numerous helpful staff at the Victoria and Albert Museum, London; the Guildhall Library, London, and the Museum of London.

Finally, I should like to thank my family, colleagues and friends for their continuing support and encouragement. My greatest debt is to my sister Paula, who has rescued me numerous times from the wilds of the manuscript and has been a steadfast and lively companion in the adventure.

Papers arising from a number of chapters have been published previously: 'The White Blackfellow', *Island*, no. 56, Spring 1993 (excerpts from chapters 3 and 8); ('In Search of the White Woman of Gipps Land', *Australasian Victorian Studies Annual*, 1, 1995, (extracts from introduction and chapters 3, 7 and 8); 'The Great "White Woman" Controversy', *La Trobe Journal*, no. 63, Autumn 1999, (part of chapter 7); 'Cribb'd, Cabined and Confined' in *Bodytrade*, Pluto Press, Sydney, 2000 (section of chapter 6); 'Winning the Gloves' in '(un)fabric/ating empire', special edition of *New Literatures Review*, no. 36, Winter 2000 (part of chapter 5); 'The Heart of Gippsland: envisioning settlement' in 'The Vision Splendid', special edition of *Journal of Australian Studies*, no. 65, 2000 (part of chapter 2).

Notes on Terminology

The 1840s lexical convention of 'Gipps Land' or 'Gipps' Land' is employed where applicable rather than the later 'Gippsland', which entered common usage from around 1850.

Irregular spelling and punctuation conventions in the primary source material are retained in direct quotations. Elsewhere, where alternative spellings are used for names or places, the most commonly used is taken as the standard.

Numerous terms are used in the source material to identify the indigenous peoples of Port Phillip. These include general categories (Aborigines, Natives, Blacks); and regional groups (Melbourne Blacks, Western Port Blacks, Gipps Land Blacks). According to Charles Tyers, Commissioner of Crown Lands in Gipps Land, in 1846 there were two 'classes' of Aborigines in Gipps Land.[1] The first 'class' comprised some 200 to 300 natives of Omeo, Maneroo, the Mitta Mitta, and other districts bordering on Gipps Land, who 'lead the greater part of the year a vagabond, gipsy-like kind of life, moving in small parties from station to station, as chances of obtaining food from the settlers offer'. The second 'class'—the 'Warrigals' or 'wild blacks'—numbered probably between 800 and 1000, inhabited the mountains, the morasses, the borders of the Lakes and the sea-coast, and were allegedly very destructive of the settlers' stock. It was 'Warrigals' (more commonly spelt 'Worrigals') who were said to be holding the White Woman captive. In the light of a substantial settler presence in Gipps Land by 1846, Tyers's demarcation of the two 'classes' probably misrepresented a complex situation.

A. W. Howitt used the term Kurnai for the confederation of the five Gipps Land 'clans', which he identified as the Brataualung, Brayakaulung, Brabralung, Krauatungalung, and Tatungalung.[2]

According to Howitt, 'a number of families inhabiting a certain locality formed that aggregate which I have termed the division, so did a certain number of divisions inhabiting a larger area form that aggregate which I have termed the clan ... the aggregate of clans formed a whole, each male individual of which called himself Kurnai, or *man*'. Howitt admitted that the distinction between these aggregates was one which was well recognised by the Kurnai, but which he had found difficult to define in a satisfactory way. He also conceded that the information he was able to collect on the Kurnai was 'unfortunately very imperfect' but that it was 'all that [could] be now rescued from oblivion, and must suffice'. Variations in the spelling of the clan/tribal names occur in the numerous accounts about the Kurnai (Gunai) by historians, Gippslanders and amateur ethnographers, including missionaries in the area in the 1860s, the Revs Bulmer and Hagenhauer.

Christian De Villiers, leader of the privately funded expedition to rescue the White Woman in 1846, gives the following names and locations for the five Gipps Land tribes: *Bungel Paul Paul* (lakes), *Bungel Mageelong* (Snowy River), *Jenora* (Upper Snowy River), *Parberry Long* (mountains about fifty miles from the mouth of the Tambo, in vicinity of country termed Tongamangee), and *Canbowerib* (between La Trobe and Mitchell Rivers).[3] However there is no standardised nomenclature in the primary source documents. It is not clear whether, or how, De Villiers's five tribes correspond with Tyers's two 'classes' of Gipps Land Aborigines—or with Howitt's clans. Neither is it possible to identify a particular tribe or group by location alone. Seasonal migratory movements and the disruption of traditional patterns and locations of habitation as settlers took over Kurnai lands make such identification difficult.

Distinctions existed between the Aboriginal members of McMillan's party, some of whom accompanied him into Gipps Land from the Monaro region, and the 'local' tribes; between the several discrete Gipps Land tribes and their respective territories; between the 'Worrigals' who inhabited the more remote areas and had little contact with settlers, and those who spent time at the settlers' stations; between the Gipps Land tribes and those beyond their borders; and between those involved in the searches for the White Woman—including the Wurundjeri (Melbourne) and Bunerong

(Western Port)—and those in the Native Police who were drawn from areas throughout the Port Phillip District.

The nomenclature of the primary source documents, such as 'Worrigals', or 'blacks' is adopted of necessity, and is not meant to imply that Aboriginal people are indistinguishable or undifferentiated from one other. I follow Howitt's use of the terms 'clan', 'tribe', etc., and spelling conventions for the tribes except in direct quotations, where the original spellings are retained.

CHAPTER 1

A Climate of Receptivity

'No man who comes to this Colony and has ground and cattle and corn can
dispassionately view the subject of the blacks, their interest says annihilate
the race.'
L. E. Threlkeld, 1826[1]

'This right to Australia is a sore subject with many of the British settlers, and they
strive to satisfy their consciences in various ways.'
Pioneer settler, Port Phillip, 1845[2]

'Rumour with her hundred-tongued mouth . . .'
Port Phillip Herald, 8 January 1841.

The legend of the White Woman of Gipps Land originated in 1840
as a frontier rumour. It was said that a white woman, purportedly the
survivor of a shipwreck, was held captive by Aborigines in the wilds
of Gipps Land in the Port Phillip District—at that time part of the
Colony of New South Wales. Speculation about the woman's existence and fate resurfaced periodically in the colonial press over the
ensuing six years. In 1846, the rumours ignited a public furore which
resulted in a publicly funded expedition to Gipps Land to rescue the
hapless captive. Neither this party, nor searches conducted by government forces in 1846 and 1847, found the elusive White Woman, and
evidence for her existence remains inconclusive.

Though an insubstantial figure in 'real life', the White Woman
has been produced and reproduced as the subject of legend and
history for 160 years. Since 1840 the White Woman has appeared in
newspaper reports, parliamentary papers, official documents, historical analyses, academic research, poetry and fictional accounts. While
rumour placed her, and search parties sought her, at the fringes of
settlement, newspaper accounts and correspondence between colonial officials in Gippsland, Port Phillip and Sydney located her
firmly in the context of colonial politics and governance, and in the
arena of public debate. Literary and artistic representations of the

White Woman have further consolidated the legend's place within discourses of contesting power relations.

The White Woman stories and images, in their retellings and variant forms, have served vested interests at successive periods of post-settlement history. In 1893, George Dunderdale, deploring the violence of the early colonial period in Gippsland when the White Woman rumours circulated, termed his own era 'the age of white-wash'.[3] In the increasingly contested space of frontier expansion in the 1840s, the White Woman stories facilitated settler occupation of territory already occupied by the Kurnai/Gunai tribes. They mobilised male adventurers to go in quest of the woman and, in the process, 'discover' new land for settlement.

The story's promulgation, via the press, in the developing towns of Melbourne and Sydney bears the hallmarks and *modus operandi* of what these days would be termed an 'urban myth'—perhaps Port Phillip's first.[4] When doubts about the woman's existence were aired, these did not diminish, but rather added to, her mysterious allure. At a time when white women had limited political power, this story about one of their sex in peril on the frontiers of settlement engaged the category of 'woman' in the service of the colonising project.

Historian Don Watson has identified the symbolic and imaginative role which the White Woman story served for the early Gipps Land settlers:

> until real white women came to Gippsland the captive woman served as proof that the white settlers were civilized. So long as they pursued her they were worthy. So long as she sang Psalm 100 they were Christians. And so long as they thought of her they ceased to think of their own worst fears and their own desire. For the Highland men at least, 'Anna' was also a manifestation of their memories. She was proof of the power of nostalgia. She took them home.[5]

The issues which circulated around the White Woman in the 1840s remain relevant today. Anxieties about identity, place and notions of belonging; ambivalence about 'multiculturalism'; and unresolved issues of justice and restitution for Aboriginal people continue, despite jingoistic images and slogans which proclaim a unified

Australian culture. Historian Henry Reynolds has argued that remnant guilt for the act of expropriation—the 'whisper in the heart'—continues to undermine the moral health of the nation.[6] As a nation, Australia struggles to define and justify itself.

A society produces and perpetuates its history and identity through story telling. In this book I look afresh at the White Woman legend to examine the roles of historiography and story-telling in producing racial and cultural difference, and in the formation of local, regional and national identity.

Angus [Augustus] McMillan was one of the earliest European settlers to explore the region which in 1840 he termed 'Caledonia Australis', shortly to be officially named Gipps' Land. McMillan, like many of his compatriots affected by the sweeping agrarian reforms of the time, left Scotland in search of opportunities in the colonies. He arrived in Sydney on 23 January 1838 with a letter of introduction to Lachlan Macalister, landholder in the Monaro Plains area (southern New South Wales today), and a former laird of the Isle of Skye. As Macalister's employee, McMillan during 1839 and 1840 crossed the ranges into Gipps Land in search of grazing country. He was to contribute directly to the opening up of the central and south eastern areas for pastoral settlement. During 1840–41 he undertook several journeys of exploration to find a route from the Gipps Land interior to the coast.

While on one of these expeditions McMillan's party disturbed an Aboriginal encampment. His account of this dramatic event was published in the *Sydney Herald* on 28 December 1840 and reprinted on 18 January 1841 in Melbourne's *Port Phillip Patriot and Melbourne Advertiser* under the heading 'SUPPOSED OUTRAGE BY THE BLACKS':

> November 15.—Started from our station to discover a road to the coast with the view of running along the Long Beach to Shoal inlets, thence to Corner Inlet,—same evening, came upon the camp of twenty-five black natives, chiefly women, who all ran away on our near approach, leaving every thing they had behind them excepting some of their spears. We then

SYDNEY.

The subjoined intelligence from the *Sydney Herald* of the 28th ult., may be interesting to some of our readers :—

Supposed Outrage by the Blacks.— We call the particular attention of parties who have friends and relatives in the neighbourhood of Port Phillip, to the following letter from a station at Gipps Land or South Caledonia, the country that lies between Cape Howe and Port Phillip. It appears quite clear that murder has been committed, and perhaps the publication of the list of property found may assist in identifying the murdered party. The letter was placed in our possession several days since, but was unfortunately mislaid:—

"November 15.—Started from our station, to discover a road to the coast with the view of running along the Long Beach to Shoal inlet, thence to Corner inlet,—same evening, came upon the camp of twenty-five black natives, chiefly women, who all ran away on our near approach, leaving every thing they had behind them excepting some of their spears. We then searched their camp, where we found European articles as underneath described, viz :—Several check-shirts, cord and moleskin trousers, all be-smeared with human blood ; one German frock, two pea-jackets, new brown Macintosh cloak, also stained with blood ; several pieces of women's wearing apparel, namely, prints, and merinos ; a large lock of brown hair, evidently that of a European woman, one child's white frock with brown velvet band, five hand towels, one of which was marked R. Jamieson No. 12, one blue silk purse, silver tassels and slides, containing seven shillings and sixpence British money, one woman's thimble, two large parcels of silk sewing thread, various colours, 10 new English blankets perfectly clean, shoemakers awls, bees' wax, blacksmith's pincers and cold chisel, one bridle bit, which had been recently used, as the grass was quite fresh on it ; the tube of a thermometer, broken looking glass, bottles of all descriptions, two of which had castor oil in them, one sealskin cap, one musket and some shot, one broad tomahawk, some London, Glasgow, and Aberdeen newspapers, printed in 1837 and 1838. One pewter two gallon measure, one ditto hand basin, one large tin camp kettle, two children's copy books, one bible printed in Edinburgh June 1838, one set of the National Loan Fund regulations respecting policies of Life insurance, and blank forms of medical man's certificate for effecting the same. Enclosed in three kangaroo skin bags we found the dead body of a male child about two years old, which Dr. Arbuckle carefully examined professionally, and discovered beyond doubt its being of European parents; parts of the skin were perfectly white, not being in the least discoloured. We observed the men with shipped spears driving before them the women, one of whom we noticed constantly looking behind her, at us, a circumstance which did not strike us much at the time, but on examining the marks and figures about the largest of the native huts we were immediately impressed with the belief that that unfortunate female is a European—a captive of these ruthless savages. The blacks having come across us the next day in numbers, and our party being composed of four only, we most reluctantly deemed it necessary to return to the station without being enabled to accomplish our object. This was the more painful to our feelings, as we have no doubt whatever but a dreadful massacre of Europeans, men, women and children, has been perpetrated by the aborigines in the immediate vicinity of the spot, whence we were forced to return without being emabled to throw more light on this melancholy catastrophe, than what I have detailed above.

"AUGUSTUS M'MILLAN."

[The clue to the foregoing mystery is doubtless to be found in the robbery of Mr. Jamieson's station at Western Port, which must have occurred very shortly before the date of Mr. M'Millan's excursion. The European dead child and living woman, are we suspect mere creatures of the imagination.—ED. P. P. PATRIOT.]

Angus McMillan's reported 'sighting' of the White Woman.
Port Phillip Patriot and Melbourne Advertiser, 18 January 1841
(reprinted from *Sydney Herald*, 28 December 1840)
Reproduced by permission of La Trobe Collection, State Library of Victoria.

searched their camp, where we found European articles as underneath described, viz:—Several check-shirts, cord and moleskin trousers, all besmeared with human blood; one German frock, two pea-jackets, new brown Macintosh cloak, also stained with blood; several pieces of women's wearing apparel, namely, prints and merinos; a large lock of brown hair, evidently that of a European woman, one child's white frock with brown velvet band, five hand towels, one of which was marked R. Jamieson No. 12, one blue silk purse, silver tassels and slides, containing seven shillings and sixpence British money, one woman's thimble, two large parcels of silk sewing thread, various colours, 10 new English blankets perfectly clean, shoemakers awls, bees' wax, blacksmith's pinchers and cold chisel, one bridle bit, which had been recently used, as the grass was quite fresh on it; the tube of a thermometer, broken looking glass, bottles of all descriptions, two of which had castor oil in them, one sealskin cap, one musket and some shot, one broad tomahawk, some London, Glasgow, and Aberdeen newspapers, printed in 1837 and 1838. One pewter two gallon measure, one ditto hand basin, one large tin camp kettle, two children's copy books, one bible printed in Edinburgh, June 1838, one set of the National Loan Fund regulations respecting policies of Life insurance, and blank forms of medical man's certificate for effecting the same. Enclosed in three kangaroo skin bags we found the dead body of a male child about two years old, which Dr. Arbuckle carefully examined professionally, and discovered beyond doubt its being of European parents; parts of the skin were perfectly white, not being in the least discoloured. We observed the men with shipped spears driving before them the women, one of whom we noticed constantly looking behind her, at us, a circumstance which did not strike us much at the time, but on examining the marks and figures about the largest of the native huts we were immediately impressed with the belief that the unfortunate female is a European—a captive of these ruthless savages. The blacks having come across us the next day in numbers, and our party being composed of four only, we most reluctantly deemed it necessary to return to the station without being enabled to accomplish our object. This was the more painful to our feelings, as we have no doubt whatever but a dreadful massacre of Europeans, men, women and children, has been perpetrated by the aborigines in the immediate vicinity of the spot, whence we were forced to return without being enabled to throw more light on this melancholy catastrophe, than what I have detailed above.

                    'AUGUSTUS McMILLAN.'[7]

McMillan's account involves a complex conjunction of historical, 'forensic' and ideological elements. Fixed on the page as news for wide circulation, the account exerts a degree of authority and permanence. Its powerful effect and lasting influence indicate that his narrative struck a responsive chord. McMillan's representation of the woman as a just-glimpsed, always already absent figure would be endlessly repeated in subsequent 'sightings' and in numerous fictional versions and historical accounts. He established a model of presenting the White Woman as an insubstantial trace whose 'proof' of existence depended on circumstantial evidence, physical, verbal or textual. He extrapolated from the clues a colonial narrative: ocean voyage, shipwreck, survival then massacre or, worse, captivity amongst 'ruthless savages'—a script which was to be followed with little variation. McMillan's contention that a captive white woman existed derived authority from his position as reporter at first-hand, but a speculative leap was required of the reader. In a colonial culture, familiar with the perils of sea voyages and receptive to contemporary ideologies of race, class and gender, the ambiguities and gaps in McMillan's account might have been filled by readers who would understand, make sense of, and complete the story.

McMillan was to take a central role in producing and perpetuating stories about the White Woman. He announced her appearance in 1840 and, seven years later, her end. When the remains of a female, reputedly those of the White Woman, and a child were discovered at Jemmy's Point, Gipps Land, in October 1847, McMillan assisted with an 'inquest upon the remains'. His assertion, published in the *Port Phillip Herald* of 5 November 1847, 'that there could not be an atom of doubt of one of them being that of a white female, which was easily evident from her head', provided the pretext for the cessation of government and public efforts to recover her.[8]

McMillan's account provided the basis for a foundational myth. Gananath Obeyesekere maintains that 'myths are bound by time and context and reflect controversies or "debates" of the period in which they were written'.[9] The issues which McMillan raises are central and recurring preoccupations throughout the substantial body of textual material on the White Woman. The dominant themes—cultural dislocation, anxiety about sexual contact with the Aboriginal 'Other', ideals and ideas about women in early Victorian society—speak for broader concerns within an emigrant settler community struggling to come to terms with, and find ways of articulating, its relationship to a 'new' land and its Aboriginal occupants.

At the time that McMillan penned his 'sighting' of the White Woman, there was no overland route from the small but rapidly developing township of Melbourne to Gipps Land. The publication of his account in Sydney and Port Phillip, the two key centres of colonial administration, brought to public attention his efforts as a pioneering explorer in the Gipps Land region. McMillan wrote himself into the history of British exploration and settlement in Gipps Land and signalled the arrival of what was to become a strong Scottish presence. His narrative of the White Woman thus enters the realm of public discourse at one of the earliest recorded points of post-settler Gipps Land history.

McMillan's account presents like a journal entry, dated and with the day's events summarily described, as though a page from an explorer's record. The last sentence makes clear that the account was written some time after the party had been 'forced to return' to the station. The account's rhetorical strategies and superabundance of detail suggest a keen sense of audience. As he (re)produces the campsite scene, McMillan positions himself as mediator, interpreter and authoritative eye-witness, and invites the reader's vicarious participation in a dramatised moment of frontier history.

McMillan provides extraordinarily detailed evidence to support his claims for the story. The catalogue of personal and domestic effects is so comprehensive that it seems unlikely that McMillan, or any other member of his party, could have recalled them without an *aide-mémoire*. He does not suggest in the account that anyone in his party took an inventory at the site.

Though chronicling a scene of disarray, the list, and the range and nature of the items described, reconstruct an orderly world, a complete, civil community. The list is not haphazardly compiled.

Items are clustered according to materiality and/or purpose. Wearing apparel (men's, women's then children's) and cloth items are followed by a purse and money, women's domestic items, household hardware and tools, glassware, weaponry, newspapers, metal containers, and books and papers (educational, devotional, legal).

In describing the objects McMillan evokes their now-absent owners and implies foul play. The men's working clothes, he says, are besmeared with human blood, a point reiterated a few lines later. How could blood at this time and place be identified as *human*? Why the need to stress that it was *human* blood? In describing it thus McMillan works towards a conclusion of massacre.

The objects, presented as though violently dislocated from their rightful place in a European domestic space, symbolise the dangers for pioneering settlers in the bush. The items conjure up for a colonial readership an imagined community, with all that was valued 'back home'—familial relationships and a genteel, comfortable and carefully husbanded economy. Though arguing a different point, Peter Hulme has noted, similarly, of *Robinson Crusoe*'s discovery of three hats, one cap, and two odd shoes, which prefigure the collection of limbs he later finds on the same shore, that the clothing 'is but a metonym for Crusoe's dead companions whose bodies, though "devoured", are whole'.[10]

McMillan's speculation drives the narrative. It anticipates and makes plausible the later breaches of logic on which his conclusion will be based. The 'evidence' bridges 'fact' and fancy, what is 'seen' and what is imagined (the imputation of massacre). A lock of brown hair—an item which might in other circumstances be no more than a sentimental keepsake, or an item of ladies' coiffure—in this context bespeaks painful severance (intimations of scalping?). The meagre amount of weaponry—one musket and some shot and one broad tomahawk—makes implicit the group's inability to have defended itself. The grass on the bridle bit, attesting to recent use (being still 'quite fresh'), creates urgency and pathos. McMillan's party is *just* too late.

A child's frock and children's copy books evoke familial scenes. Women's paraphernalia—a blue silk purse, clothing, a thimble and silk sewing threads—conjure images of female gentility and house-wifely industry. The London, Glasgow and Aberdeen newspapers of

1837 and 1838, and the bible printed in Edinburgh, June 1838, connote a literate and God-fearing Presbyterian community, authenticate the nationality of the 'victims', and delineate a time frame for events.

The inventory culminates with National Loan Fund regulations and medical certificates. These legal, commercial and medical documents, which record the insured or insurable value of (European) human life, imply the expectation and realisation of peril.

The inventory prepares the reader for the 'conclusive' piece of evidence—the dead body of a child enclosed in kangaroo skin bags. According to McMillan, Dr Arbuckle (a member of McMillan's party) pronounces the child to be 'beyond doubt . . . of European parents; [as] parts of the skin were perfectly white, not . . . in the least discoloured'. What does McMillan mean by 'discoloured' (a curious term)? Is he referring to decaying skin or pigmentation? His juxtaposition of 'perfectly white' and 'discoloured' skin on the same body produces white corporeality as an unstable entity. The primary marker of racial difference—the intact white body—is ambiguous. The fleeing female, too, is not noticeably 'white'. McMillan construes her 'whiteness' from the patches of perfectly white skin on the child's body.

Arbuckle's status as medical practitioner provides authority for a conclusion which seems to rely as much on sentiment as on science. As reported by McMillan, the sole finding of Arbuckle's examination relates to the child's racial identity. There is no indication that Arbuckle attempted to establish the cause or time of death. Neither does he suggest that the child has met a violent death. What then constituted Dr Arbuckle's 'professional' examination? Would a partial *post mortem* on a perhaps decomposing body determine skin colour or racial category, as suggested? Was Arbuckle's determination really beyond doubt, as McMillan claims?

Arbuckle's determination that the child was of European parents provides another link in McMillan's chain of 'logical' connections. McMillan presents the white-skinned child as *prima facie* evidence of a white mother. In doing so he employs a form of circuitous logic; the authentication of the child's European identity is dependent upon there being a white mother, while the existence of a white woman is deduced from the body of the dead child.

This conclusion precludes other, more likely, explanations for the presence of a fair-skinned child, notably the existence of mixed-race children, the result of sexual relations between white men and black women. In the face of this widespread and tacitly accepted colonialist practice, McMillan's conclusion asserts mid-nineteenth-century European moral values, under threat in a colonial situation.

Despite the abundant detail, there are significant gaps and ambiguities. McMillan moves directly from his discussion of the child's body to a description of 'the men with shipped spears driving before them the women, one of whom we noticed constantly looking behind her, at us'. The chronology of events is not clear. McMillan mentions three encounters with Aborigines. Is this the same group reported three times? The first-mentioned group—'twenty five black natives, chiefly women'—is depicted as non-threatening. They run away at his party's approach. If this is the group which ran away on McMillan's party's approach, they have changed over the course of the account from 'chiefly women' to 'men', from timid to hostile. If a different group, where do they fit into the chronology of events?

In retrospectively interpreting the woman's backward glance as evidence of her connection with the imagined community of Europeans, McMillan telescopes to a particularised vision of a sole survivor. The woman is invested with the accrued emotional, moral and cultural values of the 'massacred' group, now lost to the colony. The presence of the bible and the claim that the woman was saved while men and children perished links the account to narratives of providential intervention, and notably to American captivity narratives, which were popular in the 1830s and 1840s. In Australia, Eliza Fraser's story provided a recent and local variant.[11]

The 'captive' woman, described in a mere half-dozen words, is invested with drama and mystery. In the woman's just-glimpsed absence, her presence is established metonymically as the tasselled purse, the lock of hair etc. Her retreating, silently entreating, figure constitutes a dramatic rather than a physical presence, one through which the body of 'evidence' at the campsite can be elucidated and given meaning. She is constructed as a silent yet eloquent presence facing some unknowable/unspeakable future. McMillan's party, like subsequent search parties, arrives too late to confirm the woman's existence or to rescue her.

The arrival next day of Aborigines 'in numbers' (yet another group?) justifies McMillan's party leaving the area without attempting to recover the woman. The story is left without resolution or a call to action on the woman's behalf. The reader is unclear whether the 'object' which McMillan says his party was unable to accomplish was the discovery of a 'road to the coast', or the recovery of the woman.

McMillan's contention that the 'unfortunate female is a European —a captive of these ruthless savages' is based in part on his examination of 'marks and figures about the largest of the native huts'. What were these marks and figures? Were they the origin of later stories of the woman having carved a heart on the ground?

McMillan's account appeared in the *Sydney Herald* six weeks after the date ascribed to the events he recounted. The slightly qualified sensationalism of the headline 'Supposed Outrage by the Blacks' suggests that the editor was not wholly convinced that an 'outrage' had occurred, although he did direct attention to 'parties who have friends and relatives in the neighbourhood of Port Phillip' who might be able to identify the 'murdered' party. The 'captive' woman, and the possibility of retrieving her, went unremarked by the editor and unchallenged by readers.

The editor's admission that 'The letter was placed in our possession several days since, but was unfortunately mislaid' could indicate that it was not handled with the care one might expect for an important news item. Perhaps the editor considered it a titillating item worth holding over to enliven the period between Christmas and the New Year when business and political news wanes. The timing may have worked against its reception as a news item requiring immediate action, and might account for the article not stimulating a call for action from either contributors or editor.

When the *Port Phillip Patriot* reprinted McMillan's account from the *Sydney Herald* for Melbourne readers on 18 January 1841 the editor dismissed McMillan's conclusions:

> The clue to the foregoing mystery is doubtless to be found in the robbery of Mr. Jamieson's station at Western Port, which must have occurred very shortly before the date of Mr. McMillan's excursion.[12] The European dead child and living woman, are we suspect mere creatures of the imagination.

The *Patriot's* assertion, spoken with the authority of knowledge of the robbery, and made plausible by McMillan's mention of a hand towel marked 'R. Jamieson', framed the story as the product of an overstimulated imagination, rather than one requiring action. Despite its dismissal of McMillan's contentions, the *Patriot* published his account. The story's topicality and regional relevance might have been expected to excite the curiosity and previously held fears of readers in Sydney and Melbourne, particularly those who had lost family or friends in shipwrecks along the Gipps Land coast.

It has generally been assumed by commentators that McMillan sent his account to the *Sydney Herald* for publication. However, there are indicators that it may have been a private communication handed on to the newspaper by the recipient, with or without McMillan's knowledge or permission. As printed, it lacks the conventions for a published letter (address, salutation); there is no standard introduction; it was published in the editorial column rather than under 'Original Correspondence' where letters to the editor usually appeared; and the *Herald* commented that it was 'placed in our possession'.

At around the time that McMillan's account was published, fictional or factual accounts of violent crimes or murder trials citing circumstantial evidence as 'irrefutable' proof frequently appeared in the colonial newspapers.[13] These stories employed the structuring conventions of the suspense narrative (identified by semiotician Roland Barthes as the hermeneutic code), which invited vicarious participation in examining evidence presented in such a way as to lead the reader by question, response, partial disclosure and revelation to eventual resolution.[14] McMillan's rhetorical strategies and emotive terms—'beyond doubt', 'evidently', 'examined professionally', 'immediately impressed with the belief', 'no doubt whatever' —which work to persuade the reader to accept his assertion that a European party had been murdered suggest that McMillan was familiar with these conventions.

A different framework for interpreting the import of the child's body can be found in descriptions of Kurnai funerary rites which appear in accounts by early settlers and ethnographers: one which connotes care and respect for the dead, rather than murderous intent. Chief Protector George Augustus Robinson noted of Aboriginal burial practices in Gipps Land and the Maneroo District in 1844 that 'In some instances especially when a Chief Man dies, the body is frequently kept Eight or ten days, and carried by the Tribe to the favourite resort of the deceased; the bodies of children are at times kept for an indefinite period.'[15] A. W. Howitt, writing of the Kurnai some forty years later, described similar practices involving grieving rituals which could last several days and include self-mutilation.[16] This could suggest one alternative to McMillan's explanation for the blood-stained clothes.

McMillan's description does not read as though he considered the child had been put into the kangaroo skin bags as part of a funerary rite. He might have had no knowledge of such practices. This might explain his party's interference with the interred body: an act comparable, for Europeans, to disturbing a grave.

On 9 July 1840, six months prior to publication of McMillan's 'sighting' of the White Woman, the Sydney *Colonist* published a letter written by McMillan to his employer, Lachlan Macalister, in which he describes an event which reads as a prototype (albeit less detailed or dramatic) for the campsite scene of the 'sighting'. In this letter McMillan writes:

> The blacks are very numerous down at the coast and always ran away and burnt their camps whenever they saw us, sometimes leaving everything they had behind; the day before we returned we found one of their net bags with a carpenter's auger in it, which they must have got from some vessel . . .[17]

The same elements—fleeing Aborigines, items left behind at the campsite, a search by McMillan's party and the finding of a European artefact in a bag—are present. In this instance, however, McMillan does not assume that the Aborigines came by the 'carpenter's auger' by foul means. Why, in the later account, did he not make the connection between the two 'finds'? And why did he not attribute to the second, larger body of items a similar, relatively innocuous origin?

At the time of his reported 'sighting' of the White Woman, McMillan was in competition with the Polish scientist and explorer Paul Strzelecki for the title 'discoverer of Gipps Land'.[18] Strzelecki's status as a Count (albeit a disputed title), his scientific methods, and the patronage of dignitaries such as Sir John Franklin and influential grazier James MacArthur, who accompanied Strzelecki through Gipps Land, eclipsed the lesser known and less well-connected McMillan. Strzelecki was feted on his arrival in Melbourne. When glowing reports of his 'discoveries' were made available to the public, land speculators in Sydney and Port Phillip moved into Gipps Land. Competition was intense because it was unclear at this time whether Gipps Land came under the jurisdiction of Sydney or Port Phillip. Strzelecki's official report concerning the discovery of Gipps Land was forwarded to England by Governor Gipps, and his map was printed in the House of Commons papers of 1841. Strzelecki was awarded further recognition with the publication of his book *Physical Description of New South Wales and Van Diemen's Land* in London in 1845.[19] Meanwhile, colonial newspapers polarised the debate:[20] The *Sydney Herald* aligned the claims of Sydneysiders with McMillan, and those of the 'grasping "Land sharks" of Port Phillip' with the 'shameless effrontery' of 'Stretlitzky'.[21]

Prior to publication in the *Sydney Herald* of his 'sighting' of the White Woman, McMillan had been engaged, unsuccessfully, in attempts to gain public recognition for his own role as explorer and namer of the region. A copy of a letter written by McMillan to his employer Lachlan Macalister, dated 18 February 1840, was published in the Sydney *Colonist* of 9 July the same year. In this letter, which also contained the prototypical description of the campsite scene, McMillan detailed and claimed his 'discoveries' and asked Macalister to publicise them. According to McMillan, Macalister did not make the details public, as requested.[22]

Recalling this early period of exploration some years later, McMillan claimed that Strzelecki had passed through McMillan's station at Numbla-Munjee on the Tambo River on 27 March 1840, where:

> Mr. Matthew Macalister, who was one of my party in January of the same year, accompanied them one day's journey, and . . . left them upon my tracks on the coast range leading to Gipps-land, and which tracks Charley, the Sydney black-fellow, who accompanied Count Strzelecki, said he could easily follow.[23]

The issue of primacy, enshrined officially in the practice of naming, was central to McMillan's bid for recognition. McMillan's 'Caledonia Australis' had become Strzelecki's 'Gipps' Land',[24] named in honour of Governor Gipps. McMillan was particularly aggrieved that traces of his own exploration—his naming of geographical features—had been erased by the adoption in official government charts of Strzelecki's names:

> Mr. Townsend, the Government Surveyor . . . had instructions from Sir Thomas Mitchell, the Surveyor-General, to establish all the names I had given to the most remarkable places in the country I travelled over. As a foreign importer, the Count had no claim on the discoveries of another . . . The most conspicuous mountain [Mr. Townsend] named after me—Mount McMillan—afterwards changed by Mr. Tyers, one of the commissioners, to Castle Hill, which I consider *piracy*.[25]

McMillan's outrage, in the light of his own claim for authority as 'discoverer' and 'namer' of land already known to, and named by, the several Kurnai tribes who occupied the region reads now as unintendedly ironic. It is a reminder of the ingrained nature of cultural assumptions, then as now.

In making his case as primary explorer, McMillan appealed to cultural prejudices in the community. His distrust of the 'foreigner' Strzelecki appears as an attempt to mobilise, within a predominantly British culture, support for his own claim and, more broadly, for the incipient Scottish presence in Gipps Land. J. D. Lang, in *Phillipsland*, published in Edinburgh in 1847, articulated the not-so-subtle distinctions within the category of 'European', on which his championing of the Scot, McMillan, over Strzelecki, depended:

> The credit of having been the discoverer of [Gipps Land] . . . is commonly given to the Polish traveler, Count Strzelecki, by whom, at least, the merit of the discovery has been assumed; but it is pretty generally believed in New South Wales that the discovery was really effected by Mr. A. McMillan, a respectable Scotchman, who was then employed as a superintendent or overseer by Lachlan and Matthew McAlister, Esqrs, J.P.—two gentlemen from the Highlands of Scotland.[26]

The case against the 'foreigner' had been more strenuously put by the Sydney *Colonist* when in 1840 it published McMillan's letter to Macalister: 'There is something very disingenuous in [the Count's] concealment; it may correspond with Streletzki's notions of honor to usurp or pirate another man's discovery, but it is anything but handsome in the estimation of a genuine Englishman'.[27]

McMillan's assertion that he found among the items at the Aboriginal campsite a bible printed in Edinburgh and some Glasgow and Aberdeen newspapers, ascribes to the locale a Scottish presence, and to the 'captive' woman a national identity. Other national contenders (English and Irish) for the woman's identity would emerge in subsequent accounts.

The Scottish presence in Gipps Land was to gain emphasis and focus in November 1840 with the much-publicised arrival in Melbourne and Sydney of Aeneas Ranald Macdonnel, the Chief of Glengarry.[28] As a distinguished visitor to the colony, much was made of Macdonnel's status. Over ensuing months, speculation about his intention to settle in Gipps Land added lustre to the region's already glowing reputation. Melbourne readers were advised in early May 1841 that 'Mr. Lachlan Macalister and the Chief of Glengarry, . . . started for the "promised land," [Gipps Land] about a week ago'.[29] The Chief's 'highly flattering and favourable account' of the region was reported in the *Sydney Monitor* of 19 May and the *Port Phillip Patriot* of 3 June. Macdonnel arrived at Port Albert in mid-July 1841, with an entourage of some twenty servants, clansmen, tartans, bagpipes and, according to one historian, 'two elephants acquired on the journey out'.[30] McMillan's dreams for the region as a transplanted homeland, a haven for his 'starving countrymen', must have seemed close to realisation with the Laird in their midst. Macdonnel, however, stayed a bare twelve months before returning to Scotland.

McMillan had arrived in New South Wales in 1838, the year in which the now infamous Myall Creek massacre occurred, in which twenty-eight Aborigines, including women and children, were rounded up by stockmen and murdered. The hanging of seven Europeans charged with the crime was intended by Governor Gipps to convey unequivocally the message that explorers and settlers could not murder Aborigines with impunity.

It has been argued however by historians in recent years that in Gipps Land reprisals against the Kurnai continued well into the 1840s and that the main perpetrators—the so-called 'Highland Brigade'—conducted their forays under a cloak of secrecy. Historians and commentators generally agree that the 'Highland Brigade' played a central role in subduing Kurnai resistance to settlement. Some argue that the 'Highland Brigade' was responsible for a number of massacres of Aborigines in the early years of settlement, although opinions vary as to how many Kurnai were killed in defending their territory.[31]

The absence of any government presence in Gipps Land prior to the arrival of Charles Tyers, Commissioner of Crown Lands, in January 1844 would have facilitated the concealment of evidence of violence against the Kurnai. Local justice had hitherto been administered by magistrates—the Highland Chief Macdonnel (briefly) and W. Odell Raymond—who were also squatters. Even with Tyers's arrival, settler reprisals against the 'depredations of the blacks' did not cease. As late as April 1846 Henry Meyrick, newly arrived in Gipps Land, wrote to his mother that the 'settlers there thought nothing of shooting Aboriginal men, women and children on sight' and that 'no wild beast of the forest was ever hunted down with such unsparing perseverance'. Meyrick states that he had protested against the shootings of women and children at every station he had been to in Gipps Land, 'but these things are kept very secret as the penalty would certainly be hanging'.[32]

McMillan was to recall the early period of exploration and settlement in a speech at a public dinner given in his honor at Port Albert in March 1856 and in two accounts written during the 1850s in response to requests for particulars of his early experiences in Gipps Land.[33] The first written account, dated 25 August 1853, was to C. J. La Trobe, then Lieutenant-Governor of the Colony of Victoria.[34] The second, dated 8 February 1856, was to James Bonwick.[35] These accounts differ, but both provide detailed descriptions of McMillan's trips of exploration during 1839–41.

The accounts are presented in journal format, with dates and detailed descriptions of directions taken by McMillan's party, events which occurred along the way and general information, including topographical information and references to other settlers in the region at the time. However, the accounts are written retrospectively, and with the benefit of hindsight, for the purpose of providing a record for posterity. There is no entry in either account for 15 November 1840—the date on McMillan's *Sydney Herald* account of his 'sighting' of the White Woman. Neither is there any mention of his party having found European items at an Aboriginal campsite nor of having 'sighted' the White Woman. This is a significant omission given McMillan's centrality in reporting and perpetuating the story, at least until 1847. There are, however, events recorded pertaining to the period around November and December which might shed light on this curious oversight.

In his letter to Bonwick, McMillan records an unsuccessful attempt to find a way through to the coast, made shortly after he established a station, Bushy Park, on the River Avon in October 1840. Between this entry and the next mentioned date of 9 February 1841, McMillan describes how, in his absence from the station, 'wild blacks' had attacked and driven off the station hands. In response, McMillan 'started at once for the station, accompanied by Dr. Harbuckle, John McDonald, old Bath, Cohn MacLaren, and three others, seven in all; had a desperate skirmish with the natives'.[36]

The entry relating to this incident is briefer in McMillan's letter to La Trobe: 'in about the month of November 1840, the aborigines attacked the station, drove the men from the hut, and took everything from them, compelling them to retreat'.[37] There is no mention of a 'desperate skirmish with the natives'. What are we to make of McMillan's selective recollections? It seems unlikely that he would have forgotten incidents as dramatic as the White Woman 'sighting' or the 'desperate skirmish' with the Aborigines, both of which he said had occurred in November 1840.

In a further version of the Bushy Park attack, supplied to Richard Mackay in 1862, McMillan admitted to killing, in self-defence, one Aborigine.[38] He did not say whether other Aborigines were killed, but it would be reasonable to assume that with the arrival of a party of seven armed men, intent on defending the station from attack, there would have been Aboriginal deaths. Peter Gardner, noting the discrepancies between McMillan's several versions of the Bushy Park incident, and the perhaps unintentional release to Mackay, in his later years, of scant indications of truth (his killing, in self-defence, one Aborigine), considered this an example of how 'the truth was obscured by omission'.[39]

We can't know whether McMillan's 1840 account of the campsite 'sighting' reflected accurately what his party found. Nor can we know whether he believed that a white woman was being held captive or that a 'dreadful massacre of Europeans, men, women and children' had occurred nearby. However, the excessiveness of detail and the gaps and elisions revealed in this close reading of the account, taken with McMillan's omission of the incident from his later records, indicate that other, more complex, factors were also in play.

Is there a connection between the 'desperate skirmish' at Bushy Park and the imputed massacre of Europeans at the campsite scene? Was McMillan (unintentionally or otherwise) transposing anxiety about his own party's culpability onto the Aborigines? Albert Memmi, in his study of the ways in which the colonial situation manufactures both colonialists and colonised, identifies such a process by which usurpation tries to pass for legitimacy.[40] According to Memmi, the colonist's disquiet at his own position and resulting thirst for justification require him to extol his own merits while harping on the usurped's demerits, 'so deep that they cannot help leading to misfortune'. However, the usurper's triumph confirms his guilt and establishes his self-condemnation in a self-defeating process which oppresses him and causes him to wish the disappearance of the usurped such that 'if the necessity arises, [they] will become convinced of the necessity of massacres'.

Was McMillan articulating obliquely what could not be openly expressed or acknowledged? The enduring nature of the White Woman legend suggests that it articulated some deeply felt need or anxiety about settlement.

McMillan's report of the White Woman was made plausible by the loss, twelve months earlier, of two brigs in Bass Strait—the *Britannia* in November 1839, *en route* to Sydney, and the *Britomart* in mid-December 1839, bound for Hobart. When in early 1840 news reached Sydney that Aborigines had reported finding a small boat on the Ninety Mile Beach (on the east Gipps Land coastline), Governor Gipps twice despatched the revenue cutter *Prince George* to search for survivors.

The *Port Phillip Herald* reported on 24 March that Captain Moore had located the small boat (said to have belonged to the ill-fated *Britannia*), and that the government cutter *Vansittart* had found parts of the missing *Britomart* and documents and personal items assumed to belong to passengers, on Preservation Island in Bass Strait. It was speculated that the *Britomart* had been plundered by pirates who had massacred the survivors.[41]

Captain Moore's official report of 11 April 1840 states that he was unable to get more information about the fate of survivors of the *Britannia*, as the Aborigines who had reported finding the boat had since left the area.[42] The *Port Phillip Herald* reported in more sensationalist terms Captain Moore's opinion 'that our ill fated countrymen, who landed in the boat must have been murdered by the natives'.[43]

The *Britomart* and *Britannia* were two of many ships lost in Bass Strait. Like stories of people lost in the bush, such reports fed fears in a community of newly arrived colonists. The newspapers, which took a prominent role in reporting ships wrecked or missing, and in publishing fictional tales which dramatised the perils of sea travel, contributed to a climate of receptivity for McMillan's narrative of (implied) shipwreck and survival, followed by murder and captivity.

McMillan's account appeared in the context of already circulating published material which provided ready-made components for, and should have given currency and plausibility to, his story. Indeed, *had* McMillan set out to fabricate the story—which is not to assert that this was the case—all the principal themes and elements of the drama were ready to hand.

McMillan's catalogue of diverse household and personal items echoed advertisements in contemporary newspapers which, similarly, invoked the sense of a complete 'household'.[44] European articles, presumably from shipwrecks, were routinely reported washed up along the coastline, attesting to the dangers of sea travel in these waters and providing a model for McMillan's insistence on material items as authentication for his claim of absent 'murdered' Europeans. A lock of female hair found beside the body of a man washed ashore from a boat wrecked outside the Port Phillip heads, in November 1840,[45] parallels the lock of brown hair in McMillan's account as a relic of tragedy and loss.[46]

News of violent encounters between shipwreck survivors and Aborigines, as posited by McMillan, appeared contemporaneously in the newspapers. The *Patriot* on 1 October 1840 reported the murder by Aborigines, 'under circumstances of every brutal ferocity', of the unfortunate crew and passengers of the *Maria* and the *Fanny* in South Australia.[47] Less than a fortnight after McMillan's account appeared, the Melbourne press reported more optimistically the rescue of crews and passengers from two wrecks: the *Isabella* near the Port Phillip heads, and the *Clonmel* at Corner Inlet on the south Gipps Land coast.[48] The *Clonmel* incident, which occured within sixty miles of McMillan's 'sighting', provided an example of shipwreck, survival and rescue in geographic and timely proximity to the events described by McMillan.

Two contemporary examples of Europeans who survived with Aborigines in the bush before returning to white society might also have offered hope for the White Woman's recovery. Eliza Fraser's experience as a female 'captive' and her much publicised rescue, in August 1836, has obvious parallels with the White Woman story. However, comparisons between the two women were never made in the press, not even when a poem on Eliza Fraser appeared in the *Patriot* in 1844.[49] This is a puzzling omission, as a number of people in Port Phillip when McMillan's account was published knew of, or had been associated with, Eliza Fraser's rescue.

George Cavenagh, founding editor of the *Port Phillip Herald*, had been an editor with the *Sydney Gazette* when news of Eliza's rescue began appearing in the Sydney papers and when public interest in her was at its most intense. Cavenagh was to be instrumental in promoting the White Woman cause in 1846. Other Port Phillip newspapermen who probably knew of Eliza were Thomas Strode, former chief printer of the *Sydney Herald*, and George Arden. Strode and Arden had come together from Sydney in 1838 to establish the *Port Phillip Gazette*.[50] As three newspapers attempted to establish their viability and credibility, there was intense competition in 1840 for readers in Port Phillip. One might expect that any one of the editors would have drawn parallels with Eliza Fraser's rescue to capitalise on the White Woman story's newsworthy potential. Yet only the *Patriot* reprinted McMillan's account for Melbourne readers, and then with a dismissive editorial commentary.

Captain Foster Fyans, the first magistrate of Geelong, who arrived in Port Phillip in 1837, might also have made the connection with Eliza Fraser. Fyans, as commandant of the Moreton Bay penal settlement, the site of recovery of Eliza and other survivors of the *Stirling Castle*, had orchestrated the rescue mission and lodged an official report on the rescue. In his *Memoirs*, published years later, Fyans described his several conversations with Eliza during her convalescence at Moreton Bay.[51]

Fyans also knew William Buckley, the escaped convict who lived for thirty-two years with the Wathaurung people in the (now) Geelong area, prior to the arrival of colonists. Buckley acted as interpreter for Fyans's party when Fyans took up his appointment at Geelong in 1837. It seems surprising that Fyans (or someone else) did not nominate Buckley to act as go-between with the Kurnai, to aid investigations into the White Woman report or to negotiate for her recovery. Fyans had employed another 'transculturated' convict, John Graham, as a diplomat–rescuer of Eliza Fraser, with success. Buckley had removed to Hobart by the time McMillan's report was published, but could, presumably, have been recalled to Melbourne or Gipps Land if so required.

Captain Lewis, the harbour-master of Port Phillip, might also have offered or been called upon to try to rescue the White Woman. In 1836, as captain of the *Isabella*, Lewis had rescued two survivors from the brig *Charles Eaton*, wrecked in the Torres Straits several years before. A sensationalist account of the *Charles Eaton* rescue appeared in the *Sydney Herald* on 26 October 1836, at around the time that Eliza Fraser's rescue was making news. The two stories were published as companion pieces in John Curtis's *Shipwreck of the Stirling Castle*, published in London in 1838. In Port Phillip, Captain Lewis rescued numerous shipwreck survivors, including those from the *Clonmel*.[52]

The White Woman story was not taken up at this time, despite circumstances which should have been favourable to its reception. Given the controversy which attended Eliza Fraser's return to England, was her rescue considered to be a failure which everyone wanted to forget? Was McMillan's report considered to be unreliable? Or was the task of rescue in such a remote and inaccessible area as

Gipps Land simply too difficult for the infant town of Melbourne, with its limited resources, to contemplate?

McMillan's story of the captive White Woman reflected and reproduced colonists' anxieties about civilisation at risk in remote, unsettled zones. Like the rumoured fabulous beasts, bunyips, and aprocryphal creatures reported in the Port Phillip newspapers in the early to mid 1840s, the White Woman figure was a manifestation of the fears and fantasies of emigrants coming to terms with life in an unfamiliar country.[53]

The White Woman story and representations of Aboriginality therein, produced Gipps Land and the Kurnai as subjects of knowledge within colonial discourse. The story mediated contestation between rival centres of colonial administration (Sydney and Melbourne); between township and 'untamed frontier' zone; between citizens and squatters; and between Europeans and indigenous peoples in both Melbourne and Gipps Land.

At the time McMillan's account was published, Melbourne had been established for four years in territory belonging to the Woiworung people—part of the Kulin confederation of tribes.[54] According to contemporary commentator Garryowen (Edmund Finn), there was a strong Aboriginal presence in and around Melbourne in 1840 and Aborigines could be met on the streets 'at almost every turn'.[55] The European population in the small but rapidly growing town numbered almost 4500. In the twelve months since La Trobe had taken up his appointment as superintendent of the district, the population had swelled by some 2500 new arrivals, mainly 'overstraiters' from Van Diemen's Land and the first immigrant arrivals from Britain, in addition to some 'overlanders' from New South Wales.

The establishment of Melbourne was a capitalist enterprise, with a flourishing mercantile sector. Melbournians were encouraged by the newspapers to consider the settlement's modest beginnings with pride, as evidence of connection with the larger, civil world. The *Patriot* enthused in December 1839: 'The whole country only a few short months ago was uninhabited, save by the aboriginal black man. Now . . . the harbour rejoices in the rush of many keels . . . The diligence and the provident care of man—of civilised man'.[56] History is being constructed here not just from events, but from narratives

about events, perceived and articulated from within mutually supporting dominant ideologies—imperialism, capitalism, Christianity,
patriarchy. Thus a stretch of water, renamed and reconceptualised
as a 'harbour', 'rejoices' in its new-found mercantile function. The
'aboriginal black man' and the 'civilized [white] man' are produced as
mutually generative stereotypes; one constituted as the absent, ana-
chronistic *negative* to the other's unbridled, providentially sanctioned
positive.

Such stereotypes incorporate the three major ideological components of colonial racism identified by Albert Memmi, namely 'the
gulf between the culture of the colonialist and the colonized . . . the
exploitation of these differences for the benefit of the colonialist . . .
[and] the use of these supposed differences as standards of absolute
fact'.[57] They facilitated the taking of Aboriginal land for the development of Melbourne as an outpost of European civilisation.

The government infrastructure was rudimentary and, prior to
April 1841 when a branch of the Supreme Court was opened, all
legal cases except those of a minor nature had to be heard in Sydney.
There was no coroner, official mail service, harbour, pilot, or wharf
accommodation, and no local town council, although a Marketing
Committee had since 1837 exercised certain limited powers of local
government.

Although primitive by standards which might have applied to a
provincial town in England, Melbourne already had in place by 1840
many of the institutions and societies which replicated the social,
intellectual, political and religious climate of 'home' for the expatriate population.[58] Melbournians had access to three locally produced
newspapers, as well as those from Sydney, Van Diemen's Land and
South Australia, and British papers and periodicals. The circulating
library in Collins Street offered books and English-language newspapers and journals from all over the world. A Mechanics' Institution
had been established for the 'diffusion of scientific and other useful
knowledge among its members and the community generally'.[59]

The European population was predominantly male, young and
single. The March 1841 census identified only two Melbourne inhabitants over the age of sixty.[60] Men outnumbered women in the
towns, and in the squatting districts the sex imbalance was even more
pronounced, with nearly 90 per cent being males. The social con-

sequences of such an imbalance led to major campaigns to encourage female immigration during the 1840s, although for many years women constituted a minority.

Among the middle and upper classes, men eclipsed women in commercial, civic and public life, having access, through political, business or cultural affiliations such as clubs, to decision makers and decision-making processes. Their dominance in public life was reflected in the newspapers. The major network of society for middle-class women was the convention of private calls.[61] Women rarely made 'news'. When they did receive mention the context was likely to be social. Alternately, the tone was admonishing and the intent cautionary.[62] For example, 'Severus' in April 1839 berates 'a certain female, that solitary rides through the lonely forest, with a Military Officer, and that Officer, a YOUNG and SINGLE man, does not add to the credit, or respectability, of any married woman'.[63]

The 'fair sex' were discouraged from venturing out unescorted on the unmade and ill-lit streets of Melbourne after dark, in the item 'Ladies Beware', which describes how a 'respectably dressed female' who was 'deceived by the darkness' had mistaken 'a mass of mud and filth for *terra firma*'. In this instance, the bravery of the passer-by who fortunately heard the exclamations for assistance of the 'forlorn fair one' and 'plunged into the quagmire' to extricate her, enhanced the effectiveness of the representation of the helpless, because unsuper-vised, female.[64] Occasionally a feisty woman made the news.[65] More commonly, genteel women were alluded to indirectly in advertise-ments for female apparel or in information about the latest overseas fashions.

The cultural conditions and influences of the period were in temperament romantic and, like McMillan's account, emphasised woman's vulnerability. Fictional stories which appeared in the news-papers represented ideal femininity as beautiful, virtuous, and lacking agency. Heroines were defenceless and pliable, or indolent and ener-vated. 'The Forsaken', published in the *Patriot* in February 1840, typified the melancholy interest in, and validation of, the death of beautiful young heroines.[66] In 'A True Tale of Shipwreck' a young woman dies 'wounded, and crushed, and pale, and bleeding',[67] while the title of the poem 'She is Withering Away' is sufficiently descrip-tive to require no further elaboration.[68] It is unclear to what extent young women identified with these representations of women as victims of physical terror, suffering, sometimes death. However, the numerousness of examples indicates—as Susan K. Martin has argued —that stories of the dying virgin in nineteenth-century fiction provided 'one site among many for the working out of middle-class female subjectivity'.[69] Sensationalist representations of helpless and virtuous femininity were to characterise the many fictional accounts of the White Woman story which would emerge over subsequent decades.

Grace Darling provided an alternative model of British womanhood, which both opposed and reinforced the stereotype of the helpless heroine. On 7 September 1838, aged twenty-two years, Grace with her father rescued nine survivors from the steamer *Forfarshire*, wrecked off the coast of Northumberland, England.[70] Grace almost immediately became a national heroine, lauded for her intrepidity and self-sacrifice as an exemplar of the virtues of early Victorian womanhood. Wordsworth eulogised her as 'pious and pure, modest and yet so brave'. Her exploit was commemorated in biographies, portraits, paintings of the rescue, songs, dramatic performances and items of memorabilia.

Grace Darling, as *rescuer*, provided a counter to the image of the helpless White Woman awaiting rescue. Grace's dramatic act demonstrated women's strength, resourcefulness and bravery, as well as their self-sacrificing tendencies. Nevertheless, she was also portrayed as the exception which proved the rule. Whilst few women of Grace's era could demonstrate agency and resourcefulness in such a compelling manner, women were not all the stereotypically helpless, fainting creatures of popular fiction. Though restricted by convention, middle-class women engaged in numerous activities. They managed large households and working in paid employment. Some conducted businesses. They attended social functions and took on charitable or philanthropic duties. Reading the newspapers of the day, however, one gets little sense of women's engagement in the wider world. Their invisibility in the public domain was echoed by E. M. Curr who, arriving in Melbourne in 1842, remarked on the 'total absence of women from the streets'.[71]

By the early 1840s a growing number of colonial women accompanied their men to stations in outlying areas. Early Port Phillip women, such as Georgiana McCrae, Annie Baxter and Lavinia Hassell Bennet, recorded the hardships, anxieties and adventures of settler life in diaries and letters.[72] For women in isolated areas, McMillan's story of massacre and captivity by Aborigines possibly exacerbated fears for their own safety. Mrs Katharine Kirkland, arriving at Point Henry in the Western District of Port Phillip in January 1839, 'kept looking round, expecting every moment to see some of the dreaded savages rushing upon us', as she 'had heard such accounts of them in Van Diemen's Land'.[73] Mrs Kirkland, her children and the servant Mary later had a frightening experience when, with her husband and brother away:

> seven wild natives [ran] past our hut at a little distance, all naked, which gave us a great fright; I thought Mary was going to have a fit. I got my pistol, which I had hanging in my room, loaded; Mary then went for hers, and we walked up and down the hut for about an hour. My husband was at the settlement during all the anxious time . . .[74]

The White Woman *story* (regardless of whether the woman existed) was a cultural production emerging from a particular historical period and within a particular context. McMillan's narrative about helpless femininity held in thralldom by 'savages', emerging as he opened up another frontier to European settlement, was a powerful counter to pro-Aboriginal sympathies which threatened to impede the squatters' access to, and use of, tribal lands. The story mediated aspects of colonial experience, including real and imagined dangers for colonial women in outlying areas, which shaped perceptions about the yet unknown country and its Aboriginal inhabitants.

The expectation that Aborigines in Gipps Land would take European captives was perhaps a response to the American frontier experience, where thousands of settlers (men, women and children) were abducted by Native Americans. As influential as these actual abductions were the hundreds of narratives about captivity which circulated and were widely read in America, England and the colonies from the late seventeenth century. It has been argued that the propagandist value of the captivity narrative fuelled anti-Indian feeling and aided European expansion into Indian territories.[75]

In Port Phillip, attitudes to Aborigines were hardening by 1841. John Fawkner, the editor of the *Patriot*, had argued in early 1840 that the Aborigines were the 'rightful owners of the soil', 'the only REAL LORDS of the soil', and railed against the Government of New South Wales for having 'seized upon the whole of the land of the native possessors and owners of the soil,—and . . . [having] made no provision in any way adequate to their support'.[76] Fawkner did not go so far, however, as to suggest that squatters should relinquish their stations or retreat from the land.

In Port Phillip, as in all areas within the colony, competition for land precipitated violence between settlers and Aborigines. Newly arrived squatter Niel Black in 1839 noted that one could 'take up a new run, provided the conscience of the party is sufficiently seared to enable him without remorse to slaughter natives right and left . . . sometimes by wholesale'. After taking up his station Black wrote to his partner: 'A few days since I found a Grave into which about 20 must have been thrown. A Settler taking up a new country is obliged to act towards them in this manner or abandon it'.[77] From 1836 the Crown Land Act provided squatters with a legal right to occupation and—the squatters claimed—to government protection.[78] Debates from around 1837, when George Langhorne established an Aboriginal mission in Melbourne, had centred on who should have responsibility for, and bear the cost of, controlling and 'civilising' the displaced Aborigines.

Sir George Gipps arrived in Sydney in early 1838 as the new governor, with instructions to use the full force of British law to protect the Aborigines. To this end, the British Government also appointed in 1838 a 'Black Protectorate' for Port Phillip, with George Augustus Robinson (late of Van Diemen's Land) as Chief, and four Assistant Protectors. The *Sydney Herald* vehemently opposed the scheme, arguing that '[Port Phillipians] are to have, it seems, a whole tribe of "protectors" quartered on the Colonial funds . . . The whole gang of black animals are not worth the money which the colonists will have to pay for the silly documents upon which we have already wasted too much time'.[79] The Protectorate, which was in place when La Trobe arrived, proved ineffectual. By 1840, La Trobe wrote that '[a]fter a year's experience, I have almost despaired of the

desired result being obtained by the labours of the Assistant Protectors as at present directed'.[80]

While Port Phillipian John Helder Wedge, in London in 1839–40,
was petitioning Secretaries of State for the Colonies, Lord Glenelg,
and later Lord Russell, to intervene so as to prevent a 'war of extermination' in Port Phillip, such as had occurred in Van Diemen's Land,[81]
the colonists were petitioning for an efficient, itinerant mounted
police force to preserve their property from being plundered and
destroyed.[82] The three police forces—Mounted, Border and Native
—charged with maintaining order between Aborigines and colonists
in Port Phillip did not alleviate the conflict. However, despite a rapid
decline in their numbers, Aborigines with varying degrees of success
fought back, adapted and survived the invasion.

As settlers moved into the Western Port, Portland Bay and
Goulburn districts during 1839–40, these areas became sites of conflict. The Port Phillip newspapers reported in inflammatory language
almost daily attacks by Aborigines on squatters' stock and property
and occasionally the killing of unnamed whites (mainly shepherds).
Newspapers, official reports and private correspondence also reported
shootings and poisonings of Aborigines by settlers and parties under
the control of government officers in all areas.[83]

While Aborigines were fighting to retain their land, battle lines
were being redrawn in domains to which they had no access: the
clubs, salons, council chambers and places of business, the halls of
government and the House of Commons, and not least in the pages
of newspapers and journals. In the commerical and administrative
centres of Sydney and Melbourne, squatters worked relentlessly to
influence government policy in their favour. Many hundreds of
thousands of words were written each year about, on behalf of, and
against Aborigines. Without literacy Aborigines had little opportunity to make their own case in print or in court. Others who spoke
for them, even when well-intentioned, did so from their own positions and with their own political or philanthropic ends in mind.

According to contemporary theories of racial hierarchies, Aborigines were classified as amongst the lowest, if not *the* lowest, on
the scale of humanity: as 'nothing more than the connecting link
between the human and the brute creation'.[84] According to capitalist

ideologies they were deemed to have no legitimate claim to land which they had not made 'productive', and numerous schemes were devised to convert their 'desultory habits' into 'those of settled industry'.[85] According to the tenets of Christianity they were 'heathens'. Under the mantra of 'progress' they were pronounced 'savages' or 'cannibals' to be controlled and 'civilised' or consigned—by some regretfully—to extinction.

Such representations fixed Aborigines as remnants of a stone-age past and not fully human. A correspondent in the Sydney *Colonist* (pre-empting the arguments of anti-colonial theorists by more than a century) perceived in 1838 that the first step in oppression 'is to degrade the objects of our hate, and, if possible, to convince ourselves, or others, that the beings we have to do with, are not entitled to the full rights and privileges of humanity; and the oppressor will be still more successful if he can assert that his proposed victims are not men'.[86]

In the administration of justice, the legal status of Aborigines was ambivalent. Although defined as 'subjects of the Queen' and having 'an equal right with the people of European origin to the protection and assistance of the Law of England',[87] Aborigines were not permitted to give sworn evidence, and charges by Aborigines against Europeans could not be upheld in court unless corroborated by a European.[88] The *Patriot* in 1841 lamented: 'All our legal proceedings with regard to the Aborigines are, in the present state of the law, *ex parte*, and therefore monstrously unjust; indeed legal protection for the sable sons of the forest exists but in name'.[89]

A cluster of Aboriginal deaths while in police custody in the early months of 1841 reinforces the impression of systemic violence against Aborigines within the legal system. All the deceased were pronounced by the Colonial Surgeon, Dr Cussens, as having 'Died from the visitation of God'. In the most widely reported of these cases, because it went to court, two Mounted Police troopers were indicted for the manslaughter of an Aboriginal, Jagerrogger, 'by compelling him to walk from the Goulburn to Melbourne, a distance of 80 miles, with a dog chain round his neck, and a pair of handcuffs on his wrists, in two days, on the 10th of January 1841'.[90] Jagerrogger was suspected of burning haystacks on a settler's station. Evidence given at the trial reveals that Jagerrogger walked or was run some 200 miles between

28 November and 5 December, chained to the trooper's horse. The charge relates only to the final Goulburn–Melbourne section of the journey, when Jagerrogger was ill. The case was brought to trial on 17 May 1841 after La Trobe and Police Magistrate William Lonsdale instigated an enquiry. Dr Cussens, who attended Jagerrogger on his arrival in Melbourne, told the court:

> I do not think that travelling with a pair of handcuffs on, and a chain round the neck in the month of December would have caused mortal effects provided no pressure on the neck took place; but I should say it was better avoided; I made no *post mortem* examination on the body; I did not consider it necessary.

The jury, without retiring, returned a verdict of not guilty.

The Mounted Police troopers' inhumane treatment of Jaggerrogger, and McMillan's claim that Aborigines had massacred Europeans, occurred in the context of reports of settler/Aboriginal violence in every area of the district. The *Patriot* of 3 June 1841, for example, contained four such articles. An editorial headed 'The Blacks' informed readers that 'the blacks, in different parts of the colony, are again committing outrages' and cited complaints of their conduct in the vicinity of the Ovens River and at the Clarence, where the murder of a shepherd had been reported. The second item, an extract of a letter from the Ovens River, reprinted from the *Sydney Monitor*, advised that '[t]he blacks are now past all control; they are slaughtering cattle in every direction, and when Mr. Commissioner Bingham was spoken to on the subject, he calmly placed his arms akimbo, and very cooly replied—"Catch them"!!!'.

The other two articles are gruesome and sensationalist. One, a letter from Thomas Grant of Mustham, in the Portland Bay District, reporting the murder of two Europeans, recounted how Grant had found what he thought was a 'white log, with a large eagle hawk pecking upon it', but which, on closer inspection, was found to be the remains of 'poor Mr. Morton':

> He was stripped quite naked and lying on his face, the greater part of which was actually cut away, his head is one mass of frightful wounds, and many bruises on different parts of his

arms and body, which is torn by birds of prey. About fifty yards nearer the dray, lay the remains or skeleton of Larry, from whose bones the flesh had been completely cut off. The skin was cut a little above the wrists and ancles with a sharp knife or instrument, from all other parts the flesh was cut and nothing left but bare bones. God only knows whether they did not this before life was extinct, as the struggle with him had been long and dreadful, his arms were extended and were speared through the wrists to the ground.[91]

The image of Europeans tortured and murdered—Morton as though crucified—then left naked for birds of prey to feed off, is a realisation of colonial nightmares. The scene, recounted in graphic detail, with intimations of cannibalism, and read in conjunction with the adjacent reports of 'outrages' occurring in other parts of the colony, stirred antipathy towards Aborigines. The report might have triggered the 1841 'battle' at nearby Lubra Creek in which men, women and children of the Morpor tribe are said to have been murdered by settlers.[92]

The *Patriot*'s framing of the letter under the heading 'Local Intelligence—The Blacks—Fresh Outrage from Portland' validated Grant's allegations. In contrast, an allegation of an outrage perpetrated upon Aborigines by a European appears on the same page under the heading 'Misrepresentation' and prefaced by the editorial comment: 'We find the following outrageous falsehoods in an advertisement signed "F. J. Sloman" which appears in the *Sydney Gazette* of the 22nd' [May 1841]:

I see by the *Gazette* of this day, that the blacks have again been spearing some white people to the southward, which we take amiss and call it an outrage; but, Sir, permit me to ask you what you call murdering a whole tribe, which massacre took place a short time since, at a station 150 miles from Melbourne, Port Phillip; and at this present moment while I am writing this to you, ——— has forty two human heads, stuck upon poles around his house, and nailed to his door posts. Pray, Sir, will you call this an outrage committed by us? I would ask you, Sir, who cut off the heads of these forty-two unfortunate people, and what became of their bodies?—are they burnt or left to be

torn in pieces by wild dogs and birds of prey?—and, Sir, I
would further ask who murdered eight more of these poor
people at the same time, and threw their bodies into the creek,
on the road side between ———'s station and Melbourne,
which were seen by the same gentleman who visited there a
short time ago and saw all the heads as before described!

Sloman articulates another nightmare of the colonial imagination
—the European who has 'reverted' to a state of 'savagery'. The image
of the impaled heads shocks, because it turns colonialist representations of indigenous peoples as 'headhunters' and 'cannibals' back
upon itself. The editor's discrediting of Sloman, at the conclusion of
the article, as a drunkard and a 'notorious swindler', and his concluding statement that 'It is perfectly unnecessary to say that his story has
not the slightest foundation of truth', does not dispel the spectre
which Sloman had raised.

Although the *Patriot* was, at other times, to rail at the 'blood-
thirsty and villainous atrocities . . . committed in all parts of these
Colonies, by men whose skins we regret to say are white', in this case
it did not credit the report.[93] Perhaps the binarisms 'civilisation' and
'savagery' were in danger of collapsing around the image of the
impaled heads: an image which several decades later Joseph Conrad
would use in *Heart of Darkness* to indicate the depravity of Kurtz, the
European who has gone 'native'.[94] Or perhaps the English tradition
from previous centuries of exhibiting the heads of those executed as
traitors, mounted on pikestaffs on London Bridge as a salutary warn-
ing, provided a model in a new colony to quell Aboriginal resistance.

Stories like that of the White Woman anchored abstract notions
about colonists' rights to occupy the land in the specifics of a moment
in frontier experience, and provided a powerful anodyne to assuage
any lingering feelings of guilt attached to the colonising project. In a
small and scattered European population, such stories would help to
maintain the binarisms on which colonising discourses relied for
their authority, and colonising practices for their justification. Without the *idea* of her, and in light of the devastating impact of colonialism on the Aboriginal population, the contradictions inherent
in the project might have weakened, if not undermined, its authoritative address.

CHAPTER 2

The Progress of Discovery

Three years after McMillan reported sighting a captive White Woman, the story was revived briefly. In November 1843 the *Port Phillip Herald* published a descriptive three-column article on Gipps Land by a commentator using the *nom-de-plume* X. Y. Z.[1] In one sweeping sentence X. Y. Z. related what he termed a 'romantic tale':

> Here on a rising bank close to the high reeds which extend along the river, when Mr. McAlister's party first arrived, an encampment of blacks was found, who, as soon as they saw the whites, descended into the high reeds, there were women and one old man with them, hurrying onward, one of whom it was supposed was a white person male or female, probably the latter; at their deserted encampment were found many articles of clothing, blankets, broken bottles, childrens' dresses, a prayer book, &c.; and on the ground recently formed by some sharp instrument the figure of a heart of large dimensions, with a little path leading from its extremity to the swamp.

The story of the heart emerged during—and was integrally linked with—post-settlement development in Gipps Land. The wreck of the steamer *Clonmel* in early 1841 opened the way for coastal trade with east Gipps Land and ushered in a period of intense interest in the region. Captain Lewis, while rescuing the crew and passengers from the *Clonmel*, discovered the very fine harbour and inland lake at Corner Inlet. News of Lewis's discovery focussed public attention on Gipps Land and gave impetus to moves already under way to open a road between the Gipps Land coast and the interior.[2] Rescuers, salvage operators, and speculators converged on Gipps Land in early 1841, as McMillan continued his efforts to find a route from the interior to the coast. McMillan's party eventually reached Port Albert on 14 February 1841 to find already there members of the Gipps Land Company who had arrived by sea to investigate the area's potential for cattle grazing; a marine survey party from Melbourne examining the wreck of the *Clonmel*; and a salvage crew sent from Sydney.[3]

The *Patriot* of 4 February 1841, suggested in passing that as Captain Lewis was to conduct a survey of Corner Inlet, this would provide:

> a favourable opportunity for ascertaining the accuracy of Mr McMillan's statements relative to the captivity of a white female among the Gipps Land blacks, published in a late number of the *Patriot*, for although not disposed to place much confidence in the report ourselves, we still consider it possible that some of the passengers of the 'Sarah', 'Yarra Yarra' or 'Britannia' may have gained the coast in safety, and subsequently fallen into the hands of the savages. This is rendered the more probable by the circumstance mentioned, in Mr. McMillan's communication, of the post mortem examination by Dr. Arbuckle of the body of the infant found in the blacks' camp, and declared to be that of a white child. The idea that a female of European birth is detained in durance vile by these ruthless savages is horrifying in the extreme, and we think the government would be greatly to blame if such an impression should gain ground in the public opinion and no effort be made to ascertain its truth or falsity.[4]

The 'favourable opportunity' was not, however, seized by the government, Captain Lewis, McMillan, or anyone else. The article's title 'Corner Inlet' suggests that enthusiasm for the new 'promised land' of Gipps Land was the *Patriot*'s overriding concern. Discussion of the White Woman issue which, it might be argued, deserved its own space and title, was subsumed.

The *Patriot* in calling for a survey of Corner Inlet organised from Melbourne attempted to exert pressure on La Trobe to secure the strategic advantage to Port Phillip which Captain Lewis's discovery offered.[5] Although recent regulations had made Gipps Land 'part and parcel of *Australia Felix*', the area was still a contested zone, with Sydney and Melbourne vying for control.

Uncertainty over whether Gipps Land was to be governed from Sydney or Melbourne was not resolved until 1843, when Governor Gipps issued a proclamation re-setting the northern boundary of Port Phillip in line with the present Victoria–New South Wales border, and formalising La Trobe's powers as Lieutenant-Governor over the territory within the prescribed boundaries.[6] In this context of potential mercantile interests at Corner Inlet, and development and settlement of Gipps Land by squatters and speculators from Port Phillip and Sydney, lands occupied by Aborigines were being increasingly appropriated.

In late March 1841 the *Beagle* was dispatched from Sydney to conduct a regular survey of Corner Inlet's bay and rivers.[7] On 26 April the *Patriot* reported that the Gipps Land Company from Melbourne was surveying the River Albert; that a special survey was also being conducted by Mr Rutledge; and that there had been numerous applications for passage from parties desirous of seeing the 'land of promise'.[8] An expeditionary party of speculators from Melbourne was also hopeful of finding coal deposits in the region.[9]

McMillan could have recruited assistance from any of these people who arrived in Gipps Land within weeks or months of his 'sighting', to attempt to locate or rescue the captive woman. Despite all of the activity in the area over several months, there is no indication that he did so, or that anyone made enquiries about the White Woman or attempted to ascertain whether there was any basis for belief in the story. Neither did the numerous newspaper reports on the region mention the White Woman, even when details from William Brodribb's journal which might have recalled McMillan's account were published in the *Patriot*. Brodribb, a member of the Gipps Land Company, recounted that during the party's journey from Port

Albert into the Gipps Land interior, they found at a 'black fellow's camp' an English newspaper, dated 16 June 1838, and they 'had a hearty laugh at the idea of the Gipps Land blacks taking in the news'.[10] Brodribb's party was following tracks previously marked by McMillan. However, neither he nor the *Patriot* speculated whether this might have been the campsite where McMillan ostensibly had sighted the White Woman and where his party found 'London, Glasgow and Aberdeen newspapers, printed in 1837 and 1838'.

Brodribb did not mention finding any of the other items catalogued by McMillan and did not impute to the Aborigines sinister actions in acquiring the newspaper. For Brodribb, the newspaper represented a marker of cultural difference; a relic from a major centre of European culture, made incongruous by its location in the camp of illiterate Aborigines.

Brodribb's comment hints at the importance of the written text— the English book or, in this case, newspaper, in securing colonialist domination. This is not because the 'emblem' of the English book is one of the 'signs taken for wonders' by the colonised, displacing the authority of their own experience, as post-colonial theorist Homi Bhabha has argued of British colonisation in India.[11] Rather, Brodribb represents the Aborigines 'taking the news' in parodic or mimetic terms which negate the text's authority *for Aborigines*. It is Brodribb's account of the Aborigines' *inability* to respond to the authority of the English text which makes them the butt of his party's 'hearty laugh'.

The hopes of Melbourne speculators and individuals who arrived in Port Albert intending to buy land under regulations issued in March 1841 were soon dashed. It was not until July 1843, when surveying was completed, that the first land sales could be held. In the interim, the tiny but bustling settlement languished. When William Odell Raymond arrived in Gipps Land about June 1842, the European population was a meagre 'one hundred and forty-four free men, thirty-three bond, twenty-six free women, and seventeen children'.[12]

X. Y. Z.'s glowing article on Gipps Land, published in Melbourne in November 1843, might have been aimed at reviving interest in the area. The anonymous X. Y. Z. was Melbourne surveyor, architect, writer, artist and Melbourne Club member Robert Russell, who visited Port Albert twice in 1843 to undertake work on Reeves

Survey at Tarra Ville.[13] After completing the survey in October 1843 and while awaiting a return voyage to Melbourne, Russell travelled from Port Albert through the interior as far as the Avon River. His published report on Gipps Land included details observed by, and reported to, him on this journey. He related the story of the White Woman as a 'romantic' tale which had given rise to the naming of Mr Foster's station on the Glengarry (now Latrobe) River—'The Heart'.

Russell had passed through Foster's station on his way to the Avon River. Upstream was McMillan's station, Bushy Park. The locale for the incident described in the story was (as far as can be determined) near the main track from Port Albert to McMillan's and Macalister's stations (approximately where the present-day South Gippsland Highway crosses the Latrobe River at Sale). This was one of the tracks forged by McMillan *en route* from Bushy Park to the coast when in November 1840 he 'sighted' the White Woman.

Although X. Y. Z.'s version of the story varies significantly from McMillan's account, there are sufficient similarities to suggest a common origin. The story of the heart provides an example of the mutation or hybridisation which was to characterise the White Woman's story in subsequent years. The version related to X. Y. Z. reflected modifications which might have been made at any time between 1840 and late 1843.

X. Y. Z. makes no mention of the crucial piece of evidence in McMillan's account: the body of a child thought to be of European parentage. In its place is a new component: 'the figure of a heart of large dimensions', recently formed on the ground by some sharp instrument, 'with a little path leading from its extremity to the swamp'. The heart—a readily recognisable European symbol—refocusses the story from McMillan's imputed massacre of Europeans to a sentimental tale, its import being that the ground drawing was carved by the white person who was, in all probability, female. X. Y. Z.'s acknowledgment that this was a 'romantic story' signals a note of caution about its veracity.

McMillan made no reference to a ground carving. Though, as noted in chapter 1, he alluded to 'marks and figures about the largest of the native huts', he did not indicate what these might have been.

It is unlikely, however, that in such a detailed account, McMillan would have omitted an item of such singular significance as a large heart cut into the ground. Russell, who had a romantic turn of mind, might have fastened on a minor aspect of the story and developed it. Or was he—a naive townsman—being 'gulled'? Perhaps X. Y. Z.'s position as an outsider, a visitor to the area, led him to suggest that the story be given some credibility:

> the report of a white person being amongst the blacks has been again raised, and there are not wanting men who affirm that they have seen a white person, male or female, amongst the natives, who when observed drove the white person before them. Such a circumstance surely demands enquiry.

As X. Y. Z. acknowledged elsewhere in the article, there were twenty-two stations in the area by that time, 'leaving but small space for new comers'. It begs the question why, if the captive existed, did she not make contact with a station.

McMillan's account was anchored in a narrative of exploration. The story of the Heart belongs to a later phase; that of the developing post-occupation history of the Gipps Land region. It marks the earliest example of the story's emergence as a local legend and it signals a change in perception and reception of the story. As a 'romantic' tale it relegates the events related to a 'once-upon-a-time' realm of a myth of origin.

From an early twenty-first-century vantage point it is difficult to determine what meanings in the 1840s might have been ascribed to the symbol of the heart. However, within Western culture the heart has for centuries been designated as the seat of feeling, an emotional, ethical and moral register, and a polyvalent and powerfully evocative symbol. In 1840 when the White Woman story emerged, the symbol of the heart conveyed, economically and powerfully, the concerns of a post-Romantic age, which emphasised the primacy of emotional response, moderated by a concern with moral and spiritual rectitude.

X. Y. Z.'s description of the heart intersected by the little path leading to the swamp invites visual comparisons with traditional artistic depictions of profane love (Cupid's piercing arrow) and—

in the pierced heart of Christian iconography—sacred love. These associations represent binary notions of womanhood in which the White Woman could be at once sexualised subject (the 'concubine' of at least one 'savage paramour'), and idealised, genteel Christian lady who reads the bible (and deserves to be rescued).

Like other alleged traces of the White Woman's existence— messages carved on trees, footprints on a sandy beach—the figure of the heart engages woman and landscape in an interplay of meanings. The detail of the heart shifts the focus from what was in McMillan's account a concern with violation and miscegenation to that of romantic intent; from woman and location defiled by violence, to woman and land as objects of desire and possession. In interpreting a ground marking as a heart, the settlers may have been projecting their desire for the company of absent wives and sweethearts, or seeking legible signs to render the landscape readable.

The story of the heart was not taken up when X. Y. Z.'s article was published in 1843 but resurfaced three years later at a time when public interest in the captive woman had revived. On 3 September 1846, the day after a public meeting was held in Melbourne to gal-vanise support for an expedition to rescue the woman, X. Y. Z. wrote to the editor of the *Port Phillip Gazette* reiterating and embellishing the story of the heart. In this later version he presented a case of more violent abduction of a female captive by spear-wielding Aborigines.[14] While claiming authenticity for the story, and his own veracity, X. Y. Z. retained his anonymity: 'my name is at the service of the committee named at yesterday's meeting', he offered, 'but there is no occasion to make it public'. His informant's identity was similarly implied, and integrity asserted, without disclosure: 'the gentleman in charge of Mr McAlister's station, in Gipps Land—one whose state-ment is entitled to the highest credit—and whose name, if necessary, can be given'.

The effect of such promised, but deferred, revelation invests X. Y. Z. and his informant (presumably McMillan) with an air of mystery and the story with the status of privileged information. If X. Y. Z. and his informant conveyed what they believed to be an accurate account, the reliability of X. Y. Z.'s recollection in 1846 of 'facts' mentioned to him 'when on the spot, nearly four [*sic*] years ago' would still have to questioned.

In this 1846 letter X. Y. Z. cited as corroborative evidence for the story of the heart his earlier article on Gipps Land, published in the *Port Phillip Herald* of 14 November 1843. He did not, however, indicate that *he* was the author of that article, and readers might mistakenly have assumed that it provided independent corroboration. X. Y. Z. also cited information provided by a man named Collins, a sometime resident of Port Albert, that 'at the time Glengarry first formed his station at Port Albert, the blacks were seen there, and with them a white person, whether male or female he could not say, but if a female she was very tall'.

X. Y. Z. further cited information provided to him by ' "Lively," a native now in Melbourne', who was supposed to have heard the story from a 'native girl from Gipps Land and now living with his tribe (but who cannot make herself understood by Europeans,) . . .'. The girl, he said, had informed 'Lively' that:

> *a white woman is with her tribe,*—that she has three children,— that for a long time she was much grieved, (plenty cry was ['Lively's'] expression,) *that when the white people approach she is led forcibly away,* (this ['Lively'] describes by his action, seizing his own arm above his elbow, as in the act of holding and leading on another.) [original emphasis]

X. Y. Z. was the only person to publicly raise the story of the Heart—in 1843 and 1846. The discrepancy between X. Y. Z.'s version and McMillan's earlier account was not remarked on by any of the newspapers. Neither did they embrace the detail of the Heart with the same enthusiasm they were to display for other anecdotal elements attributed to the White Woman, such as messages made on trees. Given his role as propounder of the story of the Heart, it comes as no surprise that Robert Russell—otherwise X. Y. Z.—took up the motif in his unpublished 1849 novella, 'The Heart'.

The romanticising of the White Woman and the region with which she was associated might suggest an attempt (perhaps unconscious) by settlers and those with interests in the region to deflect unpalatable truths about what settlement entailed. Enshrined in the toponymy of the region, the story of the heart rehabilitated from the recent past an acceptable local history which could be related to visitors like Russell and be retained for posterity.

The story of the heart feminised the landscape and invested it with human feeling. It also overwrote Aboriginal histories and traces of occupation with post-settlement narratives of European endeavour and progress. Once such a romantic story secures a place in local history, it provides a self-perpetuating process of authentication which is difficult to dislodge. Paul Carter has argued that in local histories 'the place serves much the same function as the plot in fiction: it is a means of unifying heterogeneous material, of lending it, rhetorically at least, a unique destiny'.[15] Carter identifies the act of naming as not simply a necessary preliminary to historical progress but an historical event itself; a struggle for power, which opens a space for action and which on one level 'underlines the point that successful colonization depends not only on the physical exclusion of a former people, but on the suppression of their sounds':

> Places of human significance are the consequence of naming. It is not the topography of a place that qualifies it to circulate in the collective mind, to become a site of economic speculation, a destination for travellers, an address, a home. What matters is its rhetorical identity: its name. Before this town or village became a place, it was an unclear (as well as uncleared) space. But the act of naming changed this: it created a place in the wilderness, a point towards which one might direct one's footsteps; it implied the possibility of a reply, a local resonance or, at the very least, a ghostly echo.

According to local historians, Heart Station was first established by George Curlewis in 1841 or 1842, at which time the name might have reflected an existing local toponymy. It seems more likely that John Foster, sometime licensee of the Hart Inn at Port Albert, and the station's manager at the time X. Y. Z. was told the story, named the property.

In attributing the naming of Heart Station to the White Woman story, more prosaic possibilities were foreclosed, such as its location in the broad swath of rich pastoral country designated the 'Heart of Gippsland' as noted by Commissioner Tyers in 1844.[16] Russell had referred to the 'heart of Gipps Land' in this general sense in a letter written on 30 March 1843, several months before he heard the story of the naming of Heart Station and the White Woman.[17] The Heart was also a nickname attached to Tolbooth Prison in Edinburgh, which featured in Sir Walter Scott's popular historical romance *The Heart of Midlothian* (1818). Homesick Scots in Gipps Land might have appreciated the satiric overtones of attaching such a name to a local site, as an unwalled prison for convict or ticket-of-leave station hands, or as a site connected with punitive measures taken against local Aborigines.

The story of the heart also elided a more likely explanation for such a ground carving: namely, that it was the work of Aborigines, and marked a site of ritual significance. This possibility was acknowledged locally at the time that X. Y. Z. was told the alternative version. Mr Chas. Lucas who arrived in Gipps Land in February 1844, only a few months after X. Y. Z. had learned of the story, unequivocally attributed the heart to Aborigines:

> The Heart station included the site of an aboriginal 'corroboree' ground on which was held what was known as the 'Bush Corroboree' to which only initiated males were admitted. Among the rites were a number of figures marked out on the ground, one of which was heart shaped, and this was selected as the subject most suitable for a name.[18]

A. W. Howitt confirmed in the early 1880s that ground-cut (or marked) figures formed part of Aboriginal ceremonies amongst several eastern Australian tribes. Howitt described ground figures found elsewhere which appear to resemble X. Y. Z.'s description of the heart and the little path leading from it. One was 'an oval cleared space, about thirty or forty feet in area. The edges of the space were raised about nine inches. This cleared space was connected with the top of the hill, and another cleared space by a narrow path'.[19] Another site, seen about 1844, comprised: '[a] circle of eighty to ninety feet in diameter . . . dug, or scratched, on a level piece of ground, leaving a space of four or five feet undisturbed to enter the circle by'.[20] Howitt also described an almost life-sized, earth-cut figure, which formed part of a *Kuringal* (initiation) ceremony held by the Yuin people, in the Bega region of New South Wales (abutting Gipps Land) in the early 1880s.[21]

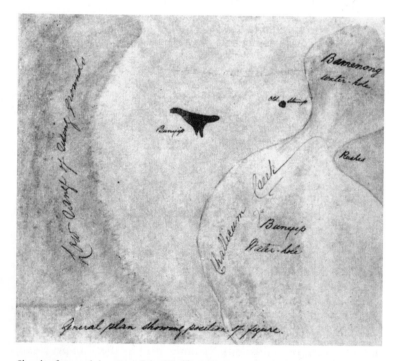

Sketch of ground drawing of the Challicum Bun-yip, by I. W. Scott (1867)
Reproduced courtesy of the Museums Board of Victoria and *The Victorian
Naturalist.*

Another report dating from around 1850 describes a large turf-cut figure of some thirty feet in length, known as the Challicum Bun-yip, at Challicum Station near Ararat, in the (then) Portland Bay District of Port Phillip. Aborigines were said to have cut the figure after an unknown animal died on the bank of the water-hole. According to anecdotal evidence, the Aborigines would visit the site periodically and would trace the Bun-yip's outline afresh. It is not known how long the figure had been there, but Aborigines reputedly said in 1856 that it had been traced long ago. Sketches of the Bun-yip were made in 1867.[22] Aldo Massola, in his 1957 article on the Challicum Bunyip, noted it was one of only three Aboriginal turf-cut figures in Victoria—the other two being the 'Heart' in Gipps Land, and an animal resembling a horse cut on the banks of the Hopkins River near Wickliffe. Massola says of the 'Heart' that 'if there was such a drawing, it could just as easily have been cut by the Aborigines for one of their ceremonies, although it certainly would not have been meant by them to represent a human heart'.[23]

In his 1846 letter to the *Gazette*, X. Y. Z. referred to the heart being 'neatly *cut*' on the '*green turf*' [my emphasis]. In his earlier article of November 1843, he described the figure 'on the *ground* recently *formed* by some sharp instrument' [my emphasis]. The slippage from 'ground' to 'green turf', from 'formed' to 'cut', reveals X. Y. Z.'s inclination to align this figure with ancient British turf-cut figure traditions. X. Y. Z.'s interpretation was possibly shaped by the context in which it was told to him. X. Y. Z.'s report, if grounded in fact, would be the first documented account of a British-style turf-cut figure in Port Phillip.

Renewed interest in turf-cut figures in Britain at around the time the White Woman rumours started might explain how she could be associated with such figures. In his book *White Horses and Other Hill Figures*, Morris Marples notes that there are nearly fifty turf-cut figures in Great Britain, a number of which date from the first half of the nineteenth century.

Marples details the regular scourings (recutting) of the famous Uffington horse—events which had the character of a fair, attracted large numbers of people from neighbouring counties (some 30 000 people attended the 1780 scouring) and were reported in the newspapers.[24] The scouring held on 19 and 20 September 1838, revived by Lord Craven to celebrate the Coronation of Queen Victoria and the birth of an heir to the house of Craven, lent contemporary relevance to turf-cut figures at the time of the White Woman story's emergence. The turf-cut figure links the White Woman indirectly with ideals of womanly virtue, as exemplified in the young Queen. The White Woman story's rehabilitative function (previously noted) parallels on a modest scale the role Queen Victoria adopted in rehabilitating a moribund monarchy and restoring its public image.

The British turf-cut figure connection also suggests another interpretation for the word 'heart'. Given that 'hart' and 'heart' are homophones, it might be that the figure initially ascribed to the White Woman as 'hart' was interpreted as 'heart'. At least one turf-cut stag/hart still exists—the Mormond Stag in Aberdeenshire—which is thought to date from around 1870.[25] The woman's association with Scotland's most characteristic animal, the stag/hart, might represent an attempt to impart Scottish identity to her. Stags are also associated in Irish and Welsh traditions with wild nature and with the forest, as intermediaries between gods and humans, as well as with the Arthurian quest and other cultural traditions dating at least from the time of Richard II, whose armorial bearings featured the white hart. Remnants of these traditions in Port Phillip in the 1840s included the Old White Hart Inn (later the White Hart Hotel) at the top of Bourke Street, Melbourne, and John Foster's previously mentioned Hart Inn at Port Albert in Gipps Land.[26]

The attachment of the story of the heart/hart to the White Woman, at a time when newly arrived colonists in Gipps Land were making Kurnai country their own, would have facilitated the inscription of old-world traditions onto a 'new' landscape, in an imaginative, if not fully articulated, sense. Before regular surveys were undertaken and when station boundaries were approximate and frequently disputed, stories such as that of the Heart must have functioned as anecdotal surveys to mediate the spatial transformation and conceptual appropriation of tribal lands.

Post-colonial theorists have explicated the symbolic nature of colonialist activities, such as mapping and renaming 'new' territories, as models of cultural dominance. Gananath Obeyesekere has argued that 'the larger the land and the sparser its population, the more easily it can be overpowered by toponymy'.[27] Gayatri Spivak notes the role of cartography in textualising and making the territory into an object to be understood.[28] Graham Huggan, too, has discussed the territorial strategies associated with maps, and the function of maps as symbols of political authority.[29] For early Gipps Land settlers, in an area still largely unmapped and unsurveyed, and with only a scattered European population, the story of the heart (even in its pre-textual form prior to X. Y. Z.'s publishing of the story) would have helped to 'world' territory unfamiliar to them by interpreting or incorporating traces of Kurnai inscription within a European cultural narrative.

The story of the Heart demonstrates the links between processes of inscription and practices of exploration and occupation. Heart Station, in allegedly deriving its name from the White Woman's act of inscription, could invoke the presence of a genteel woman and the complex meanings symbolised by the heart to perpetuate a tale of captivity which simultaneously elided and justified the taking by Europeans of Kurnai land.

Surveyor Robert Russell's presence in Gipps Land in 1843 heralded the end of the pre-survey era, at least in the more settled areas near Port Albert. With Commissioner Tyers's arrival in January 1844, regular surveys of squatters' stations commenced and station boundaries became more formally defined. By the time Russell heard the story of the heart, its cartographic role was nearing obsolescence, shortly to be overtaken by more formal measures. As a toponymous referent to the Kurnai as the brutal captors of a helpless White Woman, however, it would retain its propagandistic efficacy.

On his arrival in Gipps Land, Tyers found the settlers embroiled in a battle with the indigenous people for possession of the land. The European population in the district was at that time around 450, of whom some 325 were employed on the forty stations, and 120 were living on the special surveys at Victoria, Tarraville and Port Albert. The 'Worrigals'—the term used in the 1840s to denote 'wild' Gipps Land Aborigines—outnumbered Europeans and were, Tyers reported, 'very troublesome'. Tyers, inundated by complaints from the squatters about Aborigines spearing their stock, reported to La Trobe that 'the small police force at my disposal is inadequate to put a stop to them'.[30] Increasingly, during the period from his arrival to the revival of the rumours about a captive White Woman in 1846, Tyers's time and energies were occupied in dealing with these complaints and in subduing Kurnai resistance, as the settlers had been doing prior to his arrival.

A. W. Howitt's 'guesstimate' of the Kurnai population at the beginning of European settlement in 1839, based on the (conflicting) memories of the earliest settlers, was that they were 'very numerous' and probably numbered between 1000 and 1500.[31] Each clan occupied a discrete territory within the area stretching from Wilson's Promontory to the Snowy River and bounded on the west by the Great Dividing Range, and migrated periodically from the high country to the low, lake country, according to the seasonal availability of foods. The White Woman was at various times said to be in most of these locations, so it is not possible to attach her to any particular tribe or clan.

Anxiety within the European community about the threat of Aborigines in Gipps Land was reflected in Port Phillip, Sydney and Hobart newpaper commentaries, and expressed by settlers in the region. William Brodribb, a member of the Melbourne-financed Gipps Land Company, a speculative enterprise which established a base camp at Port Albert in 1840, described the fears which his party felt when out in the bush, when they imagined that Aborigines planned to attack them.

To discourage potential attacks, Brodribb's party 'occasionally fired off our rifles at marks on the trees, or empty bottles suspended in the air, to show them that we had arms to defend ourselves. We brought with us a small cannon, which we loaded and fired off towards the bay, and they saw the double shot strike the water.' Although Brodribb's party does not appear to have been at any time threatened by Aborigines, his fears stemmed in large part from the unknown (to him) nature of the country. Time and again his journal records his party's sense of vulnerability in unfamiliar territory. Aborigines were, he said 'never to be trusted in a *new and unexplored* country'; an '*unexplored* country, only inhabited by savages, kangaroos, and emus'; 'altogether *a new* country, and only inhabited by savages' [my emphasis].[32]

Brodribb's comments are a reminder that European occupation involved *imaginative* as well as physical appropriation. While settlers could occupy Kurnai territory with their flocks and herds, they also had to render it imaginatively familiar in order to fully possess it.

Helen Tiffen has identified the key role played by European texts—explorers' journals, drama, fiction, historical accounts and maps—in enabling conquest and colonisation.[33] Brodribb's journal, in presenting the Kurnai as the untrustworthy and threatening 'Other' to his own party, served such a discursive function.

The story of the Heart, which provided settlers with a narrative code to imaginatively familiarise and appropriate the region within a European symbolic framework, may also have served political ends. The emergence of this story in X. Y. Z.'s article only a few months after the killing near Port Albert in July 1843 of Ronald Macalister (nephew of influential squatter Lachlan Macalister, McMillan's employer)—purportedly by Aborigines—might not be entirely co-incidental. Macalister's death sparked outrage within the European community in Gipps Land and the major towns. An anonymous correspondent wrote to the *Sydney Herald* that Macalister had been brutally murdered and disfigured beyond recognition 'by the harmless, innocent denizens of the wilds of Gipps Land, bearing the anomalous cognomen of Her Majesty's most liege subjects (we give it as a gratutious opinion, most bitter enemies)'.[34] According to the *Port Phillip Herald*, Macalister was the fifth white man to be murdered by Aborigines within little more than twelve months.[35] Gippsland historians have acknowledged that Macalister's death set off a chain of reprisal massacres by the Highland Brigade. The most infamous of these incidents was the Warrigal Creek massacre where the number of Kurnai killed has been estimated to be as high as 150.[36]

The previous year, in response to reports of squatters killing Aborigines in the Portland Bay District, Governor Gipps had threatened to cancel all depasturing licences, or at least to refuse to renew them, and to 'convert the whole into an aboriginal reserve'.[37] Given the tentative legal status of squatters' occupation of land at the time, the anticipated arrival of Commissioner Tyers in Gipps Land within months of the Warrigal Creek massacre might have provided sufficient incentive for McMillan and/or others to revive the White Woman story as indemnity. The sensationalised versions of Macalister's murder which circulated in the press and which have persisted in local history might have served the same function. Settler concern about being called to account, particularly by 'do-gooder' outsiders, might explain why Russell was told the story of the heart for an article intended for publication in Melbourne, while Chas. Lucas, a newly arrived settler, learned about the corroboree site.

Concerned about the situation in Gipps Land following the Macalister murder, La Trobe asked the Chief Protector, George Augustus Robinson, to investigate. Robinson reported that '[a] few weeks anterior to my arrival the Blacks had murdered a Mr. McAlister within a short distance of the Port, and as might have been anticipated were completely dispersed'. He placed the blame for Macalister's murder onto 'depraved white men' from Van Diemen's Land and the Middle Districts, who had in 'a fit of drunkenness shot at and killed some friendly natives' (thus precipitating a reprisal killing by the Aborigines).[38] Robinson made no mention in his diary of having enquired about the rumours of the captive White Woman while in Gipps Land, although in 1846, when the rumours revived and he was questioned on this point, he indicated that he 'was disposed to believe there was no real truth in the report'.[39]

Robinson wrote positively of the Gipps Land settlers and noted that he was glad to find 'a sympathy evinced on behalf of the Aborigines and a desire for their general amelioration a feeling I felt it my duty to foster and encourage and I am happy to state that the Country generally as far as the Aboriginal and European Inhabitants were concerned was perfectly tranquil'.[40] Robinson mentioned seeing 'many Human bones and Skulls' near Lake Wellington but did not connect these with conflicts with the settlers. Rather, he attributed the rapid decline—to the point of extinction in some clans—to internecine wars and the ravages of European diseases:

> As a People the Aborigines are rapidly on the decay. They are greatly reduced. They are but Remnant Tribes. Sections are extinct. Their diminution is attributable to several Causes. In their petty feuds and intestine strifs several have been sacrificed but hundreds have fallen victims to the dire effects of European disease. Variola or Small Pox often of a confluent description, Influenza, Febris and Syphilis have extended their baneful influences to the remotest parts of the Interior. The latter is now almost general throughout the Land. Ophalmia in some parts is Indemic. Cutaneous effection is peculiar to the Natives and prevalent.[41]

In March 1844, shortly before Robinson left Melbourne for Gipps Land, squatter Patrick Coady Buckley recorded in his diary his expeditions up Merriman's Creek with other settlers and members of the Mounted Police to hunt and shoot Aborigines who, he said, had been taking his sheep.[42] This was also, according to local historian John Adams, around the time that John Macleod, newly arrived at Bruthen, 'fed the natives flour mixed with arsenic' in retaliation for their spearing of his sheep. When the Aborigines hunted the cook responsible to Orbost Station and speared him, Adams states, the Macleods 'organised a drive and followed the Aborigines back to Buchan and trapped them under the cliffs of the Murrindal River where many were shot and others killed jumping over a cliff'.[43]

Historian Bain Attwood has noted that:

> the official government reports specifically record only a handful of Aboriginal deaths, but a much higher loss of life is suggested by several sources. A private communication from Commissioner Tyers in 1847 reveals there was considerable loss of Kurnai life on Lachlan Macalister's Boisdale run, where the Braiakaulung determinedly resisted European occupation and inflicted severe stock losses.[44]

In early February 1844 Tyers organised an armed contingent of Border Police, Native Police, local landowners (including McMillan) and their stockmen to rout a party of Kurnai camped near the La Trobe River. In his official report on the incident, Tyers stated that he issued orders to not fire except in self-defence, but to rush upon them and take them by surprise.[45] Chief Protector Robinson commented of this type of manoeuvre that all European men had to do was 'ride furiously up to [Aborigines] and in a threatening attitude, when the natives would be terrified into an offensive position, which would be the signal for an attack as they would be able to swear the natives made the first attack'.[46]

In his 1843 article on Gipps Land X. Y. Z. commented that it was:

> strange that the attention of government has not been directed to the means of preserving the lives and properties of the [settlers and Aborigines]; for whilst the voice of humanity

loudly pleads in favor of the untutored denizen of the wild, justice claims a fair share of protection for the enterprizing pioneers of a new country, the early settlers. To leave the redress of injury in the hands of the whites is, to be a party to the murderous attacks to which all the natives of a new colony have been more or less subject; and yet to grant and obtain payment for squatting licenses, leaving the holder to the tender mercy of the savage under the impression that christian feeling will restrain him from defending his life and property, is to draw too largely on that spirit of forbearance which most men, if they could, would willingly evince under similar circumstances. It is indeed high time that the mutual relation in which the natives and the settlers of Gipps Land are to stand to each other should be defined by the government.[47]

Ironically, in endorsing the story of the Heart and the captive White Woman, X. Y. Z. was nourishing a rumour which was to facilitate and provide a pretext for the ongoing harrassment of the Kurnai through the mid-1840s. Tyers conceded to a select committee some years later that 'at least fifty [Gipps Land Aborigines] were killed by the Native Police and other Aborigines attached to the parties in search of a white woman'.[48]

Following publication of X. Y. Z.'s story of the heart in November 1843, no further mention of the captive White Woman appeared in the Melbourne press until 26 March 1845. The *Port Phillip Gazette* reported on that date that a white woman was being held captive by Aborigines 'on the Weimira' (now Wimmera) on the northern edge of the Portland Bay District.[49] This report shifted the focus of the story to a new location, some several hundred miles west of Gipps Land.

The report, published under the heading 'Interesting Discovery', was allegedly brought to Melbourne by 'a settler residing on the Weimira' who claimed that:

> some parties who were exploring the country beyond the last station on the Weimira, about ten days ago, discovered the name of a female cut in legible characters on several trees, and on coming up with a tribe of aborigines, they found three children of half caste complexion.

From these circumstances, and the cautious answers given by the Aborigines when interrogated, the party concluded that 'the aborigines have a European female prisoner, who is supposed to be the young lady wrecked about five years ago near Portland Bay', and for whom there was a large reward offered, or 'some female whom they have captured from an overland party to Adelaide'. This may be a reference to an item in the *Geelong Advertiser* of 15 April 1844, which reported a rumour prevailing that a large vessel had been wrecked at Moonlight Head, between Cape Otway and Port Fairy. The report was said to have been verified by a party of blacks:

> who could have no inducement to make false statements on such a subject. It is said by some that the crew and passengers have been massacred by the blacks, while others assert that only two human beings reached the shore, a lady and her child. All such particulars are, however, mere conjecture, and we must be content with the single fact that a vessel has been wrecked on the coast to the westward.[50]

The 1845 *Gazette* report of the Portland woman had been transferred anecdotally via several mediators (explorers, settler, editor), prior to reaching the reader in Melbourne, and was speculative and unsupportable on the flimsy circumstantial evidence cited. The *Gazette* did not comment on the story's lack of specificity, although almost all aspects of the account were nebulous. It is unclear, for instance, whether the settler who brought the story to Melbourne was one of the exploration party or how he had come by the information. The settler was not named, members of the exploratory party were not identified. No dates were given. The exact location of the encounter was unclear. The name of the female allegedly carved on the trees was not given. The name of the owner of 'the last station on the Weimira' was not provided. The party of Aborigines was not identified.

The lack of connection between what was presented as evidence or facts and how that information was come by, and the narrator's claim to an authoritative (but unnamed and hence untestable) source, are hallmarks of myth-making. Even if the story had some basis in fact, then the transient nature of the anecdote would mean that there was little likelihood of tracing its origin, or the captive woman. The tantalising vagueness of the report, and the repetition of details from the Gipps Land story from another place and time, lend the report a universal air. The woman serves as a protagonist in a drama enacted in an imaginative, textual space, an undifferentiated zone, rather than a specific time and/or geographic space. This repetition of events that have already happened is a characteristic of narratology and, specifically, plot formation, and point to the story's discursive function.[51]

The stories of the Portland woman and its referent—the White Woman of Gipps Land—produced and reproduced an originary narrative in which the dramatised act of possession was displaced from the usurper to the usurped, and the object of possession from land to woman. The Weimira, like Gipps Land, was in 1845 a volatile frontier zone. The story of the 'Portland' woman and her 'half-caste' children emerged from an area just beyond settlement, in that 'country beyond the last station'. Given its potential to harden public attitudes against Aborigines, the Portland report could have been a fabrication to aid and legitimise settlement, and the obfuscation a ploy to validate a nonexistent source.

Deborah Bird Rose, paying attention to gendered constuctions in outback Australia, suggests that the status of mixed-race children may be in part an index of European constructions of white male sexuality:

> In this moment of conquest, soon to be denied, the task for white male sexuality is to clear Nature—the land and the indigenous people—to make a space for civilization. The lone hero is, by his own imagining, an advance force whose guns and other masculine tools will commence the twin tasks of eradication and domestication. Only later will civilisation flourish.[52]

The Portland Bay district had for some years been the site of conflict between settlers and Aborigines. Early colonist William Westgarth says of the years 1842–44 in the area around Eumaralla and Mount Eeles that 'vengeance was taken by wholesale upon the poor

black without regard to any law save the worst of the Lynch description; and colonists were freely pointed out who had acquired a kind
of local celebrity for the slaughter of scores of their fellow-beings'.
The Rev. Hurst of Bunting Dale, Geelong, superintendent of the
Wesleyan Mission Station, reported in the *Gazette* in late 1841 that
as many as two hundred natives had been shot in cold blood to the
westward of Lake Colac by parties ostensibly going out 'kangarooing'
on the Sabbath.[53]

In April 1842, as Superintendent La Trobe called for reports into
several massacres of Aborigines in the Portland District, the settlers
and inhabitants of Port Fairy prepared a representation to La Trobe
seeking government assistance to curb alleged outrages by Aborigines
and claiming twenty-five attacks on settlers' property and stock,
principally within the previous two months. These included three
men killed, seven wounded, sixty cattle, 100 calves and over 4000
sheep and ewes taken or driven off, huts robbed and property stolen.

La Trobe's response was tempered with pragmatism. The evils
of which the settlers complained were, he said, 'those which everywhere accompanied the occupation of a new country inhabited by
savage tribes', even in cases where there was a 'well-defined frontier
or neutral ground [which] could be interposed between the civilized
and uncivilized'. In this case, he said, there was no such line and 'the
savage tribes are not only upon our borders, but intermingle with us
in every part of this district'. Furthermore, he pointed out that he
had before him 'a statement, in a form which I dare not discredit,
showing that [acts of savage retaliation and cruelty] are perpetrated
among you', namely 'a nightly attack upon a small number of natives,
by a party of white inhabitants in your district, and the murder of no
fewer than three defenceless aboriginal women and a child in their
sleeping place, and this at the very time your memorial was in the act
of signature, and in the immediate vicinity of the station of two of
the parties who have signed it'.[54]

La Trobe did, however, respond to complaints by stationing a
detachment of the Native Police Corps, under the command of
Captain Henry Edmund Pulteney Dana, in the Portland Bay District
each winter from 1842 to1849. Captain Dana also had squatting
interests in the area. He had in 1840 taken up 'Nangeela' on the

Glenelg River.[55] Captain Dana's reports for this period suggest that the Native Police under his command waged systematic and wide-ranging forays against Aborigines in the Portland Bay District, particularly during the winters of 1843 and 1844. The pretext for one of these forays was the disappearance in August 1843 of the young daughter of Abraham Ward, an innkeeper. Despite a lack of evidence that Aborigines were in any way connected with the disappearance of the child, it was claimed that they had stolen (and in the more excessive accounts, eaten) her.[56] A similar rumour was to circulate in 1846 in the Western Port area, where Assistant Protector Thomas recorded that the Aborigine Nonuptune was unjustly accused of taking 'Mr. Willoby's [sic] child'.[57]

Like the story of the captive White Woman, speculation about the fate of Ward's child mediated frontier contact. In the absence of a physical demarcation line between the 'civilised' and 'uncivilised', these stories interposed boundaries. Rumours about captured white women and children were thus used to shore up the interstices in the colonising project.

How complicit were white women in this process and what was their own investment in colonising discourses? They, too, stood to benefit from the colonial situation. I have not come across comments from contemporary white women, either in newspaper accounts or diaries, which might shed light on their views about the White Woman stories. Presumably, some shared the men's outrage and anxieties about the woman's plight. Those in remote areas may have feared that they, too, would be abducted and held captive. For some women, the story might have reaffirmed their own sense of importance as a prized object. A number of popular American captivity narratives and historical accounts, in circulation from the late eighteenth century, recorded stories of women (and men) who embraced Indian life and strongly opposed leaving their adopted Indian families. Did Australian women similarly yearn for freedom from the constraints of bourgeois life which life with the Aborigines offered, and consider that a white woman might not wish to return to her own people?

The story of the most famous of these women, Mary Jemison, was published in 1824. Remembered in legend as the 'white woman of the Genesee', Jemison was abducted in 1755 when around twelve years of age and reputedly became leader of her adopted tribe, the Seneca. Other similar cases included Frances Slocum, the 'lost sister of Wyoming', who was taken captive in 1778 by Delaware Indians and who, after fifty years with them, declined to leave them, stating that she 'did not wish to live any better, or any where else'. Cynthia Ann Parker, abducted in May 1836 by Comanche, allegedly died of grief after being brought back to her white family. These were not isolated examples. Cadwallader Colden wrote in 1747 of captives who refused to return: 'No Arguments, no Intreaties, nor Tears of their Friends and Relations, could persuade many of them to leave their own *Indian* Friends and Acquaintance[s]'. Similarly, almost all of the 200 captives on whose behalf Colonel Henry Bouquet negotiated a treaty of release in 1764 with the Delawares and Shawnees opposed return, and absconded at the first opportunity to rejoin their Indian families.[58]

In the context of widespread acts of aggression against Aborigines by settlers, and by the Native Police under Captain Dana's command, Dana's remark that if the frightful disease and mortality of the natives which had occurred over the winter of 1844 continued, they would cease to exist in the country, seems portentous. Marie Fels has noted of the efficacy of the Native Police in the Portland Bay District:

> the only terrain in which the police had not demonstrated their ability to undertake a successful pursuit [of the Aborigines] was the scrub and desert country of the wimmera and Mallee, and that was where collisions were reported in the . . . winters of 1844 and 1845.[59]

Like X. Y. Z.'s story of the Heart, which emerged briefly in Melbourne following settler reprisals against the Kurnai for the alleged murder of Ronald Macalister, the story of the Portland woman appeared in Melbourne in March 1845, during this period of 'collisions' on the Wimmera; then (having served its purpose?) almost immediately lapsed.

When news of the White Woman reappeared in the Melbourne newspapers twelve months later, the location was again Gipps Land. On 7 March 1846, the *Port Phillip Patriot* reported a sighting by one of the Native Police of 'a White Woman with two half caste children, in company with a large body of the Aborigines':

> The woman attempted to lag behind, to give the native police-man an opportunity of rescuing her, which was quickly per-ceived by her captors, who urged her before them at the point of their spears; in fact, the man who relates these facts, saw one of the savages plunge his spear into her leg to quicken her retreat. The policeman would have made an attempt to liberate her, but from the nature of the ground (a marsh) in which he was standing, up to his knees in water, he was unable to over-take the savages. The unfortunate prisoner is supposed to be Miss Lord, lost in the *Brittomart* [*sic*], wrecked near Wilson's Promontory, some four or five years since.[60]

The *Patriot* recommended that the government 'should lose no time in taking active steps for the release of the wretched woman from her disgusting fate; nay, the inhabitants should *insist* on such steps being taken without delay. The enterprise of private individuals may be excited when we inform them that one thousand pounds have been offered for the lady's recovery'. The report merged elements of the Portland woman story—the 'half-caste' children and the reward—with a detail from McMillan's account—the Aborigines 'with shipped spears driving before them' the woman. The *Patriot* signposted the political direction which the story would take over the ensuing months, as the woman's, or women's, cause became aligned on an axis of private individuals *versus* the government. The *Patriot*, while enthusiastically reporting on the offer of a thousand pound reward for the woman and lobbying for her recovery, passes over and makes no comment upon the possible fate of the 'half-caste' chil-dren. It is unclear what would happen to these children, mentioned here and elsewhere, if the woman were to be found. No suggestion is made that the children would accompany the woman back to Mel-bourne. Would she be expected to sever her ties with them? And if not, what would their reception be when they arrived in Melbourne?

Captain Henry Dana, in Melbourne at the time the report was published, was a likely source. His letter to La Trobe dated Melbourne 8 March 1846 refers to the recent sighting of the woman by Native Police in Gipps Land, while they were 'in pursuit of natives'.[61] The woman, he said, 'appeared to hang back from the rest of the tribe, but was forced on by an old native armed with spears'. The image of the woman being forced on at spearpoint has by this time become a stock scene. As a signifier of the woman's reluctance, the image functions as a shorthand symbol for captivity. It negates the possibility that she is residing with the Aborigines by choice, and produces the Aborigines as captors. If earlier versions were equivocal on this score, all doubt is dispelled by the Aborigine's action in plunging his spear into the woman's leg—an image loaded with intimations of sexual anxiety, especially as it is contrasted with the impotent figure of the watching policeman.

Tyers's official report of this incident to La Trobe on 4 April 1846 is significantly different from the version reported in the *Patriot*. Tyers relates how the troopers, when on duty a few months previously with Mr Walsh, 'protecting Mr. McMillan's cattle from the depredations of the wild blacks', had come upon a party of natives on the lower part of the ranges amongst whom they saw 'a *yellow* woman, with red or auburn hair reaching to her shoulders' [original emphasis].[62] The woman, they said, wore an opossum cloak, 'which she threw away to facilitate her escape; this was picked up by one of the troopers, who, on smelling it, was satisfied that it had not belonged to an aboriginal native'.

The striking physical description of the woman is an unlikely and unexpected image. Her 'yellow' cast of skin places her in an ambivalent situation in a narrative about government superintendence of black and white bodies: a situation which is not clarified by the enigmatic smell on the opossum skin cloak. The description is at odds with the nondescript mention of the woman in Dana's letter, on which the report of the 'sighting' which appeared in the *Patriot* on 7 March appears to have been based.[63] There is a sense of the woman's corporeality, which lends immediacy to the report. The description evokes a specific individual who acts decisively, even wilfully. This woman does not want to be rescued by the Native Police; she throws away her cloak so as to 'facilitate her escape', not from her alleged Aboriginal captors, but from Walsh and the troopers. There are marked differences between the description of this event as reported by Dana and by Tyers, although both claim to be based on the trooper's 'sighting'. Tyers, for example, makes no reference to the

Aborigines driving the woman on at spearpoint. Instead he cites the evidence of the smell on the opossum skin rug, the import of which is attributed to some undefined, arcane Aboriginal knowledge.

Tyers included, under cover, an official 'statement', reputedly made before him by Trooper Quandite of the Native Police, on 30 March 1846, and corroborated independently by Trooper Calcalo, also of the Native Police. It comprised a brief summary of information, paraphrased by Tyers:

> Trooper Quandite . . . being questioned relative to his having seen a white woman while driving the blacks from spearing cattle at the head of Mr. McMillan's run, states, that he saw a woman of a yellow colour, and that he should say she was a white woman, from the circumstance of her having long hair down to her shoulders of a light color; he saw her in some scrub; she jumped out of an opossum cloak she had on; he saw her jump out of it.

There is no way of knowing whether the information attributed to Quandite was accurate, or accurately reported, although it captures something of the cadence of speech, which gives the impression of a first-hand report.

As the officer in charge of the party of troopers while out in the field, Captain Walsh provided an 'on the site' account:

> I was out with my party of Native Troopers at the head of Mr. McMillan's run. I did not see the woman mentioned by the men. The men all assembled round the opossum cloak dropped by the woman, and smelt it, and all of them agreed that the cloak belonged to a white woman and not to a black gin, from certain circumstances which I did not exactly understand. I asked Trooper Quandite why he did not catch her; he answered, that he was so astonished at seeing a white woman among the wild natives, or warrigals, as he calls them, that he could not recover his surprise in time to follow her, as she only stood a few minutes looking at him, and then made a rush into the scrub, after which he lost sight of her all together.
>
> The troopers of my party have constantly been talking about the occurrence ever since it took place, among themselves. [64]

Walsh distances himself in his report from the troopers, both in terms of what was witnessed (he did not see the woman; they did) and in how the 'evidence' was interpreted (he 'did not exactly understand' about the smell of the cloak; they did). There is an intimation that, as a supervising officer and as a European, Walsh is excluded from the cameraderie of the party of troopers who discuss the occurrence 'among themselves'.

In his letter to La Trobe of 8 March 1846, Captain Dana mentioned a rumour that was prevalent about eighteen months previously respecting a White Woman supposed to be a captive among the natives, and for whom he (Dana), on the order of La Trobe, had made enquiries in Gipps Land and had searched for on the Wimmera. The portability of the myth—its surfacing in two regions— might be connected with Dana and his men, who passed through Melbourne regularly, and could have promulgated the story of the Portland woman, as they did the story of the Gipps Land woman. As a member of the Melbourne Club, Dana would have had numerous opportunities to repeat the story to men of influence.

On 10 March 1846, three days after the *Patriot* article appeared, the *Herald* published a letter to the editor from a pseudonymous contributor—Humanitas—who was writing in response to the recent sighting in Gipps Land.[65] Humanitas claimed that he had written to one of the newspapers twelve months previously, 'shewing that [a] lady was a captive of a tribe of blacks in the Portland Bay District'. Humanitas might thus have been the unnamed 'settler residing on the Weimira', who was allegedly the source of the previously discussed article on the Portland woman which appeared in the *Gazette* in March 1845.

Humanitas was a regular contributor to several Port Phillip newspapers, writing on topics of public interest, including Aborigines, the Melbourne School of Arts, the Cape Otway Lighthouse, the famine in Ireland and the Windsor Hospital in Sydney.[66] He was to become a crucial figure in promoting the White Woman cause by writing at least three highly emotive letters on the subject for publication and by agitating for government and civic action.

Humanitas dramatised for the reader the scene of the sighting of the woman, as though a *tableau vivant*:

> But a few days since, this lamented lady was seen by one of
> the native Troopers, and oh! what a scene *then* presented itself
> for a painter. This lady saw but a short distance from her one
> who could he have reached her, would have rescued her from
> her captivity. She lagged behind, the chance of being released
> from her wretched state gave birth to feelings in her breast
> which cannot be expressed. The wily blacks detected them in
> a moment, and in all the savage nature which they possess,
> pierced her with their spears to urge her on with greater speed
> in order to baffle pursuit.

In claiming the recently sighted woman as the same 'lamented
lady' (from the Portland District) about whom he had written the
previous year, Humanitas evinced no apparent sense of incongruity
about the change of location to Gipps Land. He unproblematically
conflated the two stories, the two locations, and the two women.
Humanitas's florid rhetoric and presumptive allusion to the 'feelings
in her breast' were calculated to excite the sympathies and indignation of the reader.

As the self-appointed spokesperson and standard-bearer for 'every
true Briton', Humanitas directed his attack specifically at La Trobe:

> If Mr. La Trobe had a daughter situated as this friendless
> woman is, what would he not do to rescue her? Would not
> reward upon reward be offered? Would not every energy be
> brought into play to relieve her? Would not the services of a
> dozen—aye, a hundred—parties be engaged in the pursuit of
> this savage tribe? Would not the bush be scoured? Would not
> its most secret places be searched? Would not every available
> means be used for the deliverance of that daughter?

There are tensions within the account generated around the trope
of the bush as ravished female which conflates land and woman as
objects of male desire. Humanitas's accusatory tone, emotive turn
of phrase, titillating imagery and insistent, rhetorical questions also
denote political intent. The *Herald*, in an editorial footnote, defended
La Trobe as 'powerless in the matter', and made a counter-accusation
that '[i]f "Humanitas" had levelled his attacks at Sir George Gipps
[Governor of New South Wales] instead of Mr. La Trobe, he would
have been nearer the mark'.

Humanitas's letter prompted an impassioned response, titled 'Miss Lord', by rival newspaper the *Port Phillip Gazette*.[67] This item asserted knowledge of the woman's identity and imparted to her a history, genealogy, social status and genteel demeanour: 'Miss Lord *was* [emphasis added] . . . the eldest daughter of John Lord, Esq., a merchant of Sydney—who, although he has been like many others, unfortunate in business—stands high as a man of integrity'. The *Gazette* castigated the Government as 'inhuman and barbarous' for thus leaving 'an amiable and accomplished female to undergo a fate worse than death itself' and, on behalf of the public, demanded that 'the Government send a sufficient force to rescue her from her savage tormentors'. However, the article's reference to her in the past tense indicates that it was already too late to retrieve her.

The article concluded, in a flourish of bravado: 'if the Government be so careless about the ruin and never-ending misery of a human being, surely the citizens of Sydney . . . ought to take up the matter, and we can assure them the citizens of Melbourne will willingly co-operate with them . . . to effect her immediate release from the clutches of these inhuman monsters'.

The *Gazette*'s plea reads as an attempt to mobilise and harness anti-government feelings within Sydney and Melbourne with a display of united civic action. The tone is militant, mutinous. If the government fails to act, the citizens should take the matter into their own hands. In light of the assumptions about the woman's 'ruined' state and shattered peace of mind, the call for action seems rhetorical rather than genuine. There is ambiguity in a call for action which emphasises relief or 'release' rather than rescue. No suggestion is made of the woman being returned to her community. The rescue consists of getting her away from the Aborigines, and hints at the problems of what to do with her if and when she comes back. The article reads as though written for the benefit of armchair humanitarians, who could self-righteously rail at the government's neglect and imagine themselves as rescuers, but not actually have to do anything.

With the exception of a brief item in the *Portland Guardian* of 17 March 1846, reprinted in the *Herald* a week later under the heading 'The White Lady', the press makes no further mention of the Portland woman. The *Guardian* was, it said, 'slow of belief' about the sightings 'in, some say, the district of Gipps Land, others say, in the Portland district'. Nevertheless, the article produced a possible history for the woman, stating that it would require no great stretch of imagination to suppose the lady to be 'one of the many females, who so mysteriously disappeared in the schooner "Yarra Yarra", between five and six years ago'. The reference to the woman as the White Lady, however, could point to an (unintended) Aboriginal source for the rumours. There was, apparently, an Aboriginal woman, said to be a 'shaman', known as the White Lady in the Portland Bay District in the early colonial period.[68]

From this point, March 1846, the location for the story was to become unambiguously Gipps Land, although the possibility that there might be more than one captive woman would remain open. The fluidity and synthesis of such stories was demonstrated over the ensuing months, as details attached to the Portland account—the woman's name carved on trees and the 'half-caste' children—were transferred to the Gipps Land woman.

As the stories circulated within the press at this time and entered the domain of public debate, competing identities, each with a national affiliation (English, Scottish and Irish), became imputed to the woman. The proponents of the stories allowed each of the main European groupings in the community to identify with the woman and to feel incensed at a complacent government which had done nothing to relieve her. The open-ended, multivalent aspects of the stories, circulating simultaneously, allowed allegiances across factions and sectarian boundaries to be harnessed in a concerted attack on the government. By this means, the alleged plight of the woman served the ends of political point-scoring.

The White Woman story assumed increased political, as well as humanitarian, relevance following the disastrous loss of the emigrant ship *Cataraqui* which struck King Island in Bass Strait on 4 August 1845. All but nine of the 423 passengers (mainly bounty emigrants including women and children) and crew perished. The distressing first-hand accounts of the wreck and its aftermath which were published in the newspapers over the ensuing weeks may have rekindled sympathy for the White Woman.[69] In the face of such horrendous loss of life perhaps the citizens of Melbourne wished to retain hope that a White Woman could have survived an earlier shipwreck.

The wreck of the *Cataraqui* had direct political consequences for Port Phillip. On hearing the news, the Admiralty in London threatened to recommend that emigrant ships not use the Bass Strait route, in which case immigrants would bypass Melbourne to disembark at other colonial ports. At a time when the Immigration Society of Port Phillip was working to attract free immigrants who were considered to be crucial to the development and prosperity of the district, the loss of the *Cataraqui* threatened to jeopardise the success of their project.[70] Disgruntled colonists increased pressure on La Trobe and Gipps to release money for a lighthouse at Cape Otway, one of the danger points for shipping in Bass Strait.

Humanitas, who had been instrumental in bringing to public attention the stories of both the Portland woman in 1845 and the Gipps Land woman in March 1846, took up the cause of the Cape Otway lighthouse—linking it expressly with the White Woman. Humanitas had castigated La Trobe for failure to act on the White Woman rumours. He now condemned La Trobe for lack of action on the lighthouse. In both cases he called on the citizens of Melbourne to take matters into their own hands. His letter to the editor of the *Patriot* published on 19 March 1846 (only one week after his scathing letter about the White Woman, Miss Lord, appeared in the *Herald*) stated in part: 'The public have already had a specimen of the conduct of the government in Miss Lord's case, and if that case could make no impression upon them, as little will be made, as to erecting a Light House on Cape "Otway"'.[71]

Humanitas's criticism of the government was, to some extent, 'after the event'. A select committee in Sydney, appointed before the *Cataraqui* disaster, had already recommended that four lighthouses be constructed in Bass Strait, and in November 1845 the Legislative Council had approved funding for work on one at Cape Otway.[72]

Similarly, Humanitas's criticism of La Trobe for having failed to investigate the rumours about the White Woman was unjust or ill-informed. During his visit to Gipps Land in early 1845 La Trobe had made 'particular enquiry' into the origin of the rumour about the woman and had traced it to, and discussed it with, McMillan. La Trobe had also at this time directed Captain Dana to investigate the rumours in both Portland Bay and Gipps Land. And on receipt of Captain Dana's 8 March 1846 report of the Gipps Land sighting by the Native Trooper, La Trobe had written immediately to Tyers requesting 'the fullest information' on the matter.[73]

If Humanitas's objective was to force La Trobe to act in the District's interests, he must have felt some satisfaction with the news within two weeks of publication of his letter about the Cape Otway lighthouse, that orders had been received from headquarters to push forward with works on lighthouses at Cape Otway and Cape Howe.[74] He, and perhaps readers of his letter, may have attributed this happy outcome to his public intervention.

Meanwhile, interest in the White Woman, which had flared briefly following the reported sighting of her by the Native Troopers earlier in March, had fizzled. Nothing further was reported until May 1846, when two brief items appeared in the Melbourne press. The first item, in the *Herald* of 12 May, was reprinted from the *Hobart Town Spectator* of 21 April. It quoted a letter from Tarraville, Port Albert, dated 8 April: 'The blacks have been very troublesome of late, and about a fortnight since speared cattle within twelve miles of the port. Mr. McMillan has captured the child of a young lady, whom the blacks stole away some years since, and for whom there is a reward of £1,000'. The *Herald* opined: '[we] once more cry shame on the Government . . . Will *no one* come forward and put the Government to the blush by leading a party in search of this truly unfortunate lady?'[75]

The juxtaposition and linking of accusations against the 'blacks' for recent and previous depredations (spearing cattle, stealing the 'young lady'), and the mediating presence of McMillan, whose counter-abduction of the young boy again places him at the centre of the speculation about the woman, strengthens the argument that the story served as a pretext or cover for ongoing retaliation by the settlers. It provides a clue to why a story which belonged to the frontier phase of Gipps Land history might have been resuscitated at a later, more concentrated, period of settlement.[76] The *Herald*'s impassioned plea, which articulated for the first time the idea of a private search party with a motive other than the rescue of the woman—namely, to embarrass the government—likewise made explicit the political possibilities which the story offered to parties in Melbourne.

The second item in the press, which appeared in the *Patriot* on 15 May 1846, reported that the 'young native' who had been in McMillan's charge for some eight months, 'says that there is no White Woman, but there are two white children', and that 'Mr Walsh of the Natve [*sic*] Police, has taken the boy with him as a guide, and started in search of them'.[77] When the White Woman story re-emerged in August 1846, again with pressure brought to bear by Humanitas, it finally 'took off'. It is not clear whose interests Humanitas was furthering. However, without his dogged determination and emotive rhetoric, the Port Phillip community might not have staked a claim in the woman's rescue and the story might never have become a civic cause.

CHAPTER 3

Agents and Agency

'I trac'd my name on many a tree, and rav'd, and wept, and rav'd!
Madness or death, were grace to me—Oh, God! what have I brav'd!'
From 'A Lay of Lament' by J. R. M.,
Melbourne, 23 September 1846[1]

The story of the captive White Woman did not 'take off' in 1840, 1843 or 1845. Its re-emergence and rapid escalation into a 'cause' in August 1846 seems to have been precipitated by the conjunction of a number of key factors, which created the right 'moment' for its production and reception. In turn, the story, and the action it engendered, reflected and authenticated the 'moment' which gave it birth.

On 20 August 1846, Humanitas, writing on the subject for the third time,[2] informed readers that the captive woman was not Miss Lord, but 'one who left this province in the *Brittania* [*sic*], for Sydney, in 1839'; that her name was 'marked on the bark of a tree in the mountainous part of Gipps Land'; and that it appeared 'that she has had four children by these blacks, one of whom is dead'. Mindful that his revelations might not be sufficiently persuasive to motivate the 'inhabitants of the town' to subscribe 'a penny or twopence [each]' to 'rescue this defenceless female from the grasp of the harpies of hell', Humanitas appended a postscripted exhortation: 'Port Phillipians! come forward and do what you can for this poor woman, and God will reward you'. His recommendation that the public directly approach 'the new Governor' and 'take care not to trouble

Mr. La Trobe' suggests that, with the arrival of the new Governor, Charles Fitzroy, the moment was ripe for those propagating the story to act, and that the reward which they sought was as much temporal as providential.

The *Herald* lent credence and support to Humanitas's letter in an editorial footnote, asserting that Mr Stratton, of Tarra Vale, Gipps Land, had told 'a friend of ours' that 'the woman's name is Ellen McPherson, formerly in the employ of Mr. John Macdonald (Scottish Chiefs)' and that 'a highly respectable settler, whose name can be supplied by Mr. Stratton, on exploring the bush in search of a run where the Whites had never before been, saw the name "Ellen McPherson" carved on a tree'.[3] The Scottish Ellen (or Ann) McPherson was to rival the English Miss Lord. A change from the formal and remote 'Miss' Lord—whose family was in Sydney—to the familiar and locally known 'Ellen' McPherson might have increased the human interest value of the story, and hence its reception, within Port Phillip.

Humanitas's letter drew an immediate response. The following day, 21 August, the *Argus* published two letters.[4] The first, from John Macdonald of the Melbourne Scottish Chiefs Hotel, corrected the *Herald* on a number of points, stating that Miss Macpherson's name was 'Ann', and not 'Ellen'. Macdonald also put forward a third possible identity for the woman—another passenger on the *Britannia*, 'the wife of a brewer in Sydney, whose name I forget'. Another pseudonymous writer, An Englishman, writing to the *Sydney Morning Herald* a week later, supplied the name of the brewer's wife as Mrs Capel, an Irishwoman.[5] Subsequent newspaper reports made reference to 'one or two' captives. This plurality of identities allowed each of the dominant European national groupings in Port Phillip to claim the captive as kinswoman. Thus, the White Woman at this point represented a kind of 'everywoman' figure, inasmuch as the limited configuration of English, Scottish and Irish represented almost the whole of the European population in Port Phillip at that time.

Macdonald, who was one of the few commentators to question the motives of the propounders of the story, challenged Humanitas's pseudonymity. He called on Humanitas to 'come forward under his

real name and impart any information he may have obtained of the
fate of this unfortunate female' so that the public would gain confidence in his statement:

> which they cannot do so long as he remains under a fictitious
> name, otherwise what can be supposed but that a subject
> which was nearly forgotten except by the friends and relatives
> of Miss Macpherson, has been cruelly revived by some person
> or persons from interested motives.

A week later Humanitas lambasted Macdonald's querying of his
pseudonymity as 'intentional insult and discourtesy . . . of so dis-
reputable a nature that it would be utterly impossible for them to
emanate from any but a grovelling mind', and appealed instead to
the reader's 'finest feelings'.[6] The *Herald*'s footnote to the letter concluded that Humanitas's opponent's [i.e. Macdonald's] remarks were
'beneath contempt', and smugly claimed credit for having urged the
government to action, advising Humanitas that 'the Government
have ordered Mr. Walsh, at the head of a party of the black police, to
proceed in the search, which is now being prosecuted with every
chance of success'.

Nevertheless, despite his reservations about Humanitas's anonymity, Macdonald was cautiously supportive of the cause, which, he
acknowledged, offered the men of Melbourne the opportunity to
assert their masculine identity through independent, civic action:
'if anything like a well grounded belief is established that Miss
Macpherson is still in the land of the living, all that can be done by
MEN, will be done to rescue her forthwith, without soliciting any aid
or assistance from the Government'. Macdonald's capitalised comment points to the ways in which the colonists created a masculinist
civic space through gendered narratives of identity. Macdonald
mobilises the figure of the helpless White Woman to produce citizens as chivalrous, independent 'MEN', and the government as
emasculated.

The second response to Humanitas's letter, published in the *Argus*
of 21 August with Macdonald's letter, put forward fresh information
which seemed to provide the proof that Macdonald sought, i.e. that
Miss Macpherson was 'still in the land of the living'. The pseudony-

mous correspondent—V—cited information obtained, he said, 'on Sunday last from a native called Yal Yal'. The purported source and authorising agent for the story's validity was a boy belonging to the Gipps Land tribe who, according to V, had told Yal Yal 'that he had seen a white woman living with the Gipps Land tribe'. The woman, it was reported, had 'lived for several years with one of the blacks, but that he is now dead, leaving her with three children now living and one dead, and that she is since living with another man'.

V's statement that 'a number of gentlemen have expressed a wish to raise a fund to defray the expense of a party', and that 'a number of the blacks belonging to the Western Port tribe have agreed to start upon the search as soon as the necessary arrangements can be made', indicates that well before the public meeting moves were already in train to organise an independent expedition party.[7]

Between 28 August and 2 September 1846, a petition appeared in the advertising columns of the *Patriot,* the *Herald* and the *Gazette*.[8] The petition, supported by sixty-two signatures, requested that the Mayor 'convene a Public Meeting, for the purpose of adopting measures for ascertaining the fate of Two Unfortunate Females who are suspected to be in the custody of a Tribe of Natives in the Port Albert district'. If readers shared Macdonald's wariness about Humanitas's motives, they might have been reassured by the publication of the names of the signatories to the petition, most of whom were members of the business community. The publication of such a document lent credibility and authority to those promoting the White Woman as a public cause. An Old Inhabitant (who nevertheless did not declare his own name) said as much: 'it is highly gratifying to observe in the [petition] the names of so many respectable gentlemen who feel an interest in [the captive's] fate'.[9]

The *Patriot* announced that three volunteers had already come forward who were willing to start at short notice 'in pursuit of the wretched woman', but did not name the volunteers or state support for any of the candidates. It did, however, put a price and a time limit on the potential rescue mission: 'Some hundred or hundred and twenty pounds, it is calculated, would equip a party for a period of three months'.[10] The *Argus* of 28 August put forward two names as men qualified and willing to take command of a 'proper party': Christian De Villiers, an outspoken opponent of La Trobe with some experience with the Native Police, and Mr Dykes. The *Argus* was dismissive of La Trobe's choice of Mr Walshe, the officer whom he had recently directed to investigate the rumours, as 'however well suited that young gentleman may be for playing at soldiers with his sable warriors, he is neither capable of leading them on such a service, nor fit to be trusted if he were'.[11]

On 28 August 1846, three of the four Port Phillip newspapers carried items about the White Woman. Each for its own purposes illuminated different aspects of the fate and identity of the captive woman.[12] According to the *Argus*, the rumour 'has now so far assumed shape, that the name of the supposed victim is given, and numerous minor details furnished, which at least give it an air of probability, seldom attaching to the many similar rumours which have from time to time been prevalent in almost every district of the colony'. The *Argus*, in dismissing Captain Dana's Native Police as unavailable to pursue the rumours because of 'the gallant Capt. and his brigade being at present engaged on active service in a distant district of the province', pressed for a publicly organised (but not completely independently funded) expedition.

Publication of the petition formalised and lent authority to what had been previously intermittent and individual expressions of concern for the woman's fate. It also brought into prominence a number of the citizens of Melbourne. The acts of 'getting up' the petition itself, and of appending one's signature in support, were presented in the press as indicators of civic-mindedness and humanitarian concern.

That the White Woman cause took the form of a petition to the Mayor—rather than to La Trobe—indicates that the petitioners, or those responsible for organising the petition, wanted the issue to be dealt with as a *civic* issue, in the public domain. At a time when Port Phillip was effectively an administrative outpost of New South Wales, and the Melbourne Corporation exercised only limited authority in local affairs, the White Woman cause provided a vehicle for opposition to La Trobe and to governance from Sydney. Did the aggrieved citizens of Port Phillip, or at least those engineering the public meeting, see the White Woman's state of captivity as analogous to that of Port Phillip, held in economic and gubernatorial 'thraldom' by Sydney? They might well have responded to the cause of the White Woman, whether they believed in her existence or not, because her *situation* provided a powerful analogy or trope for what they perceived to be their own neglected state at the hands of an indifferent but all-powerful government.[13]

The issue of separation of Port Phillip from New South Wales—pressure for which had been building since a Separation Society was formed in Melbourne in 1841—was crucial to Melbourne's transformation into a burgeoning mercantile centre. Anticipated developments in steamship navigation, which promised a boost to trade, commerce and immigration, added impetus to the separation issue in 1846. In launching the White Woman cause in opposition to the alleged inaction of an apathetic and uncaring government, the newspaper editors and organisers claimed the sphere of action and the moral high ground, and relegated the government to the role of bystander. The White Woman cause simultaneously provided the merchants and businessmen, councillors, newspaper editors and citizens of Melbourne with an opportunity to write themselves into a narrative of heroic endeavour, and to deploy 'civic mindedness' as a political strategy.

According to Melbourne chronicler Garryowen, the forum of the public meeting was from the earliest period 'regarded by the Port Phillipians as the most effective and legitimate mode in which to make the public sentiment known either in redress of grievance or a demand for justice.'[14] Public meetings provide a platform for citizens representing various factional interests to make their views known and, perhaps, to exert influence on the decision-making processes and on decision makers. However, as John Fawkner revealed of the first public meeting, held on 1 June 1836 in the newly established settlement shortly to be named Melbourne, public meetings can also be used to formalise and ratify decisions already made by members of the community who have vested interests in particular outcomes. In such cases, seemingly innocuous resolutions passed at public meetings mask other agendas.

Fawkner demonstrated an understanding of these machinations during this meeting, at which a number of resolutions were passed to maintain order in the fledgling community. Fawkner claimed in a letter written some years after the event that 'the meeting had been craftily engineered solely for the benefit of the [Port Phillip] Association'; its sole purpose, he said, had been to accept a code of regulations drawn up by that body, and to elect three of its members as magistrates. Fawkner maintained that they required all present to sign an undertaking that anyone who injured or insulted an Aboriginal should be deported either to Van Diemen's Land or New South Wales, and he implied that this was done 'to oust all those colonists who were not of the elect 15, as [William] Buckley, who was, of course, the Association's man, was the only interpreter between the Europeans and the blacks and could therefore fabricate whatever evidence he wished!'.[15]

During the fortnight prior to the White Woman meeting, published editorial items and letters to the editors make clear that the meeting's purpose was to formalise a pre-determined course of action: that there would be a search party, an expedition committee to organise it, and a fund to equip it; that De Villiers would lead it; that Aborigines would be seconded to participate in it; and that the Government would be requested to assist with funding it.

Like the meeting which Fawkner described, the White Woman meeting may have masked both an agenda and the motives of those who took the initiative to organise it. The publication of the White Woman petition raises questions about who initiated, organised and arranged for the petition's advertisement. The petition was dated 'Melbourne, Aug. 26', and it appears that the signatures were all collected on that day. The majority of signatories were men of commerce and merchants with premises in the main central business district and primarily in Collins Street. A few were professional men. The order in which the names appear on the petition suggests that the person, or persons, collecting the names went from business to business in the main commercial area of town. Some names which have eluded identification might have been customers transacting business in the stores.

Did George Cavenagh, editor of the *Herald*, whose name appears first on the list, solicit the signatures? If so, what were his motives? And what was his 'pitch' in approaching the signatories? He was to feature prominently at the public meeting, and also proposed a resolution at Mr James's premises when £20—the first donation to the expedition fund—was collected prior to the public meeting.[16] In putting their names to the petition, Cavenagh and the other signatories may have hoped to promote themselves or their business interests.

On the same day that the petition to the Mayor was being circulated, news of a massacre of Aborigines at Cape Otway reached Melbourne. The *Herald* reported that Surveyor Smythe's party had exterminated the nine remaining members of the Cape Otway tribe, eight of whom were women or children.[17] The implications for those advocating an expedition to rescue the White Woman without government sanction caused apprehension prior to the meeting. They might be held legally responsible should an injudicious choice of leader be made for the expedition, and 'lamentable results' ensue, as they had at Cape Otway.

Proponents of the White Woman expedition, like An Old Inhabitant, anxious to distance themselves and their project from the Cape Otway incident and eager to blame the Native Police's black members rather than its white leaders for that débâcle, argued for the appointment of 'a white officer, who will possess the confidence of the natives, and will be able to keep them under proper controul . . . and not allow them to indulge the feelings of revenge by which the blacks under Mr. Smythe seem to have been actuated'.[18]

While not ruling out the possibility of violence against the Gipps Land blacks by the expeditionists, An Old Inhabitant argued that this should be 'with as little loss of life as possible'. The *Patriot* endorsed this view, and stated that De Villiers was 'decidedly the man to accomplish the object in view'. The *Herald* broadened the criteria for leadership to 'familiarity with the bush, an intimate acquaintance with native habits, and a good knowledge of their language', and mentioned three individuals, including De Villiers, who had volunteered their free services and who appeared to be qualified.[19]

The question of whether or not to employ the services of the Western Port tribe of Aborigines for the expedition would be hotly debated at the public meeting, with 'some speakers proposing to employ a large number of blacks in the service, but by far the great majority objecting to their employment otherwise than as guides, lest arming them and sending them against a hostile tribe might lead to similarly disastrous results, though on a larger scale, as the late massacre at Cape Otway'.[20]

On 1 September 1846, the day before the public meeting, the *Herald* gave the first indication of the central position it would assume in promoting the White Woman cause:

> We had hoped that the local Government would have taken active measures to trace out and recover those unhappy beings [the white women] ... But no; neither Government, nor Police, nor Black Protectors, gave the smallest sign of sympathy. A newspaper—our humble selves—makes out the horrifying fact; and to the philanthropic exertions of Councillor Stephen is due the Public sympathy created by the Meeting of To-morrow, and whatever active results follow.[21]

Whether Councillor Stephen was the prime instigator, as the *Herald* suggests, is a matter of conjecture. The *Gazette*, in its report of the public meeting on 5 September, gave credit to the *Herald* for wishing to rescue the women, although it called into question Cavenagh's motives: 'while he has our thanks we do not think he has displayed the discrimination of a true philanthropist; and we are not to be led away in such a manner'.[22]

Posterity has emphasised the role of George Cavenagh in 'beating up' the story to animate public interest in the expedition party. This view is understandable, in light of his involvement at the public meeting and his appointment to the expedition committee—a position which gave him privileged access to the reports of the expeditionists. However, in the lead-up to the public meeting all of the Melbourne papers were promoting the White Woman story. While Cavenagh's involvement is not disputed, the push for a search party appears to have come, initially at least, from a number of quarters: Humanitas, V, An Old Inhabitant, and the other three Melbourne newspapers. A number of other names which recur are also likely contenders. Anonymity protects the identities of some of the key players. We can only surmise what or whose interests they served.

Similarly, the commonly held supposition that the call for a public meeting reflected widespread belief in the rumour is misleading. The sixty-two signatures on the petition were sufficient for the Mayor to convene a public meeting. The number cannot, however, be said to indicate strong interest by the citizens of Melbourne. Petitions for public meetings were regular in Port Phillip. Several years earlier, when the Melbourne population was considerably lower, more than 1400 signatures had been collected in a single day to protest the removal of Judge Willis from his office as Resident Judge of the Port Phillip province.[23]

Of the signatories to the White Woman petition, Councillor John Stephen, and three members of the Melbourne Club, George Cavenagh and squatters William Elliott and James Buchanan, might have moved in influential circles.[24] Of the remainder, few would have belonged to the social elite of Port Phillip or have been considered notable enough for inclusion in biographical or historical anthologies.

Barrister and journalist John Stephen, whose name appeared second on the list of signatories, after that of George Cavenagh, was a member of a prominent legal and literary family. At the time of the public meeting he was assistant editor at the *Port Phillip Gazette* and an elected town councillor in La Trobe ward—one of the four Melbourne wards in the Corporation of Melbourne.[25] He took an active part in Melbourne life, was involved in a number of public causes, and was seen to promote the interests of the elite in Melbourne.[26] He had connections with the *Herald* as an occasional journalist and the *Herald* supported him in the council elections.

The more influential signatories, in addition to Cavenagh and Councillor Stephen, were Alderman Augustus Greeves and businessman Joseph Ankors Marsden. Greeves, a surgeon and hotelier, was, at the time of the public meeting, alderman of Lonsdale Ward.[27] Paul De Serville describes Greeves as 'a respectable colonist outside society', a description which seems appropriate for the majority of people who signed the petition.[28] Greeves, who until 1844 had owned the *Port Phillip Gazette*, was said to have pursued a moderate course which allowed no criticism of polite society. In the mid-1840s Greeves also wrote for the *Herald*.[29]

These three 'moderates' from the aspiring middle class—Greeves, Stephen and Cavenagh—who at times worked together at the *Herald* and who pursued similar political agendas, were to emerge as key players: as signatories, attendees at the public meeting and members of the expedition committee.

Apart from Greeves, Cavenagh and Stephen, Joseph Ankors Marsden was the only other signatory who was also a donor for the expedition, a participant at the public meeting and a member of the expedition committee. Marsden was a Wesleyan lay preacher who owned a haberdashery shop in Collins Street.[30] He was involved in numerous public causes and, according to Melbourne commentator Garryowen, was 'an experienced master in the art of what is known as "taking round the hat" '.[31] His appointment to the White Woman expedition committee might have been in recognition of his abilities in that area. In supporting the White Woman cause, Marsden, as one of the outfitters of the expedition, might also have had a pecuniary interest in the project.

In addition to Cavenagh, only one of the town's four newspaper editors signed: Thomas McCombie of the *Gazette*. William Kerr, editor of the recently founded *Melbourne Argus*, though not a signatory, supported the push for an expedition in an editorial article dated 28 August 1846. Kerr had a background of civic involvement and was thought to represent democratic interests. One might have expected that Kerr would have signed the petition, if only to be seen to be supporting a civic cause, or supporting a Scottish country-woman in distress. Perhaps he was not invited or available to sign. The editor of the *Patriot*, George Boursiquot, as previously noted was not a signatory, although the *Patriot* had taken a leading role in resuscitating the rumours in March and August 1846. Former *Gazette* editor Thomas Strode, although apparently taking no prominent role, will later be seen to have been a key player.

Thomas McCombie, an outspoken opponent of La Trobe on the issue of Separation throughout the 1840s, appeared third on the list of petitioners and attended the meeting. His petition in 1848 to have La Trobe dismissed, supported by one thousand signatures and approved by the Melbourne Town Council, accused La Trobe of 'obstruction, faithlessness, and insincerity', as well as 'systematic mis-management' of money intended for public works.[32] The petition did not succeed, but its distribution indicates the depth of antag-onism towards La Trobe on the Separation issue and demonstrates the way that the Melbourne Town Council operated as an official forum for opposition to La Trobe. In 1848 McCombie would organ-ise two petitions for La Trobe's recall: one from the City Council in

June carried by nine votes to four, and the other in August from nearly a thousand members of the public.[33]

McCombie, as editor of the *Gazette*, owner of a store in Flinders Lane, Melbourne councillor and writer of history and fiction, was in a position to promote the interests of aspiring colonists. In his novel *Arabin* (published 1845), his eponymous hero argued against the establishment in Port Phillip of an exclusive circle by aristocratic emigrants: 'In fact, society must not be formed by emigrants, whatever their pretensions; it must be first decomposed, and the successful Colonists raise themselves into a superior rank by their industry and good name'.[34] The men McCombie championed were the plain-speaking, industrious mercantile class of Melbourne: men who, as he said in *The History of Victoria*, being 'unused to courtly modes of address', were frustrated by La Trobe's personal style and mode of government.[35]

In 1846 anti-government feeling ran high in Port Phillip. In the lead-up to the public meeting, views expressed in the newspapers published contemporaneously with the petition document articulated competing interests. The strength of animosity by the Melbourne Council towards Gipps and La Trobe over the 'Waste Lands' issue during 1846 can be gauged by the letter from J. F. Palmer, the Mayor of Melbourne, to the Principal Secretary of State for the Colonies and dated only days after Gipps's departure from the colony. Palmer's letter describes Gipps's measures as 'unjust and baneful in the highest degree to the landed interests of this Province'.[36] Mayor Palmer's plea followed months of uncertainty about the status of squatting tenure after the Legislative Council in Sydney had refused to renew the local Squatting Act. In May the *Patriot* had predicted that 'legislative and social anarchy' would result unless provision be made to extend the present Squatting Act, which was shortly to expire, or a new Squatting Bill be passed to retain the authority of the Commissioners of Crown Lands and the Border Police.[37]

Contention over Britain's renewal of transportation of 'exiles' (ticket-of-leave prisoners) to the colony also erupted in 1846, when it became known in August that the British government had despatched 300 male prisoners aboard the *Maitland*, to be landed at Port Phillip. The community was divided on the issue of 'exiles'. The squatters, who needed labour, were in favour of transportation, while others, mainly townspeople, considered it an evil to be resisted at all costs. La Trobe, supportive of receiving 'exiles' into the district, was criticised for bowing to pressure from the squatting interests.[38]

The year 1846 was also marked by sectarian riots in Melbourne between Roman Catholics and Orangemen. On 14 July, following an outbreak of violence at the Pastoral Hotel in which two men were shot and several others severely wounded in the ensuing mêlée, the Riot Act was read and the town put under martial law.[39] In such a climate, the Irish Relief Fund (to aid victims of the potato famine), which commenced in August and ran over several months in tandem with the White Woman subscription, provided an anodyne to the bitter divisions and factional infighting. Criticism by newspaper correspondent Humanitas that the Irish Relief Fund was dominated by Catholic interests suggests that even here there were sectarian rivalries, although the amount raised—in excess of £1360—testifies to the success of the project. Of the outcome, the *Herald* enthused:

> To see men of every country and creed, the sons of the Rose, Thistle, and Leek, the Australian, Frenchman, and Italian, congregate, as it were, round one common shrine, and thence pour forth their offerings . . . this is, sir, a gratifying fact, and will form a proud era in the historic records of Australia Felix . . .[40]

The *Herald*'s gushing attestation to the project's unifying potential (probably written by Edmund Finn, who later would use the pseudonym Garryowen) can be read as a partisan view. However, the writer's awareness of 'history', self-consciously enacted, reflects the desire for transformation and legitimation which characterised Melbourne in 1846 as it envisioned itself moving from a frontier town to an autonomous mercantile centre. The emergence of the White Woman cause at this moment, as Melbourne was assuming the proportions and characteristics of a provincial capital, provided a vehicle for the furtherance of this end.

For a community seeking transformation, the need to resolve the Aboriginal 'problem' was one of the most difficult issues to reconcile with the concept of an emergent Christian, civilised community. Ongoing anger and frustration over Aboriginal resistance to settlement erupted in the months leading up to the White Woman meeting, when Aboriginal Koort Kirrup (accused of murdering a settler) was discharged by Justice a'Beckett in March 1846 ostensibly on a point of law.[41] Melbourne newspaper editors vented their outrage in highly charged invective. In one *Herald* editorial column alone the terms 'black savage cannibals', 'black cannibals', 'cannibal savage', 'cannibal alien', and 'cannibal heathen' are used to denote Aboriginality. [42]

In this context, the White Woman cause provided a morally defensible, rehabilitative mechanism to appease any lingering sense of communal guilt for the many acts of violence against Aborigines which had occurred. It operated also to authorise those acts of exploitation and neglect of Aborigines which would continue to occur in the name of progress.

Although the term 'extinction' was entering debate on Aborigines with increasing frequency at this time, this lamented/desired outcome was by no means in sight, and colonists resented the ongoing financial burden which the Protectorate system placed on them. In this, too, La Trobe was seen as a stumbling block, because of his philanthropic leanings and connections.[43] The White Woman cause provided an opportunity to criticise the Protectorate, the 'Exeter Hall philanthropists' in London and their apologists in Melbourne. Exeter Hall, located in The Strand, was a collective of numerous religious and philanthropic groups who, having successfully lobbied in the 1830s for the abolition of slavery, then took up the cause of indigenous peoples in Britain's colonies. The re-emergence of the White Woman story at this moment appears as one element in a concerted attempt to reconceptualise contemporary debate about the Aboriginal 'question' in terms calculated to harden even the most philanthropic hearts.

The 'moment' which gave rise to the White Woman cause was precipitated by the major political upheaval in the governance of colonial Australia during 1846, when almost all senior administrators in both England and New South Wales were replaced. Sir Robert Peel resigned as Prime Minister of England early in the year and was succeeded by Lord John Russell on 6 July. Lord Stanley, Secretary of State for the Colonies, was replaced briefly by William Gladstone, who had pastoral interests in the Port Phillip District (and whose appointment was expected to advance the cause of Separation), before Earl Grey was appointed to the position in July.[44]

The colonial administration of New South Wales also changed, as Governor Gipps left Sydney in July, prior to the arrival of his replacement, Governor Charles FitzRoy, in August. In October, La Trobe left Melbourne to undertake a term as caretaker Governor of Van Diemen's Land, and Captain William Lonsdale was appointed his temporary replacement.

These appointments altered the political climate within the colony and between the colony and England. The close alliance which had existed between Gipps and La Trobe for the previous six years was severed. The arrival of the new Governor offered the potential for the relationship between Port Phillip and Sydney, and hence with London, to be redefined and redetermined along lines more favourable to Port Phillip.

The White Woman story re-emerged during that critical August, immediately following the arrival of FitzRoy, and prior to his meeting with La Trobe. By 28 August, when the *Patriot* reported that La Trobe had secretly '*crept* or rather *sneaked* away to Sydney' (to meet with FitzRoy), the White Woman story was taking on the dimensions of a cause.[45] The hastily got-up petition was being presented to the Mayor. The White Woman cause, as a humanitarian project, may also have provided a means to discredit La Trobe in FitzRoy's estimation, before the two had the chance to form an alliance. It seems probable, given the strength of opposition to La Trobe within Port Phillip and the vociferousness with which he was attacked for failing to investigate the White Woman rumours, that an element of opportunism and point-scoring was involved.

For some years sections of the Port Phillip press and members of the Melbourne Corporation had accused La Trobe of aiding the Executive Council in Sydney in plundering the land revenue from Port Phillip and in retarding separation from New South Wales.[46] These criticisms dated from a public dinner given in Gipps's honour in Melbourne in 1841, when La Trobe had unwisely quipped that he was content to play second fiddle to Gipps. La Trobe's *faux pas* earned him the title 'Second Fiddle' or the 'Twenty pound Governor', that sum being said to represent the limit of his authority.[47]

Another critical voice was added with the establishment of the *Melbourne Argus* in June 1846. It termed La Trobe a 'Monkey

Governor', a maniac, unfit to take care of himself. In time the *Argus* would set up a standing advertisement: 'Wanted, a Governor'. During 1846, La Trobe was berated for being out of touch with, and indifferent to, the interests of Port Phillip. On 25 August 1846 the *Argus*, in a pointed reference to La Trobe's 'second-fiddle' comment, expressed the hope that 'his Honor will find that Sir Charles FitzRoy's not quite such a proficient in music as his talented predecessor'.[48]

In April 1846, after years of lobbying by Port Phillipians, both within the colony and in England, Gipps and the New South Wales Executive Council had recommended to London that the southern district, or Port Phillip, be allowed self-government although, on La Trobe's advice, with a nominated Council rather than a representative Assembly. Gipps's report reached London in July 1846, just as Lord Grey took office, and although Grey accepted the recommendation as part of a planned major reform of administration of the Australian colonies, its implementation was to be delayed for over four years, as other, more pressing matters took precedence.[49]

The anticipated separation of Port Phillip in 1846 called for new narratives to define and authenticate, and rituals of public performance to enact, a process of transformation for a district poised, as it then thought, on the brink of independence. The celebrations attending the laying of the foundation stones in March 1846 for the new bridge over the Yarra River and for a new Melbourne hospital demonstrate rituals of social and political transformation. The *Gazette*'s description of the celebration in Collins Street to mark these two major public projects conjures up a town transformed:

> [presenting] to the imagination one of those enchanting scenes so vividly described in the Arabian Nights: bands playing, fifty banners fluttering in the breeze, the splendid costumes of the masons and public bodies, with the dense crowds of people, made up a perfect 'fairy scene.' The shops were shut, and everything betokened that it was a gala day.[50]

A testimonial to honour the achievements of the explorer Dr Ludwig Leichhardt, recently returned from his expedition in the northern part of the colony, provided another transformative narrative of 1846, which involved the theme of success through autonomous civic enterprise in the face of government obstructionism. Thomas McCombie, George Cavenagh and William Westgarth had several months previously been members of the committee for the testimonial. Port Phillipians responded empathetically to Leichhardt who had been, 'to the eternal disgrace of the government of Sir George Gipps, refused the sum of £1000 voted for the purpose of this expedition by the Legislative Council of New South Wales; but, not discouraged . . . proceeded on his own resources, supplemented by assistance from some colonists'. According to McCombie, Leichhardt succeeded not just in spite of, but *because* of, lack of government support. He argued that '[h]ad Dr. Leichhardt gone forth under government protection, with a large and well appointed party, it is not probable that he would have accomplished his great feat; the smallness of the party and its unencumbered condition led to compete [*sic*] success.'[51] In so doing, his expedition provides a precursor to the White Woman expedition.

Like Leichhardt's expedition, the expedition to rescue the White Woman provided a mediating and performative ritual which reconceptualised the political relationship between private citizens and government officials, between Melbourne and Sydney, and between Melbourne and Gipps Land. The narratives which engendered the venture—a helpless woman held captive by brutal savages; a heartless government which failed in its duty of care; the humanitarianism and generosity of the citizens of Melbourne who came to her aid; and the heroic endeavour by the brave men sent to rescue her— transformed vested interests into a noble cause.

The project to rescue the White Woman helped to articulate an emergent community's struggle for autonomy and recognition. In and through the figure of the White Woman, white men could strike heroic poses and a proud era of respectability could be enshrined and legitimised in the public record. The expedition to rescue her also provided a rite of expiation. The effectiveness of such rites in resolving lingering feelings of guilt and loss was demonstrated, albeit on a grander scale, by the Burial of the Unknown Warrior, performed on the streets of London on Armistice Day, 1920.[52] In more recent times, the funeral of Diana, Princess of Wales, similarly provided an outlet for an outpouring of private griefs on a global scale.

The White Woman—because she never existed or because she never returned to tell her own tale—was not party to the construction of white female subjectivity in her narratives, or the uses to which they were put. In this way, her story differs from those of the numerous white American women who published accounts of their captivity. Carroll Smith-Rosenberg argues that such women 'helped to construct white Americans as true Americans and native Americans as savages . . . by assuming the role of innocent victims of barbarous savages, by assuming the role of authoritative writers, and by authorizing themselves as an alternative white icon for America'.[53] Eliza Fraser, the only Australian white female to publish accounts of her experiences as a captive of Aborigines, assumed, or has had assigned to her by her numerous biographers and commentators, the characteristics which Smith-Rosenberg identifies. However, Smith-Rosenberg's argument is less applicable to the Australian colonial context. The degree of control which Eliza Fraser had over the production and promulgation of her story is less clear than that of many of the American examples.

As a defining event in Port Phillip history, the White Woman cause in 1846 ironically stands in place of defining narratives *by* white Australian women. As Kate Darian-Smith has acknowledged, the White Woman's 'inconclusive and unsubstantiated presence . . . has meant that the "invisible girl" has been granted more historical and imaginative space than any flesh and blood white pioneer woman'.[54] The dearth of such narratives by women in the colonial period and well into the twentieth century, by both producing and reflecting masculinist ideals and values, have shaped perceptions of national identity.

The launch of the White Woman expedition in 1846 was a constitutive event for Port Phillipians. In coming together and claiming the right to rescue a white woman, they were simultaneously producing the category 'Port Phillipian' as noble, masculine, white, and independent. Through the discursive and physical components of the expedition, Port Phillip was also being constituted territorially, as a district which incorporated Gipps Land.

Port Phillip, Hobart and Sydney newspapers had for several years provided a public domain for the dissemination of sporadic reports about the White Woman. However, the public meeting at the Royal

Hotel in Collins Street on 2 September 1846 made Melbourne the focus of action. The meeting propelled the story into what might these days be termed a publishing event. The four Melbourne newspapers reported the proceedings and the events which followed and took up positions in relation to the rescue project itself, to one another as mediators of the information for the reading public, and as competing owners of the multiple variations of the story.[55] In this sense, the contestation for ownership of news about the White Woman was as great as the contestation over the White Woman's body.

Newspaper rivalry was nothing new in Port Phillip, where the press was distinguished by its acrimonious tone. La Trobe was to complain to the Colonial Secretary in 1848 that the distinguishing characteristics of the Port Phillip newspapers were 'ignorance, disregard of truth, and a reckless and studied spirit of misrepresentation, often amounting to the most malevolent libel'.[56] The frequent litigation suits, and occasional horsewhippings and duels, which characterised relations between the various editors, reflected their headstrong and idiosyncratic personalities and the politics of colonial town life. With the establishment of a fourth Melbourne newspaper, the *Melbourne Argus*, in June 1846, the competitive environment intensified as each newspaper struggled to maintain its circulation rate and advertisers.

The White Woman cause offered an opportunity for the newspapers to boost readership and advertising. Each of the newspapers offered substantially different textual reconstructions of the meeting. The *Patriot* (the only daily newspaper in Melbourne) and the *Herald* were the first to go into print on 3 September, the day after the public meeting. The *Patriot*, presenting its summary of the meeting, considered that to report the speeches 'would be a work of recapitulation, the subject having already been exhausted'. The *Herald* supported its detailed and enthusiastic account of the proceedings with an editorial endorsement of the meeting and its outcomes. The *Argus* on 4 September reported the resolutions adopted and noted briefly that 'much difference of opinion prevailed as to the degree of reliance to be placed upon the prevailing rumours', while the *Gazette* published a lengthy article on 5 September. Together, the four newspapers present a comprehensive, though not necessarily complete, account of the meeting.

Several resolutions were passed at the meeting. The first was that, as the Government had failed to take effectual measures to investigate the rumours, the inhabitants of Port Phillip must take this duty upon themselves. This resolution formally established the meeting's *raison d'être*. Having this charge endorsed at a public meeting convened by the Mayor lent it greater authority than previous similar accusations. Further resolutions were that a public subscription be started; a committee formed and members appointed; banks be requested to accept subscriptions; and local journals be asked to promote the meeting and publicise the proceedings.

All five speakers at the meeting—Alderman Greeves, George Cavenagh, Joseph Ankors Marsden, Councillor Stephen and William Westgarth—would be appointed to the expedition committee. Alderman Greeves and George Cavenagh spoke in support of the rumours and brought forward, as evidence attesting to the woman's existence, alleged verbatim reports by Aboriginal witnesses and Gipps Land settlers. Joseph Ankors Marsden called the Mayor to account over his opening remarks that the White Woman might have 'formed connections and ties with the blacks which she might not wish to dissever'.[57] Councillor Stephen 'denounced in forcible terms the conduct of the Government in not earlier seeking for the recovery of the women',[58] and William Westgarth stated that 'from conversations he had with Mr. Robinson, the Protector, he was disposed to believe there was no real truth in the report that a white woman was detained by a tribe of the Port Albert blacks'.[59]

The *Herald* did not mention Westgarth's sceptical comments. Neither did it mention Cavenagh's response. The *Patriot*, however, did:

> [a] friend of [Cavenagh's] residing in that locality some short time ago was in search of a run, and he saw the name of 'Anne [*sic*] Macpherson' carved upon several trees in a part of the country which, there was every reason to believe had not been previously visited by Europeans. Independent of this, [Cavenagh] was prepared to produce Messrs. Pearson, Turnbull

and Reoh, who would state that some few months ago they had seen a white woman in custody of a tribe of blacks, who on being alarmed had driven her (the white woman) before them.

Why was the *Herald*, Cavenagh's own paper, reluctant to draw attention to his role in persuading the meeting of the validity of the rumours? The *Herald* seemed more intent on foregrounding the efforts of Stephen, Greeves and Marsden.

Greeves also offered anecdotal evidence in support of the rumours, namely that not long ago he had 'conversed with a settler in the Port Albert district, who averred that he had a native lad in his establishment who stated that he had frequently played with the children, the offspring of a white woman with a black chief '.[60] Between Greeves and Cavenagh all aspects of earlier rumours—from Gipps Land and Portland—except for the story of the Heart were repeated and reinforced.

In addition to the speakers, the newspaper reports also noted those who proposed and seconded the several resolutions: Messrs Baird, Davies, Kerr, Miller, O'Farrell, O'Shanassy and Robinson. Baird is unknown. John Davies was a reporter, employed on the *Patriot* and *Gazette*. Kerr was editor of the *Argus*. Miller is unknown. O'Farrell was possibly the rate collector of that name, in Collins St. O'Shanassy was a councillor and linen draper in Collins Street. Robinson was a saddler in Elizabeth Street.[61] Minor discrepancies occured in recording these names. More substantial discrepancies were to appear in the record of the meeting which John Macdonald, who was appointed Secretary to the Expedition Committee, subsequently sent to the Colonial Secretary in Sydney. These might have been the result of inaccurate minuting, or Macdonald may have had reasons for wanting other names to be attributed to the resolutions, perhaps in anticipation of its reception in Sydney.

Attendance figures for the meeting were not reported in any of the newspapers. In addition to the Mayor, sixteen people are mentioned in the several reports. Of these, four had signed the petition calling for the meeting (Cavenagh, Greeves, Stephen and Marsden). It seems that few, if any, of the other fifty-eight signatories to the petition attended. Edmund Finn, reporter at the *Herald* and attendee, was to assert later (writing as Garryowen) that those who did attend, while not numerous, were influential. The *Herald*, which published the most lengthy and fulsome report, described the meeting as 'one of the, if not *the* most interesting public meeting held in Port Phillip', although the *Argus* gave a less sanguine picture, noting that '[t]he meeting was not very numerously attended'. The *Gazette* also commented on the small number of attendees, but considered that 'those present took a most active part in carrying out the objects contemplated'.

The public meeting was less a spontaneous outpouring of concern by Melbournians about the plight of the captive woman, than validation of a project by a small group of civic-minded people. The key proponents, in putting themselves forward as humanitarians, were aided by the press, and particularly by Cavenagh's *Herald*, which assured readers that: 'Even, in the extremely improbable event of the Expedition making out that the whole of the detailed reports of the circumstances are fabricated; that no such captive is, or has been, among the blacks, a sacred duty will have been performed, and a distressing doubt finally set at rest'.[62]

The term 'fabricated' registered, albeit fleetingly, the possibility of ulterior motives in those who produced or perpetuated the reports. The *Herald*'s swift neutralising of this potentially disruptive prospect, under the authorising agency of a 'sacred duty', acted to preempt potential reader scepticism about the project and to portray the proposed expedition as humane, ennobled, and civilised. In undertaking this 'sacred duty', the meeting—a Christian, metropolitan coterie—positioned itself in opposition to the government; to the settlers in Gipps Land (the logical group to have organised a rescue mission); to the 'savages' who held the woman captive; and to those within the community (the unfeeling, the sceptical) who did not support the venture.

The meeting legitimised its proceedings by presuming to represent the Port Phillip community despite an apparent lack of interest in the cause to this point. The *Herald* claimed that the meeting was 'the most gratifying demonstration of the philanthropy and energy of Port Phillip'. However, the *Gazette*'s acknowledgement that the meeting was due to the efforts of some 'anxious to wipe away any stain on the community' hinted at the expedition's broader role as a rite of communal expiation.

Although the subject of the meeting was ostensibly the White Woman, the *Patriot*, by reporting the meeting under the heading 'The Whites and the Blacks', alluded—intentionally or otherwise—to its broader function as a polarising agent in colonial relations. If the citizens of Melbourne did not place great store in the validity of the rumours, or were not sufficiently interested to attend the public meeting, they might nevertheless have seen some merit in the employment of such a narrative on their behalf.

The Mayor's presence and his role as chair gave the meeting's resolutions an authority which they otherwise would not have had. It consolidated what was previously a number of disparate voices into a formal, civic cause. Joseph Marsden said as much when he expressed satisfaction in seeing the Mayor present at the meeting: 'for the attendance of the chief magistrate was always certain to enlist the feelings of the community, and as the head of a corporate body, he (Mr. M.) was glad to see his Worship where he was (laughter)'.[63] The laughter which accompanied Marsden's comment revealed, beneath the *bonhomie* of the meeting, an underlying nervousness about the meeting being otherwise a 'headless' body of citizens without sufficient authority to carry out its objectives.

There is a suggestion that by his presence at the meeting the Mayor demonstrated that he was with the citizens and, by implication, not against them and with the government. The purported reason for the meeting—that as the government had failed to adopt effectual measures to ascertain the positive truth or otherwise of the rumours, 'it [became] the duty of the inhabitants of Port Phillip to take upon themselves that very essential duty'—had particular import, as a report of the meeting was subsequently sent to the Colonial Secretary in Sydney for the Governor's information. The charge against La Trobe was thus moved beyond an issue of local politics into the broader arena of colonial governance in a way which demanded Governor FitzRoy's attention.

Despite the presence of a strong contingent who were pushing the same line, the meeting was not a univocal event. The Mayor's opening remarks—that the White Woman might have formed connections and ties with the blacks which she might not wish to dissever —*could* have derailed the meeting. This was a rare moment in the propagation of the White Woman story when anything close to a counter-enunciative position gained entry. In the context of the proposed project to rescue a genteel lady from 'sable villains', it articulated the unthinkable.

At the public meeting, the issue of whether the woman might not wish to be rescued was elided, and attention deflected onto the role which the Mayor was expected to play in buttressing civic unity for the cause. In response to the Mayor's remarks, Marsden told the meeting that he 'regretted such sentiments, calculated as they were to discourage the objects of the meeting with a certain class, as there were persons who would gladly avail themselves of any difficulty that might be thrown in the way of the objects of the meeting, and would hold themselves excused from not contributing by the expressions that fell from the chief magistrate'.[64]

La Trobe had made similar comments some months earlier, when in a letter to Tyers, he suggested that because of 'the peculiar circumstances of [the woman's] case . . . and the strength of the ties that she has apparently formed amongst the natives, she may be herself at present indifferent or averse to reclamation by those of her own race'.[65] La Trobe's speculations raise questions about the legitimacy of government intervention if the woman was indeed 'indifferent or averse to reclamation', and highlight gendered and racist assumptions in a government response. Would the government have felt an obligation to reclaim a white man living with Aborigines? William Buckley had lived amongst the Aborigines of the Port Phillip area for thirty-two years and was not prevented from leaving them to rejoin white settler society. And there was anecdotal evidence of Aborigines assisting white people who were lost in the bush to return to their own people.

La Trobe's comment was not revealed until late October 1846, when official correspondence relating to his investigations into the White Woman rumours was made public. By that time, the expedition to Gipps Land was under way, so La Trobe's views did not derail the rescue project, as the Mayor's remarks might have done. The *Herald*, however, considered the remarks of sufficient import to warrant a refutation, due to the 'relative official reputations of the propounders' (La Trobe and the Mayor): 'To suppose that a white woman, even one steeped in the veriest depths of depravity, could, under any "peculiar circumstances", be "averse to reclamation" or unwilling to sever the "strength of the ties" that bind her to a life of the most revolting nature amidst a pack of semi-demons, is absolutely incredible'.[66]

The force of this refutation drew in large part on 'new and horrible' details about the Gipps Land tribes, published in the same article, and provided by Sergeant Windredge of the Native Police. The *Herald* informed its readers, with great relish, that the tribes were 'not only cannibals but the actual devourers of the remains of the deceased gins, whose corpses instead of honouring with the rights of interment, they commit to the process of an aboriginal baking, and feast on the roasted flesh. This is a sickening but truthful fact!'

This exchange, which aligned the reader with the superior standpoint of the *Herald* 'in the cause of suffering humanity' over against an 'insensitive' La Trobe, simultaneously constituted the Aborigine as 'cannibal' and pandered to the reader's prurient interest in 'savage' customs. In this exchange, the White Woman, as the imagined mute witness to, possible partaker in, or potential future victim of, a cannibal feast, acts as a site for the articulation of anxiety about Aboriginal sexual appetite and about 'civilisation' being swallowed up by 'savagery'. Peter Hulme, theorising colonialist allegations of cannibalism in the Americas, has argued that 'what is to be feared from cannibal devouring is dispersal of corporeal integrity', and that the threat from cannibals 'would then be read not as the promulgation of a pseudo-ethnographic or even overtly ideological vision of the native inhabitants of the Caribbean, but rather as a graphic image of the *decomposition* of the self that is the price of failure'.[67]

The White Woman story expressed anxiety about miscegenation and cannibalism—the clichéd 'fate worse than death itself' for a white woman. It did so with a certain prurient, even salacious, interest, the effect of which was heightened by the idea of the woman as an unwilling victim to the savage lusts of half-human brutes. With a few later exceptions when the White Woman's alleged captor would be described as a handsome man, the narratives do not encourage the reader to consider that she could have found a Kurnai man desirable.[68]

The fear that captive women could be seduced by their captors was an enduring characteristic in American captivity narratives, where what was at stake was a 'battle between pale- and dark-skinned men', as noted by Kay Schaffer, following Slotkin and Fiedler. Hazel Carby and others have also pointed out the erasure of white male exploitation of Native American and African-American women through such narratives.[69] In the comparatively few narratives about Australian 'captive' white women, it is their bodies, not their affections, which are depicted as the site of contestation. Unlike the Indian warriors, Aborigines seem not to have been considered serious rivals for white women's affections in captivity narratives, despite real-life examples to the contrary.[70]

Central to the myth of Indian captivity was a recurring pictorial image of white woman as an object of lust in which she is 'tied naked to the stake and surrounded by howling Redskins'; an image, Leslie Fiedler says, which 'panders to that basic White male desire at once to relish and deplore, vicariously share and publicly condemn, the rape of White female innocence'.[71] Again, this image was not generally applied to Australian captives, although one mid-twentieth-century version of Eliza Fraser's narrative carries an illustration of such a scene.[72]

That European settlement involved the large-scale destruction of tribal life was a recognised and continuing feature of the White Woman stories. The *Gazette*, like the *Argus*, was concerned about the implications of the Cape Otway massacre and considered that it would be 'most improper to send out a party with authority from the citizens of Melbourne to rescue these white women and perhaps wage a war of extermination with several tribes of aborigines, unless under more efficient control than that of any needy adventurer, whom love of gain or notoriety may bring forward'. It had been asserted just before the meeting was convened that 'the crime might in a legal sense be construed into that of murder'.[73] The *Herald* reported that George Cavenagh cautioned 'how a person not armed with the authority of a magistrate could proceed to capture, and perhaps with the loss of life, the free savage belonging to the tribe against which the expedition would be sent'. Despite these protestations, the expedition party was expected to be heroic in its endeavour, and it was generally accepted that a rescue attempt would entail the killing of Aborigines.

These political, moral and ethical questions were raised but not satisfactorily resolved at the meeting. The project's viability as a civic venture was dependent on the establishment of its *bona fides*, and to this end the resolution that clergymen of all denominations be invited to become members of the expedition committee imparted Christian sanction to the project. The meeting also proposed to appoint a female fundraising committee. The relegation of women to the role of fundraisers reflected the gendering of roles in the public sphere in Port Phillip at a time when the community was being asked to give to several worthy causes. The highly organised Irish Relief Fund also had a female fundraising committee.[74] The annexation of the women of Port Phillip to a fundraising exercise served as a counterpoise to the 'brave men' charged with conducting the expedition. While men wrote to the newspapers, signed the petition, took part in the public meeting, formed the expedition committee and undertook the expedition, women's involvement was subsidiary. The Mayor chaired the public meeting, and the Mayoress was invited to lend her support to the raising of subscriptions.[75]

The Appeal to the Public, launched almost four weeks after the meeting, garnered moral support and called for a united response by women across divisions of class:

> surely the reflection of the hardships which must be undergone in endeavouring their rescue by the brave men who are willing to risk their lives in the venture—without fee or reward, but that of self-approval,—will be a sufficient inducement to the females in all ranks in Port Phillip to contribute towards the releasing [sic] an unhappy fellow countrywoman from the misery, the barbarous, disgusting horrors of her wretched captivity.[76]

The sufficiently ambiguous term 'fellow countrywoman' allowed the reader to construe the 'country' as the England, Ireland or Scotland of the three potential captives, or to repond to it as a call to proto-nationalist feelings in Australia.

In terms of the amount of money raised and the percentage of women among donors to the fund, the women's contributions were relatively modest. Of a total of 233 contributions, 30 small donations can be attributed to women.

The idea of a white woman 'out there' depended for its emotional charge on a counter image of other white women—wives, sweethearts, mothers, daughters—safe at home. From this dynamic, the rescue venture derived its motivating impulse and authority. Shortly after the public meeting, An Englishman writing in the columns of the *Sydney Herald* appealed directly to the women:

> I am certain that there is not a wife, a mother, or a single female in the colony, that will not each readily contribute *one penny*, which would be amply sufficient to cover the expenses necessary to be incurred in the recovery of one of their own sex, . . . one, who is compelled to yield to the disgusting passions and desires of a set of black cannibals—one, [who] however inclement the seasons, is wandering about the bush in a state of nudity—one, who is forced to subsist on the most loathsome food, the sight of which would make our hearts sicken, for it is a well known fact, that the *coolies*, or men, keep the best part of all animals for their own eating, only giving their *loubras*, or women, the entrails: such is the existence at present of a Christian, a wife, a mother, an Irishwoman.[77]

Although ostensibly directed towards the sympathies of females, the article, published under the heading 'Gross Inhumanity in a Christian Government', was calculated to incite the outrage, and inflame the passions, of bourgeois men. The invective pits the barbarism of black cannibal 'coolies' against the sensibility of genteel society. The term 'coolie', with its connotation of *imported labour*, works to displace Aborigines as indigenous people with prior occupation rights and relegate them to the lowest rungs in a hierarchy of European capitalist enterprise.

An Englishman also pits colonist against government, although his premise is unstable. Where does an 'inhuman' government fit on the civilised/savage hierarchy which An Englishman has set up? The rhetorical build-up climaxes with the plight of an *Irish* woman as an indictment of a *Christian* government by an *English* man. What is being appealed to here and what condemned? Where, for instance, might the rescue of an Irishwoman fit into the priorities of an English colonial government? Is the implication that an Englishwoman would be rescued more promptly?

An Englishman's appeal to the reader's prejudices, and his insistence on the imagined social and sexual indignities to which the woman was being subjected, quashed any notion that the White Woman might have chosen not to be rescued. The idea of one of their own wandering about in a state of nudity, and her sexual vulnerability as a naked woman, was meant to shock the reader used to contemporary proprieties of female modesty. Within European systems of cultural production, the account reads as a cautionary tale which served to buttress the idea of a proper state of gender relations in which the woman remained safe and protected in her defined domestic sphere and the man engaged with the wider (and more dangerous) world.

In one of numerous articles which delineated the roles of men and women in the enactment of the White Woman cause, the *Herald* exhorted Port Phillipians to participate in the rescue project either vicariously or (in the case of men) in actuality: 'What man is there amongst us but will not feel indignation at the cruelties such a captive must endure! What female bosom but must deeply commiserate her fearful anguish and hopeless sorrow!'.[78] Over the ensuing weeks twenty-three men, An Englishman included, would volunteer their services to the expedition committee.

Throughout September and October the White Woman cause continued to provide Melbourne newspapers with an abundance of copy. The *Herald* reported, somewhat smugly, that it had received too many letters on the subject to print more than six or seven and that the rest must await their turn.[79] Between the public meeting and the departure of the expedition party, in excess of thirty articles appeared, as well as the first 'literary' piece on the White Woman, a verse entitled 'A Lay of Lament', which came with a note to the Editor:

Sir,—the accompanying lines have been written with a view to keep alive the generous purpose of rescuing the hapless female reported to be detained by the Blacks in the forest. As the 'Herald' has not only kindled but 'fanned the flame' of public sympathy in the matter, to *its* general usefulness and 'fine impulse' the following verses are very respectfully dedicated.[80]

However, while the *Herald* fanned the flame of public sympathy for the White Woman, others wished the matter to be laid to rest. In the days following the public meeting, an anonymous correspondent had written to the editors of the *Sydney Morning Herald* seeking to forestall further publication and circulation of paragraphs about the 'fearful cruelties and diabolical inhumanities, supposed to be practised by these savages on the unfortunate victims who may fall into their hands'. The writer, Z, speaking on behalf of friends and relatives of shipwreck victims, recognised the exploitative potential of the captive's alleged state, for both the newspapers which published the articles, and readers who indulged their prurient interests:

Surely, those whose vitiated minds find in such details a pleasure scarcely less inhuman than the barbarities themselves, need not be gratified at the expense of those whose hearts are well nigh broken by the fearful state of suspense and anxiety to which their connexion and relationship with the unfortunate individuals subject them.[81]

Z's call for closure went unheeded. Anxious relatives and friends of Ann Macpherson, Miss Lord, Mrs Capel (if, indeed, all or any of these women were any more than the inventions of ambitious editors, or others with vested interests in keeping the story going) and other potential but unnamed candidates were to wait another fifteen months before the story would cease to be 'news'.

Throughout September 1846, the expedition committee awaited Governor FitzRoy's response to its request for assistance in equipping the expedition. In the interim, the committee was employed in collecting evidence, appointing De Villiers as the expedition leader, and raising funds. The difficulty of maintaining readers' interest in the cause when the expedition party could not be launched immediately, and the very real risk that the issue would go 'off the boil', must have caused concern to newspaper editors and the expedition committee. The committee members, too, may have started to lose interest; a meeting scheduled for 22 September had to be adjourned, as only two of the members turned up.[82]

The *Patriot* grew impatient with the delay. It accused the expedition committee of 'frittering away their exertions, and virtually prolonging the captivity of the wretched object of their solicitude' by taking evidence on useless points.[83] The *Patriot*'s desire to get the project under way quickly was possibly also a reflection of concern about La Trobe's impending return from Sydney. Two days later, the *Herald* remarked, in the tone of 'while the cat's away, the mice will play', that La Trobe had changed his mind about returning overland, and 'therefore, need not be expected in Melbourne for the next three weeks'.[84]

In condemning yet again La Trobe's failure as a 'public officer' the *Patriot* simultaneously produced the citizens as 'MEN' in opposition to the '*unmanly*' La Trobe, who:

> had not even the prudent decency to make a shew of that 'red tape and pigeon hole' attention, which might have been expected from the representative of the crown, to the sufferings and captivity of a British subject—and that subject, a helpless female. It wanted but this example to prove, that however indifferent his Honor may be to the welfare of the community, he is equally so in detail—his consistency is miraculous! That undertaking which is now the result of private enterprise, is properly the province of the government—and the inhuman, *unmanly* neglect of his Honor admits of no defence which *ought* to satisfy an intelligent public, not even of that unhappy excuse of our equally unhappy Mayor, that 'the woman was doubtless *reconciled to her condition!*[85]

Mr Brewster (one of the five Council members representing Port Phillip) was also raising questions against La Trobe and government officers in Gipps Land in the Legislative Council in Sydney at this time. In response to a query by Mr Brewster about what steps if any had been taken, the Colonial Secretary, E. Deas Thomson, vindicated La Trobe by advising Council that 'every exertion had been made to release her', and that the correspondence on the subject between his office and La Trobe would shortly be laid before the Council.[86] This was duly done at the October 1846 meeting of the Council.[87]

Fortunately for La Trobe and the other government officers concerned, the versions of events recorded in the official documents vindicated their actions. On 19 September, three days prior to the Council meeting, the Colonial Secretary, on behalf of Governor FitzRoy, wrote a civil but scathing response to the expedition committee's criticism of La Trobe 'that no effectual measures had been adopted'. Deas Thomson advised that His Excellency had perused the official correspondence and refuted the claim. FitzRoy declined the committee's request for assistance in equipping the expedition. In a rebuff of the public meeting's failure to follow due process, his Excellency expressed surprise 'that neither the Mayor of Melbourne who presided, nor any other person present really interested in the recovery of the unfortunate female, had considered it just and proper to apply to the Superintendent [La Trobe] for that information on the subject, which the Government, of whose presumed conduct in the affair the resolutions passed are condemnatory, was both in a position, and most willing, to give'.[88]

The effect of the Governor's terse comments, conveyed through the Colonial Secretary, is doubly reprimanding. It is clear that both parties considered that the meeting had overstepped the mark and had behaved in a way which was not good form. The letter was entrusted to La Trobe in Sydney, presumably to take with him on his return to Melbourne, for delivery to the committee secretary, John Macdonald.

In Melbourne, a critical and defensive press awaited La Trobe's return. The *Herald* on 1 October published the Colonial Secretary's letter as 'the tardy reply of an apathetic Government'. The *Herald* blamed the Mayor, 'a personal and intimate acquaintance of Mr. La Trobe's', whose opening remarks at the meeting had given the impression that 'the Government neither gave credit to the Report, nor intended any means to discover or rescue the poor creature'.[89] Evading the governor's criticism of the public meeting, the *Herald* focussed instead on FitzRoy's acknowledgment of the White Woman: 'For the first time; and—be it observed *via* Sydney, it is now officially announced that the Government credits the fact of [the woman's] forcible detention, and has used exertions, futile though they have been, for her release'.

However, while the *Herald* took a critical stance on behalf of the public meeting, Macdonald's subsequent letter to La Trobe, dated 7 October, was placatory in tone.[90] Macdonald excused the committee's failure to observe protocol, on the basis that 'at the time the Public Meeting was held Your Honor was not in the District of Port Phillip, and hence no application for any information could be made to you'. He expressed the committee's 'regret that circumstances unavoidably arising from Your Honor's temporary absence from the Province, should have led to a mis-apprehension on the part of the Government as to the views and intentions of the framers of this expedition'.

Macdonald 'respectfully' applied for information of the unfortunate female and the means in progress for her rescue and—more importantly—enquired 'whether the Government [would] interpose any obstacles to the expedition, as is reported by some subordinate officials, they intend doing'. La Trobe's terse annotation to Macdonald's letter concedes only that 'if any person or persons offered their services to assist [the government officers] ... such services could only be taken advantage of on the condition that they were performed under the express direction of the Govt under & in the manner which the Govt might judge expedient'.

Perhaps emboldened by La Trobe's departure for Van Diemen's Land, where he was to act as caretaker Governor for some ten months, the *Herald* a week later again chided 'the apathy of the Government in allowing a wretched white woman to remain forcibly detained ... and the difficulties which at every step they throw in the way of the public expedition to her rescue being started'.[91] In La Trobe's absence, William Lonsdale, as Acting Superintendent, provided tacit government sanction for the expedition party, by approving the loan of three whaleboat oars from government stores.

The context within which the expedition was mounted must have had a chastening effect on the committee. The implications of the Cape Otway massacre, and the refusal of FitzRoy and La Trobe to endorse an independent expedition, would have made the committee reluctant to place themselves in a position where they could be held liable for any 'unfortunate results' which might ensue. Thus the composition of the expedition party, the instructions with which it were sent out, its subsequent behaviour in the field and its recording of the journey for publication must have been shaped by the knowledge that they were under the scrutiny of the government and could be called to account. The project as undertaken may thus have been very different from what was originally envisaged.

The public response to the Appeal—£158.6.0—was somewhat short of the £500 which the *Herald* had confidently predicted, and substantially less than the £1360 donated to the Irish Relief Fund at the same time.[92] George Cavenagh and Augustus Greeves would have appreciated the irony, given the criticism of La Trobe for apathy to the White Woman's situation, that a substantial portion of the expedition funds was collected in La Trobe Ward. This point was not lost on those promoting the White Woman cause. The *Herald* took the opportunity to mention it again a few weeks later, when publishing the names of members of the public who were 'most nobly . . . coming to the rescue'.[93]

As the story was produced and reproduced in the context of a call for civic action to rescue the 'captive' woman, its focus shifted from the realm of text to the physical and political sphere of action: from the mobilising of an abstraction—the *idea* of a captive White Woman —to concretisation and enactment.

CHAPTER 4

'A Complex of Narratives'

'A mythology is a complex of narratives that dramatizes the world vision and historical sense of a people or culture, reducing centuries of experience into a constellation of compelling metaphors.'
Richard Slotkin, *Regeneration Through Violence* (1973)[1]

The expedition party finally embarked aboard the *Shamrock* on 20 October 1846, with the 'generous assistance of a most benevolent public . . . and with God's blessing', although not without some last-minute drama.[2] The party under De Villiers's command comprised James Warman as second in command, John Dingle, Alexander Brodie, Richard Hartnett and ten Aborigines of the Western Port Tribe including Benbow, Yall Yall, Billy Lonsdale, Beenak Mornok, Dulie Kali Kut, and others, nearly all of whom had served in the Native Police.[3] The expedition would be strengthened in Gipps Land by Donald McLeod, 'the Highland piper', who travelled over-land after having been rejected by the committee, and two other vol-unteers, 'thorough bushmen and sailors', namely Thomas Hill, '*alias the Mountain Devil*', and William Peters.[4] The party was well armed and provisioned for four months, and furnished with 'an abundant supply of fish hooks, lines, blankets and such other articles as are esteemed by the blacks, and especially with a considerable number of handkerchiefs on which are printed in English and Gaelic, a notice [to the White Woman]'.[5]

The *Shamrock* left without James Buck of Queen Street, who had been dismissed summarily from the expedition at the last moment for insubordination. Buck protested his indignation at the charge in the columns of the *Argus*. He had, he said, outfitted himself at great expense and had exerted himself by running about the town with De Villiers for six weeks to select 'respectable' recruits, entirely neglecting his business. Buck's tale of injured pride and disappointment demonstrates the seductiveness of the project and its capacity to engage the imagination of would-be heroes.[6]

George Cavenagh, as chairman of the expedition committee and editor of the *Port Phillip Herald*, was in an ideal position to capitalise on the situation and the narrative possibilities of the expedition. His appointment to the committee, much to the chagrin of the other Melbourne newspapers, ensured that over the ensuing months the *Herald* would have privileged access to the expeditionists' letters from the field and the search party journals, and would assume the role of the 'official' reporting organ. The *Argus* and *Patriot* accused the *Herald* of monopolising news in order to benefit from increased advertising.[7]

De Villiers's party left Melbourne with instructions from the expedition committee to 'report the progress of the expedition at every convenient opportunity'.[8] De Villiers and James Warman both wrote from Gipps Land, and their letters, along with Warman's journal of the expedition, were published in the *Port Phillip Herald* between November 1846 and March 1847. De Villiers's letters, and his retrospective account which appeared in the *Herald* of 11 February 1847, at times are replicated in Warman's journal, to which De Villiers refers as 'our journal'. If De Villiers kept his own field notes these were not published as a discrete document and have not (to date) surfaced. Neither is there a record of the expedition committee's letters to De Villiers's party.

Melbourne newspapers also published information gained through semi-official channels and from private sources. Rumours, too, continued, including a report which made its way back to Melbourne that the woman had been recovered and was being shipped to Melbourne aboard the *Elizabeth* from Port Albert.[9]

Warman's journal, published in three instalments in the *Herald* in February and March 1847, provided a detailed first-hand account of the expedition's movements over the three months of the search.[10] Warman and De Villiers at times went separate ways, with the expedition splitting into two parties. As Warman's journal concentrates

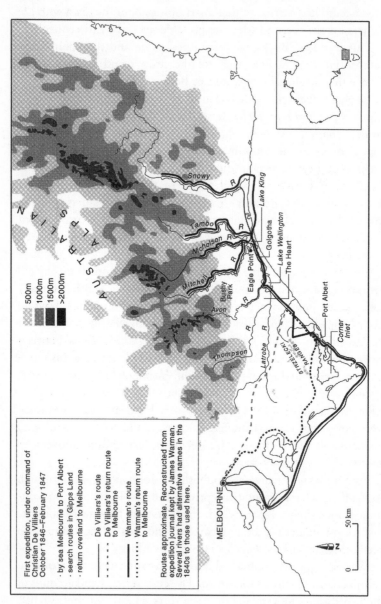

Approximate routes taken by De Villiers's expedition (October 1846–February 1847)
Details compiled by author. Map prepared by Chandra Jayasuriya, Melbourne University Press.

principally on the party to which he was attached, there are unavoidable gaps in his version of events. By the time the journal was published, many of the details already had appeared in newspapers as letters from Warman and De Villiers. The substantial column space devoted by the *Herald* to the publication of Warman's journal (reprinted due to great demand), in addition to numerous other articles on the expedition, indicates the *Herald*'s investment in the project and continuing reader interest.

The *Herald* introduced Warman's journal as 'extremely interesting, detailing among other things, the disgusting habits and character of the tribe of savages with which the wretched white woman is a heart-broken captive'. This framing comment illuminates the way in which the readers' interpretation of the search documents, and the White Woman reports generally, were mediated by editorial opinion.

The search party documents record numerous statements attributed to 'Worrigals' attesting to the woman's existence and location. Gippsland historian Peter Gardner reads these statements as evidence of a pragmatic response by the Kurnai to the frontier situation, their corroborative evidence of the White Woman's existence being 'governed by the need to avoid violence and to obtain gifts of blankets and supplies'.[11] Aside from these 'sightings/citings', Kurnai versions of the White Woman story, if they existed in Gipps Land Aboriginal oral tradition, have with few exceptions not been documented.[12] The search party documents therefore provide a one-sided version of the ways in which 'Worrigals' responded to the expeditionists and their requests for information about the White Woman.

Warman's journal conveys a sense of the immediacy and contingencies of the journey, yet universalises it within a complex of narrative conventions, themes and functions from literary genres and colonialist discourses. The grand narrative of progress, which echoes as a refrain throughout the early colonial period, provides an overarching structure. Other interconnected narrative strands include the quest and the adventure story (themes of pursuit and transformation, and picaresque embellishments); detective story (explicatory and interpretive drive, and the primacy of 'evidence'); explorer's report (appropriative assumptions and strategies, which familiarise the 'strange'); philanthropic meditation on the treatment and likely fate of the Aboriginal inhabitants of the region; polemic against settler violence; ethnographic report; and exoneration of the conduct of expedition members. Within this matrix of narrative elements and strategies, the expeditionists, settlers, Native Police, government officers, 'Worrigals', and Gipps Land itself are produced as cast and *mise en scène*. Bravado, misguided idealism, bungling and the over-reaching ambition of looking for a 'needle in a haystack', combine to produce an heroi-comic venture bordering, at times, on the Pythonesque.

Woven through the journal entries is the elusive White Woman. The unwieldiness of the task facing the expedition party in its attempts to locate her frequently overrides Warman's conscious attempts to impose narrative order. As the search party negotiates the difficult Gipps Land terrain, Warman's account, like the movements of the search party itself, twists and turns, appearing to progress before circling back and returning to the point from which it started.

The early journal entries, commencing with the party's departure from Melbourne on the steamer *Shamrock*, its voyage through heavy seas, and arrival at Port Albert three days later, focus on the adventure and dangers entailed. As the expedition progresses, Warman attempts to transform the raw discomforts of the journey into an heroic tale. The weather turns bad, the bullocks are lost, the boat is damaged in transit, the stores are water-damaged:

> At daylight commenced getting the boats and stores over the morass, a Herculean task; all hands hard at work for nine hours in water and mud; with great perseverance got the boats and stores on the banks of the Glengary [*sic*] River. Everybody thoroughly knocked up, the distance across being nearly half a mile.[13]

The discomforts and dangers which the party face soon overtake the heroic elements. Warman reminds the reader of the privations that he and the other expeditionists are undergoing on their behalf: 'I remembered your dinner hour and most devoutly wished myself there', he comments in a letter, when describing his own '*sumptuous*' Christmas dinner—coarse damper and a pot of tea without sugar.[14] His descriptions of the 'daily-ness' of the journey—the particulars of eating (or going hungry), sleeping (or rising before dawn) and travelling (or being forced to remain inactive)—convey the deprivations and frustrations.

Warman's journal provides what might then be termed a 'sketch' of European life in Gipps Land. He details the location, aspect and condition of a number of properties. Mr Cunningham's station, where they are met with the 'utmost kindness and attention' from Cunningham and his family, 'consists of a good weather-boarded house and several out-houses; an extensive dairy is carried on; the land seems poor and scrubby, but the situation of the house well chosen, situated on a hill commanding most beautiful scenery'.[15]

Warman imagines Gipps Land from a Melbourne perspective. The Glengarry River is, he says, 'much wider than [Melbourne's] Yarra Yarra'; the mouth of the straits leading into Lake Victoria are 'about the width of the Yarra Yarra at the basin'. He describes a land of promise, awaiting settlement and development:[16]

> Went up the [Snowy] river about four miles further, and encamped for the night; it is a most splendid river, nearly sixty yards wide at the place I am now writing, which is about fifteen miles from the mouth; in many places it is upwards of 100 yards wide ... at a short distance from the banks, where the hills begin to rise, it is all covered with the richest pasturage. Where we are now is one of the best runs that ever the sun shone upon, but nothing to eat the grasses. Timber of a very large growth, principally consisting of stringy bark and black butt ... The river is deep enough for good sized vessels to ply on ... Tobacco, in the wild state, in great abundance.[17]

One can imagine potential settlers or speculators in Melbourne setting off for Gipps Land, using the journal entries as a guide to suitable locations for their ventures. However, by the time that the journal was published, Gipps Land squatters were already capitalising on the expeditionists' 'discovery'. The *Herald* reported on 2 March 1847:

> During the peregrinations of the recent expeditionists, several very superior sheep and cattle 'runs' were discovered, and pointed out to some Gipps Land settlers. One is situated on

the right bank of the Snowy River, about seventeen miles from its mouth. Part of it is watered, and admirably fitted for cattle; more of it comprises the most verdant and picturesque slopes, where thousands of sheep can depasture *ad infinitum*. Mr W. O. Raymond has taken possession of this 'estate.' Another is near that locality, lately dubbed as 'Warman's Inlet;' whilst the left bank of the Snowy River is diversified with others of some magnitude.[18]

As early as mid-November, evidence of massacres and dispossession of 'Worrigals' by settlers and Native Police begin appearing in Warman's journal and letters. By January the grimmer side of the enterprise to retrieve the White Woman, and the project of settlement generally, have become principal concerns. However, Warman's *exposé* of the massacres highlights the inherent contradictions in the narrative of progress and in his own position. While Warman's sympathies were with the 'Worrigals', his quasi-ethnographic representations of 'Worrigal' savagery, promulgated in the press, served to reinforce negative stereotypes of Aborigines and thereby aid the colonising project. Warman's position reveals the 'paradox of civilization that parallels the contradictions in the very being of the civilizer himself'.[19] The primacy of the narrative of progress is not dislodged by the emerging counter-narrative of massacre, and Warman at no point suggests that his intention is to halt 'progress' in Gipps Land.

The emergence of the counter-narrative is signalled at a place named 'Golgotha':

> Fine morning, but very hot. Mr. Tyers arrived about seven a.m.; left a considerable portion of our supplies at this station, to lighten our boats, preparing for active service . . . Came on to blow fresh before we arrived at the mouth of the straits which lead into Lake Victoria . . . Arrived at a small scrubby inlet, named Golgotha; landed . . . observed several fires belonging to the Worrigals. Mr. De Villiers started about four p.m., with a party to scour the country between Reeves' Lake and Lake Victoria.
>
> . . . found the remains of many recent fires and blacks' encampments; they seem very cautious of remaining upon any open country, taking the most secluded spots near the reedy

banks of the lakes, from having been so much hunted. The general appearance of the country is scrubby, with a little grass land interspersed; it abounds with kangaroo and emu, and appears to have been a favourite hunting ground for the wild natives, from the remains of many mia mias; found in many places skulls and bones. The land we examined is a peninsula situated between Lake Victoria and Lake Reeves.[20]

What was the party's intention in preparing for 'active service'? At this point, the expeditionists had not yet encountered any 'Worrigals'. It is unclear how Warman's party proposed to act when they did. The Golgotha allusion (in Hebrew the place of skulls, and the site of Christ's crucifixion) which suggests an execution site or a charnel house is not taken up by Warman at this point.[21] He does not speculate on how the place came to be so named. Neither does he reveal who had been hunting the blacks, or comment further on the 'skulls and bones' at Lake Reeve (a comment which could be passed over as though referring to the remains of kangaroo and emu). Warman's unelaborated remarks sit uneasily in a section of entries which attest to the settlers' prosperous and comfortable occupation of tribal lands, and which acknowledge the gracious hospitality extended by the settlers to the expedition party.

The naming of Golgotha raises questions about where the killing of Kurnai might have fitted into the Christian belief system of European settlers or how they might have rationalised actions which went against the tenets of Christianity. Was Golgotha an oblique acknowledgment of settler guilt? Or was it a cynical reference to antipodean [im]morality? The White Woman's narrative, which intersects with that of the Kurnai skulls and bones at Golgotha, invests her by association wih the role of sacrificial victim—a female Christ-figure, ransomed for the atonement of settlers' transgressions. While she remained 'out there', guilt for the murder of 'Worrigals' could be appeased and the possibility of redemption retained.

In the two days following Warman's Golgotha entry—9 and 10 November—the expeditionists' path was to cross that of a party of some hundred 'Worrigals', presumably of the Tatungalung tribe, in the vicinity of the lakes. The journal entries detail the good will which was soon established between the expeditionists and this 'truly fine race of athletic savages'. On 10 November, as Warman gets to know the 'Worrigals' and hear their stories, his previous oblique references to skulls, to Golgotha and to the 'Worrigals' being hunted, re-emerge as critique: 'from all I can learn and see . . . [the Worrigals'] extermination will at no very distant day be accomplished, as all intercourse with them is with powder and ball'.[22]

However, when Warman recounted the incidents for this period in his letter of 24 November to the expedition committee, he omitted all references to the killings and harrassment of 'Worrigals'. Golgotha was not named. It was simply 'a small cove in the Lake'. No reference was made to the skulls and bones.[23] There was no mention of the tribes being 'much hunted' or under threat of extinction.

Warman's accusations of systematic and widespread murder of 'Worrigals' in Gipps Land were to be made public, perhaps without his knowledge or consent, when a private letter written by him to an unidentified party was published in the *Herald* on 21 January.[24] Alluding to the letter, the *Herald* stated: 'We have . . . been favoured with the sight of a very interesting letter from Mr. Warman . . . which we will publish in our Supplement of this evening'. It is reasonable to assume that, initially at least, Warman did not seek the role of public denunciator and was, himself, 'outed' by publication.

In this letter, Warman describes the 'great many skulls and human bones' which De Villiers's party had come across at Lake Victoria and Lake Reeve as the 'remains of Worrigals who had been shot . . . (I also found several skulls.)'. Warman attributes these killings to settlers, who 'think no more of shooting them [than] they do of eating their dinners, and from what we can learn, some fearful slaughters have taken place'. And further on: 'the "Worrigals" are most anxious to be on good terms with the white fellows; but that is not what is wanted by some of the squatters, nothing more nor less than their extermination, which they don't hesitate [to] say that they all ought to be shot'.

Warman's letter also implicates government officers:

> so long as such persons as Messrs. W. Dana and Walsh are in command of the native police, nothing can stop [the 'Worrigals'] extermination, for the native blacks are the most cruel blood-thirsty wretches alive, and nothing gives them so much

pleasure as shooting and tomahawking the defenceless savages
. . . The poor Worrigals gave us to understand about the police,
boo! boo! boo! meaning shooting them . . . I think, upon our
return, we shall be able to open the eyes of the authorities, that
is, *if they wish it*! [original emphasis]

P.S.—I should not wonder if we are subpoenaed to give
evidence in the wholesale butchery at the Snowy River.

Warman evidently was writing to someone of like mind: someone
interested in the welfare of Aborigines. Marsden or Westgarth, both
members of the expedition committee, and both involved in initi-
atives to educate Aborigines, seem likely contenders. At this time in
Melbourne, Marsden was engaged in establishing the Aboriginal
Society, a philanthropic organisation. Westgarth had recently produced a forty-page pamphlet on the condition, capabilities and prospects of Aborigines.[25] Warman refers in the letter to the need for a
Protectorate in Gipps Land. The 'copious remarks in the journal' to
which he alludes might have been recorded to further this end.

Garryowen says of Warman's appointment to the expedition:

> why he should have been chosen was a mystery. Though he
> possessed a certain sea-faring knowledge, and might make a
> good commissariat subordinate, he was about the last man in
> Melbourne to be booked on such an undertaking, literally a
> 'forlorn hope,' which could only be fulfilled by some extra-
> ordinary stroke of good luck, or dashing act of bravery or strat-
> egy, little short of miraculous.[26]

As a young man, Warman had served as a midshipman in King
George III's navy, and engaged in battles against the French and the
Americans, for which he was rewarded with a gift of land in New
South Wales. Prior to his arrival in Melbourne in 1840, he had been
twenty years in New South Wales, where he had worked for the
Customs Department in Sydney, been director of a school and
owned an hotel.[27] Nevertheless, he was not a high-profile citizen of
Melbourne and historians have not considered him important
enough to note.

On occasions, however, Warman's name appeared in the newspapers, in connection with Councillor John Stephen (who was

credited by the *Herald* for instigating the White Woman public meeting). The *Patriot* reported on 9 January 1843 that 'a worthless fellow named Warman, the father of the actress of that name', had passed himself off as a constable to take into custody two apprentices at the *Patriot* office, who were posting placards which warned 'Methodists and other Professing Christians against voting for Mr. John Stephen, a man living in the open and shameless disregard of the laws of God and Man'. The slur against Stephen's moral character alluded to his relationship with Miss Warman, the actress, daughter of James Warman.[28] On 12 January 1843, the *Patriot* reported how '[o]n Monday last Alderman Kerr set upon the worthless fellow named Warman, one of John Stephen's minions who had armed himself with a huge cudgel and did his best to use it efficiently.' In June 1844, Warman tendered his name to the court as surety for five pounds on behalf of Richard Capper, 'tragedian, comedian, scene-shifter, and candle snuffer to the Victoria Theatre', who appeared before the bench 'in obedience to an information laid by Mr Thomas Strode, of the *Gazette* office, for using threatening language, and inciting him to commit a breach of the peace'. Capper's defence was conducted by John Stephen.[29]

It seems likely that Warman's involvement with the White Woman expedition was at Stephen's instigation, possibly in recognition of services rendered. In August 1844, Warman appeared as a character witness for Stephen, the plaintiff in a Supreme Court case against Thomas McCombie, for libellous statements printed in the *Gazette* alleging that Stephen had tampered with an affidavit relating to a missing boat, which had been assigned to Warman several months previously.[30] During his sworn statement to the court, Warman described himself as 'a retired master's mate in the navy . . . own[er of] a small vessel or boat, by which I get my living'. Warman was called upon again a month later, in September 1844, as a witness in a case involving a shooting incident, in which John Stephen acted as defence for one of the accused.[31] Perhaps Stephen saw the expedition as a means of rehabilitating his own somewhat tarnished reputation with the Melbourne electorate.

On 5 January 1847 (the same day that Warman wrote to his unnamed correspondent in Melbourne), De Villiers wrote to the expedition committee a 'minute and detailed' account of the party's actions since 4 December. The previous day Warman and De Villiers had made sworn depositions before Commissioner Tyers concerning the alleged murder by the Native Police under the command of William Dana of 'a male native' and the mistreatment of an old man and a woman, on the Snowy River, at the time of the search for the White Woman (to be discussed in Chapter 5). More widespread atrocities by the Native Police were also intimated.[32]

De Villiers's letter, running to more than three columns, and including copies of letters which he had written to William Dana and Commissioner Tyers, was published in the *Herald* on 21 January 1847.[33] Warman's letter appeared the same day in the evening edition. De Villiers's main accusations were against Dana and his party. He was more moderate than Warman in implicating the settlers, noting only that the 'Natives' frequented the most inaccessible parts of Gipps Land, 'in consequence of being so constantly hunted by the native police and settlers should they dare to appear on any forest land'. In this, he might have been influenced by the views of Sergeant Windredge, who travelled with De Villiers for part of the expedition.

De Villiers's intention in writing this account appears to have been to provide a record of his own party's impeccable behaviour in the face of obstructionism from Dana and Walsh, and to forestall potential criticisms of himself or the expedition. The revelations and accusations, however, put the government on the defensive. The government party was immediately withdrawn, and Dana was instructed by Tyers 'not to continue his search after the white woman, but to confine himself strictly to the protection of the settlers, until he [Tyers] receives further instructions from his Honor the Superintendent'. The *Herald* editorial, in referring readers to De Villiers's despatch, was quick to pick up and exploit this line:

> It is painful to contrast the impetuosity and inconsiderate rashness of the Government party, which by coming into hostile collision with the tribe in possession of the white female, have destroyed the fruits of the good policy previously exhibited towards them by Mr. De Villiers . . . if the benevolent intentions of Government had not been thus for the *second* time frustrated by the folly of its subordinate agents, the poor creature would ere this have been in Melbourne.[34]

A corollary to these disclosures of violence was the allusion by Warman in his journal to the circulation of Kurnai females in a frontier sexual economy. The colonialist practice of European men taking Aboriginal women as sexual partners has been cited as a principal cause of hostility between Aborigines and whites in virtually all newly settled regions throughout the colony, and the cause of some Europeans and many Aborigines being killed.[35] The following cluster of extracts allude obliquely or overtly to Kurnai females being taken by settlers, Native Police, government officers, and perhaps expeditionists:

> Monday 9th [November 1846]:
> ... *the lubras were all young and good featured; one of them named Mary, had been stopping for several weeks at Mr. Cunningham's; she gave a very good account of the white woman, and stated she was with a man named Bungelene, in the direction of the head of the Mitchell; also, one of the men described how she 'plenty cry,' and hummed a tune exactly like the old hundredth, which he said white woman sung.*

> Thursday, 19th [November 1846]:
> *At 11 a.m. landed the three Worrigal women on the island 'Powel Powel', on account of some alledged misunderstanding between our blacks and those belonging to the Native Police, the latter claiming them on account of priority of right, as it appears those were part of the lubras that were taken by Mr. Walsh, and had been staying at the police station for some time. They did not wish to leave us ...*

> Thursday, 3rd [December 1846]:
> ... *[the Worrigals] have a custom of showing their good will to the parties by offering their lubras and females, even of the most tender years; for chastity among them is a thing very little cared for, they behaving to mere infants in a most brutal manner. There seems to be a great disparity in the sexes, not being half as many females as males.*

> Thursday, 31st [December 1846]
> ... *A disease is greatly upon the increase among the Worrigals. Something ought to be done to save that helpless race speedily; ...*

Warman's observation of the disparity in the numbers of females to males in the tribes he encountered suggests that the practice of white men taking Kurnai women was widespread. However, while white men in the colony expressed moral outrage about the White Woman's 'plight', no similar depth of public feeling was conveyed for the many Aboriginal women and young girls kept, perhaps against their will, by white men. These widely documented cases provide a counterpoint to the White Woman's imagined sexual enslavement to Bungelene and the high-minded rhetoric underpinning the expedition. Warman's acknowledgement of the attractiveness of the young 'lubras' reveals his own desiring gaze. He mentions 'a disease' being greatly upon the increase but does not attribute its introduction or spread to sexual contact with white men: a reflection, perhaps, of prevailing views that such diseases were contracted from Aboriginal women.

Warman's revelation that the White Woman hummed the Old Hundredth serves to shift the focus to another narrative register— that of providential intervention. Paul Carter has observed how, in 'eighteenth- and nineteenth-century historical writing of all kinds, Providence was regularly invoked as a convenient device to gloss events that cause-and-effect explanations seemed unable to plumb'.[36] Peter Hulme, too, notes that time and again Caribbean texts 'are set against or have introduced into them the terms of reference of a classical or Biblical text '.[37]

The Old Hundredth, a Puritan anthem, was included in its several forms in English and Scottish hymnals of the period. Its relevance to the White Woman's situation lay in its universal appeal and uplifting sentiments:

> All people that on earth do dwell,
> Sing to the Lord with cheerful voice;
> Him serve with mirth, his praise forth tell,
> Come ye before him, and rejoice.[38]

In the absence of the White Woman, the allusions to the Old Hundredth served to reinforce her narrative presence as a Christian lady sustained in adversity by faith: a rehabilitative image which countered anxieties that she had 'gone native'. As evidence of the White Woman's existence, news of her humming the Old Hundredth provided impetus to the expeditionists' quest.

The White Woman's alignment with John Bunyan's female pilgrim Christiana—whose descent into the Valley of Humiliation, in *The Pilgrim's Progress*, is accompanied by birds singing the Old Hundredth—makes Gipps Land a testing-ground for Christian faith: a zone of temptation and redemption.[39] While Gipps Land was a place of exile and imprisonment for the White Woman, for European males it represented a place of boundless opportunity, a veritable earthly paradise, like Bunyan's Valley of Humiliation, 'as frutiful a place as any the crow flies over'.

Similarly, the ideological concept of 'Manifest Destiny', defined recently by Robert Hughes—echoing Richard Slotkin—as 'America's myth of redemptive violence', which precipitated mid-nineteenth-century American expansionism was founded on the notion of a providential mission into the wilderness.[40] American Puritan captivity narratives frequently interpreted captivity as a sign of providential favour or punishment.[41]

The Old Hundredth, with its Puritan associations, evokes Gipps Land as the site for moral engagement between the forces of enlightened Christianity and ungodly 'semi-demons'. Such allegorising validated antithetical stereotypes. The hymn provided sanction for the Christianising of 'all people that on earth do dwell' and charged the settlers' efforts in 'overcoming' the Kurnai with redemptive Christian purpose. By association with the Old Hundredth, the White Woman acts as a 'moral prism' through which Gipps Land can be brought into focus as Christian (European) territory. Whether the 'Worrigals' had learned the tune of the Old Hundredth from the White Woman or settlers, or whether they hummed a melody which was taken to be the Old Hundredth is a moot point.

As the woman is never sighted by the expeditionists, these reports, descriptions and anecdotes about her provide the only evidence of her existence and whereabouts. Throughout the journal, Warman relates information received from 'Worrigals', as interpreted by members of his party including the young Kurnai boy, Jacka-wadden. The complexities of cross-cultural communication and the motives of Europeans in subjectively interpreting what was said provide cause for questioning information attributed to 'Worrigals'. In the absence of a common language, the expeditionists communicated with 'Worrigals' by signs. Presumably, these involved gesticulations, miming, facial expressions or pointed directions, and might have been augmented by verbal cues. There is no unambiguous system of signage which will transcend cultural and linguistic differences.

As the following cluster of entries demonstrates, Warman confidently presents instances of signing between his party and Gipps Land Aborigines as though they bypass the contingencies of speech. Implicit is the belief that the meaning conveyed is understood by both parties. The problems of interpreting are more complex than Warman's account suggests:

Tuesday, 10th [November 1846]
. . . All the men, when we made signs of what we came for, told us the same story and named the same man with whom she lived, and pointed out the place where she lived, and pointed out the place where she was to be found, indeed they offered to accompany us to get her, but that offer could not be accepted, they being so numerous . . .

Friday, 13th [November 1846]
Fine morning; Mr. De Villiers with two white, eight black, and our Worrigals, started at 5 a.m., with a week's provisions, for Warrdon, in quest of Bungelene and the woman. Before their going, cut on a sheet of paper two women, one was kept white and the other blackened; called the Worrigals over separately and asked which was Bungelene's lubra,—every one pointed to the white paper . . .

Friday, 20th [November 1846]
. . . At 3 p.m., we were all much surprised at seeing our friendly tribe of Worrugals come to visit us . . . They appeared highly pleased with us, and expressed themselves by signs that they knew what we wanted, and one of them gave us to understand that he had been with Bungelene and the woman only a few days back . . .

The object of the test of the paper women presumably was to reassure De Villiers's party before it left for Warrdon that the 'Worrigals' had not deceived or misled the expeditionists; or that they understood that the expedition party was looking for a *white* woman. The test fails on both counts. Readers familiar with the popular artistic medium of paper silhouettes would have known how to 'read' the paper figures. However, in order for the action of the 'Worrigals'— pointing to the 'white' paper woman—to have the meaning attributed to it by the expeditionists, the 'Worrigals' would have had to understand the question 'which was Bungelene's lubra[?]': a question reliant on language comprehension. They must also recognise that a paper cut-out was meant to represent a real, living woman, and to distinguish, on the basis of *colour*, the difference between the two paper women. Furthermore, a pantomimic test would be no more intrinsically reliable than a verbal test if the 'Worrigals' intention was to mislead the expeditionists, as seems implied. For all its ingenuity, the test is indeterminate. It demonstrates, as much as anything, the unstable and contingent nature of communication between the expeditionists and their Kurnai informants, and the degree to which desire to believe in the woman's existence directed the expeditionists' actions. The test of the paper women is proffered as though objective: a performative act by the whites contrived to verify verbal information provided by the 'Worrigals' that the White Woman was with Bungelene. De Villiers's comment, made elsewhere—'I have to remark, from my experience among savages, that there are many traits in their character, viz., not being trustworthy themselves, they imagine insincerity on our parts'—is unintendedly revealing in the context of the paper women test.[42]

The expedition's, and the narrative's, direction is determined by the outcome of the paper woman test. De Villiers and his party set off immediately for Warrdon in the mountains to find her on what is literally a 'paper chase'. Had the 'Worrigals' pointed instead to the 'black' paper woman, one wonders whether the expeditionists would have abandoned the search, or continued with the testing until the desired result was forthcoming.

A similar test conducted in Gipps Land some three and a half years earlier by an 'Irish gentleman' might have provided the inspir-

ation for De Villiers's test. Reported in the *Herald*, it demonstrates
the ambiguities attaching to paper women:

> Mr A. B. scrawled the figure of a woman on a piece of paper
> and shewed it to Jackey; he shouted with delight, as much as to
> say, 'I know what you want;' and off he went to the camp. He
> returned with a brace of sylvan nymphs, and presented one to
> me, and one to Mr. A. B.[43]

The 'Worrigals' may have assumed, similarly, that the expeditionists were asking for sexual services from Kurnai women.

For the readers in Melbourne, the description of the paper women
test added a *frisson* of local 'colour' to the journal entries, and the test
might have been conducted with this in mind. The association of
paper dolls with nurseries also pandered to European assumptions
that Aborigines were childlike. It is tempting to read metaphorical
significance into the 'emptiness' of the white cut-out figure—the
White Woman as *tabula rasa* on which the expeditionists and others
could write their own narratives—and to the two-dimensional
nature of both female figures.

The description of the test and the expeditionists' interpretation
of it represent a polyglossic moment in the journal. Despite having
passed the 'objective' test of the paper dolls, the 'Worrigals' thwart
De Villiers's expectations that they will take him to the White
Woman, and frustrate readerly expectations of narrative closure.
Instead, De Villiers's party is abandoned by the 'Worrigal' guides in
the mountains and forced to return to base camp.

> Saturday, 5th [December 1846]
> . . . *About 8, some of the Worrigals came to our camp: five . . . of
> them offered of their own accord to go to the mountains and bring
> down the white woman . . . Wrote a letter in a very plain legible
> hand, informing the woman that parties were in search of her;
> enclosed a small piece of lead pencil, for her to write in return, if
> practicable. The natives perfectly well understood that the paper,
> which was carefully wrapped in a handkerchief, was to be given to
> the woman, unseen by Bungelene.*

Sunday, 13th [December 1846]
. . . At 3 p.m. the party of native police returned from the Snowy River with two grey headed old Worrigals of the Jenerah or Snowy River Tribe, which they had taken from that place, for by the Worrigal boy (the interpretor's) account, these old men called out to the natives on the other side of the river not to give up the white woman, 'they not knowing the party had a person who understood what was said.' We have had a great deal of conversation through Taki Warren. Their information is as follows:—The white woman was on the opposite side of the river, but we could not get her, having no canoes to cross with, nor was bark for making them to be had there. They also stated that one of the Worrigals we had sent after her, with a letter addressed to the white woman, nearly succeeded in getting possession of her; that she received the letter, and commenced crying bitterly. She was in the act of writing a reply on the same paper, when Bungelene snatched it out of her hand, and nearly broke her arm, telling her she wanted to 'yabber' to white fellows; they also informed us that she was very sick; that Bungelene had been beating her about the head with a waddy . . . Being asked the reason he beat her, they said it was because she would not fetch water; but no doubt that is a falsehood; the more probable reason is, that she was endeavouring to escape with 'Carrotbit,' alias Mr. De Villiers, as they also said that she was afterwards tied by the leg; she is also cut and marked the same as the black lubras.

Warman's letter to the White Woman preempts any difficulties she might have in reading the message by writing in 'very plain legible hand'—though if in English, the message would be of little use to the Gaelic-speaking Ann [Ellen] Macpherson. He anticipates, and caters for her response by enclosing a pencil stub, although, if she responded in Gaelic, could any of the expeditionists have read her message? His quaintly polite qualifier, 'if practicable', although no doubt intended to cover her *inability* to respond, could be read (in letter-writing parlance) as covering *disinclination* on her part to do so. Warman portrays the 'Worrigals' as complicit in the subterfuge of conveying the message to the woman without Bungelene's knowledge, a move which aligns them with the expeditionists' interests over those of the tribe. Again, it is assumed that the 'Worrigals', who perhaps had never seen a written document or writing equipment before, 'perfectly well understood' the purpose of the paper and pencil, the message, and for whom these were intended.

Warman's letter-writing ritual aids narrative advancement by projecting the narrative towards an imagined future meeting when the 'Worrigals' will deliver the letter to the woman and, beyond that, to an anticipated 'happy ending'—her retrieval. The plan to communicate with the woman is thwarted when, according to Taki Warren [Jacka-Wadden], the message is intercepted.

The woman's alleged ill-treatment by Bungelene confirms the party's fears and expectations about how a 'Worrigal' would treat a white woman. The woman's reputed ability to read Warman's message and her bitter, tearful response are reported by Warman as evidence of her remnant civilised state. This is an important distinction in light of revelations of the woman as 'cut and marked the same as the black lubras'. The cicatrices, and the initiatory rites which they signify, mark her permanently with signs of cultural 'otherness'. Her description no longer matches that of the genteel and accomplished young lady who was shipwrecked. Who did the expeditionists believe they were retrieving at this point? This question problematises the ongoing quest narrative and the expeditionists' responses:

Wednesday, 6th [January 1847]
. . . I beg here to relate a conversation had between two of our friendly Worrigals, Iberett and Bungelene's brother, which will, I think, throw some light upon the marked tree:– They were asked what became of the crew? they said that six took to the boat, and were drowned in the surf or speared, adding that two of the men remained on shore and were suffered to stay with them . . . but it appears they were an incumbrance to them, not being able to get their own food, and at last were killed. Of the two women, one was taken off to the mountains, where she was killed or died very shortly after; the other was taken by one of the savages. The description of her dress is as follows:– She had on a bonnet, and something they describe as opossum skins round her neck down to her feet, (which must have been a boa), and boots on. They stripped her naked immediately, but finding she could not walk without shoes, they tied her feet in opossum skins. This female was but a short time with the Worrigal who first got her; Bungelene fought him and took her away from him, and has kept her ever since . . .

. . . one of the gins told me 'that she herself had suckled the white woman's child, when the white woman could not do it herself.' The spot where the white woman's last child was born was shewn to me too, by one of the guides, about four miles from the crossing place of the Tambo.

C. J. De Villiers to Committee.[44]

The white woman is described as tall, with a considerable stoop— deaf in one ear—and as making her miami in a different manner from the blacks—making a small mound serve as a pillow . . . a bag, an exact fac simile of a modern reticule, knitted with the European knit, and made of native grass, was found in the pos- session of one of the women belonging to the tribe amongst which she is a captive. She is said to be treated with great kindness by the savages.

Alex Brodie (member of the Expedition party).[45]

The marked tree acts here as authorising sign for the story which the 'Worrigals' relate. Their tale inverts the colonialist order. White men, instead of being resourceful and independent, are helpless—an incumbrance on the tribe. Identifying markers of European feminin- ity are erased as the White Woman is stripped of her lady's garb; only the opossum skin slippers—a concession to her tender feet—mark her difference from the women of the tribe.

Descriptions of the woman's maternity and the out-of doors location for the birth of her last child contrast with the cossetting which white, middle-class pregnant women received. Her reported inability to suckle her child—a common enough phenomenon amongst nursing mothers—could hint at suppressed or arrested maternal instincts or a rejection by the woman of the nurturing role in the situation. The bourgeois convention of the wet nurse, with its production of femininity and class differentiation in and through certain maternal functions, is also suggested.

In Brodie's account, racial difference is marked by the woman's retention of European habits and the useful arts. The 'great kindness' with which she is said to be treated reflects her integration with the tribe. The *Herald* speculated that the White Woman had been instructing her captors in the 'arts of civilization'. It advised its readers that it had 'inspected some neat specimens of basket and net work, the manufacture of the Gipps Land aborigines. One of them bears a striking resemblance to a lady's reticule, and as it was obtained from one of Bungelene's tribe, it is not improbable that the unfortunate white woman must have instructed her sable companions in such handi-work. The *material* is grass, and is characterised by much ingenuity'.[46] The *Herald* was reluctant to concede that Aborigines could produce such items themselves, even in the face of evidence to the contrary.

Warman's journal describes De Villiers's unsuccessful trip to the mountains, after which the expeditionists set off again in pursuit of the White Woman. Warman's party puts to sea. One member, Thomas Hill, is almost drowned when the boat is beached following a heavy squall. Warman commemorates his role as intrepid explorer by naming the inlet where they come ashore 'Warman's Inlet' and overwriting the history of the area's original inhabitants: 'his boat being the only one that ever went through it'.[47]

The party moves up the Snowy River in pursuit of Bungelene— further, Warman believes, than European boats have ever been before —into territory belonging to the Bungel Mageelong and Jenerah tribes. Warman's narrative construction is aided at various points as the expeditionists conduct performative or ritual acts which impart the semblance of significance and direction to the otherwise directionless journey.

> On my journey through the mountains . . . I took three men, three women, and a boy belonging to Bungeleene's tribe . . . I christined them Mr. Cavenagh, Dr. Greeves, and the third after myself; they are now known by these several names among the tribe. On our journey, our namesakes deserted our party . . .
>
> C. J. De Villiers.[48]

> It was now nearly sun down, our guides which were three Warrigals, with Taki Warren, and the lubras of two of them, then got on the alert, the men went forward in advance, and the lubras remained behind, when at my request we were all compelled to submit to a process of painting at their hands—a ceremony which is considered to be a symbol of friendship amongst the natives. In a short time, therefore, we altered our appearances, under the influence of red ochre, and our whole band presented a most ludicrous

> *aspect. I then ordered the party to prime and load without the observation of the black women; and as I imagined something alarming in the conduct of the guides, which led me to apprehend that we were in the proximity of a large band of natives. The arms were then deposited beneath a huge log, and our party was arranged in such a manner as to be prepared for any sudden onset that might be made . . . After some ceremonies it was agreed upon that the strange blacks should encamp with us that night . . . and soon after I ordered our natives to give them a corroboree, which is an unerring sign of friendship between tribes. In this performance we all took our part, but Brodie particularly distinguished himself.*
>
> C. J. De Villiers[49]

In an enterprise like the expedition, the bestowing of namesakes conformed to conventions of the adventure narrative and had parallels in, for example, Robinson Crusoe's naming of 'Friday'. De Villiers's ritual of 'christening' the male 'Worrigals' after members of the expedition committee and his party reflect the common colonialist practice of renaming Aborigines after Europeans. The Aboriginal namesakes reverberate through the journal entries as unsettling mirror images of their European counterparts. As *doppelgängers* of key figures associated with the Melbourne-based expedition—Cavenagh, Greeves and De Villiers—the namesakes remain an unintendedly ironic presence in the expedition accounts. Significantly, the namesakes elude De Villiers's authority and resist his intent, or fail to understand his command, to take him to the White Woman. This 'shadow' party circumvents the narrative and physical trajectory of De Villiers's journey. De Villiers, too, was given a 'native name'—'Nicknarock'—the name of a Kurnai man who was involved with the searches.[50]

De Villiers related the incident of the 'duplicitous' namesakes to demonstrate his party's liberal attitude to the 'Worrigals', in contrast to the alleged brutalities of the government party. When his namesake turned up after an absence of some days, De Villiers presented this as proof of the tactical soundness of his strategy, for:

> Finding that I did not shew him any ill will for the trick he served me, but treated him with great kindness, he selected of his own accord four of his tribe, and started in a few hours after

his arrival with a message for Bungeleene, taking some handkerchiefs and fish hooks as a present for him and the white
woman.[51]

In describing the namesakes incident, De Villiers produced for
Melbourne readers a moment of inter-cultural exchange by which he
projected a Melbourne presence (the names Cavenagh, Greeves and
De Villiers) onto members of the tribe said to be holding the White
Woman. The namesake ritual enacts Melbourne's proprietorial stake
in the White Woman story. Paul Carter has attributed the habit of
Port Phillip Aborigines of adopting European names to an 'Aboriginal attempt to pass beyond mimicry to kinship': a practice, he
says, which elicited from newly arrived Europeans 'a superstitious
fear of being haunted and mocked to their faces'.[52] In the expedition
journals, De Villiers's description of the namesake incident conveys
a reverse dynamic in action, in which the impetus to name appears
to derive more from De Villiers's motives than from a desire by
'Worrigals' for 'kinship'.

The ochre painting episode, too, is presented by De Villiers as
an infiltration by his party into 'Worrigal' ritual space. The ochre-
painting scene is a masquerade which allows De Villiers to write his
party into the corroboree scene as *participants*. It represents not just
the contingencies of inter-cultural communication, or the colourful
exoticising of De Villiers's party. The dominant visual marker of
racial difference (skin colour) is concealed as the expeditionists'
bodies are overlaid with Aboriginal cultural significance. The ochre-
painted expeditionists contrast with numerous pictorial depictions
of European figures standing at the fringes of corroboree scenes,
observers who are excluded from the performance.

Relinquishing the outward markers of European maleness and
'submit[ting]' to being painted by women seems to unsettle him. De
Villiers's comment that the painted expeditionists looked 'ludicrous'
could mean that they looked like white men painted up to resemble
Aborigines. Alternatively, the transformation may have been so
striking that they momentarily lost sight of themselves as Europeans.
If so, the party's action in surreptitiously priming and loading guns
reasserts that, despite appearances to the contrary, the boundary
between European and 'Worrigal' remained intact.

In the observation that 'Brodie particularly distinguished himself' there is a hint that, in entering too wholeheartedly into the corroboree, Brodie had overplayed his role. Although De Villiers presents the corroboree episode as a successful ploy to gain the friendship of the 'Worrigals', his action in usurping their ritual of ochre painting without knowledge of its ceremonial or spiritual significance and of intruding into their ceremonial space might have caused offense.

Several periods of enforced waiting, while the 'Worrigals' go ostensibly to retrieve the White Woman, have a debilitating effect on De Villiers's party and on the heroic narrative. Four consecutive entries from 21 to 24 November record that the party is 'waiting anxiously' for the return of the 'Worrigals'; on 25 November 'The Worrigals not returned'.[53]

The sub-plot of the duplicitous 'Worrigals' allows Warman, at least partially, to displace blame for his party's failure to retrieve the woman as, with each successive abortive attempt, the expeditionists' opportunity for heroic action becomes increasingly remote. Warman's depiction of the thwarting by the 'Worrigals' of the expedition's attainment of its goal conveniently suited the conventions of serialised publication. In the first section of the journal to be published, the final entry records the party still waiting anxiously for the 'Worrigals' return: a cue to the reader to anticipate the next instalment.

> Sunday 29th [November 1846]
> *Fine weather, but excessively hot; we are waiting here according to Mr. Tyers' request, as he says that the Worrigals have promised him without fail . . . that the woman was to be delivered up in a few days . . . The tribe we have made friends with are a powerful, well made people, their features not at all unprepossessing, but on the contrary their women and children mostly good looking but all exceedingly dirty in their habits, and the smell from their bodies is very disgusting; in their diet nothing goes amiss, they even eat the ant eggs, in short, vermin of every description serves them for their meals; they are also cannibals, eating even the bodies of their own women. Their hair is suffered to grow long, and is matted together with grease; almost all are in a state of nudity, without regard to sexes, the greatest part have not the slightest covering over any parts of their bodies, and they seem strangers to shame . . . They have a curious custom of carrying the bodies of their dead friends about,*

wrapped up in an oppossum cloak; the head is taken from the trunk; the legs, thighs, and arms are closely doubled into the body so as to make an almost square package, and tightly lashed in the cloak they carry it about so long that it is dreadfully offensive, smearing their bodies with the grease which exudes from the skin; at last they deposit it in a hollow tree; sometimes they make a kind of hand barrow, to convey this lump of human decomposition, instead of carrying it on their backs; it serves them also for a pillow!

Tuesday, 1st December [1846]
Fine weather. Got 60 lbs. of salt beef from N. McLeod, Esq. The Worrigals are in the habit of wearing the hands of deceased persons slung round their necks as a token of affection. They are beautifully preserved, nails and flesh with veins all perfect. Their mode of preserving them is by a curious process of stewing with hot stones.

In the absence of any news about the White Woman, and during a period when Warman's party has been ordered by Tyers not to proceed until the time for the 'Worrigals' to return with the woman has expired, Warman records a lengthy digression on the appearance and habits of the 'Worrigals'. Whether intentional or not, the effect of this passage is to distract the reader's attention from—or to provide a substitute for—the enfeeblement of party and plot.

Warman's observations are coloured by his own proprieties of modesty and ethnocentric bias. His notes constitute Gipps Land Aborigines as dirty, amoral, barbaric. The erotic and sensory embellishments of the passage, and Warman's obsession with vermin, nudity and decomposition, reveals a fascination with and prurient interest in the practices described. The passage recalls the sensationalist speculation in the period leading up to the public meeting concerning the treatment the White Woman might be undergoing at the hands of her 'savage captors' and substantiates even the most excessive statements then made.

The entry for 1 December, which juxtaposes European salted beef with 'Worrigal' stewed hands, produces racial difference in terms of the two forms of preserved flesh. The stewed hands engage Warman's interest ('a curious process') and aesthetic sense ('[t]hey are beautifully preserved . . . all perfect'). Furthermore, he informs the reader, the 'Worrigals' wear them as 'a token of affection'. Warman does not say that he saw any 'Worrigals' wearing these 'stewed' hands on the day that the entry was written. His description of this 'Worrigal' mortuary rite arises, as though logically connected, from his description of his party's receipt of the consignment of salt beef.

His choice of the term 'stewed', which in the English vocabulary is usually (though not exclusively) associated with the preparation of food, indicates Warman's concern that the bodies belonging to the hands had been eaten by 'Worrigals'. An entry two days previously informs readers that the 'Worrigals' were cannibals. Again, the remark is generalised and does not appear to have been prompted by Warman witnessing an act which he took to be cannibalism. The comment seems to relate to Sergeant Windredge's earlier report that Jacka-wadden had attested to cannibalism amongst the Lakes tribe, and may reveal Warman's anxiety about being eaten by 'Worrigals'.

Warman's 'ethnographic' digressions were possibly included for a party in Melbourne who planned a philanthropic and Christianising venture in Gipps Land (the unnamed recipient of his aforementioned letter about Golgotha?). The digressions also remind the newspaper readers (the armchair expeditionists) that the party, on their behalf, was engaged in a dangerous mission, and that the frontier of settlement was by no means a safe place for Europeans. In this way Warman re-engages the narrative of heroic endeavour at a point when the expeditionists were suffering the indignity of waiting while the 'Worrigals' were assigned the task of attempting to retrieve the White Woman. Warman's comments at this time about the Government's 'supineness' in not attempting to civilise the 'Worrigals' might in this context be read also as an attempt to deflect criticism of his own party for its supineness when public opinion expected action.

At a time when the woman's retrieval was anticipated, Warman's comments might indicate ambivalence about his participation in bringing the woman back. If the ladies of Melbourne blanched at the thought that a genteel, white woman could have been living in the way described in the journal, perhaps doubts began to arise in Warman's mind about the wisdom of bringing the woman back into their midst. The party continued to plan for the woman's rescue. Nevertheless, Warman's inclusion of details about the 'tribalised' White Woman must have prepared the way for public acceptance of an alternative form of narrative closure to that of the woman's rescue and return.

In the concluding remarks in the journal, Warman comments on why the return of the White Woman might make Gipps Land settlers uncomfortable:

> That [the native tribes of the Gipps Land district] were numerous when that portion of the territory was first located, is admitted by official records; that they are now reduced to a comparative few, is undeniable. The causes hereafter may be known, should the wretched captive ever be released to tell the tale of woe; but till then the truth will never be fully revealed.

If the woman *had* provided damning information against the settlers and government officers in Gipps Land, would her word have carried more weight than that of Warman or De Villiers? Or would she have been dismissed as mentally deranged from the effects of her ordeal, as one later quasi-historic version of the story would have it and, thus, literally silenced?[54]

CHAPTER 5

The Dream-like Arrangements of Romance

'We have had our Scott, who . . . reproduces to us his world of
feudalism and chivalry, and we live for a while amongst knights of
lofty and generous bearing; we have ladies in all their feminine loveliness and
unswerving fidelity—we have tournaments, combats and border raids, spirits of
martial adventure, the actors of which are all
tinged and inclined with an absorbing love of country.'
From speech by Mr Johnstone, Burns Festival, Melbourne, January 1847[1]

Mr Johnstone's speech at the Burns Festival in Melbourne on 26 January 1847, delivered as De Villiers's expedition was returning from Gipps Land, is a timely reminder that the expedition project was conceived and promoted in the spirit of Sir Walter Scott's chivalric model. Scott's theories on chivalry, expounded in an essay in the 1818 edition of the *Encyclopaedia Britannica* and personified in his immensely popular historical romances, gave relevance and force to the nineteenth-century fascination with medieval history, and provided an ideal of masculinity at a time when industrialisation and urbanisation were transforming British culture.[2]

Scott's importance as a national figure was recognised in events such as the Waverley Ball held in London in July 1844 to raise funds for a monument to Scott in Edinburgh. The ball, at which eighty-four guests, costumed as characters from Scott's novels, danced the Waverley Quadrille, was attended by more than 1300 persons of 'rank and distinction', including the Duke of Wellington.[3] In the colonies Scott's works were widely read. His influence on Australian fiction provided—to use Robert Dixon's phrase—an 'attempt to expel dangerous social energies by the dream-like arrangements of romance'.[4]

The De Villiers-led expedition was styled by promoters and participants as a sacred quest by heroic men to aid a damsel in distress. To this end the *Port Phillip Herald* undertook the role of its namesake—the Herald of medieval pageantry—as messenger, publicist, organiser, creator and arbiter of ceremonies, and awarder of honours. In representing the expeditionists as a 'little voluntary band of adventurers' whose dedication in the service of an ideal was untainted by pecuniary interest, and from whose efforts the community could expect to reap moral benefit, the *Herald* imbued the expedition with romantic and chivalric allusions aimed at calling forth finer feelings in its readers. The *Herald* would maintain the distinction between De Villiers's heroic volunteers, who 'without fear or reward risked all', and the government officers also searching for the White Woman who, by implication, were acting under orders as they were paid to do.

In his correspondence, De Villiers also cast the expeditionists as knights errant. Perhaps acting under instruction from Cavenagh to provide a narrative commensurate with what he, as editor, expected for publication, De Villiers attributed to the captive woman an awareness 'that the expedition was in quest of her and within no great distance'. The woman 'cried bitterly', he said, 'and often asked herself "Why did not the white men come and fetch her away".'[5] James Warman, second-in-charge of De Villiers's party, also lauded the expeditionists as 'our little band of philanthropic adventurers' and 'our small but intrepid band'.[6]

In the chivalric tradition, the fair lady sent the knight into battle wearing her favour in the form of a scarf or handkerchief. In a inversion of this narrative sequence, which draws however on the same associative elements, De Villiers's party took with it pictorial handkerchiefs on the back of which were printed messages for the White Woman. The handkerchiefs were distributed by the expeditionists to 'Worrigals', or were left in their campsites or nailed to tree trunks, in the hope that they might come to the White Woman's attention.

A surviving handkerchief, perhaps the only one, has been carefully preserved in the Buntine family for over 160 years. Its nail-pierced

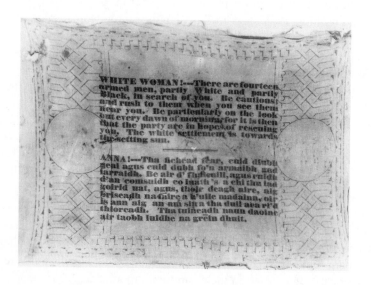

Handkerchief taken by an expedition in search of the White Woman in October 1846, with a message to the woman printed on the *verso*.
Reproduced by permission of La Trobe Collection, State Library of Victoria.
Original handkerchief sighted by kind permission of Alwynne Buntine.

edges attest to its function in the expedition and affirm its status as a relic of a foundational event in early Port Phillip history. The handkerchief is bordered on both sides with an interlocking Celtic design edged with a fine leaf pattern.

The message to the woman on the handkerchief is printed in English and Gaelic—Gaelic being the language spoken by Scottish crofters who emigrated from estates in the highlands during the 1830s and 1840s. The English version is addressed 'White Woman', while the Gaelic message, although substantially the same, addresses a particular woman, 'Anna'. This was probably written with Ann McPherson in mind, and might have been in deference to the considerable financial contribution allegedly made by her brother in Sydney to the expedition fund.[7] The English message reads:

> WHITE WOMAN! — — — There are fourteen armed men, partly White and partly Black, in search of you. Be cautious; and rush to them when you see them near you. Be particularly on the look out every dawn of morning, for it is then that the party are in hopes of rescuing you. The white settlement is towards the setting sun.

The handkerchief's message assumed the woman's literacy and gentility. Literacy served as a marker of difference between the woman, who would be expected to understand the message's purpose, and the 'Worrigals', for whom the handkerchief would be merely a decorative item or one which excited curiosity. The message, which frames the imagined rescue in the mythopoeic moments of dawn and sunset, would have had little practical value to the addressee. Why direct the woman's attention to the 'white settlement . . . towards the setting sun'—a distance of some 180 miles (300 km) across mountain ranges and through impenetrable scrub and swamps? A more suitable instruction would have alerted her to the numerous and more accessible pastoral stations in Gipps Land. The handkerchief's message seems rather to valorise the expedition party and to identify it with Melbourne. While the arena for action was Gipps Land—demarcated physically by the distribution of the handkerchiefs as the expedition moved through that region—the world to which the quest, and the expeditionists, referred was Melbourne.

The handkerchief's illustration shows an interior, domestic scene. A gentleman dozes in a chair, beneath which is a sleeping dog. Evidence of a successful hunt—a brace of water fowl, a dead rabbit, a fowling piece—indicate the cause of his fatigue. A young woman on tiptoe leans forward to kiss the sleeping man. She gestures to caution an elderly person, standing behind her in the doorway. The man and woman are wearing fashions of the late 1830s to mid 1840s.

Under the central illustration, the legend 'Winning the Gloves' refers to the convention that to win a pair of gloves one had to kiss a sleeping man, or to perform a kindly act meriting this award.[8] Sir Walter Scott incorporated this quaint custom in his historical romance, *Saint Valentine's Day; or, The Fair Maid of Perth*, as a Valentine's Day courtship ritual. Catharine Glover—the eponymous 'Fair Maid'—steals a kiss from the sleeping Henry Gow, her suitor and valiant defender. By this kiss, Catharine indicates her preference for Henry as her Valentine for the coming year, and also wins thereby a pair of gloves.[9] The association of gloves with honour and chivalry are explained by Simon the Glover, Catharine's father: 'A glove on the point of a spear is a sign and pledge of faith all the wide world over, as a gauntlet flung down is a gage of knightly battle'.[10]

The handkerchief illustration is a contemporary 1840s reworking of Scott's Valentine's Morn scene. *The Fair Maid of Perth*, the events of which are set in the fourteenth century, was written in 1828 and republished numerous times. In August 1846, it appeared in the eleventh volume of the lavishly illustrated Abbotsford edition of the Waverley novels. In timely proximity to the White Woman expedition, a dramatised version of *The Fair Maid of Perth* was performed in Surrey, England, on 26 May 1845, and reviewed in the *Illustrated London News* of 31 May 1845.[11]

At either side of the main illustration, medallions record military scenes, probably from the Napoleonic wars. An almost identical group of figures to that in the right-hand medallion can be found in a painting depicting Wellington leading a column of Highlanders, advancing to La Haye Sainte.[12] This scene depicting several prostrate 'Native' figures, seemingly dead, has a (perhaps unintended) relevance in the context of the searches for the White Woman, in which Aborigines were harrassed and killed.

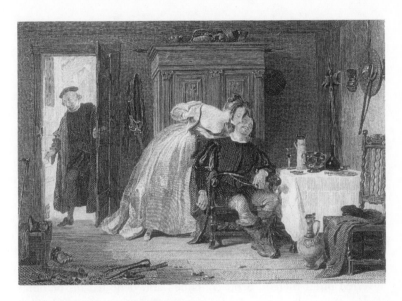

'St Valentine's Morn', by W. Allan R. A.
From Walter Scott's *Saint Valentine's Day; or, The Fair Maid of Perth* (1878 ed.)
Reproduced by permission of A. C. Black Publishers.

The woman depicted on the handkerchief is a phenotype of the young Queen Victoria, indicating the way in which characteristics of romance, valour, honour, and virtue attaching to literary and historic figures were attributed to her. The handkerchief image of Victoria-as-Fair-Maid-of-Perth mirrors a representation of Victoria-as-Grace-Darling, dating from around the same period.[13] These works, like numerous others, deploy Victoria's image as a reflexive model of ideal womanhood and highlight her role in promoting ideologies of domestic femininity.

The Winning the Gloves scene, as the depiction of a courtship ritual initiated by a young woman, could be read as a discreet allusion to Queen Victoria's proposal to Prince Albert on 15 October 1839, when 'she summoned him to her room, and, taking full advantage of her royal station, abruptly offered him marriage'. It was, she told her aunt, the Duchess of Gloucester, 'a nervous thing' to do, but, she added, it would not have been possible for Albert to propose to the Queen of England as 'he would never have presumed to take such a liberty'.[14] Immediately prior to proposing to Albert, the Queen 'spoke of the great tournament which had been held at Eglinton Castle' in her honour.[15] The Eglinton Tournament, held in August 1839, and to be discussed shortly, emerged in the wake of an unfounded rumour revealed in the *Court Journal* of 8 July 1837, that Victoria was planning a tournament at Windsor in which one hundred Knights of England would be called to defend her name against the challengers, and that she would crown the victor and make him her Prince.[16] Victoria's allusion to the Eglinton Tournament may have offered her an introduction to the delicate matter at hand, her need to choose a consort.

The Walter Scott connection similarly provided an ideal narrative and iconographic vehicle to displace any lingering feelings about the unseemliness of the young Queen's action. In incorporating the 'winning the gloves' convention into a Valentine's Day ritual and to the inverted order therein, Scott contained and deflected his heroine's display of female agency. As a personification of virtue and idealised femininity, the Fair Maid of Perth provided an effective model to neutralise anxieties about female power and assertive female sexuality, and the polarities of virgin/fecund woman, which the Queen's proposal brought into play.

It is possible that the handkerchiefs used for the White Woman search were printed as a commemorative item to mark the Queen's celebrated visit to Perth, Scotland, in 1842, and were amongst those which fluttered so gaily when she was everywhere met by 'deafening cheers and waving of handkerchiefs from casements'.[17] The Fair Maid in the handkerchief illustration wears a tartan shawl, which, according to Scott, 'women of ... fair character and decent rank' universally carried around with them when they went abroad.[18] Victoria wore such a shawl during her 1842 visit, and was welcomed by the ladies of Perthshire 'dressed in plain white gowns and tartan scarfs', like the Fair Maid.[19] As a married woman and mother, the Queen could not, of course, be referred to directly as Perth's 'Fair Maid'. Nevertheless, given the fierce competition amongst towns in Scotland to outdo each other in lavish displays of welcome and allegiance, Perth's advantage in being able to claim the Queen as its 'Fair Maid' was obliquely made in in the press during her visit to Perthshire. In reporting her visit to Inverkeithing, the *Times* acknowledged that this was the location for an event 'which Sir Walter Scott has interpolated into his romance of the *Fair Maid of Perth*'.[20] When the Queen was given the keys of the city of Perth, the *Perth Courier* reported the happy coincidence that 'according to some authors of note, the ancient Romans designed the now Fair City of Perth by the auspicious word "Victoria" '.[21]

How did the handkerchiefs come to be in Melbourne in 1846? Who selected the handkerchiefs for the expedition and organised the printing of the White Woman message thereon? How was the illustration intended to be 'read' in relation to the expedition? In the absence of any visual representations of the White Woman, the illustration by default provided an image which represented the virtues which the searchers hoped she was able to retain. As an indispensible item in a lady's wardrobe, the handkerchief evoked (as had McMillan's list of items) the White Woman's genteel status. The cosy domesticity and comfortable elegance depicted in the illustration envisages her proper sphere. The expeditionists, and those philanthropic Melbournians who performed a kindly act by supporting the expedition fund, hoped to win if not gloves then (as the *Herald* urged) the laurel crown. For the expeditionists, too, after several months of living rough in Gipps Land and perhaps feeling out of touch with the more cultured world of Melbourne, the handkerchiefs would have been a reminder of the values which the expedition represented. The image of the sleeping man caught off guard, as the young woman steals up to kiss him, was also a timely reminder of the need for the expeditionists to remain vigilant.

In the mid-1840s missionary societies and philanthropic groups from Exeter Hall in London provided pictorial handkerchiefs for distribution amongst Aborigines and other indigenous peoples in Britain's colonies. The decision to take handkerchiefs to Gipps Land might have been influenced by this example. In Port Phillip, Protector Robinson distributed handkerchiefs showing an image of a 'lady and woman and horses and dogs' to Aborigines during his sojourns amongst them in the Western District in 1841.[22] This practice was presumably to promote Christianising and civilising, although whether through contemplation of the illustrations or through the adoption of the use of handkerchiefs as a European hygienic practice is not clear. The former purpose is suggested by a comparable practice, implemented by Governor Arthur of Van Diemen's Land in the late 1820s, of nailing to trees in outlying areas handkerchief-sized boards painted with didactic illustrations depicting the punishments which would be meted out to Aborigines who breached European laws.

Whatever the expeditionists' intent, the 'Worrigals' found their own uses for the White Woman handkerchiefs. James Warman reported that:

> At 3 p.m., we were all much surprised at seeing our friendly tribe of Worrugals come to visit us . . . one of them gave us to understand that he had been with Bungelene and the woman only a few days back. He also said she had seen the handkerchiefs . . . he having two of them tied round his head . . .
>   Entry for Friday, 20th [November 1846][23]

As noted previously, the Gipps Land woman was associated with the ships *Britannia* and *Britomart*—names which invoke Britain and empire in an interplay of history and myth and incorporating devices of allegory and personification. Britannia, a poetic name for Britain, was from 1672 personified as a woman with helmet, shield and trident. She symbolised the connection between empire, militarism and the economy.[24] From the 1840s, and particularly at times of national crisis, Queen Victoria was frequently depicted as Britannia to rally national spirit and to promote Britain's image as a major European power. Victoria's emblematic role was acknowledged during her visit to Antwerp in 1843, which was celebrated with a street procession featuring a gigantic effigy of Britannia.[25] By the mid-nineteenth century, Britannia, in the person of the young Queen, could accommodate emerging British bourgeois definitions of woman as the allegorical standard-bearer of civilisation.

Britomart, an Amazon in Edmund Spenser's late sixteenth-century romance, *The Faerie Queen*, linked Arthurian legend with Britain's female monarch. Britomart was one of several guises attributed by Spenser to Queen Elizabeth I, another being Gloriana, the 'Faerie Queen', the object of Prince Arthur's quest.[26] The accession to the throne in 1837 of Queen Victoria, whom Benjamin Disraeli was to term 'the second Faerie Queen', put Victoria at the centre of the nineteenth-century revival of interest in medievalism in Britain and her colonies. Lord Tennyson in his series of Arthurian poems, the earliest of which is *Morte D'Arthur* (1842), modelled his King Arthur on Queen Victoria's husband, Prince Albert. The new monarch's reign was thus celebrated as a living link with the chivalric tradition.

The expeditionists encouraged the Britannia and Britomart icono-mania. James Warman sent back to Melbourne from Gipps Land a 'most interesting relic'—the butt of a tree on which were carved the initials 'H B', and the outline of a cutter, underneath which could be traced the letters 'BRIT' with other indecipherable letters running on.[27] It was claimed by Humanitas that the initials on the tree were those of his 'esteemed friend Commissary Bowerman', a passenger on the *Britannia*.[28]

The *Herald*, announcing the tree's arrival in Melbourne, con-curred that 'the carving is unquestionably the labour of some ship-wrecked person' and supported earlier speculation that 'the party who cut the letters must have belonged to either the "Britannia" or the "Brittomart".' Neither the *Herald* nor anyone else connected the initials with H. B. Morris, a member of the Gipps Land Company who was in Gipps Land in 1843, and whose report, 'A Trip to Gipps Land in April 1843', was published in the *Herald* on 19 May 1843, under the pseudonym 'H. B.'. The 'relic' was exhibited at the *Herald* office and later at the Mechanics Institute Museum.

In Scotland in 1839 the chivalric revival was celebrated in a spec-tacular medieval-style tournament hosted by the 13th Earl of Eglinton at his castle in Ayrshire to celebrate Queen Victoria's coron-ation. The Eglinton Tournament emerged in the wake of an un-founded rumour, previously mentioned, that the Queen was planning a tournament at Windsor and would crown the victor and make him her Prince.[29] The emerging national infatuation with medieval romance was expressed in the tournament, in the Gothic revival in architecture (for example in the new Houses of Parliament), in litera-ture and art, in the revival of heraldry, and in entertainment. In 1838 tens of thousands had attended the new museum at the Tower of London to see the display of Queen Elizabeth's Armoury, including the suits of armour of twenty knights, arranged historically from Henry VI in 1450 to James II in 1685, and weapons.[30] Three years after the Eglinton Tournament, in May 1842, the Queen and Prince Albert were to hold a medieval-style costumed ball at Buckingham Palace.[31]

Lord Eglinton's flamboyant gesture immediately captured the public imagination. Possibly inspired by Scott's representation in *Ivanhoe* of the tournament at Ashby de la Zouch—renditions of which had become a standard in theatre repertory since 1820 when *Ivanhoe* was first published—the Eglinton Tournament attracted more than 100 000 spectators from all over Britain to watch fourteen knights compete in the events.[32] The knights were magnificently outfitted and equipped and had practised their skills at a purpose-built tiltyard near Regent's Park.[33]

The Eglinton tournament was to be represented in fictional form by political statesman and novelist Benjamin Disraeli in his 1880 historical novel *Endymion*.[34] One of Disraeli's characters, Nigel, articulated the significance of the event in contemporary terms. The tournament represented, he said, a 'great revivification':

> Chivalry is the child of the Church; it is the distinctive feature of Christian Europe. Had it not been for the revival of Church principles, this glorious pageant would never have occurred. But it is a pageant only to the uninitiated. There is not a ceremony, a form, a phrase, a costume, which is not symbolic of a great truth or a high purpose.[35]

Disraeli, however, omitted the torrential downpour which marred the great day at Eglinton Castle.

Compared with the splendour and extravagant display of the Eglinton Tournament, the expedition to rescue the White Woman was a modest affair. Nevertheless, for the citizens of Port Phillip who had read of the Tournament from afar, the rescue expedition provided the opportunity to enact a knightly undertaking.[36] In a community with few aristocratic connections, and where social distinctions were carefully maintained, the quest to rescue the White Woman offered merchants, businessmen and squatters who aspired to gentility the semblance of an 'aristocratic' undertaking.[37]

The nineteenth-century chivalric revival was embraced by Port Phillip society. Melbournians with ambitions to gentility had the opportunity in late 1844 to have their arms and seals engraved by an artist newly arrived in Port Phillip.[38] Societies such as the Masonic Brethren, splendidly bejewelled and outfitted as Knights Templar, Knights of the Holy Sepulchre, and Knights Rosicrucian, enhanced the ambitions and reputations of its members and satisfied a desire for exclusivity, pomp and display through chivalric references and through secret signs, symbols and regalia.

The physical and psychological elements of the White Woman expedition—the journey through unfamiliar territory, meetings with the racial 'Other', contestation for possession of the prized object— were heightened and rendered intelligible within the European literary tradition of the medieval quest. Quest narratives provide discursive explorations into unknown territories, which objectify the places and peoples described. In a colonial context, the quest for the White Woman served numerous functions. It provided a morally elevated enunciative position from which to describe events in Gipps Land. It provided a dominant structuring device for the expedition, giving form and meaning to the wanderings of the expeditionists, and casting them as the embodiment of the chivalric ethos. The quest also provided the opportunity to produce and disseminate information about the land.

The story of the lost White Woman—a colonial originary narrative —was thereby recast, with European men assuming the role of knights, and the Aborigines cast as the infidel. European women were expected to endorse this role-playing. As Leslie Fiedler has argued of the 'Walter Scottification' of the American western, the hero —who risked his life to defend the good white woman at home against the forces of savagery—sought only 'that she recognize the legitimacy of the means by which he makes her existence safe, and give up any vestigial Christian scruples against the use of violence'.[39]

As an emblematic figure, the White Woman's representation could not be fixed. She slips from the personification of Britannia to the wilful yellow woman of Trooper Quandite's report. X. Y. Z.'s story of the Heart was one narrative mechanism for stabilising her as romantic heroine. The Heart's place in quest narratives dates at least from the fourteenth century, when Sir James Douglas, carrying the heart of Robert Bruce to the Holy Land with the intention of burying it at Jerusalem, fell in battle with the Saracens of Andalusia.[40] The heart was also the subject of the fifteenth-century quest narrative *Livre du Cueur d'Amours Espris* [The Book of the Heart Possessed by Love], in which the heart was symbolised by the Knight 'Cueur' whose helmet was emblazoned with a large red heart flanked by wings.[41] Queen Victoria, too, was feted as the 'Queen of Hearts'. Given that X. Y. Z. revived the story of the Heart in the *Gazette* immediately after the public meeting, it is surprising that those promoting the expedition as a 'sacred quest' did not exploit the potential of the Heart as a motif.[42]

In the Arthurian quest narrative tradition, the pursuit of a desired object is linked to processes of transformation and restoration to wholeness of the hero and the land, which, from the twelfth century, assume specifically Christian spiritual dimensions. Recovery of the desired object, although providing the pretext for the journey, was of secondary importance to the quest itself, and the knowledge thereby gained. In medieval narratives, questing knights must embody the chivalric virtues, resist temptation, thwart danger, solve riddles, and prove their bravery, chastity and honesty.

While De Villiers's expeditionists confined themselves to the role assigned by the Expedition Committee—to find and retrieve the White Woman—they appear to have met with little opposition from the settlers in Gipps Land. De Villiers wrote from Port Albert on 28 October that the locals, 'so far from their being averse to our humane undertaking . . . have expressed their readiness to give me every assistance . . . and we leave the settlement with the best wishes for our success by all parties here'.[43] However, experiences in the field necessitated a radical re-evaluation by De Villiers and Warman of what they saw as the ambit of their roles. Contrary to the idealist, universalising themes of the quest narrative, the expeditionists found themselves embroiled in the pragmatic 'here and now' of frontier politics.

As the expedition progressed, readerly expectations of a seamless quest or adventure narrative were frustrated as competing narrative strands threatened to eclipse the expeditionists' tale of heroic endeavour which the *Herald* had worked so hard to promote. The publicly funded expedition was unable to contact or retrieve the woman and, therefore, the concomitant drive for closure was continually deferred or thwarted as the hoped for, and promised, meetings with the woman failed to eventuate.

In November 1846, a month after De Villiers's party had left Melbourne, Acting Superintendent Lonsdale had authorised a government contingent comprising 'Mr. [William] Dana, jun. and 25 black troopers', to proceed to Gipps Land. Tensions between these government officers and De Villiers's party were to culminate in public denunciations, slander and recriminations. The *Herald* had divisively created a climate of rivalry between De Villiers's party and the government officers. Cavenagh, however, had not anticipated the extent to which an adversarial situation in Gipps Land would result in the development of a counter-narrative which would challenge assumptions of European civilised behaviour, upon which the expedition project had been premised. Ultimately, the quest was confounded by reports by De Villiers and Warman which took the form of a political *exposé*.

The efforts of De Villiers's expedition would be reported regularly to the expedition committee and be published in the *Herald*. In contrast, the Windridge-led government expedition was subject to scrutiny by Commissioner Tyers, who, in turn, was instructed 'to report from time to time [to the Superintendent of Port Phillip] for the information of His Excellency the Governor'.[44] The government correspondence relating to the White Woman searches was not meant for public dissemination in the way that the reports of the privately funded expedition were. However, should the government be called to account, official correspondence could be made available to the public.

The public nature of the crisis, and the political furore which it precipitated, as played out in the pages of the Melbourne newspapers and in the official correspondence throughout 1847, would embarrass all participants in the saga: the government, members of both search parties, and the expedition committee. Accusations by De Villiers and Warman concerning misconduct by Dana's government party, in particular their brutality to the Gipps Land Aborigines, would become public knowledge when published in the *Herald*. The officers of the government expedition would in turn bring counter-accusations against De Villiers of misconduct, ineptitude, cowardice, drunkenness and misappropriation of public funds.

Intimations of the schism which was to develop emerged soon after the arrival of the expeditionists in Gipps Land. On 23 November 1846 De Villiers made an official deposition to Charles Tyers over alleged hostility towards his party by Sergeant Walsh of the Native Police who, he said, 'had gone up to two of the natives in De Villiers's party with a Tomahawk to strike them'.[45] In his letter written the following day to the Expedition Committee, Warman did not mention the incident. He presented instead a positive report. However, the details were to be made public in January 1847. In subsequent reports, De Villiers and Warman would raise further, more serious, and more sweeping allegations against government officer Mr William Dana, the Native Police under Dana's command, and the Gipps Land settlers.

Such untoward behaviour could be accommodated, at least in part, within the chivalric narrative tradition, in the form of wicked 'black knights', mercenaries who terrorised helpless peasants, dishonoured ladies, desecrated churches, and brought knighthood into disrepute.[46] The black troopers of the Native Police could be, and indeed many times had been, cast unproblematically in such a role, the massacre of the Cape Otway tribe being a recent example. Warman claimed that 'part of Mr. Dana's party [in Gipps Land] were those who assisted at the Otway massacre'.[47] However, if De Villiers and his men were the crusading knights, and the Native Police were their sinister *bêtes noir*, the charges against the settlers and the government officers (Walsh and Dana) placed them ambiguously and uncomfortably in between.

As 1847 began, De Villiers's expeditionists were still in Gipps Land, their provisions exhausted and clothing worn out, awaiting instructions on whether to return to Melbourne or continue the search. Hopes that De Villiers's party would rescue the captive woman were, by this time, becoming increasingly remote. However, by late January 1847 the *Herald* was again collecting subscriptions to extend De Villiers's time in Gipps Land. Acting Superintendent Lonsdale also sought assistance for De Villiers's party from the Governor. Lonsdale, who had already authorised Tyers to provided limited assistance to De Villiers, must have been dismayed at the Governor's terse response, conveyed by the Colonial Secretary on 2 February:

> The issuing of Rations, or affording aid in any shape or under any circumstances, to the private expedition, must in some measure connect it with, without making it responsible to, the Government and whenever the latter is called upon to assist, it ought also to have the right and the power to control. It is with much pain therefore, that the Governor feels compelled to express His regret at the step which Your Honor has taken; and which His Excellency cannot but apprehend may tend to embarrass the Government, more especially as Mr. Tyers was already fully authorized to take any steps, short of violence, for the recovery of the woman.[48]

The *Gazette*, less connected than the *Herald* with the promotion of the private expedition, recognised that inter-party rivalry was jeopardising the rescue project. 'What avails a search under these circumstances?', it asked on 23 January:

> If the leaders of such parties criminate and recriminate each other as they are now, and have hitherto been doing—if they watch each other's proceedings, as is evident they do, from the tenor of their dispatches, what results are the public to expect?—The failure of the expedition—probably the death of the woman, if she exists, and the useless and profligate expenditure of monies on as ill an organised party as ever left Melbourne.[49]

On 10 February 1847, as predicted by the *Gazette*, De Villiers returned to Melbourne without having sighted, let alone rescued, the White Woman, but 'fully determined to return without delay, and leave no effort untried to win success'.[50] The *Herald* defended De Villiers: 'His sole reason for returning without success is the straits to which himself and his gallant little band were reduced for provisions and stores of every description, as well as a positive refusal, on the part of Mr. Commissioner Tyers, to co-operate with them in any manner'. The *Herald* was quick to reassert the narrative of heroic endeavour over the more conspicuous narrative of failure, which De Villiers's return signalled:

> Mr. De Villiers is . . . not to be deterred from the prosecution of the honourable and humane cause in which he has embarked—that the woman is there a prisoner has been established—that she will yet be rescued from her horrible condition, he feels highly confident, and he is therefore fully determined to return without delay, and leave no effort untried to win success . . . We cannot close without recording our unqualified approbation of the manner in which Mr. De Villiers has labored in the good and toilsome cause—the coolness, determination, and experience evinced by him—and the resolution with which he has bore up against obstacles of no light nor fanciful nature. Every philanthropist must feel more or less indebted to him; and we are assured that it only requires time and patience to consummate the objects of the expedition.[51]

De Villiers's own 'account of the failure of his expedition' casts doubt on the distinction which he, Warman and the newspapers had previously drawn between the exemplary 'heroic' conduct of De Villiers's own party towards the Gipps Land Aborigines, and the behaviour of the government officers, Walsh and Dana. For example, De Villiers told the tribe with which his party was on friendly terms that he 'considered their conduct was all "gammon", and that in consequence of such deception on their parts it was my intention to go back to Melbourne and bring all the white men and blacks to Gipps Land to punish them'.[52]

On 16 February, Sergeant McLelland of the Native Police, writing to the editor of the *Patriot*, contested the 'calumnious falsehoods reported by De Villiers and Warman, concerning the conduct of the Native Police, in Gipps Land'.[53] McLelland's spirited defence of the actions of the Native Police is of less interest here than his accusations that De Villiers had been 'lying about Lake King for upwards of six weeks in a state of inactivity' and that De Villiers's motives in undertaking the search for the White Woman were not entirely disinterested. 'Report in Gipps Land', he wrote, 'says, that De Villiers is aiming for the Protectorship should one be required [and a]ny person with the least discernment reading Warman's statement which appeared in the Melbourne papers, might understand, that he is putting in a word for his brother muff.' De Villiers had previously expounded his ideas for a scheme to replace the Aboriginal protectorate in the *Herald* in July 1846.[54]

De Villiers's leadership and integrity were also challenged by expedition party member Mr Brodie. The *Patriot,* citing Brodie, described an incident in which De Villiers rushed up to a 'Worrigal', 'presented his gun at the savage's head and roared out "You lie, you lie you run away!"—this was what Mr. De Villiers called "bouncing the man"'. When De Villiers prevented the party from taking hostages, 'the whole party expressed their conviction of the utter uselessness, under De Villiers guidance . . . [and] resolved to return to Melbourne—galled, vexed, and out of heart at the imbecile conduct of their leader'. Brodie accused De Villiers of putting up at a public house at the Glengarry [River], 'drinking during the entire time and when in a state of intoxication violently abusing the men under his charge—trying to make them fight—and saying his life was in danger, refused to travel in company with his party to Melbourne'.[55]

McLelland's and Brodie's criticisms proved difficult for the Expedition Committee to counter. However, Cavenagh's powers of persuasion were considerable, and he turned them to discrediting McLelland and to reviving public interest in the rescue cause and renewing confidence in De Villiers. In the *Herald* of 18 February 1847, Cavenagh's defence of the expedition project brooked no dissent:

> Mr. De Villiers's expedition has shown by the anxiety of the Blacks to prevent her capture, by their precautions to prevent her escape, by their care to obliterate all traces of the white woman's footsteps, by their repelling scrutiny; by their offer of a black lubra in exchange, by their avowal that she was detained as *a hostage* against an exterminating attack by the whites; above all by the strictly consentaneous accounts given by the aboriginals north, south, east, and west of Gipps Land, detailing without alteration the minute particulars of her history and condition; and last but not least, the decisive letter of Mr. McMillan—an old and most respectable settler—such a body of evidence has now been established to prove the existence of the white woman among the Blacks, as is perfectly irresistible.[56]

In the same edition of the *Herald*, Cavenagh published Angus McMillan's recent letter to the Expedition Committee, which lent credibility to the private expedition and concluded with McMillan's offer of assistance, made to the expedition committee and not to the government contingent: 'AS A PROOF, I AM NOW WILLING TO GIVE MY SERVICES TO ASSIST IN HER RECOVERY, WHICH I THINK CAN BE ACCOMPLISHED BY PROMPT MEASURES, ESPECIALLY AS BOATS ARE ALREADY ON THE LAKES TO FACILITATE THE OBJECT' [original capitals].[57]

In the *Gazette*, A Fellow Colonist speaking out in support of De Villiers said he had the publicly expressed recommendation of such 'influential private parties as Messrs. Raymond, McMillan, Meyrick, &c., amongst the squatters, and of Serjeant Wainridge of the Local Native Police'.[58] However, general feeling in Melbourne was against De Villiers's involvement in a further expedition, at least until allegations about his leadership of the first expedition had been investigated.

The *Patriot*, argued that 'neither the *first* nor *second* "in command" of the recent expedition should be again permitted, at least at the expense of the public, to accompany "expedition" number 2'. The *Patriot* also advocated harsh measures against the Gipps Land Aborigines:

FORCE MUST BE USED, AND OUGHT TO BE USED, when other means fail—not the force of indiscriminate slaughter, but such 'force' as every man of observation will admit, would, if used in the recent expedition, have by this time relieved the wretched female from the repulsive thraldom of a savage. There appears to exist a degree of sensitive apprehension for the safety of the savages, which bid fair to overshadow all healthy sympathy and exertion for the release of their unhappy captive—such pharisaical philanthropists deserve the reputation of Sterne's humanity—a humanity that could 'weep over a *dead ass*, but neglect a *living mother*.' The matter comes to this—the blacks declare that the woman shall not be given up unless captured by force ... Is then the woman to remain in their brutalizing dominion, until the ultima ratio be adopted? Let any European practice a similar oppression upon his fellow, and disregard conciliatory attempts ... how long would *force* be unemployed?—are the shot and shell used against the slaver, not fatally pointed for the release of 'aliens' to British soil, laws, and complexion—and shall babblers prate against *force* being used to release a British subject, and that subject a helpless woman, from a slavery worse than death?[59]

The *Patriot*'s view reflected the strident arguments of squatting interests in Gipps Land and elsewhere. The reference to slavery, which targeted the 'Exeter Hall philanthropists', capitalised on anti-philanthropic discourse in order to discredit those who 'blew the whistle' on Dana, Walsh, the Native Police and the settlers in Gipps Land for their ill treatment of the Kurnai. The criticism also applied indirectly to those in colonial government—notably La Trobe and Gipps (by now returned to England)—who had, at least officially, endeavoured to pursue humanitarian policies in settler–Aboriginal relations.

In late February 1847, La Trobe returned from Van Diemen's Land to Melbourne as the furore raged over De Villiers's and Warman's allegations. After perusing the correspondence on the searches for the White Woman which had accumulated during his absence, La Trobe concluded that the evidence for the woman's existence was 'far from conclusive'.[60] Nevertheless, following a persuasive deposition by the expedition committee on 26 February, urging further action, and perhaps anticipating public approbation, La Trobe authorised Tyers to 'push forward the search with a view to her release by every possible means' and 'without regard to expense'.[61]

La Trobe also approved the appointment of five members of De Villiers's party whose 'general character & qualifications would appear to recommend them' to be engaged on government pay and rations. La Trobe did not nominate De Villiers, Warman or Brodie, 'it being . . . distinctly understood that the expedition was to be under the control of the Government, headed by Mr. Tyers, and Serjeant Windridge, leader'. Sergeant Windredge may have been appointed as expedition leader because he was the only senior government officer in Gippsland (apart from Tyers) not implicated in De Villiers's and Warman's allegations of bloodshed at the Snowy River.

Official investigations into the allegations against William Dana, Walsh and the Native Police were as yet incomplete. When Dana had not submitted his report on the Snowy River incident by 9 March, La Trobe wrote to Dana's supervising officer—his brother, Captain Henry E. P. Dana—advising that he had 'been directed by His Excellency the Governor to call upon Mr. William Dana to explain why he did not furnish the report required of him by Mr. Tyers'. La Trobe appears to have been uncomfortable about Dana's presence in Gipps Land and requested that Captain Dana 'require Mr. William Dana to return to Head Quarters . . . & that you should make another arrangement for the Command of the party of Native Police still in Gipps Land'. La Trobe must have suspected that the Native Police were being directed by unauthorised persons, presumably settlers, while in Gipps Land. He instructed Captain Dana that in future they were to be considered 'specially & solely under the control of the Crown Commissioner to whose assistance they are expressly sent'.[62]

Cavenagh's and the expedition committee's involvement with the Windredge-led expedition was to be substantially curtailed due to the negative publicity surrounding the allegations made against De Villiers, which were still under consideration by the expedition committee when Windredge's party left Melbourne on 4 March.

On 10 March the *Gazette* informed readers that De Villiers was proceeding to Gipps Land 'with a view of obtaining the most direct and tangible proofs of the injustice with which he has been treated . . . Should he succeed, as doubtless he will, Mr. de V. will offer his services to Mr. Tyers as honorary volunteer, for the rescue of our unfortunate and enslaved country woman'.[63] To this end, a meeting of the 'Friends of Mr. Christian De Villiers' was held at the residence of George Arden (former editor of the *Gazette*) on 10 March. Those in attendance declared 'their entire confidence in [De Villiers'] ability and integrity' and considered that he was 'entitled to some public aid to enable him to return to Gipps Land, in pursuance of the object with which he was originally charged'. Two days later, an advertisement appeared in the *Argus* inviting subscriptions, to be sent to Arden, who had chaired the meeting and was to act as treasurer.[64]

The expedition committee subsequently cleared De Villiers of the serious charges, namely, 'useless delays, pusillanimity, and misappropriation of funds', although the committee considered that 'a want of discipline appears to have prevailed among the party, and that due care was not had towards the economical consumption of the stores'.[65] If DeVilliers did subsequently offer his services to Tyers, they were apparently not accepted, as his name does not appear as an expedition member in any of the reports.

Although qualified support for De Villiers and the private expedition was forthcoming from all of the Melbourne newspapers, the quest narrative was exhausted.[66] Nevertheless, as subsequent chapters will reveal, numerous other contemporary and nostalgic discourses imbricated in the expedition project provided fruitful avenues by which the White Woman story could continue to be articulated and acted upon.

Within weeks of the publicly funded search party setting out for Gipps Land, news of its progress began arriving in Melbourne. Between October 1846 and February 1847, the months in which the searches were conducted, communications from the expedition were published regularly. These reports, culminating in the publication in the *Herald* of Warman's journal of the expedition, in three instalments from 23 February to 2 March 1847, were to provide sufficiently detailed descriptions to enable readers to chart the general progress of the search.

At around the time that Warman's journal was published, a second expedition was preparing to leave Melbourne for Gipps Land to attempt to retrieve the White Woman. It was at this time, also, that Thomas Ham's *Map of Australia Felix* went on sale to the public. Ham's map provided the citizens of Melbourne with the opportunity to situate the events related by Warman and De Villiers, and to trace the new expedition's journey into the farthest and (to Europeans) least-known reaches of Gipps Land. The expeditionists' reports from the field, read in conjunction with Ham's map, provided the wherewithal for town-bound armchair adventurers to participate vicariously in a narrative of heroism and adventure.

Drawing on numerous sources, Ham provided the public, for the first time, with a comprehensive cartographic record of the Port Phillip District. The map incorporated information collected over the previous decade in government surveys, reports from Commissioners of Crown Lands, and records of explorers, settlers

Detail from *Map of Australia Felix* (1847), compiled and engraved by Thomas Ham. Reproduced by permission of La Trobe Collection, State Library of Victoria.

and government officers. The *Herald*, advising readers of the map's imminent availability, noted that 'it is most gratifying to find that the official trammels which have hitherto thwarted every attempt to give the public plans of these surveys which the public have paid for, have at length been broken asunder'.[67]

As a document of colonial expansion, Ham's map was a timely addition to the records of recent 'discoveries' by explorers and surveyors which had been streaming in to colonial headquarters in Sydney from all areas of the colony.[68] The map provided up-to-date information for the would-be immigrant, settler, speculator and capitalist. It mediated in Western cartographic conventions the *idea* of the Port Phillip District as a space of unbounded capitalist potential.[69] The *Port Phillip Gazette* recommended it 'to settlers for use, and to persons who might send it home, to show those interested in the colony, its vast extent and capabilities', while the *Sydney Morning Herald* suggested that 'mercantile men in the colony will find it to their advantage to possess one'.[70]

Ten weeks after the map's publication, and while the second expedition party was still in Gipps Land searching for the White Woman, George Arden, freelance writer and former editor of the *Port Phillip Gazette*, reviewed Ham's map in a series of newspaper articles published in the *Port Phillip Herald*.[71] Arden had taken a prominent role in promoting the Port Phillip district as early as 1840, with the publication of his book *Latest Information with Regard to Australia Felix*. His lecture entitled 'Progress of Discovery in Australia', presented at the Melbourne Mechanics' Institute on 5 June 1846, and his exposition of Ham's map the following year, celebrated the development of a thriving province and anticipated an unprecedented era of trade, commercial development and prosperity.

The publication of Ham's map, like the White Woman cause, provided Arden (who signed the petition for the public meeting) with a vehicle to protest his dissatisfaction with the Gipps government for having failed in its duties to the citizens of Port Phillip. Ham was a privately employed engraver, and Arden presented the publication of the map as a triumph of civic endeavour over government obstructionism, and a vindication of the colonists' long-denied rights to such information. Almost one-third of Arden's review was devoted to an attack on Governor Gipps who, he claimed, had conspired 'to detain the colonists from a knowledge of the "land they live in"'.

Ham's map operated as a palimpsest on which details of European presence reinscribed Aboriginal territories as colonial space. The map represented the district as European territory, exclusively for the benefit of European (and largely pastoral) pursuits. It included details of more than one thousand squatting stations, as well as land purchased from the Crown or open for occupation, with the description of soil and timber and geological features and structures of settlement such as post offices, roads, inns, towns, villages, punts and bridges.[72] The language of the map legitimised European occupation. However, traces attesting to Aboriginal presence register on the map in the form of Anglicised renderings of Aboriginal names attached to geographic features.

The role that such systematic charting and mapping has played in the European acquisition of foreign lands has been identified by Gananath Obesekere as:

> not only a major scientific activity but . . . also simultaneously a symbolic activity whereby the alien land is mapped out, identified, and systematically renamed with familiar English names. The larger the land and the sparser its population, the more easily it can be overpowered by toponymy.[73]

Ham's map provided an unprecedentedly detailed pictorial representation of European knowledge about, and occupation of, the land at a particular historical moment. While the blank spaces were rapidly being filled in, some large stretches of territory in the high country and to the east of Melbourne, north of the Great Swamp, marked 'Unsurveyed Country' awaited, it would seem, the arrival of the surveyor and the European settler to bring them into 'productive' existence. These unmapped regions, along with the more sparsely detailed remote areas, included large parts of Gipps Land where the searches for the White Woman were being undertaken.

Arden's review extrapolated from the map what these days might be termed a 'travelogue'. Taking Cape Howe as his starting point— that being the easternmost tip of the border between Port Phillip and the Middle District—Arden's exposition followed the contours of the coastline toward Melbourne. Along the way he embellished his description with historical and anecdotal information to 'flesh out' the points of reference on the map and to bring them into three-dimensional relief as sites for the enactment of *vignettes* of European exploration and settlement.

In describing the Gipps Land coastline, Arden alluded to the loss of the *Britannia* in December 1839, and to the existence 'beyond dispute' of a white woman 'residing for several years amongst the black natives'. As proof of the woman's existence, Arden cited 'the discovery of a marked tree upon one of the coast ranges bearing rudely carved, the name of that vessel, the initials of the owner and captain, a date and a figure of the vessel itself'. In his review, he applauded the efforts of the expedition party which was at that moment in Gipps Land to recover the 'wretched female' and anticipated that she would be 'speedily delivered up by her savages and embruted captors'.[74]

In situating the White Woman 'in' Ham's map, Arden deployed her as an unwitting agent of spatial politics. It was not necessary for the woman to exist, or for expeditionists to encounter or rescue her, in order that the space of frontier conflict be reconceptualised as the site of the woman's degradation and enslavement. Reports of her having been 'sighted' in particular locations, 'her' marks on the landscape, and the expeditionists' presence in, and journeyings across, the territory in pursuit of her, acted—at least at a narrative level—to this end. The woman was thus imbricated in (to use J. B. Harley's term) the 'representational hierarchy' of the map, and functioned as a metaphor for the feminised land as contested possession between white and black men.[75] In American pioneering history such metaphors facilitated the processes and practices of European conquest of the land and the subjugation of Native Americans.[76] The journal of expeditionist James Warman, second-in-command to De Villiers, insistently locates the rescue project in the on-going conflict between European settlers and Gipps Land Aborigines for possession of the land.

Arden's review, like X. Y. Z.'s story of the Heart, conflated geography, history and romance. At the same time as the land was represented as the site of the White Woman's 'horrible thraldom', the *possibility* of her existence, the ever-present *possibility* of sighting her, imbued the terrain with a numinous, romantic quality. Arden's review encouraged readers—the people of Melbourne who, he noted, had fitted out the expedition parties 'with their usual liberality'—to 'imagine' the countryside as though ennobled by the 'gallant undertakings' of the expeditionists. Arden suggested that the history of William Buckley, who had lived with Aborigines in the Port Phillip Bay area for thirty-two years, 'together with that of "Lundican", the white woman now in captivity amongst the blacks of Gipps Land, would form a most singular romance of real life, although curiously and painfully interesting'.[77] Once beyond the spatial containment of the narratives and the map, Arden seems to suggest, the White Woman would be bracketed off, with Buckley, as a pair of historical and social curiosities. If Arden was also promoting a real-life *romance* between 'Lundican' and Buckley, this could be read as a projected change of status for the White Woman, should she return to civilisation.

CHAPTER 6

Scapegoats and Figureheads

'. . . to make the farce complete, we would have suggested to them the propriety of
again starting, taking the precaution of having amongst them a newly-arrived
female emigrant, who, for a 'consideration,' might be induced to take a part in the
hoax, and returning with the lady after she has become tolerably sun-burnt, load
themselves with earthly honors and emoluments, and hand their names down to
posterity as the "liberators of the white woman".'
Port Phillip Patriot, 7 April 1847[1]

The second expedition party, led by Sergeant Windredge, left Melbourne on 4 March 1847. Windridge, two 'Worrigals' and two Western Port blacks, 'Lively' and 'Charlie', who had also accompanied De
Villiers's party, proceeded overland to Gipps Land. There they were
joined by the five members of De Villiers's expedition nominated by
La Trobe who sailed to Port Albert aboard the *Elizabeth*. The *Herald*
anticipated that Tyers would select additional expeditionists in Gipps
Land and that altogether the party would 'amount to twenty-five
men, chiefly whites'.[2] The Expedition Committee in its report noted
that it was:

> happy to observe, that His Honor has instructed the new
> Expedition that 'great discretion, prudence, and patience,' can
> alone promise success; instructions entirely coinciding with
> those which were given by the Committee to the former party
> . . . [and trust that] upon no account whatever, will those
> cruel threats be suffered to be put into execution—'of going to
> work with the blacks'—which can only end in disaster and
> disappointment.[3]

The Expedition Committee had supplied the expeditionists with
'trinkets as presents for the natives, consisting of looking glasses,

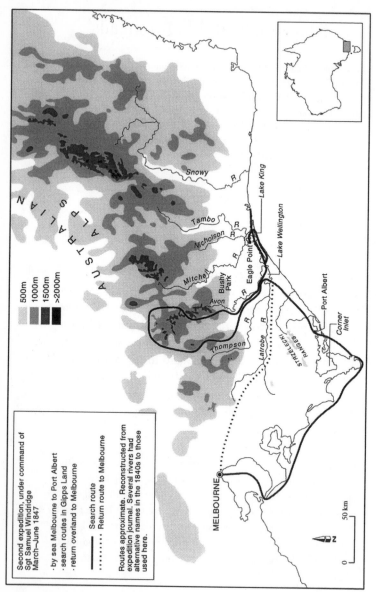

Approximate routes taken by second expedition (March–June 1847)
Details compiled by author. Map prepared by Chandra Jayasuriya, Melbourne University Press.

sailors' knives, Jews' harps, fishing hooks and lines, tomahawks, &c., all of which are highly prized by the blacks'. The looking glasses, like the handkerchiefs distributed by the earlier search party, carried a message:

> White Woman! A strong armed party, headed by the Govern-ment, is now in search of you, *determined* to rescue you. Two Worrigals, named Boondowal and Karrowutbeet, are with the white party. Be careful so far as your own safety is concerned, and do every thing to throw yourself into the hands of this party. Inform the person who detains you, as well as his tribe, that he and they will be handsomely rewarded if they will give you up peaceably; but if they persist in detaining you they will be severely punished.—Melbourne, March 4, 1847.[4]

Printed in large type, this message differed from the message on the pictorial handkerchiefs. There was no mention of 'Anna'. Neither was the message duplicated in Gaelic. In the months following the printing of the handkerchiefs and their distribution by De Villiers's party, reports had come back to Melbourne that the woman was marked and scarred like a 'lubra', stooped and partially deaf. There seems a terrible irony in using mirrors as the medium for a message to a woman believed to be scarred or physically diminished by her experiences.

The message on the mirrors, like those on the handkerchiefs, appears as concerned with lauding the '*determined*' and 'strong armed party', and with recording that the expedition originated from Mel-bourne, as with providing useful information and instructions to the White Woman. How relevant, for instance, would the provision of the date be to a woman who had been without a calendar for several years? The threat that the 'Worrigals' would be 'severely punished' if they 'persisted in detaining' the woman reads ominously, particularly in the light of expressed views that 'force' should be used to retrieve the woman. The message gives the impression that, contrary to its instructions, the party had been given *carte blanche* to 'go to work' on the 'Worrigals'.

The expeditionists had barely arrived in Gipps Land before further 'sightings' of the White Woman were in circulation both in Gipps

Land and Melbourne. In addition, there were 'absurd stories . . . such as Bungelene endeavouring to carry off Mrs. Windridge, wife of the Sergeant, and that he had been speared by the interpreter boy Taki Warren'.[5] News arrived in Melbourne by the *Elizabeth* from Port Albert on 23 March 1847 that 'a shepherd informed the party who landed from the "Elizabeth" that *he had seen* the unfortunate captive'.[6] The *Herald* reported on 15 April that the 'Worrigal' named 'one eye', who had accompanied De Villiers to the mountains as a guide in January had 'informed Mr. Tyers, through the interpreter boy Take Warren [*sic*], that after he ran away from the party on the mountains, *he saw the White Woman* with a Worrigal named Rangholegen'.[7]

Some Gipps Landers, however, were incredulous of the rumours and were amused by the gullibility of the Melbourne press. The *Herald*'s 'own Correspondent' wrote from Tarraville on 10 May 1847:

> The report of a white woman is looked upon by all of us as a clever hoax. From first to last we were convinced that no white woman is or was lately alive; and we could only laugh at the exaggerated statements which appeared in the Melbourne papers, and which now and then found their way to this out of the way District.[8]

Tyers, Captain Dana and Walsh also expressed scepticism concerning the White Woman's existence at various times. The *Patriot* on 7 April 1847 reported that 'Captain Dana, and the government party who proceeded to Gipps Land in search of the white woman . . . have returned to town after having convinced themselves that their sympathies and those of the public have been enlisted in behalf of an imaginary being', and that the affair 'appears to have originated in a joke upon the part of a few waggish settlers in the district, with a view to test the gullibility of the "Herald"'. The article continued: 'Mr. Tyers, we understand, has become heartily tired of the undertaking, from a conviction . . . that the white woman, respecting whom so much has been said and written, is an "invisible girl", a mere creature of the imagination, or perhaps a feminine Bunyip'.[9]

However, if Tyers was sceptical, as the *Patriot* claimed, he did not disclaim the White Woman's existence in his letter to La Trobe on 26 April.

Newspaper reporting of the second expedition was substantially reduced from that which had accompanied De Villiers's expedition. The second expedition did not appoint an official chronicler to provide regular despatches directly to the expedition committee, and hence to the *Herald*, as De Villiers and Warman had done. However, the *Patriot* complained in early March that 'Mr. Cavenagh has succeeded in securing another three months monopoly of "Earliest Information" from Gipps Land, to say nothing of the stray advertisements therefrom accruing'.[10]

Expedition leader Sergeant Windredge was obliged to report through the official government channels to Tyers. While some information trickled through to the newspapers from official sources, or informally from private, unnamed correspondents, there was not a reliable, regular stream of correspondence to the expedition committee or to the *Herald*. Reports which did come through lacked the strong personal presence of De Villiers and Warman. After the second expedition party arrived back in Melbourne in July 1847, the expedition committee had to apply to La Trobe for access to the official correspondence and seek his approval before it could be published in the newspapers.

De Villiers and Warman had put together cogent, publishable reports. The unpublished journal of the second expedition is a far less polished piece of writing. Clues in the journal establish that the anonymous author was Donald McLeod, who had also been a member of De Villiers's party. McLeod's expression, grammar, punctuation and spelling are idiosyncratic, and his penmanship inexpert. The journal's revelation that not all members of the first expedition were as literate and well-educated as De Villiers and Warman undercuts to some extent the effect which had been promoted in the press of the first expedition as a gentlemanly undertaking. This might explain why his journal was not published in the *Herald* or elsewhere, which underscores the role which the expedition committee and the *Herald* played in controlling and mediating representations of the expedition party and the expedition venture.

Such information as was published intermittently in the news-papers included diary extracts from another unnamed member of the second expedition, who can now be identified as Peters.[11] Infor-mation brought to town by Tyers, Captain Dana, McMillan and other settlers also appeared in the press.[12] The *Herald* on 6 May referred the sceptical to 'Mr. Tyers and Mr. McMillan [who] are in town, and willing to give every information on the subject'.[13]

In the absence of regular news reports, the Port Phillip newspapers on several occasions kept alive reader interest by promising but deferring disclosure.[14] The *Herald* inventively created news out of no news, in reporting that '[t]he "Elizabeth" from Port Albert, having been three weeks on her passage to Melbourne, does not bring intel-ligence respecting the fate of this wretched captive'.[15]

Meanwhile, McLeod was recording in his journal the expedition-ists' frustration at the unreliable, even duplicitous, 'Worrigals':

> they are Greatly Given to fibs more Especialy if they Expect any thing for the information Given—which unfortunately has been so very frequently the Case with since we Came amongst them from first to Last if you Give them one pound of Bread they will say any thing you wish them that is if they understand what you are in want of . . . [16]

Tyers also stated that 'from former experience of the want of ver-acity among the wild blacks, some doubt must hang over every state-ment they make'.[17] Although one can not rule out the possibility that the 'Worrigals' might have been 'gammoning' the expeditionists, they might have had good reason for doing so. The *Argus* in March 1847 reported: 'The natives of Gipps Land seem of late, since the destruction of their brethren on the Snowy River, to have taken the notion that on the surrender of the white woman a party of whites will be sent into their country with orders for their extermination'.[18]

The dialects of the five Gipps Land tribes varied considerably, as noted by Walsh. The expeditionists and government officers in Gipps Land claimed that they used interpreters to overcome diffi-culties in communicating with the 'Worrigals'. But this did not guarantee that translations were accurate or that understanding would be achieved. Jacka-wadden, aged about eight, was the principal interpreter throughout the searches for the White Woman. 'Yal Yal' and 'Lively' from the Western Port tribe, who had accompanied De Villiers's party, also functioned as guides, interpreters and negotiators for the second expedition. They had previously been stationed with the Native Police in Gipps Land and might, or might not, have gained some knowledge of Kurnai languages. The expeditionists also took 'Worrigals' with them as interpreters. It is questionable whether any of these interpreters were sufficiently adept with dialects other than their own, or with English, to perform the role effectively.

At the end of his journal, McLeod included 'A List of Warigle names or words with an English Explanation Affixed to Each'. The 123 words and their English counterparts were possibly compiled as a phrase-book reference by McLeod to assist in his communications with the 'Worrigals'. McLeod does not indicate to which of the five Kurnai language-groups the words pertain. If used across, and understood by, the several different language groups, the words probably comprised composite linguistic elements, and would thus provide a crude record of a Kurnai *lingua franca* from the early colonial period. McLeod did not, however, attempt the extensive 'ethnographic' observations which Warman included in his journal.

By July 1847 the second expedition, unable to achieve its declared objective of rescuing the elusive woman, drew to a close. Most members returned directly to Melbourne. However, McLeod, accompanied by Kelly and one of the Western Port 'blacks', travelled to McMillan's station, Bushy Park, where 'McLeod [was] invited up to the house' while the others were put up at the men's hut. McLeod's journal reveals that during the five days he spent in the company of McMillan, Macalister and Dr Arbuckle, he played 'some fine Pibrochs and Highland Reels for their Amusement . . . which pleased the Gentlemen very much'. While at Bushy Park, he records 'partys Every night'. The Bushy Park entries confirm that the chronicler was McLeod, the 'Highland piper'. The entry for Thursday, 17 June reads: 'Mr. Macalisters wants to Engage me as his piper to Go with him to hobart and from there with him to Sydney New South Wales at a Salary of 60/ per annum'.

McLeod was singled out for preferential treatment in being invited up to the house. This might have been because he was a fellow Scot. Macalister's offer to him of a position as his piper possibly reflected the goodwill generated by a convivial evening and/or the superior nature of McLeod's playing. However, other interests might also have been served in getting McLeod on side.

On a previous occasion, on 2 June 1847, McLeod had also stayed at McMillan's head station while the other expeditionists remained at the outstation. These visits reveal the familiarity which existed between the three Scottish squatters most closely associated with the White Woman story, McMillan, Macalister and Arbuckle, and selected members of the expedition party, such as McLeod. The potential for collusion in this association is self-evident. The generous hospitality enjoyed by McLeod on these occasions might have caused him to modify his entries in his journal so as not to paint the Gipps Land settlers in a bad light, as Warman had done. McLeod may also have acted as an informant to his countrymen and this might have influenced the course of events throughout the searches.

Tyers blamed the failure of attempts to recover the woman on the 'bad faith of that chief [Bungelene]'. Perhaps under pressure for results, and in order 'to be no longer duped by this wily Black', Tyers 'thought it advisable to try the effect of a compulsory detention of himself and his family, intimating that concession to our demands is the surest means of recovering his freedom'.[19]

The fate of Bungelene, his wives and children, forms a parallel narrative to that of the searches for the White Woman. From mid-1846 Bungelene was cast as a key figure in the drama, the *bête noir* to the woman's genteel white humanity. His participation—both real and imagined—in the narrative, and his presence and co-operation in the searches, provided the pretext for much of the expeditionists' action. His capture, interrogation and incarceration kept public interest at a premium when the search parties floundered about in Gipps Land with little of interest to report. The scapegoating of Bungelene when the second search party returned unsuccessful, without the woman, her body, or any tangible evidence of her captivity, and his subsequent death in custody, is a cruel counterpart to the rescue project and the high-minded rhetoric which gave it shape and substance.

Bungelene was an influential and esteemed tribal elder. Tyers was to acknowledge him as 'Chief of the Gipps Land Tribes', and while the title might be inaccurate in terms of Kurnai tribal structures, it reflects the importance he was accorded in Gipps Land by Europeans. De Villiers had represented Bungelene as 'a man of middle age, and great influence with the *Parberry Long* tribe . . . a man of considerable strength and dexterity, although left handed . . . rather older [than his brother Patko] but more savage and ferocious'.[20] Tyers reported to La Trobe: '[j]udging from the deference and respect the Gipps Land Blacks pay him, there is no doubt Bungeleene is a man of no small consideration among them . . . This may account for the want of success hitherto attending the search after him'.[21]

Trooper Owen Cowan, in his journal entry for 26 January 1847, does not describe Bungelene as either an elusive or threatening figure: 'Bungeleene came up to the Station accompanied by 100 Blacks—offering us a Black Gin and calling her Loondigon (the name we understood the white female was known by). He wanted Blankets—The Gin had Two children—Bungeleene is a left handed man, rather old'.[22] Expeditionist Donald McLeod presented him as 'a fine Looking man apparently about 45 years of age and well made very kind to his women . . . he is very fond of the Highland Pipes'.[23]

Throughout the first expedition, Bungelene had been a continuing enigmatic presence in the search party's letters and journals. The second expedition focussed its energies on capturing and holding him and members of his family hostage until the White Woman was delivered up. On 10 April 1847 Bungelene was apprehended by Sergeant Windredge and brought to Commissioner Tyers's headquarters at Eagle Point. He remained there under guard until early May, when the expeditionists took him with them to the mountains to try to locate the White Woman.

Although Bungelene's capture and 'compulsory detention' were ostensibly to facilitate retrieval of the White Woman, their significance goes beyond that. His incarceration, while bolstering white confidence, would have been aimed at demoralising the tribe and reducing its capacity to wage guerilla warfare upon the Gipps Land squatters. The killing or capture of a resistance leader was a well-known strategy of warfare. The English had used it with effect against the Scots to quell Jacobite rebellions during the eighteenth century. If the settlers had wanted Bungelene removed from Gipps Land so as to break Kurnai resistance, the story that he held the White Woman proved an effective means to that end.

When the 'compulsory detention' of Bungelene at Eagle Point did not result in the White Woman's retrieval, Tyers had an official document drawn up—a Memorandum of Agreement—to which Bungelene was induced to put his mark. The publication of the Memorandum in the *Herald* in July demonstrated to the people of Melbourne that the government was taking serious measures to deal with the recalcitrant Bungelene.[24]

> Memorandum of agreement entered into this day between Charles J. Tyers, Esq., on the part of Her Majesty's Government, and Bungelene, Chief of the Gipps Land Tribes:—
>
> I, Bungelene, promise to deliver to Charles J. Tyers the white female residing with the Gipps Land blacks, provided a party of whites and Western Port blacks proceed with me to the mountains at as early a day as may be convenient, for the purpose of obtaining her from my brothers. I also agree to leave my two wives and two children with the said Charles J. Tyers, as hostages for the fulfilment of my promise. And I, Charles J. Tyers, promise, on the part of Her Majesty's Government, to give Bungelene one boat, with oars, a tent, four blankets, a guernsey frock, some fish-hooks and a fishing-line, and a tomahawk for the said Bungelene's own use, and six blankets, two tomahawks, three guernsey frocks, and other articles between three or four men of the said Bungelene's tribes who may be instrumental in the recovery of the said white female, conditioned that the said Bungelene fulfil his part of the agreement.
>
> BUNGELENE   x his mark.

Although no formal charges against Bungelene had been made, at the time he 'signed' this document he had been held in custody at Eagle Point, closely guarded, for over a month. His command of English was minimal. He was not literate. The memorandum, with its implied legal status, made Bungelene an unwitting party to his own detention and that of his wives and children. In a private communication to La Trobe, Tyers stated that Bungelene 'seem[ed] thoroughly to understand the nature of the agreement, and that it is equally binding on both parties'. Neither La Trobe nor Governor FitzRoy, to whom Tyers's correspondence was duly forwarded, questioned this assertion, or objected to the undertaking.[25]

The Memorandum of Agreement with Bungelene was foreshadowed in February 1847 in a letter to the editor of the *Gazette*, pertaining to the removal of Aborigines from Van Diemen's Land to facilitate white occupation. In suggesting how the second expedition to rescue the White Woman should be conducted, the anonymous correspondent—'A Fellow Colonist'—recommended:

> sending forth a competent leader, in company only with some two or three blacks as guides, interpreters, and negotiators. It was in this way, and this way only, that Chief Protector Robinson succeeded in bringing the hostile tribes of V. D. Land into Hobart Town, and causing them to enter into a treaty of deportation to Flinders Island, [after] Military, Police, and posse comitatus of the colony, had failed in coercing them to the same end.[26]

There was little precedent for such a document in Port Phillip and its legality must have been questionable. An earlier 'treaty' which John Batman, on behalf of the Port Phillip Association of Van Diemen's Land, had attempted in 1835 to effect with the Port Phillip tribes was ruled invalid by Governor Bourke and the Colonial Secretary, in London.[27]

As contracted in the Memorandum of Agreement, Bungelene accompanied the expedition party on an arduous fourteen-day trek through the mountain range due west from Eagle Point, in search of the White Woman. The party followed a direction different from that taken by De Villiers's party, and ventured into country which the 'Worrigals' called 'Bo Bo' towards the Murray River. As with the first expedition, much importance was attached to ephemeral 'evidence' of the woman's existence which the party encountered along the way. McLeod's journal records that on 25 May the party made its fire 'on the spot where [Bungelene] pointed out as been the Identical spot where the Londicon Slept'; on 27 May the party stopped at one of Bungelene's camps 'where he pointed out to us the Mia Mia which

the White woman Lay in when with him'. On 29 May the party
came upon 'the remains of three Mia Mias where we found a Log of
wood which the boy said was used to tiy to the White Womans Legs
the Grass was still on the Log'.

Sergeant Windredge marked trees in several of the campsites and
McLeod left written messages for the woman:

> Intimating on them that there were a strong Armed party out
> in Search of the White female Detained by the Aboriginal
> Natives telling her in Case that she found them to Look out for
> any opportunity of Escape which she might find or Observe
> fires in her Neighbourhood for a week or ten days from the
> 24th of May the Date of our Arival in that vicinity.
> Extract from McLeod's journal, Tuesday, 25 May [1847]

On 31 May, after ten days' travelling in extremely cold and difficult conditions, and with no sign of the 'fugitives' or the White
Woman, the expeditionists 'upbraided [Bungelene] with his Du-
plicity' and threatened to 'shoot him for Leading us astray'. The party
arrived back at Eagle Point in the early hours of 4 June. McLeod
vented his frustration at the failure of the venture by blaming
Bungelene:

> it is my firm belief that he would have Given up the woman
> only that he is afraid that she will tell about the murder of the
> Crew of the Vessel who have all Indoubtedly been murdered by
> him and others of his Brutal Tribe the woman would very soon
> be Given up to us if we were allowed to put him in Irons and
> Give him nothing but the ration Given by Government but in
> place of that he is fed and Coaxed by Every one . . .
> Extract from McLeod's journal Saturday, 5 June [1847]

On 8 June, McLeod recorded that:

> the old man is very uneasey . . . we have been telling him that
> the White people are Comming from Melbourne to Shoot the
> blacks on the Islands and in the Mountains and that we are to
> bring him to Melbourne there to be hanged all which he
> beleives which makes him rather Down hearted and frightened

while out with us in the Mountains he asked Tacka Warron if
we would alow him to bring his Lubra to Melbourne with him
that shews that he has No Great Intention of Giving up the
woman.

Extract from McLeod's journal Tuesday, 8 June [1847]

On 11 June, still at Eagle Point, Bungelene allegedly told the
expeditionists that 'Nick Narrot has the woman towards the Buckan
country and wishes us to Go out in Search of him and the White
Woman'. Apparently the information was not taken seriously as, on
12 June, McLeod noted that some of the expedition party had
'Started for Melbourne taking with them the Man Bungalenie [sic]
and his family with them on the road'. According to information
provided by another, unnamed, member of the expedition party:

> Bungelene, two lubras, and two picaninnies, were consigned to
> the charge of William Peters, who with the expeditionists, Hill,
> Kelly, Hartnett, and four blacks escorted them overland from
> Gipps Land to the Narra Narra Warren police station, and then
> handed them over to the safe keeping of Capt. Dana . . .[28]

The euphemism 'safe keeping', like the catch-phrase 'died from
the visitation of God' which, as noted previously, was used to explain
the numerous Aboriginal deaths in custody in the early 1840s, masks
the brutality which prisoners at times experienced at the hands of
police. Assistant Protector Thomas was to testify in 1861 to the
Central Board appointed to watch over the interests of Aborigines
in the Colony of Victoria that Bungelene 'was brutally chained to a
gum tree for many days and nights' at Narre Narre Warren, until
Thomas 'brought the matter officially under the notice of the
Government'.[29]

Although the purpose and legality of Bungelene's detention at
Narre Narre Warren was never established, none of the government
officers appears to have been willing to make a decision to release
him. Tyers passed responsibility to La Trobe: 'I have . . . no means of
detaining Bungaleene, his women and children, but have requested
Mr. Dana . . . to take charge of them at Head Quarters until your
Honor shall decide what further steps are to be taken'.[30] Captain

Dana, too, wrote to La Trobe requesting instructions.[31] La Trobe replied to Dana that he had not yet received intelligence from Tyers and did not know under what circumstances he had sent up Bungelene. 'All I can say is that he may be detained till I see what the dispatches I suppose the party brings with them'.[32] La Trobe, who a short time before had expressed scepticism as to the White Woman's existence, now sought instructions from the Governor as to the course which Dana was to pursue and 'to the degree of restraint which he is to impose upon Bungeleene's movements'. La Trobe acknowledged that:

> It is true that Bungelene cannot be detained by legal forms, and I am very doubtful whether any good can be expected to result from his detention; but it is also true that as far as his own acts and supposed admissions can be received in proof, he may justly be charged with holding a European female as his Captive, as it may be presumed, against her will.[33]

La Trobe's hope that the mystery would be cleared up by information provided by one of Bungelene's wives proved vain. Protector Robinson, sent by La Trobe to Narre Narre Warren to make a report, was not able to elicit any additional information. Bungelene's replies were, Robinson said, reluctantly given, vague and unsatisfactory, and his own scepticism about the White Woman remained unaltered.[34] Robinson, however, did not challenge Bungelene's detention, nor did he as Protector act as advocate for Bungelene. Governor FitzRoy also declined involvement.[35]

Despite paper-shuffling and buck-passing between the various government officers, the 'lady-killer' (as the *Gazette* called Bungelene) remained in custody at Narre Narre Warren for a further fifteen months, until his death on 21 November 1848.[36] Dana had proposed, and La Trobe had authorised, Bungelene's return to Gipps Land in January 1848, and it is unclear why this did not occur.[37]

The Day Book of the Native Police Station at Narre Narre Warren chronicles the sorry saga in half a dozen entries from 28 June 1847 when '[t]he late Gippsland Expedition Party arived Bringing Bungeleena and two lubras with their Five Picaninies and handed them over to commandt of Native Police for the consideration of the government'. The Day Book records that Bungelene was kept 'in custody' at the station, 'but as little confined as possible to prevent his escape. A Sentry Placed on the wach house with the door open to let in the air'. He was allowed '2 hours exercise every day for the benefit of his health'. On 1 July 'Mr. Wm Dana went to Melbourne to acquaint His Honor the Superintendent of Bungeeleena', and La Trobe's visit to the station the following day to see Bungelene is recorded. On 28 July Bungelene was 'Very menancolly being detained so long'. On 8 August he was moved from the watch house to the tailors shop, and on 9 August to the thatch house. On 15 September he was issued with 'two pair new Blankets'. There are no further entries for 15 months until, on 21 November 1848, 'Bungelena died', and on 22 November, 'Bungeleena buried—all the men on the Station attended'.[38]

Bungelene's detention did not bring about the retrieval of the White Woman. Bungelene did, however, help the expeditionists to locate the figurehead from a wrecked colonial vessel, which was in the possession of the Lakes tribes. Commissioner Tyers informed La Trobe on 10 April 1847 that Bungelene had described the figurehead 'as an image of a white woman, with a Cap on her head, curly hair and her arms broken off at the elbow holding a spear'. The figurehead, Tyers said, 'is preserved in the Scrub, near the beach, and can be obtained'.[39] The pursuit of the figurehead was an ongoing preoccupation for the members of the second expedition throughout April, and its retrieval provided a provisional form of narrative closure. On 20 April, the *Herald*, citing an unnamed informant writing from Eagle Point, informed readers that Bungelene had told Windredge 'where the latter could get the figure-head of the wrecked vessel out of which the white woman came, and by the description he gave of the head, Sergeant Windridge feels certain that it was the "Britannia," brig'.[40]

After numerous attempts over several weeks, the figurehead was recovered. Windredge claimed it had been 'repeatedly hidden in different places, although repeatedly promised to be given during a period of six months'. McLeod records the retrieval:

> Bungalenie was in Great Glee when we understood his Meaning about the figurehead of the Vessel which he says he will Bring us to in the morning if we Chose. the Arms were Cut of at the Elbows the Breasts Large Like a hoorlots and the Hair Long

and that him Carry one big waddy like him Corong stick and
Tree Like um spear which they point out by the three fingers
meaning the Trident which Brittania Invarably Carry . . .

Extract from McLeod's Journal, Friday, 9 [April 1847]

Sergeant Windradge and a boats Crew Left head quarters at
9 O'clock A.M. for the purpose of finding the often promised
figurehead they sailed over to the back of Phoul Phoul in a
back water off Lake Reeves when they Suceeded in finding the
article so much Desired and proceeded Immediately home-
wards where they arived about 9 O'clock A.M. and secured the
figurehead in Sergeant Windradges house for the night it is
only the Bust of a Woman which has hade something fastened
on the temples which has been removed and part of both
Breasts Cut with some blunt instrument it seems to have been
painted a Coper Colour and Green where it was fastened to the
stem of the Vessel to which it formerly belong it looks as if
wrenched of by some force where are marks of two nails on
Each side of the neck and on the breast below the Chin as if
there hade been stays on suporters to the figure from the Dread
Nord as a Guard for the face which is frequently the Case in
Ship to prevent the stays on the port ropes from Chafing the
paint off them in bad weather . . .

Extract from McLeod's Journal, Saturday, 1 May [1847]

The *Herald* reported that '[a]round the "figure head" it seems
the natives repeatedly danced, and they held it in high veneration.
No wonder then that the white captive is so difficult to recover'.[41]
The *Argus*, citing Commissioner Tyers, on 7 May similarly informed
readers that the figurehead 'was in possession of the blacks, and
treated as an idol, forming the centre around which they danced
their most solemn corroborees'.[42]

The description of Aborigines dancing around the figurehead, as
a fetish, is more a product of overactive European imagination, than
of events which might have transpired in Gipps Land in the mid-
1840s. Depictions such as these, like references to cannibalism and
infanticide, are stock features in colonial adventure narratives and
tales of empire. From these clichéd images of Aborigines as fetishistic
'savages', it is a short step to defining them as less than human.

In contrast, Bungelene's gleeful response when he realised that the expeditionists wanted the figurehead seems a moment of reversal—a reminder that it was Europeans, not Kurnai, who were guilty of fetishism. So firmly entrenched was the connection of the 'captive' woman with the report of the lost *Britannia* that the figurehead was imagined to resemble 'Britannia', with trident. McLeod's disappointed response when he saw that 'it is only the Bust of a Woman' reveals the expeditionists' emotional investment in retrieving a 'Britannia'.

In his 14 June letter to La Trobe, Charles Tyers described the figurehead in his possession as 'the bust of a female, not quite the size of life, rudely carved, and appears to have been painted red, with the eyes white. Most of the red paint is worn off leaving the priming of a dark color. The figure-head has evidently belonged to a small craft, probably Colonial—but certainly was never intended to represent Britannia'.[43]

An unnamed correspondent writing to the editor of the *Argus* in late July 1847 identified the figurehead as that belonging to the *Yarra Yarra* which 'sailed under the command of Captain Lancey from Launceston, about the beginning of 1839 with passengers, of whom were the Captain's own family, and the Misses Seargantsons who kept a school at Launceston'.[44] The introduction of Misses Seargantsons offer a belated further possible identity for the White Woman.

The alleged repeated assertions by Kurnai that the White Woman did exist and a 'sighting' of the White Woman by a stockman, on the Sydney side of the Snowy River, reported in the *Argus* in July 1847, shortly after the expeditionists had returned to Melbourne, prolonged speculation and made it difficult for the government to close the case.[45]

Even after the two unsuccessful expeditions, and searches over eighteen months by government and private parties, the 'idea of a young, lovely, and accomplished female, being "cribbed, cabined and confined" in the Harem of one of the petty chiefs of a barbarous tribe of the wretched aborigines of New Holland', as the *Gazette* put it, could not be completely dispelled.[46] The *Herald* in October 1847 proposed 'appeal[ing] to the sympathy of a Port Phillip public to enable the Gipps Land Expedition Committee to send off a fresh party in pursuit'. However, the matter does not appear to have been taken further.[47]

On 5 November the *Herald* in an Extraordinary edition reported, under the heading 'Murder of the Captive "White Woman" at Gipps Land' (the use of inverted commas for 'White Woman' seems to mark the figure's conversion into legend at this point), that the remains of a white female and child had been discovered at a place called Jemmy's Point, about four miles from Commissioner Tyers's residence. This intelligence was conveyed to the *Herald* by Mr David Campbell 'from the station of Mr. McMillan'. The ubiquitous McMillan, requested by Tyers to attend an inquest upon the remains of the woman and child, had stated to the *Herald*'s informant:

> that there could not be an atom of doubt of one of them being that of a white female, which was easily evident from her head—that Mr. Tyers had collected all the official information he could upon the point, which would be duly forwarded in a few days to his Honor the Superintendent, and further, that the bodies were to be decently interred the following day . . . upon which occasion a number of the neighbouring settlers had signified their intention of being present.[48]

It was fitting that McMillan should be present at the inquest. He had initiated the rumour and had kept it alive for over six years.

According to the *Herald*'s informant, after Bungelene's arrest, the woman had fallen into the hands of his brother who, after a fight, and 'according to barbarian custom' had lost her to 'the conqueror'. Bungelene's brother 'brooding over the loss of his white prize, meditated a deed of vengeance'. He lay in wait one night 'and murdered the woman and her child'.

The charge that the White Woman had been murdered, published by the *Herald* and iterated in less sensational form in the *Patriot* of 6 November,[49] did not concur with Tyers's official report to La Trobe.[50] Tyers advised on 2 November that he had learned from Patco, the son of Bungelene, that 'the unfortunate female was drowned in Lake King by the upsetting of a canoe, during a Gale of wind, while crossing from Tambo Bluff to the opposite shore about four or five months ago and her body, being recovered by Patco was placed in a tree near the spot'. Tyers organised a crew of four native troopers 'with a view to ascertain if this story had any foundation— and if so, to the removal of the remains for burial to some civilized part of the country'. The desire to retrieve the body to a 'civilized' place distinguishes the treatment accorded a white woman from that of many white men who died in the bush and were buried in unconsecrated ground.

After two ineffectual searches, the four native troopers returned with bones, 'which the boy said were those of Toondigan the white woman'. The deceased, Tyers said, appeared to have been 'about 5 feet 4 inches in height of Middle age—with Black and Grey hair'. Tyers stated that he intended to seek confirmation from Dr Arbuckle as to whether the remains were those of a white female. If he did so, there is no record that Tyers communicated the result to La Trobe. Given the efforts expended by both government and private parties over many months, and given that Bungelene was still being held in custody at Narre Narre Warren pending charges, it might be expected that the Melbourne coroner would have been required to examine the remains. If the body was that of a white female, as claimed, efforts could then have been made to establish the woman's identity. The condition of the remains may have made identification impossible. Perhaps the identity of the female was irrelevant if closure of the case was the principal aim of the exercise.

La Trobe wrote to Tyers on 20 November advising that he saw no reason to doubt 'the probable truth of the real existence . . . of such female . . . and [saw] nothing improbable in the account now given of her death', but suggested that 'a tolerably conclusive proof that the remains recently brought to you were those of the European Female as represented would be obtained by its being ascertained that the deceased had actually left a child and that that child was an half caste'. There is no record of any further communication between Tyers and La Trobe regarding the identity of the body of the woman. Thus, the government preferred to let matters rest.

The extent to which the White Woman's story was used as a vehicle for anti-Kurnai propaganda is reflected in the differences between McMillan's version of how the woman and child met their deaths (published in the *Herald* and *Gazette* of 6 November 1847) and Tyers's (unpublished) version. George Cavenagh had written to La Trobe on 5 November soliciting particulars of the 'authentic intelligence . . . just . . . received by the Govt respecting the murder of the "White Woman" & her child . . . for publication in an Extraordinary issue of the P. P. Herald to be published this afternoon'.[51] La Trobe's reply, printed at the end of the article, referred only to a hasty note which Walsh had addressed to Mr Dana advising him of the finding of the body and that Tyers had gone down to investigate. This was, the *Herald* said, 'the only intelligence which it is in the power of Mr. La Trobe to give the Chairman of the Gipps Land Expedition Committee'.

The *Patriot*, however, was unprepared to let the *Herald* report go unchallenged. It published a brief notice under 'Odds and Ends' on 23 November advising that the remains were 'said to be those of an aboriginal female, and the "yarn" about her murder by Bungeleene's brother a specimen of the [*Herald*] editor's "making up"'.[52] The *Patriot* reported on 30 November that La Trobe had started for Gipps Land and would 'investigate the rumours as to the remains of "the white woman," said to have been found on the edge of a lake'.[53] On 24 December the *Patriot* had one more jibe at the *Herald*: 'The hoax played off upon the gullability [*sic*] of the "Herald" . . . is affording no little amusement to the wags of Gipps Land. We learn from good authority that the bones found were identified as those of a lubra, and her child.'[54] Presumably, one of those 'wags' was McMillan.

By November 1847, the story had probably outlived its newsworthiness and the *Herald* recognised and took advantage of the opportunity for narrative closure. The report of the woman's death relieved the citizens of Melbourne, and the government, of the need to undertake any further efforts on her behalf. It also solved the narrative problem of how to bring about a satisfactory conclusion to a story in which the heroine's experiences would make her return to polite society difficult, if not impossible. On behalf of those who wished to believe that the remains found at Jemmy's Point were those of the White Woman, the *Herald*'s eulogy provided an appropriate sense of closure:

Death though regarded as a mishap by others, must have descended as a blessing upon this poor woman, who has undergone a trial far more harrowing and terrible than even Death's worst moments.

She is now no more—and it is a melancholy gratification that the public suspense has been at length relieved, by her discovery even in death.[55]

CHAPTER 7

Investing in a Legend

'About eighty years ago the small white community of Gippsland was deeply stirred
by strange reports that a woman of their own race had fallen into the hands of the
aboriginal tribes . . . In the mist of distant years the episode now appears as a
curious piece of Australian mythology, comparable with that of the ancient Greeks.'
'A Gippsland Mystery: Story of the Captive White Woman',
Age, 5 November 1927.

'But an old legend is hard to kill.'
William Spence Logan, 1927.

The White Woman legend has been a valued and contested cultural
property for over 160 years. Its perennial appeal for storytellers and
readers lies, at least in part, in the unresolvable narrative tension
emanating from the mystery of the woman's existence. The legend's
endurance, its emergence at regular intervals throughout the nineteenth and twentieth centuries and the particular variants which
have been promulgated as 'history' attest to its ongoing role in white
post-settlement mythology as a transformative narrative. The legend
remains a source of nostalgia, revised and sentimentalised.

The distinction between 'literary' and 'historical' adaptations of
the story are a somewhat arbitrary taxonomic device. The same
characteristics of literary production are employed: symbolism, allegory, character and plot development and narrative structuring
devices.

Short stories, poems and novellas which involve fictionalised
characters and events frequently make claims to historical accuracy
or authenticity. Conversely, historical accounts incorporate fictional
embellishments which originated in the 'literary' romances, such as
the woman being accompanied by a staghound or being rescued and
returned home to England or Scotland.[1] Selective details taken from

the early accounts, notably the wreck of the *Britannia*, messages cut on trees, the Heart, the ship's figurehead, have been picked up and perpetuated in 'reminiscences', and in family and local histories, while new features, including additional potential identities for the woman, have been introduced.[2]

The White Woman legend, whether told as history or fiction, has reflected and reproduced understandings of 'race' in Gipps Land. For Daniel Bunce, in his 1857 *Australasiatic Reminiscences*,[3] the legend provided more than an anecdotal framework within which to present his travels through Gipps Land. Bunce relates how his party meets two people associated with the White Woman: James Warman 'the leader [*sic*] of the party who went in search of the white woman', and Pack Bullock Jack, the overseer of a station on the Snowy Mountains. Bunce attributes the rumour's origin to Jack, though Jack's version differs from the reports in circulation throughout the 1840s:

> on one occasion while searching for cattle, [Jack] suddenly surprised a number of blacks who seeing him took to the Snowy River. Upon jumping into the water, the hair of one of the women expanded on the surface like a horse's tail, as he expressed it, and from this circumstance he concluded that it must have been a white woman.[4]

Jack does not employ other primary markers of racial difference. Instead he arrives at his conclusion that the woman is white by comparing her hair with a horse's tail. Aborigines commonly were described in colonial documents in animalistic terms. H. B. Morris in 1843 evokes a disparaging menagerie when he describes a Gipps Land Aboriginal woman as having a 'fine foxy smell; a skin of an Indian buffalo; the lantern jaw and flat nose of a baboon; and the mouth of a hippopotamus'. When he gives her a looking glass she 'put her paws behind the glass, like a cat'. As he approaches the camp, the 'gins' run away into the bush like 'so many emus'.[5] One might therefore expect that the horse's tail analogy would have been presented as evidence that the woman was Aboriginal.

The horse's tail recalls the lock of hair from McMillan's report, which is also taken to signify absent European femininity. Female hair played an important role in the way Victorian women were represented in fiction. In the context of European definitions of middle-class female subjectivity, hair was held to be expressive of a range of female characteristics including sexuality, beauty, vulnerability, domesticity, and magic.[6]

Jack's story of the White Woman, like others which paste white 'history' over an already occupied landscape, is decontextualised from the conflict accompanying settlement. In recording the White Woman stories for posterity in local histories, a few notable variations acknowledged that Aborigines were killed by the search parties. Fewer have acknowledged or confronted the sweeping accusations made by Warman and De Villiers against the settlers and the Native Police under the white leaders Dana and Walsh. Versions of the White Woman story, recorded as memories, have elided elements of local and family histories which later generations of Gippslanders either were unaware of, or did not wish to confront, or perpetuate. For subsequent generations, the story is perpetuated in the guise of quaint, mythic, colourful, or romantic tales.

The historical documents also produce the White Woman legend as contested cultural property. Commentators or historians writing from outside Gippsland have in general located the legend within Melbournian or Port Phillipian history, and have emphasised the role which Melbournians took in promoting the White Woman cause. Gippslanders have isolated the story as a Gippsland event and focussed on its place in Gippsland history, with some acting as advocate for, or custodian of, a family or local story, and others, such as the Rev. G. Cox and W. C. Cuthill, taking a broader, more regional perspective. Competing claims for historical accuracy and for ownership of the story are enacted around the notion of local history as embedded in oral narratives and family memory *versus* history as text, located in archival records and authenticated by historical societies.

In 1874, the White Woman story was recapped by A Melbournite of '38, in an article published in the *Australian Journal*. Despite the authoritative claim of the article's title, 'The Early History of Victoria', the subtitle—'Being Reminiscences of Bygone Days'—acknowledged the subjectivity of a process which entailed nostalgic recollections of past events from a vantage point of some forty years later. Few readers in 1874 would have remembered the events of the mid-1840s when the White Woman story was news in Port Phillip.[7] 'A Melbournite' claimed residency from almost the earliest days of European settlement and his *nom-de-plume* asserted his authority as eyewitness to early Melbourne history. He preserved for posterity, as 'history' and 'reminiscence', a unified and closed narrative which did not encourage the reader to ask questions about the broader historical context within which the story was produced and circulated.

Thomas Strode, one-time editor of the *Gazette*, was almost certainly A Melbournite of '38.[8] A Melbournite claimed that 'the unfortunate creature [Mrs. C., or the White Woman] accompanied the family of the writer from Sydney in October 1838'. Strode, with his wife and children, arrived in Melbourne on the *Denmark Hill* from Sydney in October 1838.[9] His is the only family listed among the passengers.

Similarly, An Englishman, in a letter written to the editor of the *Sydney Herald* in 1846, had claimed that 'Mrs. Capel . . . accompanied my family to Port Phillip, in the "Denmark Hill," at the close of the year '38'.[10] The letter, which carried a Sydney address was presented as the opinion of a private citizen, unconnected with the Melbourne newspapers. If, as the clues indicate, An Englishman was another of Strode's *noms de plume*, this would place Strode alongside George Cavenagh and the, as yet unidentified, Humanitas as central figures in the development of the White Woman cause in 1846.

In a postscript on the fate of the White Woman, A Melbournite said that after many years she was recovered:

> though unfortunately in an idiotic state, and unable to utter a single word of her native language, or understand any question put to her, therefore no tidings of the fate of her ship companions could be elicited; and notwithstanding her husband ministered to all her wants, and made her as comfortable under the circumstances as care and money could bestow, yet the pitiable woman never recovered her reason, the shock to the system being beyond medical aid and all the unwearied attention lavished upon her.

There is no comparable ending to the story in either historical or literary versions, although 'A Lay of Lament' by J. R. M. intimated derangement in the line '[s]ad, sear'd, and craz'd she seem'd to be, fast verging to despair'. Given the imagined horrors to which she was said to have been subjected, the representation of the woman in an 'idiotic state' was narratively consistent. It satisfied the reader's desire to know 'what happened' while (because of her speechlessness) precluding possibilities of disclosure about her experiences. This version, which overrode the failure to recover the woman, avoided the unresolved doubt about the woman's existence which characterised the actual events. Through A Melbournite, the woman and the legend are reclaimed from Gipps Land, for Melbourne.

Melbourne commentator Edmund Finn further consolidated Melbourne's claim to the White Woman. Finn attended the White Woman public meeting in 1846 as a reporter for the *Port Phillip Herald* and possibly contributed White Woman articles throughout 1846 and 1847. Under the *nom de plume* Garryowen, Finn represented the story in his *Chronicles* of 1888 as a composite ten-page version of the rumours and events leading up to and including the several searches for the White Woman (or women).[11] He acknowledged the story's consumption by the newsmakers and public of Melbourne: 'it was the universal topic of conversation, and any scrap of information tending to throw light on the terrible mystery was eagerly devoured'.[12]

He included 'White Women Captured by the Blacks' and an account of William Buckley as contrasting formative events in interracial relations from Melbourne's early colonial period. His account of Buckley is restrained. His highly charged account of the White Woman indicates an emotional and territorial investment in the legend. His opening lines establish a privileged position for the event in the (then) fifty-year history of the district (later state), and for his self-defined role as chronicler:

> There is not in the whole history of Victoria a more harrowing episode than the capture and detention of three European women by the Gippsland Aborigines; or one, now more utterly forgotten, and of which no lengthy or complete narrative has appeared in any publication, if the disjointed accounts printed in some of the early newspapers be excepted.[13]

Garryowen's account, although more comprehensive than A Melbournite's version, nevertheless was selective, partial, and in places incorrect. He gave no impression that those involved in perpetrating the rumours or organising the public meeting were motivated by anything other than altruism. Elsewhere in the *Chronicles*, however, he acknowledges the cut-and-thrust of public life in Melbourne and comments that George Cavenagh was 'utterly insincere, figuratively as hollow as "the big drum," a *sobriquet* by which he was known'.[14]

In stressing the noble ideals of the public cause, Garryowen avoided its racist and political implications. References to the allegations by De Villiers and Warman of settler and Native Police brutality against the Kurnai were not mentioned. Of De Villiers's despatch which detailed charges against Walsh and Dana, he noted only that 'it was mostly taken up with reference to altercations with the Government party, and contained nothing of import to this narrative. It, however, testified to various kindnesses on the part of Commissioner Tyers, and the good-tempered efficiency of Trooper-sergeant Windridge'.[15] Bungelene and his family, he stated, 'after being detained . . . for some time . . . were released'.[16]

By the mid-1880s when the *Chronicles* were in preparation, Melbourne, as a thriving capital city, was a testament to the dreams and aspirations of the earliest settlers. Garryowen described writing the *Chronicles* as a 'retrogressive pilgrimage', 'a pleasure-trip to the region of Long-ago—an excursion to Phantom-land'.[17] His project invited a favourable, indeed nostalgic, assessment of Melbourne's humble beginnings. The positioning of the White Woman saga as an heroic Melbourne narrative reflected his own involvement in the White Woman cause and his awareness of its transformative function in Melbourne's development from settlement to provincial town. His revival of the charge of cannibalism amongst the Kurnai reproduces the devouring indigene, whereas European colonists are presented as architects of the metropolitan centre of Melbourne.

The ongoing claim by Melbourne for possession of the White Woman story as cultural property continued into the twentieth century. Pseudonymous writer Historicus, writing in the *Argus* of 25 May 1912, centred the claim on the journal of the second expedition: 'a modest manuscript volume in Mr Armstrong's cabinet of treasures in the Melbourne Public Library'.[18] The journal was, for Historicus, an historical curiosity and a 'fit companion' for the other works in the cabinet of treasures:

> John Batman's journal of his expedition from Launceston to Port Phillip, from May 10 to June 6, 1835, and . . . the Field Book of John Helder Wedge, containing notes and sketches made while surveying Port Phillip a few months later—. . . and making with it a trilogy of bold and earnest endeavour in the early days of Victoria's history.[19]

Historicus's standpoint for the story was Melbourne. Here the expedition was organised by the benevolent Melbourne public. And here the journal now took its place in the Melbourne Public Library's historic collection. Gippsland in 1843 was, Historicus says, 'almost a terra incognita'. While it may have seemed so from Melbourne, it was not *terra incognita* to the Kurnai or to Gipps Land squatters, although large parts were still unexplored by white people at the time. Historicus's recognition of the journal's significance as a public document contained in a State Library collection illustrates (to borrow from cultural theorist Chris Healy) 'the association between paper records in museums and the work of social memory'. Healy argues for the centrality of the explorer's role in forging historical imagination by 'invent[ing] the ground on which history was being made'.[20]

Putting forward an alternative view, Allan McLean's 'Recollections of Early Gippsland', published in the *Bairnsdale Advertiser* of 31 January 1905, anchored the story in personal memory and Gipps Land folklore. McLean recollected that a white woman was supposed to be living with the Aborigines in Gippsland when he was a boy, and he located McMillan's 'sighting' of the woman 'about two miles and a half east of where Sale is situated now . . . The spot has been known as "The Heart" ever since'. McLean's admission that bloodshed occurred in the searches for the White Woman–'[h]undreds of aborigines were killed in conflicts with them, but the pursuit yielded little or nothing', and that ' "Bringelina" . . . died in prison without saying anything'—is unusually candid.

Personal memory—this time Aboriginal—was also cited as authentication for one of the more unusual versions of the story. George

Illustration of White Woman drowning (artist unnamed). From George
Hermann's 'The Broken Honeymoon: An Extraordinary Tale of a White Woman
among the Blacks' (1913).
Reproduced by permission of La Trobe Collection, State Library of Victoria.

Hermann's 'The Broken Honeymoon: An Extraordinary Tale of a
White Woman among the Blacks', published in *Life Magazine* of
1 August 1913, propagated the tale as 'the true version' of 'one of the
strangest happenings of the early days of Australian colonization',
which he maintained 'has not so far as I know appeared before in
print, and is known only to a few'.[21] The story of the woman's fate,
he said, had been gathered from a missionary to the Gippsland
blacks and corroborated by Jimmy Scott, an Aborigine who lived for
many years on the Ramahyuck Mission Station and claimed to be
the last living man who had been implicated in the raid to rescue the
woman.

In Hermann's version, a settler and his bride were on their honeymoon at the Stockyard Creek and Turton's Creek diggings in South
Gippsland when the woman mysteriously disappeared. She was
carried off because she wore a brooch with a peculiar stone which the
Aborigines believed to be a very rare charm 'which combined the
power of bringing luck to the tribe and of conferring unlimited
power of life and death on the wearer'.[22] She was held as a 'mascotte'
by the tribe. After some five years, when rumours about the woman
reached the Rev. F. A. Hagenauer, the missionary in charge of the
Ramahyuck Mission Station, he persuaded the authorities to provide
assistance to search for her. A 'long, stern chase' ensued across the

lakes to Jimmy's Point. Success seemed within their grasp, when in midstream:

> the poor woman jumped to her feet and holding out her arms to her rescuers, called to them in agonised tones to be quick. Whether her sudden movement capsized the frail canoe or split the bark from which it was made is uncertain, for Jimmy Scott, who told me the story, was in another canoe. At any rate it sank and under the very eyes of the rescuers the woman was sucked down by the current and never seen again.[23]

Unlike other versions of the story, this account places the events well beyond the period of exploration and early settlement. The story is framed within two defining moments of later colonial endeavour in Gippsland—the gold rushes and the arrival of missionaries. During the 1860s, the two missionary reserves, Ramahyuck, under the control of the Rev. Hagenauer, and Lake Tyers, run by the Rev. John Bulmer, were to play a central role in confining the remnant Kurnai population. For the Kurnai, gold discovery and missions brought further competition for tribal lands and concerted efforts to break them from their traditional lifestyle.

Hermann's/Jimmy Scott's orally transmitted version was disputed by the Rev. George Cox, 'hon. secretary South Gippsland sub-centre Historical Society of Victoria'. Cox stated that the writer broke new ground with the story but did not touch the real mystery of the White Woman, which had its origins from 1840, whereas the [Stockyard Creek] diggings dated only from 1870.[24]

The debate continued in the January 1914 issue of *Life Magazine* with Cox producing 'historical facts' to discredit Hermann's story that the tribe was large enough to have taken and kept a woman captive.[25] Cox's facts comprised statistics from a Parliamentary report on Aborigines, dated 1853–54, which put the population of the Corner Inlet [Bratauolung] tribe at a mere fifteen men, nine women and eight children, and the *Victorian Year Book* for 1874, which indicated that the European population in Gipps Land was, by that time, 1057. Hermann defended his story on the basis that it had been told to him by Mr Hagenauer and corroborated by Mrs Hagenauer: 'Because it was unknown and unrecorded and strange, does not take away from its accuracy.' Cox's rejoinder was denied publication, and the debate ceased.

Hermann's version was also raised, and discounted, by Mr W. M. Buntine (M.A.) in an article in the *Victorian Historical Magazine* in June 1914. Buntine dismissed as unreliable the version of the story 'supplied by an old blackfellow of Rahmayuck Mission Station', as '[i]t is well known that the . . . blacks . . . have a propensity for giving such a story as they deem will be most acceptable to the listener'. Buntine considered, however, that there were some facts which brought the story 'out of the realm of mythology into that of actual history, and as such are worthy of being preserved'.[26] These 'facts' included information supplied by Mr John Buntine, Senior, of Echuca, who was a member of a party of pioneers which about 1841 had disturbed an encampment of blacks near Port Albert. Buntine Senior's version of the event—a variation on McMillan's account— does not include a 'sighting' of the woman, and in place of the plethora of items catalogued by McMillan, the party finds only a towel and an article of female attire which had been used to block the ends of a canoe. Buntine Senior reported that the party had found 'the figure of a heart cut in the soft earth, with a line from it pointing to a dense bank of ti-tree scrub into which the blacks had fled' at another recently deserted camp, in the district now known as the Heart.[27]

The article included a reproduced photograph of the *verso* side of one of the White Woman handkerchiefs from 1846, showing the printed messages to the woman. Buntine stated that the handkerchief, which had been carefully preserved for nearly seventy years, constituted 'the only existing piece of concrete evidence connected with the story of the lost white woman'. While dismissing the first-hand account of the 'old blackfellow of Rahmayuck', Buntine privileges a first-hand account by (presumably) an elderly relative, and 'concrete evidence' in the form of the handkerchief message, as 'actual history'.

Buntine's article was also cited in the *Argus* of 30 May 1914.[28] The *Argus* placed little store in the veracity of the story, although it acknowledged its enduring appeal to 'numbers of good, sympathetic folk' for whom 'the mystery had a charm, and gave scope for a

pleasurable exercise of the imagination'. Robert Russell, Henry Gyles
Turner and A Melbournite of '38 had also, the *Argus* said, been
unwilling to relinquish their fond delusions of the woman's existence.
However, in presenting an extensive extract from Buntine's article,
including the reproduction of the handkerchief, the *Argus* in turn
contributed to the perpetuation of the legend.

Buntine's article was influential. Details from it were published in
the *Oban Times* (Scotland) on 26 April 1919,[29] and his version of the
story was to reappear periodically in various guises, including 'Old
Black's Tale' by J. A. F. which appeared in the *Argus* of 29 March
1947; Charles Barrett's 1948 book *White Blackfellows*, which cited
Buntine and quoted extensively from his article;[30] and Charles Daley's
1960 'The Story of Gippsland'.[31] These reproductions of the Buntine
version have consolidated its place in regional history.

Two other early Gippsland settlers' accounts, by William Spence
Login and Mr J. Hodges, published in the 1920s, indicate how inte-
gral the White Woman legend has been to the production of Gipps
Land history.[32] According to Login, 'the history of the "Old Days in
Gippsland" would not be complete without a short account of the
Search for the White Woman'. Hodges's account differs from any
earlier account, both in details of the story and in presenting a positive view of the Kurnai. His story involves a young boy named
Jimmy King, whose father gave him a merciless thrashing with a
stock whip which permanently deprived the lad of one eye. When
news of the father's cruelty reached the child's heavily pregnant
mother in Sydney, she undertook the arduous journey to Gippsland
where, being repulsed by a callous and brutal husband, she sought
sanctuary with a remnant of the Flooden Creek (Sale) tribe. 'Amid
this terrible loneliness, broken only by the humanity and pity of
aboriginals, an infant girl was born.' The woman on recovering her
strength returned to Sydney. It was only after all this had happened,
said Hodges, that the white settlers learned of the presence of a white
woman among the blacks. Hodges's version does not appear to have
gained support.

The story's re-emergence at periods of national crisis during the
twentieth century—World War I, the Great Depression and World
War II—suggest its role in articulating racial, cultural and gender

difference as a counter to the levelling effects of great social upheaval. One 1945 account, published in the last months of World War II, linked the captive White Woman directly with wartime defence measures, conducted from the Gippsland air base built at the site of the Heart. The article explained how the Heart, once the home of 'the black man in primitive state', had become a symbol for the modern RAAF base, from whence 'brave airmen' served their country in 'Russia, Europe, Malaya and New Guinea':

> The mystery of the heart remains . . . it was never solved. But now on the place where those carvings were found there has been constructed a modern airport. A place where men fly in giant machines of the air. A place where a day's work may mean a trip to Melbourne or Hobart or Sydney—and return . . . A place where, when the men row or run, they wear the sign of the heart on their singlets.[33]

The story about a female captive reflected, also, at this time concerns about the fate of numbers of Australian Army nurses taken prisoners of war by the Japanese after the fall of Singapore in World War II. The women who survived until liberation in August 1945 told harrowing tales of hunger, privation and daily humiliations by their captors. Their published stories were a cause for national pride and found a ready audience. Betty Jeffrey's book *White Coolies*, for example, ran to three editions and seventeen reprints in the decade following publication in 1954. The death of Vivian Bullwinkel, one of the nurses, made national front page news in 2000.

In Britain in the years immediately prior to World War I, a related anxiety about corruption of the nation from within found expression in large-scale agitation about captive white women—the White Slave Market. According to the white slave literature, and the Bill brought before Parliament to try to stop the white slave traffic, unsuspecting British girls were being abducted and sold into prostitution in Europe and Singapore by 'Western Men with Eastern Morals' (the title of one of the pamphlets).[34]

Herald correspondent, E. M. Webb, who in January 1934 was touring Victoria and writing articles under the heading 'Rediscovery of

Victoria', recorded two versions of the White Woman legend. In one, the woman was rescued, married a Mr Fraser (a linkage to Eliza Fraser?) and returned to Scotland.[35] This version was supported by a reputed 'sighting': 'it was even stated that a Miss McLean who resided in Sale, saw the woman later when she was on a trip to Scotland'. Arthur H. Bradfield's article in *The Journal & The Record* in October 1949 offered the legend as refutation of the contention that Australia was 'a land without history and devoid of adventure'.[36] A story published in the *Gippsland Times* in March 1950 provided for the White Woman yet another identity, Miss Annie Weddon.[37]

Mabel Brookes's 1967 book chapter 'The Lost and Abandoned', in *Riders of Time*, presents a jumbled version of the story from numerous sources, and is notable mainly for the accompanying illustration by Harold Freedman, which is one of the limited number of pictorial representations of the White Woman.[38] In the illustration, the White Woman stands to the rear of a group of Aborigines, holding a small child with two larger children at her side.

She is elevated pictorially above the Aborigines as though, literally, 'on a pedestal', like a classical or religious statue. Her imposing stature is all the more significant given that Brookes describes the 'Pawl Pawl' tribe as 'immensely strong and tall; Bungeleene, the so-called chief, being six feet six inches'.

The Aborigines (static figures) range across the middle distance, interposed between the woman and the handkerchief pinned to a tree trunk in the left foreground which has the rescue message addressed to her. From its position, it seems likely that the message will escape her notice. The woman, distanced spatially from the Aborigines, and culturally remote from them (she is the only clothed figure), maintains her European looks and fair complexion. The woman's children, whose nakedness and stance aligns them with the Aboriginal men, allude to the story's sexual dimension.

A debate on the White Woman story was enacted from late 1959 until 1962 between Gippsland resident Mr R. E. Jeffs of 'Mill Farm', Carrajung Lower, and Mr W. C. Cuthill, historian and former stipendiary magistrate of Gippsland, in successive editions of the Traralgon newspaper *The Journal & The Record*. This debate demonstrates the way in which competing rivalries for ownership of the

White Woman, Aborigines and handkerchief with message pinned to tree, detail of illustration by Harold Freedman. From Mabel Brookes's *Riders of Time* (1967). Reproduced by permission of Heather Freedman.

story pitted oral tradition against textual record and local memory against regional perspectives. Sharon Payne has argued of this exchange that, in their imagining of the White Woman as a victim of Aboriginal savagery, Cuthill and Jeffs unite in their positioning of 'the white man' as the true local South Gippslander.[39]

The debate, sparked by Cuthill's article 'The White Woman With the Blacks', which was serialised in the Traralgon *Journal* in November 1959, highlights the fierce strength of attachment to rural mythology. In response to the Cuthill article, the *Journal* of 17 December 1959 published another White Woman story, the tale of the White Woman Waterhole, related by Mr Jeffs, whose grandparents had arrived at Port Albert in 1852.[40] Cuthill's version, the *Journal* noted, had been 'substantiated by official records . . . and read to the Royal Historical Society of Victoria'. In contrast, the *Journal* presented Jeffs's version as having been 'handed down from grandfather to grandson'. The *Journal* stated that 'Mr. Richard Jeffs—our informant's father' had learned of the story from *his* father, Thomas Jeffs, who had collected some of the planks from the shipwrecked vessel and 'was one of the volunteers at the meeting where the subsequent rescue was arranged'.

In Jeffs's version, set in the Won Wron area in about 1854, the woman survived the wreck by clinging to her kangaroo dog and, after some eighteen months with the Aborigines, her presence 'was accidentally discovered through a stockman cracking his long whip to amuse the blacks at their camp on the banks of the waterhole now known as White Woman's Waterhole'. The stockman, 'the late P. C. Buckley of Yarram', discovered a charcoal message written on the trunk of a tree—'Please rescue Me. Be very careful. Closely guarded.' In response, the stockman wrote—'Be at this spot day after tomorrow mid-day'—then returned to Yarram and raised a party of 'twelve of the best mounted' settlers. The woman's rescue was effected when she made a 'flying leap on to [the stockman's] horse behind him'. The captive woman was rescued by a party of whites and subsequently returned to her parents in England.

As proof of the story's accuracy, Jeffs attested that the rescuers had received a letter of thanks from the woman's parents and an English newspaper 'describing the rescue of the woman by these brave men from a "horde of niggers"'. The tree with the messages, he said, 'was sent to the London museum, but as far as the narrator is aware, no acknowledgment was ever received'. The location of the rescue and the stump of the tree had been shown to Jeffs. The plank of wood from the shipwreck was still in possession of his family.

The *Journal* gave some credence to Jeffs's story. In the following issue, it afforded Jeffs the (admittedly modest) title 'Carrajung Lower Historian'. The article described how the *Journal*, in company with Jeffs, was 'taken on a verbal visit to the scene . . . to the tree upon which was written, in charcoal, so long ago: "Please Rescue Me!" . . . We were right on the spot!'[41] This validation of a verifiable site lent authenticity to Jeffs's account, even though the 'tree' could be only a stump, the part with the message having been, according to Jeffs, despatched to England.

While Jeffs claimed the story as part of his family history, the *Journal* located the event within the history of post-settlement development of the Won Wron site, including later sawmilling and charcoal industries, the coming of the railway, and the modern era:

> To the whine of a jet overhead we leave White Woman's Water-
> hole with its memories of the past—the aboriginals, the rescue,
> the stockman who used to camp with his stock . . . the sawmill,
> and the railway and forest undertakings; to await the coming of
> who can tell what next?

Cuthill responded to Jeffs's story in the *Journal* of 4 January 1960 by calling on P. C. Buckley's diary as documented evidence of a different version of the shipwreck story, associated with a later period (1852–54) and not involving a captive woman. Cuthill established his position and credentials as historian by citing the locality and availability of archival material which he had consulted, commenting on the reliability of other commentators's versions of the story, discounting Dunderdale as '[h]e did not have access to the records which are now in the archives at the Public Library of Victoria', and endorsing the Rev. George Cox as the first reliable Gippsland historian on the basis that '[m]any letters passed between him and the Historical Society of Victoria questioning the accuracy of data received'. Cuthill's comments reflect as much his position as the arbiter of the many and conflicting accounts as they do his validation of the historian's methodology over oral traditions. Cuthill's conclusion which appeared under a sub-heading 'Fascinating Romance'—perhaps an editorial intervention—left little doubt that Cuthill placed small store in Jeffs's story:

> I must leave it to your readers to judge whether the story now
> propounded by Mr. Jeffs has not been coloured and amplified
> by the passage of time, and whether the two accounts have now
> been dovetailed into a fascinating romance of which Paddy
> Buckley's version is the only historically correct one.[42]

It was more than eighteen months before Jeffs's riposte to Cuthill appeared in the *Journal* under the banner 'Won Wron Rescue no Fascinating Romance' and with an explanatory paragraph, bordered and headed 'Mr. Jeffs Retaliates . . . !'[43] The extended row of full stops culminating in an exclamation mark conveys the *Journal*'s acknowledgment of Jeffs's blustering indignation. The *Journal*'s view of the relative status of the two men's positions as purveyors of local history was further emphasised in its deference to 'well-known historian Mr. W. J. Cuthill'.

Where Cuthill had called on public records to substantiate his position, Jeffs cited the integrity of his oral sources. He called to his defence old-fashioned standards which were taught in the local Won Wron school, where he first presented the story at a Back-to-School celebration held at Easter in 1959:

> I wish 'The Journal' readers and all interested to know that we old scholars of Won Wron school, including my father and myself, were never educated to propound colourful and amplified stories to interest ANYBODY'S imagination much less a fascinating romance as Mr. Cuthill puts it. We were there taught to at all times keep to the true facts of our case . . .

Also crucial to Jeffs's argument as custodian of local history was the standing of those within the local community who attested to the story's accuracy. William Paragreen 'was known throughout South Gippsland where he lived all but six years of his long life, as a man whose word and honor were beyond reproach . . . So clear was his intellect and accurate his stories that what he related was taken without question'. Mr. William Bodman:

> a life-long resident of Won Wron and former pupil of Won Wron school too, remembers his 'Uncle Harry', over 40 years ago, pointing out to him the place where the rescue took place. 'Uncle Harry', the late H. G. Bodman, M.L.A., was a shire councillor, Justice of the Peace, and at his death a Member of Parliament for Gippsland South. A man whose statements were accepted without question.

Jeffs's comment that '[a] study of his criticism shows plainly to us South Gippslanders that Mr. Cuthill is not a kindred spirit' indicates the fierceness of attachment to, and emotional investment in, the story as local history. As an outsider, Cuthill's greatest offence, as another old Won Wron 'Schoolboy' acknowledged, was to presume to know more about Won Wron history than the locals and to attempt to take ownership of the story out of their control. Jeffs describes the response of the old 'Schoolboy' on being shown Cuthill's article:

Standing up to his full height, 'The Journal' waving in one
hand, reading glasses in the other he exclaimed, 'What right
has a man who has not even lived in the district, to challenge
statements made by men like the Jeffs and William Paragreen
and backed up by statements from Harry Bodman (late H.G.
Bodman, M.L.A.) to say nothing of the rest of us old Won
Wron residents, who have been familiar with the story of the
rescue all our lives . . . If historians don't believe it, can they tell
us why the place is named White Woman's Waterhole, ask
them that?' our Won Wron 'Old Boy' concluded.

A month later, when the *Journal* published a further, and final,
instalment in what it termed 'the great "white woman" controversy',
Cuthill's standing was further enhanced. Possibly reflecting the bias
of a Traralgon newspaper for a Traralgon-based historian, the *Journal's*
descriptions of Cuthill over the course of the debate became increasingly deferential, from the brief and lower case 'historian' (first
article), through 'well-known historian' (second article), to the effus-
ive and capitalised 'Noted Historian' and 'Well-known Stipendiary
Magistrate and dedicated Traralgon historian' (final article).[44] Cuthill,
drawing on a wide range of source material—official correspondence, Gippsland and Scottish newspapers, the Private History Collection in the Public Library of Victoria, the C. J. Tyers report of
1853, Robert Russell's story 'The Heart', and other published
accounts, fictional and historical—identified at least eight different
versions of the White Woman story.

Whereas Jeffs had battled to privilege his version of the story as *the*
authentic one, to retain local ownership of the story, and to locate it
within his own family and local history, Cuthill positioned the story
as merely one of numerous 'romantic tales of the various white
women' in the Gippsland region which had appeared over the previous century. The weight of scholarship which Cuthill brought to
bear on the debate, the authority he claimed as historian, and his
privileging of documented and archived sources over locally known
oral accounts, silenced Jeffs, at least in the public domain. However,
Jeffs's version of the story retained local status, as it has in recent
years been promulgated in an official tourist brochure for the Won
Wron area.[45]

Cuthill has played a significant role in documenting and promulgating the White Woman story. His 1959 paper to the Royal Historical Society of Victoria, which was subsequently published in the *Victorian Historical Magazine*,[46] brought the story to the attention of professional, as well as amateur, historians. Cuthill's main contribution has been in locating, collating and typescripting the substantial body of archival resource material on the White Woman now held in the La Trobe Collection of the State Library of Victoria. This impressive achievement has secured for Cuthill a central place in ongoing research on the White Woman and continues to influence amateur, scholarly and creative interest in the story. His diligence in this exercise reveals Cuthill's own narrative of pursuit of the White Woman story. The manuscript material puts the researcher on the path shaped and directed by Cuthill's meticulous tracking of the story's textual manifestations. In shaping the reading of the history of the White Woman story, the archive preserves and produces cultural memory.

Cuthill's White Woman manuscript material ceases in the late 1970s. Since this period the story has continued to figure in Gippsland histories which, in the main, present the story as a colourful episode in early Gippsland folklore. A number of historians, however, including Peter Gardner, Don Watson and Phillip Pepper, have examined more critically the story's role in the quashing of Kurnai resistance to European settlement.

Peter Gardner has argued:

> If the 'end' in this affair was securing the release of the captive white woman then the violent 'means', from the hunting and killing to the holding of Bungelene hostage were failures. If on the other hand the 'end' was the destruction of the Kurnai Tribe of Gippsland, and the 'means' to attain this the 'captive white woman story', then the means certainly achieved the desired end.[47]

Gardner's speculation that the 'end' of the White Woman affair was the destruction of the Kurnai is persuasive, although he acknowledges that 'there is no evidence to support such a conspiracy in early Gippsland history'. Nevertheless, the destruction of the Kurnai was not absolute as Gardner's comment suggests. The Kurnai have not died out or relinquished claims to their land. In April 1997 the Kurnai (or Gunai) people, numbering some 4500, lodged a claim for native title over all Crown land and water in the Gippsland region.[48] While this claim has not at the time of writing been settled, gains are gradually being made. The Indigenous Land Corporation in 1998 purchased the freehold title to a 166-hectare property, Windarra, and returned it to the Kurnai people. The purchase of Windarra is part of a national lands acquisition strategy on behalf of Aboriginal people, aimed at restoring their contact with their traditional lands and strengthening indigenous culture.[49]

Since his book, *Gippsland Massacres*, was first published in 1983, Gardner has drawn attention to frontier violence in Gippsland. In so doing, he has discomforted those who would prefer to forget this aspect of Gippsland history. *Gippsland Massacres* was republished in 1993 by Ngarak Press, Gardner's own publishing house, in a revised, enlarged and more scholarly edition. With his other books, *Through Foreign Eyes* (1988) and *Our Founding Murdering Father* (1990), Gardner has established a case which is difficult to ignore, that settler violence against the Kurnai in Gippsland was systemic.

Gardner's books now appear on reading lists for university courses in Australian colonial history and have been instrumental in un-settling positivist histories of the region. However, while gaining respect outside Gippsland, Gardner's works have yet to attract local support comparable with that given to biographies on McMillan such as Kenneth Cox's *Angus McMillan, Pathfinder* (1973). Perhaps in polemicising and foregrounding post-settlement violence, Gardner, as a Gippslander, is considered to be disloyal to the region or to be airing 'dirty washing' in public. His allegations, even if refuted by locals, have cast into doubt the previously untarnished reputations of Gippsland's early settlers, including 'founding father' Angus McMillan.

Gardner's claims have been taken up in other revisionist histories including Don Watson's *Caledonia Australis* (1984), Phillip Pepper's and Tess D'Araugo's *The Kurnai of Gippsland* (1985), and Bruce

Elder's *Blood on the Wattle* (1988). Like Gardner, these writers have emphasised the violent means by which Europeans—and, as Watson notes, principally Scotsmen—took possession of the land.[50]

Contrarily, historian Marie Fels in her account of the Port Phillip Native Police, *Good Men and True* (1988), has disputed the number of Kurnai killed by the Native Police in the searches for the White Woman.[51] Against Commissioner Tyers's later evidence to a select committee, that 'at least fifty [Kurnai] were killed by the Native Police and other Aborigines attached to the parties in search of a white woman', Fels states that official reports of 'collisions' in Gipps Land between 1845 and 1847 list only six Aborigines killed and two wounded, including the one death at the Snowy River which was reported by Warman and De Villiers.[52] She argues that Warman's and De Villiers's imputations of a massacre on the Snowy River were erroneous and that the stories told to them by Kurnai of killings by the Native Police were 'merely a fabrication dreamed up for "a lark" by a man who furnished it as grist for the mill of the feud between de Villiers and the Native Police Corps'.[53] Nevertheless, she acknowledges that reports by Walsh, Windridge and Tyers of collisions between Kurnai and the government party, while in search of the White Woman during 1846, are evasive and must be doubted for what they leave out.[54]

Following Fels, historian Michael Cannon, in *Who Killed the Koories?* (1990), rejects what he terms Warman's 'red-hot version of the affray' on the Snowy River although Cannon makes his own case for widespread massacres of Aborigines by settlers in Gippsland. Like Fels, Cannon opts for Tyers's explanation 'that these extravagant claims had been spread by a man called Yorky, in the service of John Foster, licensee of the Heart [*sic*] Inn at Port Albert . . . "for a lark"'.[55]

Until recently, local histories have not invited too close a scrutiny of the actions of pioneering settlers or of government officers in dispersing Kurnai from land wanted for European occupation. More recent works tend to challenge the pro-European assumptions of earlier publications, although few go so far as Gardner or Watson. Since the 1960s a number of Gippsland shires have celebrated their centenary anniversaries. These events have provided the impetus for the commissioning and funding of commemorative publications which celebrate, rather than critique, the region's achievements and development since European settlement.[56] Nevertheless, a number of these histories have, like earlier records, implicated McMillan and the Highland Brigade in the massacres of Kurnai.[57] However, a predominant tendency in these works has been to rationalise the massacres of Kurnai as unfortunate but necessary retributive justice for attacks by them on settlers' stock and property. These retellings, which have created a renewed interest in Gippsland history, further consolidate the White Woman story's originary status in colonial history, even where the projects involve a re-evaluation of history, history making and nation building.

Phillip Pepper attributes one version of the White Woman story to Kurnai oral history: 'they remember Lohan-tuka as a legend of "a big pale coloured woman with long flowing red hair who lived by herself. She came out of her cave to frighten the people and little children"'.[58] This hermit-like figure—solitary, independent, intimidating—provides a counter to constructions of the White Woman's subjectivity as a helpless 'captive'. Annette Kolodny has written of a comparable American figure, the lady in the cave, the subject of an enormously popular 1787 fictional narrative, the 'Panther Captivity'.[59] Kolodny argues that this narrative, in displacing the male adventure narrative with one of female adventure, and in replacing a masculinist frontier economy of hunting with a settled, agricultural economy, offered the 'fantasised possibility of a civilized white woman's lone survival in the wilderness places of America'.[60]

Historian Kate Darian-Smith has examined the centrality of the White Woman incident 'to a *specific Gippsland history* of white settlement' [original emphasis], the story's endurance at a regional level, and its place as 'one of the founding myths which constitute the collective memory of modern Gippsland, and through which the unique history and identity of the region have been expressed'.[61] Given the European bias of historicising practices, to what extent are Kurnai memories incorporated in 'the collective memory of modern Gippsland'? Does the story of the White Woman constitute for Aboriginal Gippslanders, as it apparently does for those of European origins, a myth of colonisation? If not, this might indicate that the story did not have currency amongst the Kurnai in the 1840s or does not today. In the light of its repercussions for the Kurnai, the White Woman story may seem to some the reverse of a founding myth—an apocalyptic narrative akin to that fictionalised by Mudrooroo (Colin Johnson) in *Doctor Wooreddy's Prescription for Enduring the Ending of the World*.

Over the past three decades, in the wake the sweeping reforms introduced by Labour Prime Minister Gough Whitlam in the early 1970s, Aboriginal rights have come under intense public and juridical scrutiny. The policies and practices of Australian governments have been examined and found wanting by Royal Commissions in 1985 (British nuclear testing in the 1950s, notably at Maralinga);[62] 1989 (Aboriginal Deaths in Custody); and 1997 (the forced removal of Aboriginal children from their families—the 'Stolen Generation').

Aboriginal political activism has also gathered strength, particularly since the 1988 celebrations for the Bicentenary of European occupation in Australia. The excessive outpouring of national patriotic fervour which characterised the Bicentennial year was countered by accusations of 'settlement by fraud', and by unease about the failure of successive governments to improve the quality of life of Aboriginal Australians. Aboriginal political activists such as Burnum Burnum and non-Aboriginal Australians who rejected the superficiality of Bicentenary jingoism took the opportunity, while the world's attention focussed momentarily on Australia, to draw attention to the disadvantage which Aboriginal Australians continued to suffer in areas of health, legal and human rights. The year of the world's indigenous peoples in 1993 provided another sustained period of scrutiny, and international agencies continue to monitor Australia's performance on issues of human rights for Aborigines.

Historian Henry Reynolds, who has written prolifically since 1972 in support of Aboriginal sovereignty and land rights, has also been instrumental in reshaping public opinion from the prevailing Anglophilic view that 'white is right' to a more critical assessment of the processes and practices of domination which have occurred and their repercussions. More broadly, theoretical developments and critical practices in the areas of cultural, literary, feminist and postcolonial studies have in the past two decades produced a rethinking within academe of what constitutes 'history'. In drawing attention to the constructedness of knowledge, meaning, subjectivity, identity, these theoretical movements have in different ways and on a number of fronts countered the hegemony of the grand narratives of European history, and have facilitated the production, promulgation and reception of alternative histories, including those of women and colonised peoples.

Autobiographical, fictional and academic writings by Aborigines in the past two decades have challenged continuing colonialist attitudes towards, and treatment of, Aboriginal people. These include Roberta Sykes, 'The New White Colonialism'; Ruby Langford Ginibi, *Don't Take Your Love to Town*; Philip McLaren, *Sweet Water —Stolen Land*; and Ian Anderson, 'Re-claiming Tru-ger-nan-ner', to name just a few.[63]

However, sensitiveness to anti-colonial views remains. This was evidenced by the vetoing in 1996 of five artworks by Aboriginal artist Ray Thomas, commissioned by Melbourne City Council. The artist's sister, Marlene Young, was quoted as saying that the works were not put on public display because they were considered to be 'too controversial'.[64] One piece, which depicted the head of an Aboriginal man impaled on the sword of justice, was to have been installed outside the Supreme Court. Other works included ceramic mosaics depicting Aboriginal deaths—bones and skulls—to be installed near the King Edward VII monument and the Queen Victoria monument. A fifth piece, a map of Aboriginal massacre sites in Victoria which was to have been placed at the grave site of John Batman, 'founder' of Melbourne, also was abandoned due to lack of money. The controversial aspect of the artworks was no doubt as much a result of the proposed locations for their installation—sites symbolic of settlement, and of colonial and Imperial authority—as the images themselves.

Widespread and often acrimonious public debate continues in Australia about whether, and to what extent, present-day governments and citizens should be held responsible for, or attempt to redress, the wrongs of the past. Liberal Prime Minister John Howard, following historian Geoffrey Blainey, has disparagingly labelled calls for government recognition of past wrongs against Aborigines a 'black armband' view of history. Mr Howard has resisted mounting public pressure to apologise to Aborigines and to accept the term 'Stolen Generation' for children who were removed from their families earlier this century under government assimilationist policies.

Australian Olympic athlete Cathy Freeman has spoken out in the British press against Prime Minister Howard's insensitivity to the stolen generation.[65] Australia's compliance to the International Covenant on Civil and Political Rights, in relation to the stolen generation, has come under the scrutiny of the United Nations's Human Rights Committee in Geneva. The United Nations's committee has also been called upon to review mandatory sentencing laws in the Northern Territory and Western Australia in a complaint lodged by Cherie Blair, QC, wife of Tony Blair, Prime Minister of Great Britain, on behalf of four Aboriginal legal aid services.[66]

During the Bicentennial year, (then) Prime Minister Bob Hawke's Labor government instigated a national process of reconciliation between non-Aboriginal Australians and Aborigines and Torres Strait Islanders. The aims of that process have yet to be realised. Some advances in the bid to recognise native title, considered the cornerstone of reconciliation, have been made. The High Court 'Mabo' ruling in 1992, which overturned the notion of *terra nullius* (the premise which denied Aboriginal ownership of the continent prior to colonisation by Britain), the Native Title Act of 1993, and the 'Wik' High Court decision in 1997, which reasserted that native title could co-exist with and was not extinguished by the granting of pastoral leases, provided legal precedents for further Aboriginal land rights claims. Contestation of the Wik ruling, primarily by pastoralists, and the introduction of the Liberal government's compromised version (Prime Minister Howard's '10-point plan') reversed many of the advances of the Wik ruling.

As the twenty-first century unfolds, the steady groundswell of public support for reconciliation dominates the political agenda. The term reconciliation and the project it represents mean different things to different sectors of the Australian community, and to government. Reconciliation is seen by some as a salve to the conscience of 'White Australia' or as a means of deflecting criticism of Australia by overseas nations. For others it represents a genuine attempt to lay the ghosts of past wrongs and to move forward on a more positive footing.

Good will, or otherwise, for the cause of reconciliation has served to deflect attention from the cultural and political implications of the term itself. What are the repercussions of using an English term, and this particular English term, rather than an Aboriginal one to define and conceptualise the project? Reconciliation is a concept steeped in the Christian tradition of atonement and of 'turning the other cheek'. Definitions include: to make friendly after estrangement; to heal, harmonise or make compatible; or to make resigned or contentedly submissive to a disagreeable situation. By definition, re-conciliation also presupposes conciliation: an unpropitious connection in the light of George Augustus Robinson's use of the term 'conciliation' to effect the removal of Van Diemen's Land Aborigines to Great [Flinders] Island in 1832.[67]

The test for reconciliation will be to avoid replicating the same strategies of cultural domination that it seeks to redress. Colonial legends such as that of the White Woman reveal how strategies of domination come into play and operate. What stories are we, as a nation, telling ourselves at the present time? Are they stories which will advance the cause of a just society?

CHAPTER 8

Literary and Artistic Versions

'This was the last ever heard of the sorrowful story of the white woman, and
of the most pitiable and painful tragedy that ever shadowed the canvas
of the colony's history.'
Garryowen, 1888[1]

J. R. M., 'A LAY OF LAMENT' (1846)

The first literary piece on the White Woman, 'A Lay of Lament' by
J. R. M., appeared in Poet's Corner in the *Port Phillip Herald* of
29 September 1846 as the expedition committee was canvassing
funds to support De Villiers's expedition to Gipps Land. J. R. M.'s
stated aim was to 'keep alive the generous purpose of rescuing the
hapless female reported to be detained by the Blacks in the forest',
and he dedicated the verse to the *Port Phillip Herald* which had 'not
only kindled but "fanned the flame" of public sympathy in the
matter'. These references are the only indicators that the poem following relates to the White Woman. The poem itself makes no direct
reference to Gipps Land, Aborigines or captivity.

> Alone, beneath a wild wood tree, a female knelt in pray'r,
> Sad, sear'd, and craz'd she seem'd to be, fast verging to despair;
> 'Father of light and love,' she cried, 'Oh! hear, in mercy hear,
> A soul by years of anguish tried, and scath'd beyond a tear.

On the woman's behalf, J. R. M. posed the question: 'Am I by every
human heart—by earth and heav'n forgot?' The answer was to be a

resounding 'No!' For although the *Herald*'s obituary for the White Woman in late 1847 effectively laid to rest the story as a public cause, fascination with the White Woman continued long after the expeditionists returned, newspaper reports ceased and official correspondence files closed.

The verse format of 'A Lay of Lament' demarcates it from news items about the White Woman and projects the story beyond the particulars of time and place, into the universalising realm of art. Over the ensuing century and a half, writers and artists have created the White Woman character as subject, legend and phenomenon. These works include the poem 'Ode to the White Woman' by Homo (1847), Robert Russell's unpublished novella 'The Heart' (1849), Henry Gyles Turner's serialised story 'The Captive of Gipps Land' (1857), Angus McLean's novel *Lindigo, The White Woman* (1866), Mary Howitt's short story 'The Lost White Woman: A Pioneer's Yarn' (1897), and Mary Gaunt's stort story 'The Lost White Woman' (1916). The most recent fictional work is Liam Davison's novel *The White Woman* (1994). Various scenes from the White Woman story have been illustrated by Robert Russell (1849), Samuel Calvert (1860s), Sidney Nolan (1945), Harold Freedman (1967), Genevieve Melrose (1968) and Fred Baxter (1968).

J. R. M.'s 'A Lay of Lament' gives voice and presence to the previously nebulous figure. It dramatises in direct speech for the first time the woman's response to her abject condition as envisaged in the newspapers at the time. Portrayed as a stereotypically helpless early Victorian heroine, she prays for relief from her suffering either through death or madness:

> Look on this pallid cheek of woe—this broken heart
>   combine,—
> Was ever, in this world below, a fate as dark as mine?
> Cut off, and cast away, from all that holy nature blends
> In her eternal festival—home, kindred, hopes and friends:
> And doom'd—oh, heav'n! to pass my days in savage
>   scenes of blood—

In framing the verse with a quotation from Ossian, the so-called ancient Gaelic bard,—'It is night and I am alone, forlorn on the hill of storms'—J. R. M. aligns the woman's suffering with that of Ossian's tragic hero.[2] He thus transposes her human condition and abject degeneration to an ennobled form of suffering. In linking the woman with the Scottish bard, J. R. M. might have had in mind as the plaintive subject of the verse the Scottish Ann Macpherson. She, too, 'trac'd [her] name on many a tree'. With the exception of the first two lines which set the scene, the verse comprises the woman's prayer to the 'Father of Light and Love' to 'Save me from despair!', which locates the woman's suffering within a Christian teleology.

J. R. M. contributed to the *Herald* regularly throughout the 1840s, and as evidenced in his 'A Lay of Lament', his verse is extravagantly sentimental and classically referential. The form of the Lay was revived in the nineteenth century, notably by Walter Scott, whose 'Lay of the Ancient Minstrel' (1805) exemplified the form.[3] J. R. M.'s depiction of the White Woman as pale and bowed by grief was to set the tone for her characterisation in later works such as 'Ode to the White Woman', the only other poem on the woman.

HOMO, 'ODE TO THE WHITE WOMAN' (1847)

'Ode to the White Woman' by anonymous poetaster Homo was published in September 1847, two months after the second expedition had returned to Melbourne.[4] 'Ode' addresses the woman but, unlike J. R. M.'s 'A Lay of Lament', does not give her a voice:

> Unhappiest of the fairer kind;
> Who knows the misery of thy mind—
>   What tongue thy grief can tell?
> Torn from kind parents, friends and home,
> And left in the wild woods to roam—
>   With savages to dwell.

The expiatory function of the woman as a sacrificial victim or priestess is momentarily evoked—'Stript of thy silken vestments bare'. R. F. Brissenden's analysis of the emotive appeal of 'virtue in distress', the paradigm cliché of the sentimental novel, suggests why such representations of the White Woman functioned so effectively: 'even in situations which are morally neutral the implication is always made

that the suffering the characters undergo is intensified and to some
extent brought about by the fact that they are virtuous. The notion
not that virtue is rewarded but that virtue invites its own punishment
is a central theme'.[5] The poem's preoccupation is with the woman's
naked corporality and the threat to her virtue. She is 'stript . . . bare',
'left without a rag to wear'. The fashionably (now un)dressed lady
must bid—

> Farewell to gloves and silken hose
> And dresses flank'd with furbelows,
>   And the warm winter shawl;

The poem's empasis on images of sensuality from the domestic sphere
place the woman in a sexually charged space. Homo articulates both
repulsion and fascination with the woman's imagined intimate
embrace by an Aboriginal man (a dialectic which Terry Goldie defines
as 'fear and temptation') and its attendant themes of sexual contami-
nation and competition:[6]

> Expos'd to insults worse than death,
> Compell'd to breathe the pois'nous breath
>   Of a rank scented black;
> To yield to his abhorr'd embrace,
> To kiss his staring, ugly face,
>   And listen to his clack.

In depicting the privations which Homo ascribes to the woman in
her present state—the 'rude bark shed'—the poem reflects the prevailing double standard which simultaneously disparages, as 'savages',
Aborigines living in the traditional manner, and heroises, as 'pioneers', Europeans living under conditions of privation.

The poet's voyeuristic interest in the woman's degraded state
mirrors the (Christian) deity's gaze which suggests that even in
darkest Gipps Land He watches: 'That eye which pierces night's dark
shades/And all the universe pervades,/Watches thy deep distress'.
The poem finishes with the assertion that only God's hand will 'thy
sad wrongs redress'.

Similar images reverberate through subsequent literary versions of the White Woman story. In dramatising the woman's experiences at the hands of her 'savage captors', these poems and fictional works simultaneously 'produce' the Kurnai they purport to describe: a process of semiotic reproduction articulated by Edward Said in *Orientalism*:

> texts can *create* not only knowledge but also the very reality they appear to describe. In time such knowledge and reality produce a tradition, or what Michel Foucault calls a discourse, whose material presence or weight, not the originality of a given author, is really responsible for the texts produced out of it.[7]

The motif of a white man or woman held captive by 'primitive' tribes, or rediscovered 'lost' civilisations articulated theories of racial hierarchies enacted and validated in numerous works of nineteenth- and twentieth-century literary fictions. The topicality of such ideas in Port Phillip at the time of the White Woman expeditions is evidenced by a story of a 'lost' ancient civilisation with an Australian setting which was published in a Geelong newspaper in October 1847. ' "Oo–a–deen": or, The Mysteries of the Interior Unveiled', an anonymously authored novelette, appeared in three instalments in the *Corio Chronicle and Western Districts Advertiser*.[8] 'Oo–a–deen' describes a civilisation, the Mahanacumans, living in Edenic bliss in the heart of the Australian continent, their ancestors having quitted 'central earth' at some unknown 'dark time'. The narrator is a Port Phillip squatter who inserts into the tale a 'manuscript' written by a wild European man who claims to have stumbled across, lived with, and been expelled by, the Mahanacumans.

The 'lost tribe' theme enacted in 'Oo–a–deen' is revived and extended in a later antipodean variant, Rosa Praed's novel *Fugitive Anne* (1904). Written after Francis Galton's influential 1869 treatise on eugenics, *Fugitive Anne* adds the weight of later 'scientific' authority to theories of racial superiority.[9] Such fantasy civilisations, whose arrival precedes that of the 'native tribes', occupy the remoter zones of continents as yet incompletely colonised by Europeans. As first-comers, they provide a mechanism to displace indigenous populations as the earliest occupiers of the country.

Fugitive Anne picks up the lost world theme popularised in works like H. Rider Haggard's 1880s adventure novels set in Africa. In his 1887 novel *She*, Haggard's female character—a beautiful, white, seemingly immortal being with power over all things living and dead—rules a light-skinned race in a remote inland region in Africa. Fugitive Anne, the heroine of Praed's tale, is a white woman taken captive and revered as a goddess first by an Aboriginal tribe and then by a remnant, red-skinned Mayan-like civilisation hidden in the Australian interior. Anne's captivities provide the plot mechanism for the explication of nineteenth-century racialist doctrines, articulated and given authority by Anne's protector and lover, the Danish scientist-ethnographer Eric Hansen.[10]

These 'lost world' narratives are encoded to validate the ascendancy of enlightened European man. The protagonists, modern Europeans, are brought face to face with their ancient progenitors—cultured, though superstitious, light-skinned races who through some quirk or strategy have become sealed off from the outside world for thousands of years.

J. J. Healy argues that the 1890s fascination with such tales repositioned Australia as 'a land where everything—the cradle of man, the rise and fall of a primal civilization, cataclysms—had happened'.[11] These captivity narratives and stories of lost tribes take their place in a Western literary tradition of romance, adventure, and shipwreck tales, of which Shakespeare's *The Tempest*, Daniel Defoe's *Robinson Crusoe*, and Haggard's *She* are familiar examples. In such tales fantasies and anxieties about inter-racial contact and racial hybridity are offset against colonialist desires for land, mineral wealth, or adventure.

ROBERT RUSSELL, 'THE HEART' (1849)

Robert Russell's unpublished novella 'The Heart' (1849), in which each chapter is prefaced with a quote from *The Tempest*, draws upon this literary tradition.[12] As in Shakespeare's play, Russell's story commences with a storm-tossed vessel, and he locates his shipwrecked heroine, Ellen Brignell, in a landscape charged with symbolic meaning. When 'A Lay of Lament', 'Ode to the White Woman', and

'Oo–a–deen' were published, closure on the White Woman searches had not occurred and thus, theoretically, the possibility of rescue remained. By the time that Russell was writing 'The Heart', searches for the woman had been abandoned.

In the opening shipwreck passages, Russell identifies Ellen with the symbol of the heart as expressive of sorrow and maternal love. Six times in three paragraphs he describes how she clasps her young child to her 'breast', 'heart', 'bosom', 'aching bosom' and 'wearied heart'. Her physiognomy marks her as a tragic heroine. Grief is 'stamped permanently on her smooth forehead and trembling on her anxious lips'.

When their ship the *Sarah* is wrecked off the Gipps Land coast, Ellen and the other passengers and crew make shore where, in vain, they await rescue. Ellen is emigrating from England with her infant son and dissolute husband, Charles, in the hope of improving their waning fortunes. Russell creates Ellen as a genteel heroine—a personification of female virtue—who, though stranded in the wilds of Gipps Land, '[clings] to her civilized habits with womanly fondness'. Her passivity contrasts with the men's activity. She speaks deferentially, in a whisper, her steps are 'trembling', she exhibits a 'child-like simplicity' and she remains throughout timid and indecisive.

The Aborigines kill the shipwreck survivors with the exception of Ellen, her child and one sailor. Ellen and her child are taken by the Aborigines on a three-day journey through an inhospitable landscape. Having reached their destination, Ellen performs the defining act in the story, the cutting of the Heart:

> And a holy calm breathed peace around and came little healing on the heart of the lady who, now bending forward, seemed busied with a task on which all her energies were directed . . . A sweet smile was on her features. It might be peace of mind, or coming lunacy . . . upon the bright green sod, had she cut the figure of a Heart. It was of large dimensions and perfect symmetry, and, from the point leading to the water's edge, there was a little path.[13]

This act reasserts her Christian, European identity. Simultaneously, in inscribing the landscape with the Heart, Ellen marks it as a place of sanctity and sanctuary. Her mark imaginatively modifies the landscape not just for herself but for Europeans thereafter.

In a later scene reminiscent of Angus McMillan's 'sighting' of the White Woman, the heroes, two surveyors from Sydney, approach the Aboriginal encampment near the Avon River. As the 'blacks' flee, the surveyors see a female being driven on at spearpoint. At the camp-site the men find blankets, broken guns and clothing. Then, as cultured Europeans intruding onto the scene, they intuit the significance of the Heart cut into the turf:

> their eyes became rivetted on what they now beheld. It was the 'Heart' cut upon the green bank, the earth still fresh from which the sods were taken which formed its well marked outline, and, leading from it, still untrodden, was the little pathway, meet for a child's tiny footsteps. Amazed, they bent downwards, still silent as though to read the meaning of the mysterious symbol, the truth now faintly breaking in upon them.[14]

They also find an English prayer book open at the Burial Service and deduce that 'some white person, apparently a female, was amongst these savages, kept with them, too, against her will, perhaps in slavery and subjection'.

Russell interprets the woman's action and the Heart's symbolic meaning:

> Perhaps some yearnings of love towards her lost husband, or some indistinct or definite hope that the symbol might be seen by her own countrymen. There it was, however, and the moon shone on that object, calm and tranquil as though no broken heart lay throbbing beside it, and, near it, that child, whose grave perhaps that symbol consecrated, never beheld on earth again.[15]

Russell's ambivalent attitude to the Aborigines is apparent when one compares the surveyors' assumptions about the woman's slavery and subjection with an earlier tender scene depicting the empathy between the Aboriginal women and Ellen which crosses cultural and racial boundaries. The Aboriginal women 'sat around and soothed her with their wild songs'. They sang of the 'white woman's sufferings, of her boy, and of her husband killed. At each pause their old eyes fell on her with kind gaze, and their hearts softened towards her as they repeated their wild and melancholy song.'[16]

The Kurnai, even before they enter as characters, are imagined as a menacing presence. Through his characters Russell voices the prevaling ambivalence about Aborigines in the late 1840s, from the extreme—'Some say that they should all be exterminated as they were in Van Dieman's Land, and then we should have no more trouble with them'—to the humanitarian, 'Poor Wretches'.[17]

Images of the Kurnai as harmlessly animalistic—'pawing over and over the breasts and shoulders of their new friends'—are soon overtaken by images of the grotesque, irrational, monstrous:

> Then did hundreds of men and women glare wildly on the novelties about them . . . aged, broken-down hags of more fearful aspect than the heated night-dream . . . Here, with iron visage and statue-like form, stood around men of gigantic mould, whose strong arm grasped the war spear and whose look was full of horrors.[18]

Then, says Russell, 'came a scene too dreadful to dwell on'. Russell nevertheless elaborates:

> The huge fire was replenished, and the savage feast was fed by the bodies of their slaughtered victims. The flame burst upwards and their glowing countenances grew bright as they sat around . . . and, having feasted on their slaughtered foes, deep sleep came on the men.[19]

Russell's scene of diabolical, flame-lit figures, more horrific because witnessed by a Christian woman, depicts Gipps Land as a Hades-like, nether region with the Kurnai as a diabolical foe. It recalls a similar scene from Mary Rowlandson's popular and much-reprinted 1682 captivity narrative: 'Oh the roaring and singing and dancing and yelling of those black creatures in the night, which made the place a lively resemblance of hell'.[20]

American captivity narratives were precursors for articulating territorial contestation as an allegory of temptation, salvation and redemption while promulgating the myth of the Demonic Indian.

Russell's 'hags' and 'men of gigantic mould' are mythic figures, and the cannibal feast is stock fare for the colonialist tale of adventure or colonialist nightmare. Russell's note of introduction to the novella stating '[t]he character of the natives is pretty justly described' appears to endorse as accurate his vituperative stereotypes. His intention in writing this scene might have been to create a dramatic moment primarily to cater to the expectations of the overseas reader—'Gentle Reader,' he asks, 'were you ever in Australia?'

Russell refers repeatedly to Gipps Land as a 'desert', defined as both 'trackless and uninhabited country' and the land of 'the savage and the cannibal'. The term demarcates an imagined uninhabited zone where the surveyors, as 'free spirits of the desert', could enact their adventures.

Historian Henry Reynolds attributes the origin of the colonialist use of the term 'desert' to late eighteenth-century legal theory. In Blackstone's *Commentaries* the phrase 'desert and uncultivated' is used to differentiate between colonies won by conquest or treaty and those where 'lands are claimed by right of occupancy only'. Russell's use of the term 'desert' reveals how a complex legal argument which underpinned the colonising project in Australia, when deployed as a trope in a work of fiction, could naturalise settler occupation of Kurnai territory. It portrays Gipps Land as an unoccupied region, awaiting the cultivating hand of Europeans. Ellen figures as the embodiment of civilisation. Her gesture of carving the Heart transforms the desert, however tentatively, into a proto-'civilised' space.

Ellen, like the White Woman in 'A Lay of Lament', is given a voice to convey her plight to the reader:

> 'Am I,' she would ask herself, 'that Ellen Adair who, of old, could call around me lovers and friends? . . . Was it I who wedded . . . and left my home to pass the wide waters? Surely I am not that Ellen Adair . . . Yes, it is no dream. I am that wretched outcast.'[21]

At the site of the Heart, a battle to rescue Ellen from hundreds of 'savage kidnappers' ensues, shots are fired and Ellen is hit. She dies in her brother's arms. The sentimental death scene depicting Ellen as a broken lily is a standard from romantic fiction:

Half clad, her still beautiful eyes upturned, her tangled hair glossy no more, her pale features pale still in spite of sunbeams that had robbed them of their beauty, with hands half raised in prayer and half in pain, there lay poor Ellen ... On [her brother] her eyes fell languidly, drooping as a broken lilly [*sic*] she sank, her head upon his breast, one sigh, and all was still ... They buried her beneath the green turf, there, where she fell. It was her own selected spot. There, by the heart she traced, she sleeps in peace.'[22]

Although Russell's version parallels McMillan's account, Ellen's witnessed death and burial provides a degee of closure which had not been possible in 'real life'.

It is apt that Surveyor Russell has the woman's death coincide with the arrival in the district of surveyors; their official surveys would overtake the *informal* 'cartographic' role of the story of the Heart promulgated by McMillan and others. In casting surveyors as heroes in the story Russell was able to write elements of his own experience into an 'heroic' tale. In his authorial note which prefaces the manuscript, Russell states that many incidents in the story are drawn from his own visit to Gipps Land in 1843:

The spot on which the <u>heart</u> was cut I have trodden on, my companion searching for the very marks which he had seen and regarding which, & the circumstance of the European articles having been found, a communication was made with the Government in Sir Richard Bourke's time—<u>then</u> it was known that a white person was captured, <u>since</u> that time the fact has been more publicly mentioned—<u>now</u> I fear the matter is hopeless.

Russell (as X. Y. Z.) published an article on Gipps Land in the *Port Phillip Herald* in November 1843 which included a paragraph on the story of the Heart. In 1846 he revived and published the story in a letter to the editor in direct response to the public meeting. These articles provided the basis for his 1849 novella. Russell was perhaps prompted to resurrect the story at this time as a response to the news in October 1848 that Barbara Thomson, a young Scottish-born woman, had been retrieved by the crew of the SS *Rattlesnake*, after having lived for some five years with the Kowrarega tribe of Muralug Island in the Torres Straits, about twenty miles from Cape York.[23] Russell has one of his characters ask: 'Have you not heard of the female kept at Port Macquarie, a slave to [Aborigines] for months? She was but lately rescued', which reads as an oblique reference to Barbara Thomson or, alternatively, given the time at which the story is set, Eliza Fraser.

Russell's melodramatic tendencies frequently strain the narrative's serious intent. Phrases such as 'her dizzy brain had spun around' or 'He wore no cloak, but full before them stood in all his strength' indicate that Russell was influenced by the overblown prose style of popular fiction of the day. The prefacing of each chapter of 'The Heart' with an extract from Shakespeare's *Tempest*, while suggestive of Russell's serious literary intent, emphasises by comparison his novella's modest literary status.

'The Heart' manuscript has one illustration, by Russell. This illustration confirms that the story's focus is masculine adventure rather than woman's plight. It depicts the moment when the surveyors *find*, rather than that when the woman *cuts* the Heart. The White Woman does not appear in the illustration even as a background figure. Attention instead focuses on the horsemen, while the heart-shaped carving on the ground is easy for the reader to overlook. Russell's description of the turf-cut heart reads incongruously. It is even more so in visual form, resembling a romantic symbol pasted onto the landscape.

For Russell's nephew, Robert Poynder, to whom the work was bequeathed, the novella presented an opportunity for Russell's family to share in the fame of Russell as a public figure.[24] Poynder's sentiments are those of a proud nephew, acknowledging his uncle's place in early Melbourne history:

> This book was written by my Uncle Robert Russell—The Surveyor, who came to Australia Felix with Sir Thos. Mitchell, in 18 ? 34 or 35 and who laid out the Streets of the city of Melbourne.—Russell St. is named after him. His likeness is in the Public Library.[25]

Pen and ink drawing by Robert Russell, illustration to 'The Heart' (1849)
Reproduced by permission of the National Library of Australia and Mr Ian
Russell.

HENRY GYLES TURNER, 'THE CAPTIVE OF GIPPS LAND' (1857)

Unlike Russell's unpublished novella, Henry Gyles Turner's serialised
story, 'The Captive of Gipps Land', published in *The Illustrated
Journal of Australasia* in 1857, reached a wide readership. Turner sets
the story towards the close of the year 1844, when a ship is wrecked
off the coast of Wilson's Promontory. His heroine Mary Willis and a
crew member, Williams, are the only survivors. Turner's first images
of Mary, like Russell's of Ellen, stress her vulnerability and grief. In
representing Mary as a blue-eyed, pale-skinned young woman, Turner
enforces her gentility as an 'English Rose'. As a character, however,
Mary's role appears to be primarily to activate and justify a plot of
male derring-do.

Mary is plunged into a world of the bush and the tribe when she
is taken captive by the Aboriginal Chief, Gomul. The chief's poly-
gamous habits are made more repellent by his intention to add a
European to his harem: 'White lubra sit down 'long o' chief—the
great man, Gooroomul—have four gins now—like have one white
more'.[26] Williams forestalls Gomul's marriage to Mary and, making

for the nearest squatter's station, organises an armed party to effect Mary's rescue.

Mary's action in leaving a message on bark, to guide Williams to her when he returns with the rescue party, suggests a capacity for resourcefulness. Her character, however, is not further developed. After the early establishing scenes the story progresses for some thirty pages without a glimpse of her. She is present only in Williams's imaginings:

> She was a captive, alone, amidst a hundred; none to console her; none to advise her; none to sustain her in her trials; a poor fluttering pigeon in a nest of vultures; a pure, gentle, trusting woman, in the hands of a horde of the most debased and degraded savages, who, to crown the horror of her situation, were now eagerly seeking the life of the man she most loved on earth.[27]

She reemerges in the final scene when Williams, fleeing after a bungled rescue attempt, hears a 'female shriek' and turning, sees: 'At a distance of about two hundred yards, in the midst of a confused mob of women and children . . . the struggling form of Mary Willis'. At this point the drama is seen from Mary's perspective:

> The first emotion was heartfelt gratitude at finding herself again within reach of his protecting arm; but even while she rejoiced her joy was turned to mourning. She saw that his purpose was evidently flight: she cared no more; but as the sense of her great desolation stole over her—as she saw him she so loved deserting her in the hour of her extreme need, she felt her very soul grow sick with misery, and, uttering the piercing shriek that had arrested the young sailor, she sunk in a swoon to the ground. When Williams turned at the cry, she was being raised in the arms of the women and carried away.[28]

Williams is speared through the heart and has time only to mutter 'Dear Mary, God help thee!' before expiring.

In the opening scenes Turner describes the Aborigines as dignified and conciliatory. However, as the narrative progresses, as in other literary adaptations of the White Woman story, the Kurnai revert to 'type', becoming 'cruel and blood-thirsty', 'black devils', 'naked niggers'. They utter 'demoniac yells', spring 'like tigers', swarm like 'black ants', exercise 'cruel ingenuity', 'play hide and seek with the devil himself', present 'a seething mass of ferocity'. The benign and childlike *versus* the violent and demonic Aboriginal is a recurrent textual theme which reflects, as Terry Goldie has argued, 'a general system of indigene-linked terminology, which includes a variety of elements from the idyllic to the satanic, extending to the emotive indigenisms emblematic of the standard commodity of violence'.[29]

Two of the four published episodes of 'The Captive of Gipps Land' are accompanied by illustrations by Samuel Calvert, entitled 'The Conference' and 'The Reconnoitre'. 'The Conference' depicts an early scene in which Williams negotiates with the dignified Aboriginal leader Gomul. Between these two foreground figures stands the interpreter Peter, an Aboriginal in European clothes. They are surrounded by seated Aborigines. The figure of the White Woman, poke-bonnetted and non-participative, is assigned to the background. So small that she might be a figure painted on a backdrop, her representation reflects the story's preoccupation with masculine action over feminine adversity.

The second illustration, 'The Reconnoitre', foregrounds the European rescue party. Hidden from view from the wrecked ship, where the Aborigines have Mary held captive, the men are depicted with rifles at the ready, poised for heroic action—comrades-in-arms prepare to dash from cover and bear down on and disperse the 'wild mob'. In positioning the viewer behind the screening trees as eyewitness to the impending attack, Calvert aligns the reader visually with the heroes.

Turner's version of the story, foregrounding squatters (rather than expeditionists or surveyors) as the heroic would-be rescuers of the captive woman, appeared in 1857, the year after Angus McMillan was publicly honoured in Gipps Land for his pioneering efforts.[30] Turner's valorising of the squatters as a 'civil cavalry', 'civilised foe' and adventurers 'made of the right stuff' reflects an emergent nostalgic reassessment of the ageing early squatters as veterans of a frontier war. The story was published a year after the end of the Crimean War (1853–56). Turner's military terminology 'civil cavalry', picked up in the title of Calvert's illustration, 'The Reconnoitre', might therefore

THE CONFERENCE.

'The Conference', by Samuel Calvert. Illustration from H. G. Turner's 'The
Captive of Gippsland' (1857)
Reproduced by permission of La Trobe Collection, State Library of Victoria.

be read as an oblique tribute to, and a transposition into a local context of, the valour, gallantry and disregard for casualties exhibited by
British and allied forces in the Crimea.

Turner describes frontier justice in action, aided and sanctioned
by the law. When only two of the 'valiant party of five sturdy [white]
warriors' return to the station after the failed rescue mission, 'immediate were the demands upon the native police, and the available
forces, for taking immediate vengeance upon the blacks . . . Many
were the expeditions organized'. Turner, however, downplays the
results of punitive actions by the avenging parties—'A few stray
Aborigines were caught, and treated with ill-judged harshness'.[31]

Although Turner employs the conventional dramatic opening of a
fictional work—'One wild, stormy night . . .'—he concludes on a
note which implies historical authenticity:

Years have rolled by since the events narrated above occurred, and the race which at that time added its quota of terrors to a life in the bush has now dwindled into an object of curiosity and sympathy. We look in vain for deeds of noble daring, for actions of heroism, or even for samples of ordinary courage, amongst the debased and degraded remains of the aboriginal population; and yet we cannot divest ourselves of the truth, that we, a civilized and Christian people, have done this for them: we have taken from them the little in their character that was noble, and have implanted in its stead the vices of drunkenness, avarice, and lying.[32]

Turner's lament reflects the 'dying race' hypothesis which was to gain strength from the mid-1850s, by which time the European population—massively swelled by the influx of gold seekers—had vanquished Aboriginal resistance in the south eastern states. The sentiments expressed by Turner reflect a new phase in the regulation of Aborigines, leading to the establishment in the 1860s of Aboriginal mission stations in Gipps Land, as elsewhere.[33]

ANGUS McLEAN, *LINDIGO, THE WHITE WOMAN; OR, THE HIGHLAND GIRL'S CAPTIVITY AMONG THE AUSTRALIAN BLACKS* (1866)

Angus McLean's novella *Lindigo* was printed in Melbourne in 1866. Like Turner's 'The Captive of Gippsland' and other later works on the White Woman story, *Lindigo* owes as much to imagination as to history. McLean, an early Gipps Land settler, would have known of the circumstances surrounding the searches for White Woman and has incorporated selected historical elements into the story. He may have been the 'worthy Scotchman named McLean' who was the first to head the list of donations for the White Woman fund, with a 'handsome donation of £10'.[34]

McLean's heroine, Bella McKay of Kinlochlinn, Scotland, becomes the lost white woman Lindigo, following her shipwreck and captivity in Gipps Land. The novel proceeds initially through a series of convoluted scenarios which provide background but are largely unrelated to her captivity and rescue. Though ostensibly about Lindigo it is principally a travel tale of colonial fortune.

McLean transposes Bella, the idol of the Western Highlands, a renowned beauty admired by Queen Victoria, and counterpart to the Fair Maid of Perth, into Lindigo, the prized and resourceful captive of Aborigines. In an opening scene in which Bella is awakened by her lover's kiss, McLean flags the fairytale plot and intimates a happy ending. Bella, like Sleeping Beauty, will be released from 'living death' (as the White Woman's captivity was frequently described) and restored to life. Unlike Russell's tragic heroine Ellen and other White Women who are enervated, longing for madness or death, Bella, destined for survival, is 'lively', light stepping, cheerful, and benevolent. McLean, through dialogue, creates a strong sense of Bella as a character, and she is at the forefront of most of the Lindigo section of the book.

Bella is sailing to Australia to join her fiancé, Charlie Stuart (a nod to Bonny Prince Charlie), bringing with her Charlie's staghound Bran. When the ship founders, Bella survives by clinging to Bran. Cast ashore, her time with the Aborigines as Lindigo, unlike the captivity experiences of most of her fictional counterparts, is comfortable, her position is respected, and there are no taints associated with her cohabitation with the Aborigines:

> Her least wants and comforts were attended to with the most scrupulous nicety. Her clothes were made of the finest skins of the *Tuon* (a small squirrel), and her food consisted of the most delicate game . . . so that her captivity became more endurable every day, as she became more reconciled to her fate.

Lindigo, strongly identified as a Highlander, is more resilient and enterprising than her fictional English counterparts who succumb to their grief. Both before and after the shipwreck, she takes a central role in the action and frequently behaves as an intermediary who resolves conflict. At crucial times she acts with uncommon self-possession. The Aborigines see Lindigo as a spiritual being sent to confer benefits upon them, and she performs her role as a beneficient spirit by using the ship's medicine chest to cure their illnesses and by becoming the protector of an orphaned Aboriginal boy, Takawarrant. Her arrival heralds a period of peace and plenty for the tribe.

McLean attributes Lindigo's privileged treatment to Bungilina's belief that the staghound Bran is a reincarnation of his drowned father. Beliefs such as these, commonly attributed to Aborigines by European commentators, have the effect of explaining away, as misguided superstitions, acts of kindness and generosity by Aborigines towards Europeans.

McLean also employs as a narrative device a superstition from Highland folklore. Charlie's servant Donald, glimpsing Bran in the Gipps Land bush, takes him to be the Cu-Glas, a portentous 'tuhich' or follower, in the shape of an animal which on certain occasions, such as before a death or any important event occuring to a descendant of an 'old' family, would make itself visible. The decisive role which the staghound is assigned in the story enables McLean to exploit the superstition of an uneducated servant, without having his educated Highland character, Charlie, subscribe to it. McLean's utilisation of the Cu-Glas motif and Lindigo's occasional lapses into Gaelic remind readers that Highlanders brought with them ancient Gaelic beliefs and heritage. This figure from Gaelic folklore (like the Gaelic messages on the White Woman handkerchiefs) invests Gipps Land with the associations and cultural attributes of the Highlanders' native land, including the paradisaical associations emphasised by eighteenth-century poet Alexander MacDonald:

> Adam spoke it,
> even in Paradise,
> and Eve's Gaelic
> flowed in its lovely wise.[35]

Some Highland clergy maintained that the Scottish land clearances of the early nineteenth century, which reduced many Highlanders to poverty and starvation, represented divine retribution for sin. Emigrant Highlanders could—particularly through positing the White Woman as a Gaelic speaker—imagine Gipps Land as their own Paradise regained.[36]

McLean's depictions of the Kurnai, despite touches of local colour, seem more a projection of fictional representations of American 'Indians' than Australian Aborigines. McLean was possibly influenced by American frontier tales such as Fenimore Cooper's *Last of the Mohicans*. Lindigo's appeal to her friend Matoka, worded, she says, 'according to the custom of the tribe', reads like a precursor to the stilted language of the ubiquitous 'Indian brave' of Hollywood westerns:

> The brave Matoka knows well that a poor woman who was never used to living in the thick forest, or swim the deep water, or paddle the canoe like his own native women, is unable to make her escape without the help of a warrior![37]

Matoka is wary, but Lindigo wins him over, promising that if he helps her to escape: 'We will make him a great chief over all the tribes! We will clothe him like ourselves, and give him back his hunting-ground'.[38] McLean invites the reader's endorsement for Bella's ploy. However, as a European entering Gipps Land in the early 1840s when the story is set, McLean would have known that the squatters would not give the Kurnai back their 'hunting-ground' under any circumstances, 'captive' White Woman notwithstanding. McLean, in having the escape plan fail, is able to sidestep the ethical dilemma which Lindigo's unrealisable promise has set up. Nevertheless, the promise sits unsettlingly at the centre of the story.

In true adventure narrative fashion, Lindigo, tied to a tree, is rescued at the moment she is to be speared to death by the tribe. An attack on the heroic rescuers ensues, and Bungilina and Charlie, locked in a deadly embrace, teeter on a cliff edge. Charlie is saved by the staghound, which with Bungilina plunges to its death.

McLean avoids the overt sexual references which characterise other fictional White Woman figures. Lindigo's first words to her rescuer—'Charlie dear, I have been true to you'—reassure Charlie, and the reader, that Lindigo's virginal status has not been compromised. Lindigo, despite years of captivity, retains her own language and is immediately recognisable to Charlie, unlike several real-life counterparts who lost facility in their own tongue and were initially unrecognisable as Europeans. Lindigo's sun tan and fur dress, like an exotic costume, make her 'more charming than ever'. She can shed the outward signs of indigenisation and return to her former position as Bella, the European.

Bella and Charlie, having come into a colonial fortune, return to Scotland, taking with them Aborigines Tackawarrant, Quandak and Maria. Exhibited as antiopodean curiosities, the Aborigines entertain the Highlanders with a corroboree. Aboriginality as a 'diabolical' force is thus ultimately contained and defused as spectacle: 'The dark spectres . . . reminded the spectators of . . . inhabitants of the lower regions'.[39]

Calvert's cover illustration for *Lindigo*, like his illustrations for Turner's 'The Captive of Gipps Land', depicts Lindigo as a passive seated background figure. However, in the dramatic scene which Calvert has chosen to depict, Lindigo plays a decisive role; her prompt action saves Charlie's life. Visually, Lindigo's pale skin, cloaked form and parted, drawn-back hairstyle make her immediately recognisable as an early Victorian woman. Her illuminated form, though distanced from the foreground figures, provides a focal point which contrasts with the dark female form of an Aboriginal woman alongside her. However, the primary focus is on the menacing figure of an Aborigine brandishing a tomahawk, who is silhouetted against the fire-lit tree in the foreground. Charlie's staghound sniffs at the base of the hollow tree inside which, the reader knows, Charlie is concealed. The book's title *Lindigo* over-arches the scene, while the subtitle—*'The White Woman'*—serpentines across the cover like a wreath of smoke, providing a spectral mood.

At 198 pages, *Lindigo* is considerably longer than Russell's or Turner's works. Like many of the White Woman stories, *Lindigo* reads like the work of an amateur writer and may have been intended only for circulation amongst McLean's circle of family and friends. Copies would, no doubt, have been sent 'home' to Scotland, McLean's birthplace, as an entertaining colonial tale and as testament to the success of early Scottish immigrants in Gipps Land.

Published the year after Angus McMillan's death, *Lindigo* was perhaps McLean's tribute to McMillan. McLean's descriptions of the exploratory journey into Gipps Land of Bella's fiancé, Charlie, echo McMillan's accounts of his own expeditions over the same terrain. A number of incidents between Charlie's men and Aborigines closely follow McMillan's anecdotes. 'Takawarrant', the 'Worrigal' child kidnapped from his tribe by Charlie, and 'Bungilina' the chief, appear alongside fictional characters.

Cover illustration by Samuel Calvert to Angus McLean's *Lindigo, the White Woman; or, The Highland Girl's Captivity Among the Australian Blacks* (1866) Reproduced by permission of the National Library of Australia.

McLean concludes the story with a mock-historic postscript:

> after Charlie Stuart's departure from Australia, vague rumours
> of the captivity of a white woman being among the Warrigal
> tribe, daily increased . . . Consequently an expedition was set
> on foot by some philanthropic and chivalric colonists for her
> rescue.
>
> After a great deal of fatigue and expense, this was abandoned,
> little expecting that she was settled comfortably at home with
> her husband. The band of natives who witnessed the rescue of
> Lindigo, and the death of their leaders, became so alarmed that
> a similar fate awaited them, that they sought the security of the
> snowy mountains, never afterwards holding intercourse with
> the other tribes. They sometimes visited the 90-mile beach, but
> always kept aloof from civilized society.[40]

This interpolation presents the eviction of the 'Warrigal' tribe
from their territories under the guise of voluntary exile which, conveniently, leaves their lands uninhabited and open to settlement. In
their absence, Gipps Land becomes the realm of 'civilised society'.

SAMUEL CALVERT, 'THE WHITE CAPTIVE' (1872)

Samuel Calvert produced several original illustrations of the White
Woman. In his engraving for Turner's 'The Captive of Gipps Land'
(1857), Calvert depicts the woman as a small, poke-bonnetted background figure. In his cover illustration to McLean's *Lindigo* (1866),
he visualises her as a dark-haired woman, seated unobtrusively behind
the foreground figures.

'The White Captive', Calvert's engraving in *The Illustrated Australian News* of 1 February 1872, brings the woman into the foreground. Her fair hair falls loosely about her shoulders. She wears no
bonnet and her clothing is plain and unadorned.[41] The brief article,
also entitled 'The White Captive', which Calvert's engraving ac-
companies refers to a different lost white woman: a young bride who
becomes separated from her husband while they are travelling with
stock to take up 'unclaimed pastures on the River Murray, near
Moorunde'. The woman, found wandering by the blacks, was led to
their camp where, 'tired and distressed, she sank down in confusion

'The White Captive', by Samuel Calvert. Illustration from 'The White Captive',
The Illustrated Australian News (1872).
Reproduced by permission of La Trobe Collection, State Library of Victoria.

at the feet of the stalwart chief [Onkaatunga], who gazed wondering
in her face'. Onkaatunga possesses 'restraining virtues' and the
woman is eventually restored to her husband.

The anonymously authored story might have been written to
accompany an unused engraving left over from Calvert's previous
assignments to illustrate works about the White Woman of Gipps
Land. Calvert's scene shows the White Captive as the recipient of
solicitous attention from an Aboriginal couple. There is kindly concern in the demeanour of the man as he inclines towards the White

Woman, his elbow almost brushing hers, his gaze fixed intently on her face. The standing Aboriginal woman looks on attentively and even the infant peeping over her shoulder appears interested in the white stranger.

Calvert's composition places the White Captive as the focal point of the work. Diagonal lines formed by the edge of the bark shelter, the man's extended leg and his hunting weapons converge on her, as does the gaze of the man and the standing woman. The viewer's eye is directed towards the White Woman, whose modest gaze is downcast and her arm slightly raised. Interposing between the Captive and the Aboriginal figures is a crude cross, formed by the pronged upright support and cross beam for their bark shelter. This symbol intimates divine protection for the White Captive. As a pictorial device, it also works to divide the composition vertically. The right side of the scene is light- and space-filled: an effect created by the Captive's blonde hair, white skin and light clothes, and the open spaces stretching to the horizon behind her. In contrast, the left side is darker, the picture plane more crowded with figures, and the pictorial space rendered shallow by the bark shelter and overarching foliage immediately behind the figures. These visual cues link the white woman with those unbounded spaces and the future, while the Aborigines are confined spatially and, as the accompanying text confirms, relegated to the past.

The author of the article attests to the centrality of white women to the success of colonisation. In providing the settler with children she will secure his place as 'a pillar and foundation of an important future'. The article suggests that, in contrast, Aboriginal women 'scarcely realise the position accorded to the wives and daughters of our own social life, and in this we may accept a very reasonable explanation for the speedy decline of the aboriginal savage races'.

MARY HOWITT, 'THE LOST WHITE WOMAN: A PIONEER'S YARN' (1897)

Mary Howitt's 'The Lost White Woman: A Pioneer's Yarn' was written in 1897, fifty years after the searches for the woman. The story was published as Christmas reading in the *Australasian* newspaper of 18 December 1897 in a column entitled 'The Storyteller'. Mary

Howitt was the first female author to write about the White Woman. Her depiction of the White Woman, the Loan-tuka, marks a major departure from all previous versions of the story. The Loan-tuka is an escaped convict, not a genteel lady. The story was presented for the narrator's fictive bushmen audience, as a 'pioneer's yarn', a genre which employs personal experience, hearsay, historical details and legend, embroidered with fiction:

> You want a yarn of the early days, boys. Well, light up your pipes, and we'll sit over there in the shade of the wattles. It isn't often you get me in the humour, but what happened fifty years ago, on a Christmas Day like this, has been in my mind all day, so I may as well get rid of it at once.

The 'yarn' includes elements from the original newspaper reports —the piece of a bible found at a camp near Lake Wellington, letters cut on trees, the figure of a heart cut in the ground, the ship's figure-head—most of which have also been incorporated into previous fictional versions. However, the details are shrouded in the mists of time and the discoverers, in traditional rumour mode, are anonymous —'someone', 'someone else', 'most people'.

Mary Howitt was the daughter of Alfred William Howitt, noted 'authority' on the Kurnai, and the grand-daughter of William Howitt, writer of fiction and author of *Colonization and Christianity*, an indictment of colonisation, published in 1838. According to Allan McLean, Mary Howitt 'obtained the materials for the sketch from her father . . . who, as is well known, is the repository of a vast collection of aboriginal lore, particularly Gippsland lore'.[42] The reader's knowledge of Mary Howitt's privileged access to information through her father, and the revelatory tone of the introduction, would have lent credibility to her depiction of Aborigines, and the story.

The use of colloquial language sets the tone of opportunist colonial heroes who make good. The events are set in the context of Kurnai resistance to settler occupation, and renewed exploration at a place which the narrator calls 'Doruk country'—'a place to make your mouths water, boys . . . Grand, open flats on each side of the river, with grass up to the stirrup-irons . . . The finest lightwoods I ever saw were dotted here and there, while mobs of emus stalked about as bold as brass'.[43] The story is replete with anecdotes depicting the 'blackfellows' as foolish, irresponsible, lacking in judgment, superstitious, and so forth. One scene presents an old Aborigine who, after shaking hands with the narrator and his companion Bob, proceeds gravely to shake the bridles of their horses, which replicates an incident from McMillan's account of his early journeys of exploration into Gipps Land.[44]

The narrator and his partner Bob establish a run in Doruk country, with a view to looking for the White Woman. While chasing 'a great yellow dingo', the narrator is thrown from his horse. Evening comes on. He catches sight of a figure walking towards him in the bush:

> Imagine my surprise to see the tall figure of a woman, clothed in skins, and a mantle of her own magnificent black hair falling past her waist.
>
> She carried a yam stick like all gins, but her skin was white!
>
> It was the Loan-tuka at last, and out I jumped, regardless of all dangers, to attract her attention.
>
> She came silently up to me, and said in a low, rather hesitating voice:
>
> 'I am the white woman you have looked for. I come to warn you.'

The Loan-tuka, acting as guide, shows him a safe pass back to his station, avoiding the ambush which the Aborigines planned for him. She is 'more than a match for [him] in speed, barefooted though she was, and must have known the country well, for she never hesitated, but walked on'.

Before they part, the woman tells her story. She, with her husband and another convict have made their escape from Tasmania. The two men die in the boat and she is cast up on the beach. She is welcomed into the local tribe as Bolgan, the drowned wife of the chief, Bungil Woornin, brought back to life by his magic, and she has lived with him ever since. When pressed by the narrator to leave the Kurnai and return with him, the Loan-tuka declines: 'I belong to the Kurnai now . . . Good Bye! You will never see me again, and your greatest kindness is to leave me free'. Howitt concurs with earlier authors that the woman's story can only be reconciled with her death. The narrator, in concluding his story with the report some time later of Bungil Woornin's death—he had been shot in a row with settlers—reveals also that 'the Loan-tuka had been drowned, with her half-caste child, through the upsetting of a canoe in Maclellan's Straits'. He intimates that her death was suicide.

As an escaped convict, Howitt's Loan-tuka figure problematises assumptions of female freedom *versus* female subjectivity which underpin most accounts of the White Woman's captivity. The woman's freedom and status amongst the Kurnai stand in opposition to her ignominious incarceration in Van Diemen's Land. Although her life with the tribe could be seen as another type of incarceration, she refers to herself as 'free'. She is not the passive, simpering captive awaiting rescue by heroic males, but the rescuer of the narrator and a dignified queenly figure, in command of her own destiny.

She says that the tribe never allowed her near the narrator's station 'for fear of losing me, for they love my long hair and my white skin'. Like transculturated American captives Mary Jemison (also known as the White Woman) or Eunice Williams, who refused to return to the white community, the Loan-tuka of her own accord remains with the Aborigines.[45] The Loan-tuka's death by suicide, though open to interpretation, suggests agency on her part within the limited range of possibilities open to her.

MARY GAUNT, 'THE LOST WHITE WOMAN' (*c.* 1916)

Mary Gaunt's collection of short stories entitled *The Ends of the Earth*, published in London around 1916, includes another version of 'The Lost White Woman' story. As the Eurocentric title of the book suggests, this story, and others from Gaunt's visits to Africa and China, are presented as anecdotes from the far-flung reaches of Empire. Gaunt neither claims, nor disclaims, historical accuracy. However, she attaches a strong autobiographical authorisation to the story, and includes as characters Captain Dana, Johnny Warrington and Captain Lonsdale.

In the preface, Gaunt recalls that when she was six years old her parents took her to Gippsland during the gold rushes. There she 'first heard, without comprehending the grim tragedy that lay behind, the story of the brig that was wrecked on Ninety Mile Beach, and the white woman who lived with the blacks and despairingly traced initials on the forest trees'.

Gaunt's heroine is Ellen Hammond who, with three crew members, is cast ashore from the wreck of the *Britannia* in November 1839. Ellen, 'hardly more than a girl . . . drew her red cloak round her and shivered drearily'.[46] Ellen's red cloak, like that of Little Red Riding Hood, signals imminent danger and places the story almost from the beginning within the tradition of folk or cautionary tales. The repetition of such tales, with their fearful but familiar tropes of good and evil, provides reassurance for the reader/listener and offers a code or moral framework for interpreting the unfamiliar.

Gaunt reminds the reader that this is a tale from the 'ends of the earth': 'in 1839 they knew less about Gippsland than we do about Central Africa'.[47] Gippsland functions in the story as a preternatural zone, perhaps comparable in the European imagination to the forbidding gloom of Europe's (then) great forests. Ellen's little party sets off, without food or water, in the direction of Twofold Bay. As night falls, the party is attacked by 'black figures, with skeletons marked on them in white, [who] outnumbered them ten to one'. The men are 'butchered before her eyes'. Ellen crouches, covers her face with long fair hair, gives a yearning tender thought of her husband at home in Sydney, and bends her head to meet her fate; in her ears, 'only the uncouth yabbering of savage tongues. How horrible, how weird, how unearthly it all seemed!'.[48]

If Ellen is Red Riding Hood, then the 'stalwart savage with a bearded face smeared with grease and a piece of bone stuck in his hair' approximates the Big Bad Wolf. He grunts in astonishment and admiration: 'Probably in all his days he had not seen anything so fair as this English girl, with the sunny hair about her shoulders and her blue eyes wide with horror and terror'.[49]

Gaunt juxtaposes the 'English Rose' with Antipodean 'savage'— she is fair, he is greasy skinned; her hair is 'sunny', his is decorated with bone; she is silent, he grunts. Gaunt panders to the reader's prurient interest in Ellen's vulnerability to sexual advance. Hand on her shoulder, the 'savage' leads Ellen through the bush to his campsite. The reader can anticipate the 'fate worse than death' which awaits her.

Throughout the story the impression that Ellen is irremediably tainted and better off dead echoes insistently. It is articulated by

Captain Dana of the Native Police who attempts, tactfully though unsuccessfully, to persuade Ellen's husband, Tom, to leave the search for her to the Native Police:

> My dear fellow, you haven't realised what the life of a woman among them is like, what she'd be after two or three months, let alone two or three years! . . . We'll hand her over to the first white woman we come across and then you shall see her when she is properly clothed and——.[50]

Tom, also, is tortured by the prospect: 'Even if he found the woman he loved, would it not be better for him and her that she should be dead? How were they ever to blot out those cruel years? And what must she have suffered! What must she be suffering still! Oh God! Oh God!'.[51] The sentiments expressed here give voice to Ellen's earlier wish to drown herself rather than to be left alone and unprotected amongst the 'horrible savages'. They also echo the unspoken fears of Howitt's Loan-Tuka, who chooses not to return to the white community.

The *dénouement*, like that in Robert Russell's 'The Heart', involves Ellen's death in a scene of wild confusion. Troopers rush the campsite, shots are fired, Ellen is hit and Aborigines flee. Ellen's enigmatic last words to Tom read as an endorsement of her own death: 'I'm glad. I'm glad, sweetheart. I have wanted you so much'.[52] They suggest that Ellen, too, considered herself irremediably tainted.

Robert Dixon states that in Gaunt's story '[t]he role of the captivity narrative as a vehicle for the regulation of female sexuality reaches its ugliest expression'. He draws attention to the 'dark undercurrent of sexual guilt suggested by its ambiguous title [*The Lost White Woman*]', with its 'explicit suggestion of moral ruin and degradation'.[53] Ellen's taintedness arises from sexual congress with an Aborigine rather than because of unregulated sexuality *per se*. This distinction is clarified by Gaunt's representation of another captive white woman in her later novel, *As the Whirlwind Passeth* (1923). In this work, the abductor is a white man who holds the woman prisoner until she agrees to marry him.[54] Although her reputation is compromised she is not depicted as fatally tainted, and eventually attains an honourable and happy resolution to her situation.

Like Russell, Gaunt emphasises the *whiteness* of the dying woman as though through death she is rehabilitated to her former pristine state: 'It was a white face that lay there among the folds of the rug, a very white face, the hair all round it like an aureole was flaxen'.[55]

Gaunt's story concludes with a *tête-à-tête* between Dana and Captain Lonsdale in which Dana reveals that Ellen's husband (unwittingly?) fired the fatal shot. Gaunt's arch closure, however, claims historical validity:

> 'She was better dead,' said Captain Lonsdale quietly: 'much better dead. But you are right, we'll keep the story quiet.' And so quiet did they keep it that many people to this day think that the white woman who was captured by the Gippsland blacks was never found.[56]

The reinvention of the White Woman story in times of war might signal its use as a metaphor for, or inversion of, white Australian identity besieged or at risk of invasion. Given the White Woman's emblematic associations with Britannia, the story's appeal might have had particular resonance at a time when Britain, with Australia's support, was at war. Gaunt resurrected the White Woman of Gipps Land story in 1916 for a First World War readership. Turner's 'The Captive of Gipps Land' (1857) appeared shortly after the end of the Crimean War. Mary Howitt's short story 'The Lost White Woman: A Pioneer's Yarn' (1897) was published as Britain prepared for the Boer War. The short tale 'Me Um White Mary' (1938) and Sidney Nolan's painting 'Gippsland Incident' (1945) respectively mark the beginning and end points of the Second World War.

'ME UM WHITE MARY' (1938)

'Me Um White Mary', subtitled 'A White Woman Held Prisoner by the Blacks of the North for 36 Years', tells the story of a white woman lost in another locale—Arnhem Land. 'Me Um White Mary' was published in the *Australian Life Digest* of 1 June 1938 and 'Claimed a True Story by "The Cornhill Magazine"', from which it was reprinted. The story, told by Cappy Ricks, appears to be a fictional composite of other literary and real-life lost white woman figures.

This one is named Ellen, like Russell's and Gaunt's heroines. She is rescued by the survey ship *Rattlesnake*, as is Barbara Thompson (though some thirty years later than Barbara Thompson). The geographic location—Arnhem Land—is where Europeans Alice Willett and her daughter May were allegedly held captive by Aborigines in the 1920s.[57]

'Me Um White Mary' and other similar hybrid works including Ion Idriess's fictionalised recreation of the life of Barbara Thomson, *Isles of Despair* (1947), Charles Chauvel's film 'Uncivilized' (1936), and the film 'Blond Captive' (early 1930s) illustrate the way in which the multiplicity of elements from the original White Woman stories are perpetuated.

The story of the White Woman of Gipps Land found reverberations in other fictional accounts of white women lost in the Australian bush. At a time when Australian literature was at its beginnings such stories, collectively, provide the first instances of women as the subjects of legend. They have the potential to become a counter to the male foundational myths which dominate Australian literature.

SIDNEY NOLAN, 'GIPPSLAND INCIDENT' (1945)

Sidney Nolan's 1945 painting 'Gippsland Incident' (reproduced on the front cover of the book) is the first work of art on the subject of the White Woman by a major artist.[58] 'Gippsland Incident' demonstrates the extent to which certain aspects of the myth had been forgotten, displaced or dissociated from the story by the mid-twentieth century. Nolan, commented retrospectively on the work in 1978:

> Gippsland Incident is based on a true event. A man struck a tree with an axe and he found embedded in it the figurehead of a ship that had been wrecked on the Gippsland coast. The figurehead had floated up, but when he hit the tree he decapitated the woman. I inscribed the tree with a heart, a rather menacing arrow (not much love here!) and the date of the painting. It was a curious incident and I do not paint such complete events as a rule . . . As with the Kellys I wanted some lyricism mixed with the rather startling drama.[59]

The 'true event' on which Nolan based the painting is a remnant version of the White Woman story, dehistoricised and depoliticised. Perhaps Nolan was interested in, and therefore retained, only the story's mythic dimension. The history of white–black relations in Gippsland, which formed the original context for the White Woman story, had, by 1945, become 'forgotten' or overlaid with other elements both in the version Nolan relates and in his painting. However, although the 'captive' woman and the Kurnai have been expunged, sufficient common elements remain—the figurehead, the heart, the markings on the tree, the Gipps Land location, the shipwreck—to establish the origins of the story. And the elemental components of European masculine endeavour and the colonial trope of land-as-female (the woman has literally become part of the tree) have survived the story's conversion into legend.

The painting's atmospheric expressionism projects the story's mythic dimensions. The landscape is hazy with a soft opalescent glow; the sun/moon is a brooding presence visible through vigorous swirls of leaves; the figurehead is anthropomorphised—a woman with soft, flowing hair, a gentle expression and a mushroom-like body/stalk which curves against the man, who stands stiff, like a wooden effigy. The decapitation of the 'woman' (Nolan's description revealingly, slips from 'figurehead' to 'woman') at the moment of her liberation, the 'menacing' arrow inscribed on the tree above the heart, and the axeman's emotional detachment create what art historian Sir Kenneth Clark has identified in Nolan's work as 'a faint colour of menace'.[60]

Nolan's comment about the 'curious' nature of the incident conveys a degree of scepticism although he asserts the story's veracity. He does not reveal where he heard the story, whether at Dimboola in the Wimmera, where he had recently completed three years' Army service; at Heide, the artistic commune of Nolan's friends and patrons John and Sunday Reed in Heidelberg, near Melbourne; or elsewhere. It may be that he had read an article published in the *Argus* in May 1945, which described how one of the early Gipps Land settlers, a man named Curlewis, had seen two strange carvings on one of the trees on his holding: 'He believed them to be the carving of a human heart and a pair of scissors. He called his property "The Heart".'[61]

The timing of the article and Nolan's scissor-like arrow on the tree suggest a connection.

Nolan's painting is unsigned. The artist has placed the date of its execution at the base of the tree trunk. So placed, it appears related to the other markings on the tree and contemporises the narrative event. Nolan thus projects into the pictorial space his own historical standpoint and presence as a witness to, or participant in, the drama.

Two years after Nolan painted 'Gippsland Incident', following estrangement from the Reeds he travelled north to Fraser Island, off the Queensland coast, the site of Eliza Fraser's 'captivity' and 'rescue'. Eliza's 'story' became the subject of four series of major paintings executed by Nolan over the ensuing four decades, and his interest in the potentially destructive aspects of the male–female relationship, foregrounded in 'Gippsland Incident', was pursued in many of his Eliza Fraser paintings. Kay Schaffer has examined the ways in which Nolan in these paintings worked through his sense of loss and his betrayal by Sunday Reed in these paintings.[62]

The differing degrees of emphasis which Nolan accorded these stories of the two 'captive' white women reflects and consolidates their respective positions in the public imagination in the latter half of the twentieth century. While Nolan's Eliza Fraser paintings have been exhibited, and reproduced for mass consumption in numerous books published by international publishing houses, 'Gippsland Incident' has received scant attention. While the story of Eliza Fraser has become the subject of works by major literary figures such as Patrick White and André Brink, the story of the White Woman of Gipps Land by comparison has, until recently, found expression on a more modest, and local, stage.

FRED BAXTER, *SNAKE FOR SUPPER* (1968)

Fred Baxter's children's book *Snake for Supper*, published in 1968, provides an alternative version of how the White Woman legend originated. Baxter's White Woman is a young girl, Kathy, who becomes separated from her pioneering family in the upper Snowy River region, as they make their way over the ranges into Gipps Land.

'The Message Tree', by Fred Baxter
Unpublished illustration to Fred Baxter's *Snake for Supper* (1968).
Reproduced by permission of Thelma Rawlings.

Kathy's life is saved by Aboriginal children—Jirri, Gurawin and Babbilla—and together the children undertake the long journey along the coast towards the lakes. On the way, Kathy is captured by tribesmen and held until her young Aboriginal friends rescue her. Later, the children come upon a White Woman handkerchief pinned to a tree. Kathy wonders whether the message is meant for her: 'It says *white woman*. Why should they call me a woman, a grown-up', she ponders.

Fred Baxter produced his own illustrations for *Snake for Supper*. However, these were not used and the book was published with illustrations by Genevieve Melrose [now Rees]. Melrose's depiction of the message tree scene shows the children in close-up and with Kathy fully engaged in touching and reading the message. Kathy is clothed in a European-style shift, now somewhat tattered, and her fair hair is tied back in a 'pony tail'. Baxter's version of the same scene, 'The Message Tree', shows the little group from a distance. Kathy is identifiable by her long blonde hair. She holds the hand of one of her

Children finding message to White Woman, by Genevieve Melrose.
From Fred Baxter's *Snake for Supper* (1968).
Reproduced by permission of Lansdowne Press, Children's Literature Collection,
Rees State Library Collection, and Genevieve Rees [Melrose].

companions and points towards the message tree. The children appear to be in the locality of (now) Paynesville, with Raymond Island just offshore.

In Baxter's story, as Kathy stands puzzling over the message, she is again abducted by a group of black warriors, who then vanish into the scrub, 'taking the squirming white girl with them'. The book's conclusion is a re-enactment of Russell's and Turner's rescue dashes, as Kathy's brother and other settlers (having been guided to her by Jirri, Gurawin and Babbilla) make an armed attack on the Aboriginal captors. This time, however, the outcome is a happy one for the White Woman. Kathy is rescued, perhaps because her youthfulness removes the threat of sexual 'taint' which doomed her adult White Woman counterparts.

In the preface to the book Baxter pays tribute to the intelligence and self-reliance of Kurnai children, and to the Kurnai nation which, he says, 'no longer exists'. The conclusion to the story—which has Kathy's Aboriginal friends remaining with her to work at her father's homestead on the rich plains between the lakes—presents settlement and assimilation as though unproblematic.

LAURIE DUGGAN, *THE ASH RANGE* (1987)

Laurie Duggan's *The Ash Range*, published in 1987, is a book length prose-poem about the settlement of Gippsland, which incorporates a section on the White Woman.[63] Duggan describes the frontier 'as a place where imagination and reality [met]' for the Gippsland settlers, who fulfilled their desires for 'vast domains thickly populated with cattle, sheep and horses . . . secure tenure and great houses and servants'. Being gentlemen, Duggan argues, the settlers 'craved respectable white women and from this craving came The White Woman of Gippsland'.[64]

The Ash Range attempts to unlock the imagination and memories beneath the 'patina of Victorian heroics'. Duggan comments in the introduction that:

> At the moment when Gippslanders were pronouncing themselves responsible for a triumph of civilization over barbarism (it was happening all over the Empire) they locked away the imagination which had made it possible.[65]

The Ash Range represents a serious contemporary attempt to reclaim cultural memory by creating dialogue between documents about the early days of settlement, including the White Woman material.

Duggan, following Don Watson's *Caledonia Australis*, locates the White Woman story in the context of the dispossession of Aborigines by Highlanders, in whose minds the 'rampage' might have echoed Glencoe and Culloden. He juxtaposes snippets of White Woman articles, part of the message in English on the handkerchiefs, and the statement issued by settlers at Alberton refuting De Villiers's and Warman's charges of settler violence. In presenting sections of this original prose material in poetic form, interspersed with a linking verse commentary, Duggan conveys with economy and effect the drama of the White Woman searches, and their implications for the Kurnai peoples.

The literary and artistic works considered in this chapter provide a timely reminder of the crucial role which language, storytelling and art play in producing and conceptualising black–white relations in this country. Like numerous other stories about disappearing or captive females, real and fictional, the White Woman legend has expressed, and continues to express, unease about white occupation in this country. Ambivalence about place is evident in Joan Lindsay's 1967 novel, *Picnic at Hanging Rock*, in which three teenage schoolgirls and a schoolmistress disappear mysteriously while on a St Valentine's Day picnic at Hanging Rock near Mount Macedon, Victoria, in 1900.[66] Mystery also shrouds the disappearance of Margaret Clement, a reclusive elderly woman known as 'the Lady of the Swamp', who vanished in 1965 into the swamp at Koo-wee-rup, between Melbourne and Gippsland.[67] The disappearance of a baby girl, Azaria Chamberlain, at Uluru (Ayer's Rock) in 1980, apparently taken by a dingo, became a national obsession. The sensationalised trial of the mother, Lindy Chamberlain, for her child's murder, tapped residual anxieties about land and woman as the good–bad mother.[68] More recently, Peter Pierce has examined the figure of the lost child as an Australian anxiety which continues to haunt the national imagination.[69]

The most recent fictional version of the White Woman legend is Liam Davison's 1994 novel *The White Woman*, which dramatises the legend as a foundational event, the implications of which reverberate in contemporary debates about national identity and reconciliation. Alongside *The White Woman* are a number of award-winning fictional works about male 'White Blackfellows', also published in the 1990s by prominent Australian authors: Rodney Hall's *The Second Bridegroom* (1991), David Malouf's *Remembering Babylon* (1993), and Barry Hill's epic poem *Ghosting William Buckley* (1994). These stories focus on nineteenth-century Europeans who, by circumstance or choice, lived—or, in the case of the White Woman, were *said* to have lived—in the bush with Aborigines. These fictional constructs, along with other recent literary and creative works on 'transculturated' figures, challenge the national myths through which Australian national identity has been articulated. William Buckley's story, for instance, has in recent years been reinterpreted in a number of works including a post-colonial play, an elegiac, narrative series of paintings, a 'portrait' of Buckley, and a 1997 edition of Craig Robertson's book *Buckley's Hope* (first published in 1980), with a foreword by Wurundjeri elder Joy Murphy.[70]

Patrick White's *A Fringe of Leaves*, a 1977 retelling of the story of Eliza Fraser, anticipates these more recent works, although its emphases are somewhat different. Unlike Davison's elusive white woman, Patrick White's Eliza Fraser character, Ellen Gluyas, has a robust corporeal presence in the narrative and is a more complex and transgressive figure than the female characters presented by Malouf, Hall or Davison. Although White presents Ellen in essentialist terms, she resists simplistic readings. She partakes of a cannibal feast which supplants for her the solemn ritual of Christian communion. She eschews conventions of Victorian prudery in favour of an uninhibited sexual coupling with Jack Chance, her convict rescuer. And although she chooses to return and be reassimilated into the white community —initially the Moreton Bay convict settlement, later the Imperial centre, London—she does so from a position of increased critical consciousness.

Like the White Woman, Eliza Fraser continues to be evoked as an emblematic figure of colonisation. Since 1981, Badtjala artist Fiona Foley has produced anti-colonial art installations and paintings deploying images of the disembodied head of Eliza Fraser. Kay

Schaffer has demonstrated in her detailed analysis of Foley's art, the ways in which Foley uses Eliza Fraser's image to subvert and contest Eurocentric standpoints and versions of Thorgine (Fraser Island) history.[71]

In works such as 'Mrs Fraser Heads for Trouble III', 'Eliza's Trap', and 'Eliza's Rat Trap Installation', Foley incorporates the motif of the rat trap in complex images of entrapment and release. Eliza's bonnetted head, observing, approaching, or (in 'Eliza's Rat Trap Installation') caught in the rat trap, teases out and inverts historical renderings of Eliza as 'captive'. Foley's rat traps, painted in the red, black and yellow colours of the Aboriginal flag or juxtaposed with Aboriginal figures or motifs, also evoke the various mechanisms by which Aborigines have been entrapped since European occupation. The rat trap recalls the steel man traps which some early settlers used to trap and maim Aborigines who approached storehouses. Cultural, political, economic or social traps also come to mind. Disproportionate numbers of young Aboriginal men continue to be jailed for minor offences, to become subjected to mandatory sentencing, or to die in custody. Foley's traps, despite their menacing presence, are for the most part empty, unset or 'sprung'. The mechanism is disengaged: an indication, perhaps, of her confidence in Aboriginal self-determination, or compassion.

The proliferation of literary and artistic works on the transculturated European figure, including the White Woman, in recent years suggests the aptness of the figures themselves, and of fiction and art, to explore contemporary relations between Aboriginal and non-Aboriginal Australians. These transculturated figures have made available to non-Aboriginal writers a position from which they can write about Aboriginality: a project which might otherwise attract charges of appropriation or essentialism. Cultural theorist Chris Healy suggests a different imperative for the continuing relevance of the historiograpy of figures such as Eliza Fraser. He argues that in Australia:

> modern historical sensibilities have been constituted through
> colonial stories of 'race', territory, nation and subjects imbri-
> cated in secular time so that those whose memories have been
> trained in such modalities are not free simply to choose other
> modes of history that might be called postcolonial.[72]

As both historical figure and cultural myth, the 'White Black-fellow' marks a contentious and disruptive site in colonialist dis-courses. Enigmatic, he or she paradoxically negates and reinforces the boundaries of 'civilised' and 'savage', black and white, Imperial centre and colonised 'other'.[73] In these recent literary, performative and artistic adaptations, this figure, as a point of first contact between Europeans and Aborigines, offers a moment pregnant with latent possibilities through which writers have explored anxieties about national identity and possibilities for cultural 'hybridity' or under-standing between Aboriginal and non-Aboriginal Australians. This is not to suggest that such revisionist literature is not fraught with con-tradictions. Expatriate Australian writer and cultural commentator Germaine Greer has criticised Malouf's *Remembering Babylon* for perpetuating essentialist stereotypes of Aborigines.[74]

For twentieth-century readers, these constructs of nineteenth-century characters provide an alternative perspective to the accounts which have in large part formed our understanding of the colonising process. Each seeks, through literature to art, to make a difference to the ways in which Australian colonial history is known and under-stood. The works provide insights into the function of stories—their telling, suppression, reception or rejection—within discursive for-mations such as history. In drawing attention within their works to the ways in which the stories of their characters are made into texts, these authors remind us that the production of what is elevated as 'history' is arbitrary, contingent and provisional.

Rodney Hall, for instance, has his narrator FJ, a convicted forger who escapes to the bush in 1838 where he is adopted into a tribal group, write his 'own' story as a misguided declaration of love to a woman he has only briefly glimpsed. Hall has the woman forward the letters, unread, to the colonial administrators as part of her appeal for increased military presence in the area, as protection against attack by Aborigines. FJ's eloquent affirmation of the 'authenticity' of tribal life, and his condemnation of the 'forgery' of British settlement in the colony, are thereby (mis)used by the woman to aid settlement. This fact does not diminish the importance of his tale to the reader. Quite the reverse. The process of writing clarifies, validates and records his lived experience as, cocooned in a circle of tribal guardians, he is inducted into their ancient culture. Hall does not purport to speak on behalf of Aborigines through FJ, although he articulates their distress at the colonists' project. Rather FJ challenges imperialist assumptions about what constitutes 'civilisation'. Considered from outside the colonialist discourse within which it normally functions, the settlers' project is shown to be inauthentic:

> Please do not imagine I have forgotten what civilization is. I saw the road clearly as a road. The buildings as buildings. But I also saw, with the sight of Men, the horror of it, the plunder, the final emptiness . . . the sheer scale of violence made the sight hard to grasp, so out in the open it was, and so ruthless . . . As I saw it, he had taken a place, complete in itself, full of the food I had been living on, smashed it to fragments, then slaved at the work of carving out something in its stead, something different. But—how can I put it?—something no longer complete.[75]

David Malouf's *Remembering Babylon* is also critical of the colonialist project. The book takes its starting point from F. T. Gregory's account of James Murrells, better known to his contemporaries as Jemmy Morrill, a British sailor shipwrecked off the Queensland coast in 1846, and whose first name is shared by Malouf's protagonist. After having lived for seventeen years with Aborigines from the Mount Elliot region, Murrells reputedly walked into a stockmen's camp claiming kinship: 'Do not shoot me, I am a British object—a British sailor'.

Murrells's revealing utterance (what today might be termed a Freudian slip) captures his ambivalent position as both British subject and constructed 'object' of colonial discourse. Reading against the grain, Malouf uncovers a complex and problematic figure. The settlers are uneasy in the presence of one who disrupts confident definitions of British subject and indigene. Gemmy, who has lost his facility with English, is assisted by the local schoolmaster to write his story. Unlike Hall's FJ, Gemmy does not articulate for the reader his experience of tribal life or criticise the project in which the settlers are engaged. When he leaves the settlement to return to the bush, Gemmy attempts to reclaim his written history, but takes by mistake the essay of a primary school pupil. His story remains in the school-master's possession and with the European characters who perpetu-ate his memory.

Barry Hill's William Buckley has his story written for him by Morgan, his biographer, and Hill makes clear to what use the story will be put:

> Can he write? He can't write.
> He can't even speak. He won't talk.
> What he says, (when he can)
> that Ticket of Leave Man writes down.
> Who? That tattler, that coot from Grub Street.
> See: Mister Clay speaks, Mr Morgan inscribes.
> Each leans, one in the shade of the other
> —concocting. On paper
> it takes more than one
> lifetime to clear the country
> of savagery.[76]

The progtagonists' stories, whether accurately recorded or not, and whether used for purposes antithical to those intended by the tellers, become the property of other Europeans and enter 'history'.

CHAPTER 9

Liam Davison's Novel *The White Woman*

'A book is a deed . . . the writing of it is an enterprise
as much as the conquest of a colony.'
Joseph Conrad, *Last Essays*.

Liam Davison's 1994 novel *The White Woman* sustains the legend's
relevance for a generation of Australians struggling to come to terms
with issues of Aboriginal land rights and notions of belonging.
Davison's scholarship informs and provides an authoritative foundation for his fictional interpretation of the story, which presents as
though a first-hand account of the 1846–47 searches for the White
Woman. Drawing on archival sources, Davison brings a post-colonial
sensibility to the reading of this historical and fictional material.
However, although Davison's book shares the concerns of revisionist
historical works, his narrator cautions the listener/reader: 'don't you
presume to judge, not by your own standards. You have to see it
through our eyes and, when all is said and done, you can't'.[1]

Davison's interpretation in turn becomes part of that larger body
of textual material which constitutes the 'White Woman myth' and
might in time be read as an authenticating account. Through his
narrator, Davison provides imaginative insight into the motives
which might have led men to go off in search of the White Woman,
as well as a critique of the story, as a narrative construct. Davison's
book foregrounds frontier violence. He reanimates the grisly details
of Kurnai massacres, documented by De Villiers and Warman, which
circulated in Melbourne newspapers in early 1847. The massacre site

which Warman in his journal referred to as 'Golgotha', and which has been absent from later fictional and 'historical' accounts of the White Woman legend, is revived and given prominence by Davison's narrator. There was, he says, of Golgotha 'hardly a spot we could put our feet without a hand or a jaw-bone crumbling under us'.[2]

Published by the University of Queensland Press, *The White Woman* received critical recognition—a literary award and reviews in scholarly journals and newspapers—in the months following publication. In acknowledging assistance from the Literature Board of the Australia Council, the Victorian Ministry of the Arts and the Marten Bequest Travelling Scholarship for prose, the book asserts Davison's and the work's standing as a work of literature. The support which Davison's work attracted also demonstrates contemporary interest in the retelling of the story.

Surprisingly, despite the legend having been propagated by writers and historians for over 160 years, the White Woman, as a figure, has only now acquired popular recognition. Davison's book has brought the legend to national and, with its publication in French translation as *La Femme Blanche* in 1996, international attention.[3]

In Davison's *The White Woman* storytelling is a central preoccupation. The novel takes the form of a dramatic monologue, told by an unnamed narrator to an unnamed, silent but mediating listener who has come asking questions about his father. Davison's narrator tells a 'ripping yarn', a revelatory first-hand account of his experiences as a member of both De Villiers's party and the second expedition led by Sergeant Windredge, recalled from a vantage point some thirty or forty (the narrator is ambiguous on this point) years after the events. As a participant in the searches, Davison's narrator, in bringing the White Woman to life with words, in imaginatively constructing her out of his own desires, dramatises the way in which *the idea* of the White Woman has functioned in the service of post-settlement history-making and politics.

Davison attributes to these characters details from the archival material which connect them with particular members of the expedition.[4] He characterises the expeditionists, and defines their roles, by the items they carry. De Villiers wears a 'great watch and chain', Warman strides purposefully in new boots, McLeod cleans his carbine, Dingle fingers his rosary, Hartnett carries a book in which he writes Kurnai words. These items symbolise the discursive, material and social practices of colonialist expansion (historical time, the march of progress, gunpower, organised religion and the written word).

Although the story is presented from the narrator's late nineteenth-century standpoint, the insights which he offers and the literary style he uses reflect more late twentieth-century sensibilities. While the literary model is traditional, recalling Samuel Taylor Coleridge's *The Ancient Mariner* and Joseph Conrad's *Heart of Darkness*, Davison uses post-structuralist strategies of intertextuality—notably his evocation of the archival material and textual subversion—to undermine positivist notions of history and history making. Davison's narrator rejects the notion of history as a totalising, 'master' or 'meta' narrative, acknowledging that what passes as history can only be provisional, partial and biased, and is always open to interpretation and dispute.[5] He points to what remains unsaid in historical data and within his own text: 'There were things which couldn't be uttered, dark things that swelled beneath our talk but never broke';[6] and 'It wasn't so much lies that shaped our accounts of what went on out there as silence'.[7] His promise to 'tell you my truth anyway for what it's worth; the truth I hold onto . . . I'll tell you . . . the unspoken and the unspeakable', is qualified by his admission on the previous page that 'there are still things which shouldn't be revealed'.[8] He also acknowledges that once the story becomes the property of the listener, he will change, edit and modify it to suit his own needs: 'No doubt you'll alter it to suit, or choose what you want to hear—which bits will become history and which will not'.[9]

History, as Davison through his narrator reminds us, is constructed out of the present and from the standpoint and experiences of the history maker. However, he also invokes a dynamic concept of history, which intrudes uninvited into the present and which overrides individual subjectivity and interpretation:

> That's the problem with the past—the choice it offers. The advantages of hindsight. Things don't unfold before your eyes. You have to give it shape. And even then, when you think you've got it nailed—the right events in the clearest possible order—it squirms into the present and changes things.[10]

The narrator's 'problem with the past' is also, of course, Davison's. He, too, has had to 'give [the story] shape', to take up and foreground certain aspects from the archival material and to give less emphasis to other aspects—perhaps leave them out altogether. He synthesises a version of the story which encompasses knowledge gleaned through three years of research, including visits to Gippsland sites where key events took place. Thus, he relates his interpretation of the story to its historical and fictional antecedents. In having his narrator keep a scrapbook of newspaper cuttings—'all the yellowing pages of her harrowing ordeal'—Davison is able to include large excerpts verbatim from the primary source material, without straining credulity. The narrator's obsession with the past and with the archival material is, in turn, also Davison's and Cuthill's, and mine.

For Davison, as for Paul Carter's explorers in *The Road to Botany Bay*, history is experienced in engagement with, and in response to, the physical world. Davison locates history spatially. His expedition-ists travel across Gipps Land, marking it with traces of their own passing and 'reading' in it traces of earlier travellers, other intersecting narratives. For the narrator, history inheres in the landscape. More than just a repository for evidence of the past, the physical world acts as a moral field which reifies, echoes back as a grotesque parody, the dark deeds to which it has been witness:

> When we stopped to rest our legs we heard . . . the unnerving mimicry of lyrebirds deep inside the forest: the 'thock' of axes against trees, dull sounds like shattering bone followed by low, drawn-out wails of mock grief and the sharp discharge of carbines. A whole repertoire of stolen sounds echoing through the still bush as if the birds bore witness to some horrifying massacre.[11]

This narrative strategy of ornithologic mimicry allows Davison to displace the responsibility for moral or ethical judgment from the implicated and fallible human narrator, onto nature, although as the disclosure of what nature reveals comes via the narrator this must be taken with the same caution as any other part of his narrative.

Like Coleridge's Ancient Mariner, and Conrad's Marlow, Davison's narrator seems driven by a compulsion to disclosure. In part, this satisfies his own role as story-teller, with the pleasure and sense of power which this brings. In part, it fulfills a compact with the listener —as an obligation or burden to discharge, a debt of honour. The primary motive, however, seems to be a personal and moral imperative to tell the untold story: the unspoken and 'unspeakable' story behind the news cuttings, to keep the memory of past events alive by passing the story on to the younger listener. Time is running out. The narrator claims that he is possibly the only expeditionist left. This rhetorical strategy is used by him to authenticate his story: no one lives to contest his claims. He is an old man. Insanity and dementia run in his family, or so he confesses. In implying his own fallibility, the narrator deliberately unsettles the reader's trust and risks undermining his own authority. Paradoxically, however, his candour works to establish his authorial integrity; it pre-empts, and thereby partly disarms, readerly cynicism or resistance and clears a space for the reception of his story.

Davison uses rhetorical strategies to create the presence of the listener, to move the narrative forward, and to align the reader with the narrator's ethical judgments about the events which are being disclosed. The listener never addresses the reader directly; his responses are mediated through the narrator. If the listener is merely a figment of the narrator's imagination, he nevertheless exists, like Coleridge's wedding guest, as a mediating presence. When the narrator invites the listener to imaginatively recreate particular events, the reader, too, responds: 'Can you imagine it?';[12] and 'See how the jaw fits';[13] and 'But look close, feel the texture of it between your fingers, the elaborate stitching, see the faded letters printed on it. Do you recognise the words? Can you make them out?'.[14]

Through his narrator, Davison critiques the primary source material, paying attention to the way in which meaning is constructed, the modes of production and reception. In offering McMillan's original 1840 account of the 'sighting' of the White Woman, for instance, Davison punctuates the recitation (in *italics*) with the narrator's critical comments:

> *We came upon a camp of twenty-five black natives* . . . Yes, it comes easier to me than the Lord's Prayer now. Read it, tell me if I'm wrong [. . .] *We then searched their camp* . . . Yes, they

searched the camp. Imagine how I felt when I read it first . . . *where we found European articles as underneath described* [. . .] *several check shirts, cord and moleskin trousers, all besmeared with human blood; one German frock; two pea-jackets, new brown mac-intosh cloak also stained with blood* . . . Notice how the blood repeats itself [. . .] *one Bible printed in Edinburgh, June 1838, one set of National Loan Fund regulations* [. . .] The holy books, you see. Everything's accounted for: the oil, the vessels for pouring water [. . .] All the elements of her story are there. The blood. The broken glass. You can almost see her face staring back at you, pleading for your help [. . .] You see where this story leads, what licence it would have given him? You have to ask, would a man like McMillan make it up?[15]

Davison's narrator imagines what the women of Port Phillip might have thought of the exercise. He depicts them as complicit in the project to retrieve the White Woman, and attributes to them motives other than altruism. He echoes what he imagines to be the women's anxieties not only about how the White Woman will fit back into female society in the tiny colony but also their own fears about how they may be received when they return to that larger world of British society. He offers one possible scenario for the White Woman's return. In dramatising this moment, he depicts her as constrained in another form of captivity, as a drawing room curiosity or trophy:

They must have contemplated the horrors she endured and prayed to have her back among them, safe in their parlours where she belonged. What a prize she'd be! To have her sitting there, poor girl, sipping tea. Saved from a dreadful fate by their own generosity.

Even before we'd left, they'd started to make their plans: the guest lists, the subjects to be cautiously avoided. They'd staked their claims, and who could argue that they had a right to her after all the years of isolation they'd endured themselves, removed from the centres of civilization? No doubt they saw themselves in her.[16]

This scenario throws into relief the story's function in the 1840s in reinforcing social mores for women in a colonial situation. It poses the questions—is her return possible? Would she want to come back?

The ladies might sit down to tea with this woman in their midst, but would she be one of them? The unspoken questions, the 'cautiously avoided' subjects, suggest otherwise. The scenario, of course, is Davison's narrator's version of how the ladies might have responded. Perhaps in 'real life', women might have reacted differently. Eliza Fraser's experiences in the months following her return suggest that for a woman reassimilation was fraught with problems, even when the period spent in the bush with Aborigines was relatively brief. Eliza's story was appropriated by her London biographer, John Curtis, and turned into a myth of Empire.[17] Perhaps she was complicit in the process. But the final glimpse we get of Eliza, peddling her increasingly exaggerated story around the streets of London, effectively marginalises her as sideshow freak, while Curtis's version becomes the authenticating account.[18]

In creating the collective voice of the genteel females in the colony, albeit briefly, Davison draws attention to a conspicuous area of silence in the archival material: the almost complete absence of women's voices. The narratives, both historical and fictional, are almost exclusively male constructs, and their focus, though ostensibly the White Woman, is more closely concerned with male endeavour. Like 'the intended' in *Heart of Darkness,* the White Woman provides a pretext for the male enterprise of colonial activity but is excluded or protected from knowledge of that activity. As Conrad's protagonist, Kurtz, explains: 'Oh, she is out of it—completely. They—the women I mean—are out of it—should be out of it. We must help them to stay in that beautiful world of their own, lest ours gets worse'.[19]

Davison's White Woman, though ostensibly the subject of her narratives, remains a silent and elusive figure unable to participate in the construction or telling of her own story. She is, the narrator suggests, an *idea*, called into existence out of the desires and needs of men:

> You see why we had to find her? Why we had to believe? Which story would you prefer to hear; the virtuous woman lost in the bush, held by savages against her will, *left to undergo a fate worse than death itself* unless we rescue her. Or the other one about ourselves? . . . You see what we'd have to face without her? [original emphasis][20]

This statement indicates the way in which the category 'virtuous woman' was invoked to legitimise the colonising project. The 'other story' of frontier violence, occluded and justified by the narratives about the captive 'virtuous woman', represents the 'horror' which the narrator finds at the heart of the colonial project, civilisation, and within himself. As Cavenagh's 'happy band of bold adventurers!' pursue the object of their quest up the river into a vast, impenetrable and brooding landscape, beyond the last outposts of settlement, the White Woman becomes increasingly a locus for unspeakable knowledge and self-revelation. The 'unspeakable' is confronted at the place where the White Woman was said to have given birth; expressed in terms of anxiety about the female body, ambivalence about sexual possession, and through an inversion of the central Christian trope of redemption (the virgin birth):

> It's not what we wanted to find, you see. Not like that. It's not how she was meant to be. Holding a child perhaps—swaddling clothes and a shining babe in arms—or else standing flat-bellied before us, all intact . . . And the blood! You see how it altered things. How she could never be the same again? It was as though we'd stumbled across something we should have known all along but didn't want to see, some undeniable truth about ourselves, and everything was changed because of it.[21]

At this point the White Woman's taintedness—her closeness to the abject—stands in opposition to the inviolate 'intended' in *Heart of Darkness*. Davison's *The White Woman* thus brings into focus, as previous versions of the story do not, the ways in which white women have been positioned in colonialist stories to prop up discourses of colonisation and masculinity. In this respect, Davison's novel intersects with wider contemporary concerns with how traditional definitions of history have tended to marginalise or stifle the voices of non-dominant groups, including women and Aborigines.

In terms of Davison's rewriting of history as fiction, in having the narrator confess to his own and the story's limitations, Davison avoids making truth claims for the version which the narrator presents. Davison does not, however, claim a disinterested position. The desire to retell the story, and the form which it takes is, after all, his. Hence the book. Despite the qualifiers regarding the narrator's reliability, his incisive critique of how the story was produced and functioned clearly bears Davison's authority; at such moments Davison appears to collapse the distinction between author–narrator function and to address the reader directly. In demonstrating the seductiveness of the story, its power to move white men to action, whether that be folly, heroism, violence, *The White Woman* problematises what might otherwise be simplistic responses to the past.

Davison articulates a political as well as an ethical position. While his narrator cautions the reader against making judgements about historical events, Davison presents a critique of frontier violence which resonates in contemporary politics. The story his narrator tells acts persuasively as evidence that actions cannot be divorced from their political consequences, or the present from the past.

Abbreviations

Argus	*Melbourne Argus*
CCL	Commissioner of Crown Lands
Col. Sec.	Colonial Secretary
GA	*Geelong Advertiser*
ILN	*Illustrated London News*
J&R	*The Journal incorporating the Traralgon Record* (otherwise known as *The Journal and The Record*)
LC	Legislative Council, New South Wales
MS	Manuscript
OC	Official Correspondence
PPG	*Port Phillip Gazette* (from August 1845 *Port Phillip Gazette and Settlers Journal*)
PPH	*Port Phillip Herald*
PPP	*Port Phillip Patriot & Melbourne Advertiser* (from October 1845 *Port Phillip Patriot & Morning Advertiser*)
PRO	Victorian Public Records Office, Melbourne
SH/SMH	*Sydney Herald* (*Sydney Morning Herald*)
SLV	State Library, Victoria, La Trobe Collection
VPRS	Victorian Public Record Series

Notes

PREFACE

1 The Cuthill material on the White Woman is in MS 10065, bags 1–6.
Related material comprises photoprints of the handkerchief taken by expedition
in search of the White Woman, 1846, MS 10720, box 286/6; 'Journal of an
expedition which started from Melbourne 6 March 1847 in search of a white
woman supposed to be detained amongst the aborigines of Gippsland', H4224,
box 18/11 (copy at box 32/12); Robert Russell, photocopy of 'The Heart', a
novel, May 1849, MS 12795, box 3561/5; Ella Sellars, biographical notes on
Selina Bartlett Blake (née McLeish), James Warman and Lucinda Watson,
c. 1990. MS 12866, box 3630/11.

NOTES ON TERMINOLOGY

1 Tyers to La Trobe, 'Report by the Commissioner Crown Lands, Gipps Land, on
the Aborigines in his District, dated 9th December, 1846', 46/1923 PRO, VPRS
19/P, unit 87.
2 Fison and Howitt, *Kamilaroi and Kurnai*, pp. 15–16. See also Howitt, *The
Native Tribes of South East Australia*.
3 *PPH*, 18 February 1847, 'Gipps Land Expedition', letter from C. J. De Villiers
to G. Cavenagh, Esq., Melbourne, 15 February 1847.

1 A CLIMATE OF RECEPTIVITY

1 Cited in Reynolds, *Frontier*, p. 106.
2 Cited in Reynolds, *Frontier*, p. 162.
3 Dunderdale, *Book of the Bush*, p. 237.
4 Rush, The White Woman of Gippsland: Rumour and Anxiety, MA, 1994.
5 Watson, *Caledonia Australis*, pp. 178–9.
6 Reynolds, *The Law of the Land*, pp. 4–5.
7 *SH* version. Slight variations in typesetting occur in the *PPP* version.
8 *PPH*, 5 November 1847, 'Murder of the Captive "White Woman" at Gipps
Land' [extraordinary ed.].
9 Obeyesekere, *The Apotheosis of Captain Cook*, p. 50.
10 Hulme, *Colonial Encounters*, p. 194.
11 Kay Schaffer has written a definitive account of the Eliza Fraser narratives. See
Schaffer, *In the Wake of First Contact*.

12 The robbery of Jamieson's station was reported in *PPH*, 6 October 1840. For Jamieson's comments on the robbery see Bride, *Letters from Victorian Pioneers*, p. 90.

13 For example, *PPP*, Monday, 22 March 1841, 'Fisher's Ghost: A Legend of Campbelltown'.

14 Barthes, *S/Z*, p. 17. For an exposition and critique of theories of narratology see Brooks, *Reading for the Plot*.

15 Mackaness (ed.), *George Augustus Robinson's Journey into South-Eastern Australia, 1844*, pp. 11–12, 19–20.

16 Howitt, *The Native Tribes of South East Australia*, p. 459.

17 McMillan's letter with editorial comments reprinted in Lang, *Phillipsland*, pp. 218–22.

18 An account of Strzelecki's expedition was published in *PPH*, 23 June 1840.

19 Strzelecki, *Physical Description of New South Wales and Van Diemen's Land*.

20 For example, Hobart *True Colonist*, 19 August 1842, quoted in *PPP*, 29 August 1842, and Sydney *Colonial Observer*, 7 September 1842.

21 *SH*, 18 February 1841.

22 Lang, *Phillipsland*, p. 218. The accompanying editorial supported McMillan's claim.

23 Bride, *Letters from Victorian Pioneers*, p. 208. See also Bonwick, *Port Phillip Settlement*, pp. 492, 495–6, 498, and 'Report by Count Streleski', in Bonwick, p. 499.

24 The possessive apostrophe claims the region for Gipps (and Sydney).

25 Bonwick, *Port Phillip Settlement*, p. 494.

26 Lang, *Phillipsland*, p. 217.

27 Cited in Adams, *The Tambo Shire Centenary History*, pp. 34–5.

28 For reports of Macdonnel's arrival see *PPG*, 9 January 1841, reprinted from *Sydney Herald*; the poem 'Welcome to Glengarry' by R. H. H., *PPG*, 7 April 1841; and Garryowen, *The Chronicles of Early Melbourne*, Vol. II, p. 651.

29 *PPP*, 6 May 1841, 'Gipps Land'.

30 Collett, *Wednesdays Closest to the Full Moon*, p. 35.

31 Watson, *Caledonia Australis*, pp. 164, 167; Gardner, *Gippsland Massacres*, p. 39.

32 Meyrick, 30 April 1846, H15789–15816, SLV.

33 McMillan's speech is reproduced in McCombie, *History of the Colony of Victoria from its settlement to the death of Sir Charles Hotham*, pp. 79–80.

34 McMillan's 'Memorandum of Trip by A. McMillan, from Maneroo District, in the Year 1839, to the South-West of that District, Towards the Sea-Coast, in Search of New Country', in Bride, *Letters from Victorian Pioneers*, pp. 201–9.

35 McMillan to Bonwick, 8 February 1856, in Bonwick, *Port Phillip Settlement*, pp. 488–94.

36 *ibid.*, p. 493.

37 Bride, *Letters from Victorian Pioneers*, p. 208 and footnote 7, p. 209, which states that 'McMillan returned with a party of seven and the Aborigines were driven from the run after desperate fighting'.

38 Appendix to Mackay, *Recollections of Early Gippsland Goldfields*. Cited in Adams (ed.), *Notes on Gippsland History*, Vol. I, p. 43.

39 Gardner, *Our Founding Murdering Father*, p. 32.

40 Memmi, *The Colonizer and the Colonized*, pp. 52–60.

41 *PPH*, 24 March 1840, 'Shipping Intelligence'.

42 Moore to Collector of H M Customs, 11 April 1840, encl. with letter from Collector of Customs to Col. Sec., 24 April 1840. Item 5 in the Schedule of Correspondence on the White Woman tabled in the Legislative Council on 21 October 1846. Typescript copy in MS 10065 SLV, bag 6.

43 *PPH*, 14 April 1840, 'Shipping Intelligence'.

44 See Merchants Campbell & Woolley's advertisement, *PPP*, 26 December 1839, 'for sale ex *Mary Anne*', which listed almonds, French olives, pickaxes, morticing, felling and grubbing axes, coach wrenches, hooks and hinges, white lead, black and green paints, buckets and piggings, ladies' black and white satin shoes, black and white Beaver hats, medallion table covers, haberdashery, etc.

45 *GA*, 28 November 1840 [reprinted from *PPG*], 'Wreck of the Prince Albert'. Extract from a letter dated Point Nepean, 19 November 1840.

46 See Lovell-Smith, 'Out of the Hair Tent', pp. 67–76.

47 *PPP*, 1 October 1840, 'South Australia—Execution of Two Natives—Two Others Shot'.

48 *PPP*, 7 January 1841, 'Loss of the *Clonmel*'.

49 *PPP*, 'A Fragment' by Anon., 1 February 1844.

50 Walker, *The Newspaper Press in New South Wales, 1803–1920*, p. 43.

51 Brown (ed.), *Memoirs recorded at Geelong, Victoria, Australia, by Captain Foster Fyans (1790–1870)*, pp. 163–71. Fyans's official report of the rescue is reproduced in Dwyer & Buchanan, *The Rescue of Eliza Fraser*, Appendix 8, p. 37.

52 The editor of the *PPP* was shortly to champion Lewis's cause as rescuer of the survivors of the *Charles Eaton*. See *PPP*, 29 March 1841, 'Corner Inlet'.

53 For example, *PPP*, 17 February 1847, 'The Bunyip' (reprinted from *SMH*); *GA*, 17 September 1847, 'Extraordinary Sea Monster' and 'Marine Bunyip: Another Account'.

54 Shaw, *A History of the Port Phillip District*, pp. 18–22; Presland, *The Land of the Kulin*, p. 71.

55 Garryowen, *The Chronicles of Early Melbourne*, Vol. 1, p. 110.

56 *PPP*, 26 December 1839, editorial comment.

57 Memmi, *The Colonizer and the Colonized*, p. 71.

58 De Serville, *Port Phillip Gentlemen*, Vol. I, p. 41.

59 Garryowen, *The Chronicles of Early Melbourne*, Vol. I, p. 419.

60 Boys, *First Years at Port Phillip*, p. 117; Garryowen, *The Chronicles of Early Melbourne*, Vol. I, p. 493; Shaw, p. 101.

61 Russell, *A Wish of Distinction*, pp. 18, 58–61.

62 There were numerous articles advising 'ladies' how to behave. For example, *PPP*, 7 January 1841, 'Advice to Young Ladies'.

63 *PPP*, 10 April 1839, letter to the editor.

64 *PPP*, 12 July 1841, 'Ladies Beware'.

65 *PPH*, 31 December 1846, 'Furious Driving'.

66 *PPP*, 10 February 1840, 'The Forsaken' (republished from the *Standard*).

67 *PPP*, 1 June 1840, 'A True Tale of Shipwreck'.

68 *PPP*, 30 August 1841, 'She is Withering Away' (reprinted from *Pickwick Papers*, 1840). Other variations on this theme include 'A Father's Welcome to his Widowed Daughter', *PPP*, 25 January 1841; 'The Dying Girl's Lament', *PPP*, 3 March 1843; and 'The Blind Beauty of the Moor', *PPP*, 16 March 1843.

69 Martin, 'Good Girls Die; Bad Girls Don't', pp. 11–22.

70 For an overview of the Grace Darling phenomenon, see Mitford, *Grace Had an English Heart*. An excerpt from Wordsworth's poem is printed in Mitford, p. 81.

71 Curr, *Recollections of Squatting in Victoria*, cited in Shaw, *A History of the Port Phillip District*, p. 216.

72 Niall, *Georgiana*; Frost, *A Face in the Glass*; Bennett, 'Account of a Journey to Gipps Land', pp. 172–94; Franklin, 'Excursion to Macquarie Harbour', in Bassett (ed.), *Great Explorations*, pp. 112–15.

73 Kirkland, 'Life in the Bush', p. 176.

74 *ibid.* p. 196.

75 For example, Pearce, 'The Significances of the Captivity Narrative'.

76 *PPP*, 17 February 1840, editorial.

77 Black, 'Journal of the first few months spent in Australia, September 30 1839 – May 8 1840', typescript copy, MS 11519, SLV.

78 An Act to restrain the unauthorised occupation of Crown Lands, passed by the Legislative Council, 29 July 1836. Reproduced in Spreadborough & H. Anderson, *Victorian Squatters*, pp. 277–9.

79 *SH*, 8 October 1839.

80 Kenyon, 'The Aboriginal Protectorate of Port Phillip', p. 136.

81 Wedge to Oranmore, 7 December 1839; Wedge to Fowell Buxton, 24 July 1840. In Bonwick, *Port Phillip Settlement*, pp. 507–9.

82 *PPP*, 6 May, 1841, letter to the editor, signed 'CENSOR'.

83 According to some, 'No-good-damper' station, swamp and Inn, near the present-day Melbourne suburb of Caulfield, were so named *c.* 1840 because troublesome Aborigines were given poisoned damper by a settler. For example, Rev. G. Cox, 'Notes on Gippsland History', *Gippsland Standard*, 30 October 1912; Dunderdale, *Book of the Bush*, pp. 277–8. For more widespread claims of poisonings of Aborigines, see: *PPP*, 5 August 1839; *PPP*, 2 April 1840. On arsenic poisoning in the Western District 1842–43, see Clark (ed.), *The Port Phillip Journals of George Augustus Robinson*, p. 104.

84 *PPP*, 28 May 1840. See McCombie's summary of contemporary classifications of the various races of men in *History of the Colony of Victoria*, pp. 84–6. Street, *The savage in literature*, discusses criteria for classification, and hierarchy and racial theory, pp. 55–105.

85 For example, despatch from Lord John Russell to Governor Gipps on the treatment of the Aborigines of New Holland (No. 133), 25 August 1840, and enclosed report by Captain G. Grey, *Report upon the best means of promoting the Civilization of the Aboriginal Inhabitants of Australia*, published in *PPP*, 12 July and 15 July 1841. The *PPP* recommended that the government should give the Aborigines education in farming, implements and seeds. *PPP*, 17 February 1840, 'The Aborigines'.

86 Quoted in Reynolds, *Frontier*, pp. 104–5.
87 *PPP*, 5 August 1839, 'Vide Govt Notice on the Subject of the Aborigines, May 22'.
88 See 'An Act to allow the Aboriginal natives of New South Wales to be received as competent Witnesses in criminal cases, 1839'. Royal Assent refused. Repealed by Act 34 of 1924. In McCorquodale, *Aborigines and the Law*, A131, p. 19. See also Cannon, *Historical Records of Victoria*, Vol. 2B, pp. 758–9.
89 *PPP*, 31 May 1841, 'The Herald and the Protectorate'.
90 The trial was reported in the *PPP*, 20 May 1841, 'Supreme Court—Criminal Side'. Other reports and comments on the case appeared in *PPP*, 31 December 1840; *PPP*, 6 May 1841; and *PPP*, 24 May 1841.
91 *PPP*, 3 June 1841, 'Local Intelligence—The Blacks'.
92 Massola, *Journey into Aboriginal Victoria*, p. 55.
93 *PPP*, 17 February, 1840, 'The Aborigines'.
94 Conrad, *Youth* and *Heart of Darkness*, pp. 142–3.

2 THE PROGRESS OF DISCOVERY

1 *PPH*, 14 November 1843, 'Gipps' Land'.
2 *PPP*, 21 January 1841, 'Important Discovery'.
3 *PPP*, 28 January 1841, 'Corner Inlet'; *PPP*, 1 February 1841, 'Gipps' Land'; *PPP*, 4 February 1841, 'Corner Inlet'; *PPP*, 15 February 1841, 'The Clonmel'; *PPP*, 22 March 1841, 'Gipps' Land'.
4 *PPP*, 4 February 1841, Local Intelligence, 'Corner Inlet'.
5 For example *PPH*, 19 January 1841, 'An Important Discovery'.
6 *NSW Gazette*, 1843, p. 861. See also *PPP*, 3 February 1842 (reprinted from the *Colonial Observer*).
7 *PPP*, 29 March 1841, 'Corner Inlet'.
8 *PPP*, 26 April 1841, 'Gipps' Land'.
9 *PPP*, 31 May 1841, 'Gipps' Land'.
10 *PPP*, 15 April 1841, 'The Progress of Discovery'.
11 Bhabha, 'Signs Taken for Wonders'.
12 Raymond, 15 August 1853, in Bride (ed.), *Letters from Victorian Pioneers*, p. 240.
13 Russell acknowledged authorship of the article in letters dated November 1843 and December 1843, Port Albert Maritime Museum.
14 Letter to the editor, signed X. Y. Z., Melbourne, 3 September 1846, in *PPG*, 5 September 1846.
15 Carter, *Living in a New Country*, pp. 123–4.
16 Tyers to La Trobe, 'Report on state of Gipps Land District', Alberton, 15 July 1844, in Bride (ed.), *Letters from Victorian Pioneers*, p. 228.
17 Russell's letter to unnamed correspondent, 30 March 1843, Port Albert Maritime Museum.
18 Adams (ed.), *Notes on Gippsland History*, Vol. IV, p. 3; Also *Argus*, 27 August 1912, 'Notes for Boys—Peculiar Stones', p. 9, and *Argus*, 17 September 1912, 'Notes for Boys—The Heart Estate', p. 9.
19 Howitt, *The Native Tribes of South-East Australia*, p. 572.
20 *ibid.* p. 575.

21 *ibid.* pp. 494–5, p. 553, and fig. 32.

22 Massola, 'The Challicum Bun-yip'; Massola *Journey into Aboriginal Victoria*, pp. 80–1; Massola, *Bunjil's Cave*, p. 147; Worsnop, *The Prehistoric Arts, Manufactures, Works, Weapons, etc.*, p. 168. See R. E. Johns' Scrapbook No. 1, Museum Victoria, for I. W. Scott's sketches of the Challicum Bun-yip, 1867.

23 Massola, *Journey into Aboriginal Victoria*, p. 186.

24 Marples, *White Horses and Other Hill Figures*, p. 57.

25 *ibid.* p. 119.

26 The White Hart Inn, Bourke Street, listed in the *PPG*, 11 September 1844, 'Publicans' Licenses'.

27 Obeyesekere, *The Apotheosis of Captain Cook*, p. 12.

28 Spivak develops this argument in 'Three Women's Texts and a Critique of Imperialism' and in 'Criticism, Feminism, and the Institution', p. 1.

29 Huggan, *Territorial Disputes*.

30 Tyers to La Trobe, 15 July 1844, 'Report on Gipps Land', in Bride, *Letters from Victorian Pioneers*, pp. 231–3.

31 Fison & Howitt, *Kamilaroi and Kurnai*, p. 181.

32 Brodribb, *Recollections of an Australian Squatter 1835–1883*, pp. 33, 34, 38.

33 Tiffin, 'Post-Colonial Literatures and Counter-Discourse', p. 97.

34 *SH*, 6 Sept 1843, reprinted in *PPH*, 21 September 1843, 'Gipps Land'.

35 *PPH*, 'Extraordinary', 29 July 1843, 'Murder at Gipps Land'.

36 Gardner, *Our Founding Murdering Father*, p. 43; Gardner, *Gippsland Massacres*, p. 8. Also Cannon, *Who Killed the Koories?*, p. 171; Elder, *Blood on the Wattle*, p. 87; Green, *The Gippsland Lakes*, p. 20; Porter, *Bairnsdale*, p. 54; *Bairnsdale Advertiser*, 7 April 1952, 'An Absentee Pioneer: The Story of Lachlan Macalister' by N.B.

37 McCaughey et al., *Victoria's Colonial Governors 1839–1900*, p. 20; Critchett, *A 'distant field of murder'*, pp. 118–19.

38 Mackaness (ed.), *George Augustus Robinson's Journey into South-Eastern Australia, 1844*, p. 10.

39 *PPP*, 3 September 1846, 'The Whites and the Blacks'.

40 Mackaness (ed.), *George Augustus Robinson's Journey into South-Eastern Australia, 1844*, pp. 33–4.

41 *ibid.*, p. 33.

42 Journal of Patrick Coady Buckley, Port Albert Maritime Museum, entries for March 27 [1844] and March 30 [1844].

43 Adams, *The Tambo Shire Centenary History*, pp. 59–60.

44 Attwood, Blacks and Lohans, PhD, p. 61.

45 Tyers's report cited in Watson, *Caledonia Australis*, pp. 164–5.

46 Cited in Critchett, *A 'distant field of murder'*, p. 29. Robinson makes a similar point in relation to Dana's Native Police in the Portland Bay District, cited in Fels, *Good Men and True*, p. 140.

47 *PPH*, 8 November 1843, 'Gipps Land'.

48 Cited in Fels, *Good Men and True*, p. 177.

49 *PPG*, 26 March 1845, 'Interesting Discovery'.

50 *GA*, 15 April 1844, 'Wreck at Moonlight Head'.

51 For an analysis of narrative repetition see Brooks, *Reading for the Plot*, pp. 99–100.

52 Rose, 'Nature and Gender in Outback Australia', p. 403.

53 Westgarth, *Victoria; Late Australia Felix*, pp. 94–5; *PPG*, 29 December 1841, 'Original Correspondence'.

54 The petition was published with La Trobe's reply in *GA*, 4 April 1842, 'The Aborigines'. See also Critchett, *A 'distant field of murder'*, pp. 168–9, and Kiddle, *Men of Yesterday*, pp. 124–5.

55 Bride (ed.), *Letters from Victorian Pioneers*, p. 438.

56 *PPH*, 13 October 1843, 'Portland Bay Extracts. The Blacks', and *PPP*, 9 October 1843, no heading (reprinted from the *Portland Mercury*).

57 Thomas, 'Brief Account of the Aborigines of Australia Felix', in Bride (ed.), *Letters from Victorian Pioneers*, p. 408; *PPH*, 27 February 1846, 'Child Lost'; *PPH*, 5 May 1846, 'Child Stolen by the Blacks'; *PPH*, 6 May 1846 'Child Stolen by the Blacks'; *PPH*, 8 May 1846, 'A Feeling Reply'.

58 Derounian-Stodala & Levernier, *The Indian Captivity Narrative, 1550–1900*, pp. 5–8. See also Kolodny, *The Land Before Her*, pp. 68–75; Kestler, *The Indian Captivity Narrative*, pp. 17–20, 114–18, 123.

59 Fels, *Good Men and True*, p. 149.

60 *PPP*, 7 March 1846, 'White Woman Detained By the Blacks' (reprinted in *Portland Guardian* 17 March 1846).

61 H. P. Dana to La Trobe, Melbourne, 8 March 1846. 46/421, PRO, VPRS 19/P, unit 80.

62 Tyers to La Trobe, 4 April 1846. 46/665, PRO, VPRS 19/P, unit 81.

63 *PPP*, 7 March 1846, 'White Woman Detained By the Blacks' (reprinted *Portland Guardian*, 17 March 1846).

64 Walsh, statement declared before Tyers, 30 March 1846. No. 6 in schedule of correspondence tabled in the Legislative Council, 21 October 1846. Typescript copy in MS 10065, La Trobe Collection, SLV, bag 6.

65 *PPH*, 10 March 1846, 'Miss Lord', letter to the editor.

66 *PPG*, 24 April 1839, 'The Aborigines'; *PPG*, 4 May 1839, 'Aborigines No. 2'; *PPG*, 15 May 1839, 'Aborigines No. 3'; *PPG*, 11 May 1839, 'Aborigines No. 4'; *PPG*, 1 June 1839, letter to the editor; *PPP*, 23 October 1846, 'The Aboriginal School at Merri Creek'; *PPH*, 16 February 1844, 'Fellow colonists'; *PPP*, 19 March 1846, 'Cape Otway' (reprinted in the *Portland Guardian*, 31 March 1846); *PPP*, 17 August 1846, 'The Famine in Ireland'; *SMH*, 5 February 1847, 'Windsor Hospital'.

67 *PPG*, 11 March 1846, 'Miss Lord'.

68 For references to the White Lady, see Dawson, *Australian Aborigines*, p. 55; and Massola, *Journey into Aboriginal Victoria*, pp. 53–4.

69 A comprehensive coverage is given in *GA*, 17 September 1845. For details on where the passengers and crew members had come from in Britain, see Lemon & Morgan, *Poor Souls, They Perished*. A dramatic performance entitled 'Shipwreck of the Emigrant Ship "Cataraqui",' was performed to a full house in

Melbourne on 18 September 1845. Garryowen, *Chronicles of Early Melbourne*, Vol. I, pp. 474–5.

70 *PPH*, 20 August 1846, 'Immigration' (reprinted from the *Colonial Times*, 4 August) [on convicts]; *PPH*, 20 August 1846, 'Immigration' [a different article, on plans to bring immigrants from New Zealand]; *PPH*, 10 March 1846, letter to the editor, 'On board the *Shamrock*, at sea, 24th February, 1846' [on immigrants from Europe].

71 *PPP*, 19 March 1846, 'Cape Otway', letter to the editor (reprinted in *Portland Guardian*, 31 March 1846).

72 Shaw, *A History of The Port Phillip District*, p. 212.

73 Dana to La Trobe, Melbourne, 8 March 1846, 46/421, PRO, VPRS 19/P, unit 80; La Trobe to Tyers, 10 March 1846, 46/237, PRO, VPRS 2142, reel 3, pp. 74–5; La Trobe to Col. Sec., 6 May 1946, 46/368, PRO, VPRS 2142, reel 6, p. 148.

74 *PPP*, 28 March 1846, 'The Superintendent'.

75 *PPH*, 12 May 1846, 'Poor Miss Lord!'.

76 At the end of April 1846, the European population of Gipps Land was 852 (612 males and 240 females). *PPP*, 26 May 1846, 'Census of Port Phillip'; *Argus*, 12 June 1846, 'Census for the District of Gipps Land' (supplement).

77 *PPP*, 15 May 1846, Local Intelligence, 'Miss Lord'.

3 AGENTS AND AGENCY

1 *PPH*, 29 September 1846, 'A Lay of Lament'.

2 *PPH*, 20 August 1846, 'Miss Lord', letter to the editor, from Humanitas. Again, Captain Dana was in Melbourne shortly prior to Humanitas writing to the press. *PPP*, 24 August 1846, 'The Native Police', announced Dana's arrival on 17 August.

3 *PPH*, 20 August 1846, editorial footnote to Humanitas's letter.

4 *Argus*, 21 August 1846, 'Original Correspondence', letters to the editor, from John Macdonald, Scottish Chiefs, Melbourne, 20 August 1846, and from V, Melbourne, 20 August 1846.

5 *PPP*, 10 September 1846, 'Domestic Intelligence—The White Woman with the Blacks' (reprinted from *SMH*), letter to the editor, from An Englishman, Sydney, 29 August, headed 'Gross Inhumanity in a Christian Government'. Extracts from the letter also appeared in *Argus*, 8 September 1846, 'The Gipps Land Blacks', and *PPG*, 9 September 1846, 'The Gipps Land Expedition'.

6 *PPH*, 27 August 1846, 'Ellen McPherson', letter to the editor, from Humanitas, Melbourne, 22 August.

7 The identity of V might have been Christian De Villiers who, within days, was to put himself forward as a prospective leader of the expedition.

8 The advertisement appeared in: *PPP*, 28 August–2 September (incl.); *PPH*, 28 August, 29 August (extraordinary ed.), and 1 September; and *PPG*, 2 September. The names of the petitioners appeared in *PPH* and *PPP* of 1 September

but did not appear in every edition. Instead the statement: 'Here follow sixty-two signatures' was inserted in the notice. Minor typographical differences appear in the several newspapers. The quotation cited here is from *PPP*, 28 August.

9   *PPP*, 29 August 1846, 'Original Correspondence', letter to the editor, from An Old Inhabitant, Melbourne, 29 August 1846.

10 *PPP*, 28 August 1846, 'White Woman Among the Blacks'.

11 *Argus*, 28 August 1846, 'The Gipps Land Blacks'; *PPP*, 28 August 1846, 'White Woman among the Blacks'; *PPH*, 28 August 1846, 'Public Meeting'.

12 *Argus*, 28 August 1846, 'The Gipps Land Blacks'; *PPP*, 28 August 1846, 'White Woman among the Blacks'; *PPH*, 28 August 1846, 'Public Meeting'.

13 For example *PPP*, 12 August 1845.

14 Garryowen, *The Chronicles of Early Melbourne*, Vol. II, p. 661.

15 Billot, *John Batman and the founding of Melbourne*, pp. 203–4.

16 *PPH*, 1 September 1846, 'The White Females Detained by the Blacks'.

17 *PPH*, 28 August 1846, 'Extermination of the Cape Otway Tribe of Aborigines'. For background to Smythe's expedition see *GA*, 8 July 1846, 'Mr Surveyor Smyth'; *GA*, 8 August 1846, 'Return of Mr Surveyor Smythe'; *PPH*, 20 August 1846, 'Cape Otway'.

18 *PPP*, 29 August 1846, letter to the editor, from An Old Inhabitant, states that De Villiers in 1837 led a successful expedition against the Yarra Yarra, Geelong and Mount Macedon tribes.

19 *PPH*, 1 September 1846, 'The White Females Detained by the Blacks'.

20 *Argus*, 4 September 1946, 'The Gipps Land Blacks—Public Meeting'.

21 *ibid*.

22 *PPG*, 5 September 1846, 'The Report of Two White Women Being Detained by the Blacks'.

23 *PPP*, 3 July 1843, 'To the Honorable and Worshipful the Mayor of Melbourne. Melbourne, June 24, 1843'.

24 De Serville, *Port Phillip Gentlemen*, Appendix II, pp. 189–91.

25 Mouritz, *Port Phillip Directory, 1847*, p. 23. Stephen's term of office was due to expire in November 1847.

26 De Serville, *Port Phillip Gentlemen*, p. 21, and Appendix III, pp. 206–7.

27 Mouritz, *Port Phillip Directory, 1847*, p. 22.

28 De Serville, *Port Phillip Gentlemen*, p. 21.

29 Garryowen, *The Chronicles of Early Melbourne*, Vol. II, p. 833.

30 Marsden arrived in Melbourne in March 1841, after a short period as a Methodist missionary in India from 1838. *A Biographical Register 1788–1939*, Vol. II L–Z, p. 82; Mouritz, *Port Phillip Directory, 1847*, p. 109; *Australasian*, 17 August 1889 (obituary); *Argus*, 12 August 1889 (obituary), p. 5.

31 Garryowen, *The Chronicles of Early Melbourne*, Vol. II, p. 672.

32 Cannon, *Old Melbourne Town*, p. 458.

33 Gross, *Charles Joseph La Trobe*, p. 63; Shaw, *A History of The Port Phillip District*, p. 246.

34 McCombie, *Arabin or the Adventures of a Colonist in New South Wales*, p. 103.

35   McCombie, *History of the Colony of Victoria from its settlement to the death of Sir Charles Hotham*, pp. 57–8.

36   Published in *PPH*, 12 May 1846.

37   *PPP*, 15 May 1846, 'Breakers A-Head'.

38   For example, *PPH*, 10 March 1846, letter from J. D. Lang, 'On board the *Shamrock*, at sea, 24th February, 1846'; *PPH*, 20 August 1846, 'Immigration'.

39   *PPH*, 20 August 1846, 'The July Riots'; McCombie, *History of the Colony of Victoria from its settlement to the death of Sir Charles Hotham*, pp. 119–20.

40   *PPP*, 18 August 1846, 'The Irish Relief Fund'; Garryowen, *The Chronicles of Early Melbourne*, Vol. II, p. 671; *PPH*, 27 August 1846; *PPP*, 17 August 1846, letter to the editor, from Humanitas.

41   *PPH*, 17 March 1846, 'Koort Kirrup' (report of the trial).

42   *PPH*, 17 March 1846, editorial article.

43   McCombie, *History of the Colony of Victoria from its settlement to the death of Sir Charles Hotham*, p. 57; Gross, *Charles Joseph La Trobe*, pp. 46–7.

44   *PPH*, 12 May 1846, 'A Distinguished Squatter'.

45   *PPP*, 28 August 1846, 'Mr. La Trobe'.

46   McCombie, *History of the Colony of Victoria from its settlement to the death of Sir Charles Hotham*, pp. 60–1, 116–18.

47   Shaw, *A History of The Port Phillip District*, pp. 175, 245; Garden, *Victoria: A History*, pp. 63–6; Gross, *Charles Joseph La Trobe*, pp. 79–80.

48   *Argus*, 25 August 1846, 'The Superintendent'. See also the satiric public notice in *Argus*, 7 July 1846, 'The Superintendent of Port Phillip', signed C. J. La Punch, and *Argus*, 23 October 1846, 'La Trobe's Last Kick'.

49   Gross, *Charles Joseph La Trobe*, pp. 72, 92, 93; Shaw, *A History of The Port Phillip District*, pp. 153–7, 177, 238–48.

50   Quoted in McCombie, *History of the Colony of Victoria from its settlement to the death of Sir Charles Hotham*, p. 118.

51   *ibid.* pp. 122–3.

52   Fitzsimons (ed.), *Heraldry & Regalia of War*, p. 78.

53   Smith-Rosenberg, 'Captured Subjects/Savage Others, p. 179.

54   Darian-Smith, 'Capturing the White Woman of Gippsland, p. 20.

55   The reports of the public meeting cited in this chapter comprise: *PPP*, 3 September 1846, 'The Whites and the Blacks'; *PPH*, 3 September 1846, 'The Gipps Land Expedition' and 'White Woman Meeting'; *Argus*, 4 September 1846, 'The Gipps Land Blacks—Public Meeting'; *PPG*, 5 September 1846, 'The Report of Two White Women Being Detained by the Blacks'.

56   Garryowen, *The Chronicles of Early Melbourne*, Vol. II, pp. 828–9; Garden, *Victoria: A History*, p. 44.

57   *PPH*, 3 September 1846, 'White Woman Meeting'.

58   *ibid.*

59   *PPP*, 3 September 1846, 'The Whites and the Blacks'.

60   *ibid.*

61   Mouritz, *Port Phillip Directory, 1847*, pp. 58, 102, 122, 123, 130.

62   *PPH*, 3 September 1846, 'The Gipps Land Expedition'.

63 *PPH*, 3 September 1846, 'White Women Meeting'.

64 *ibid.*

65 La Trobe to Tyers, Melbourne, 5 May 1846, 46/486, PRO, VPRS 2142, reel 3, pp. 119–20.

66 *PPH*, 26 November 1846, 'The White Woman at Gipps Land'.

67 Hulme, *Colonial Encounters*, pp. 194–6.

68 *PPP*, 18 February 1847, 'Gipps Land Expedition', report of De Villiers.

69 Schaffer, *In the Wake of First Contact*, p. 50; Slotkin, *Regeneration through Violence*, pp. 247–59; Fiedler, *The Return of the Vanishing American*.

70 An example is in Lady Broome's *Colonial Memories*, pp. 116–18.

71 Fiedler, *The Return of the Vanishing American*, pp. 92–3.

72 See frontispiece to R. Gibbings, *John Graham Convict 1824*, A. S. Barnes & Company, New York, 1957.

73 *PPH*, 3 September 1846, 'White Women Meeting'.

74 *PPP*, 7 September 1846, 'The Ladies' Meeting'.

75 *Argus*, 29 September 1846, 'Gipps Land Expedition Committee'.

76 *Argus*, 29 September 1846, 'Appeal to the Public'. The appeal notice was also published in *PPH*, 13 October 1846; *Portland Guardian*, 13 October 1846; *PPH*, 20 October 1846.

77 *PPP*, 10 September 1846, 'Gross Inhumanity in a Christian Government' (reprinted from *SMH*).

78 *PPH*, 29 September 1846, 'Gipps Land Expedition'.

79 *PPH*, 10 September 1846, 'Notice to Correspondents'.

80 *PPH*, 29 September 1846, 'A Lay of Lament' by J. R. M.

81 *SMH*, 9 September 1846, letter to the editor, from Z, Sydney, September 7 [1846].

82 *PPP*, 23 September 1846, 'The Female Mission'.

83 *PPP*, 7 September 1846, 'The Recovery Expedition'.

84 *PPH*, 11 September 1846, 'Mr La Trobe'.

85 *PPP*, 7 September 1846, 'The Recovery Expedition'.

86 *SMH*, 23 September 1846, 'Legislative Council, White Woman Among the Aborigines'; *Argus*, 29 September 1846, 'Legislative Council, Tuesday, September 22, Gipps Land Blacks'; *PPP*, 2 October 1846, 'Legislative Council Tues. 22 Sept., White Woman Among the Aborigines'.

87 *SMH*, 22 October 1846, 'Legislative Council (Wednesday 21/10/46), The White Female in Gipps Land'.

88 Col. Sec. to Macdonald, published in *PPH*, 1 October 1846, 'The Gipps Land Expedition', and *Argus*, 9 October 1846, 'The Gipps Land Expedition'.

89 *PPH*, 1 October 1846, 'Gipps Land Expedition', editorial column.

90 Macdonald to La Trobe, Melbourne, 7 October 1846, 46/1473, PRO, VPRS 19/P, unit 85.

91 *PPH*, 13 October 1846, 'The Gipps Land Expedition'.

92 *PPH*, 24 December 1846, 'Gipps Land Expedition', lists donors, receipts and expenditure; *PPH*, 11 September 1846, 'The White Woman and the Blacks'.

93 *PPH*, 13 October 1846, 'The Gipps Land Expedition'.

4 'A COMPLEX OF NARRATIVES'

1   Slotkin, *Regeneration Through Violence*, p. 6.

2   *PPH*, 29 October 1846, 'Strange Circumstance'.

3   *Argus*, 20 October 1846, 'Gipps Land Expedition'.

4   Warman gives the details about Thomas Hill and William Peters in his letter to the expedition committee, 30 October 1846, in *PPH*, 1 December 1846, 'Gipps Land Expedition'. *PPP*, 1 December 1846, 'The Gipps' Land Expedition', provides details about McLeod and Hill.

5   *PPH*, 20 October 1846, 'The Gipps Land Expedition'; *PPP*, 20 October 1846, 'The Gipps Land Expedition'; *PPG*, 21 October 1846, 'The Gipp's Land Expedition'. The handkerchief will be discussed in Chapter 5.

6   *Argus*, 27 October 1846, letter to the editor from James Buck; *PPH*, 29 October 1846, 'James Buck'; *Argus*, 6 November 1846, letter to the editor from James Buck.

7   For example *Argus*, 1 January 1847, 'The Gipps Land Expedition'; *PPP*, 8 March 1847, 'Gipps Land Expedition'; *PPH*, 9 March 1847, 'Wrong Again'; *PPH*, 8 April 1847, 'The White Woman'.

8   De Villiers to Committee, 28 October 1846, Port Albert, in *PPH*, 19 November 1846, 'Gipps Land Expedition'.

9   *PPP*, 25 January 1847, 'The Gipps' Land Expedition'; *PPH*, 26 January 1847, 'The White Woman'.

10 *PPH*, 23 February 1847, 25 February 1847, and 2 March 1847 respectively, all under the heading 'Gipps Land Expedition'.

11 Gardner, *Our Founding Murdering Father*, p. 48.

12 Phillip Pepper attributes one anecdote about the White Woman to Aboriginal sources. Pepper & De Araugo, *The Kurnai of Gippsland*, p. 76.

13 *PPH*, 23 February 1847, 'Gipps Land Expedition'. Entry for Sunday, 1 November [1846].

14 *PPH*, 21 January 1847, 'Gipps Land Expedition', letter from Warman to unnamed correspondent, 5 January 1847.

15 *PPH*, 23 February 1847, 'The Gipps Land Expedition'. Entry for 6 November [1846].

16 See Mary Louise Pratt, *Imperial Eyes*, pp. 60–75, for an examination of the 'fantasy of dominance and appropriation' that is built into the landscanning European gaze.

17 *PPH*, 25 February 1847, 'Gipps Land Expedition'. Entry for Wednesday, 23 [December 1846].

18 *PPH*, 2 March 1847, 'Gipps Land'.

19 Obeyesekere, *The Apotheosis of Captain Cook*, pp. 13–14.

20 *PPH*, 23 February 1847, 'Gipps Land Expedition'. Entries for Saturday 7 and Sunday 8 [November 1846] respectively.

21 Golgotha—a place of interment, a graveyard, a charnel-house. *Oxford Shorter English Dictionary*; *New Testament*, John 19.17.

22 *PPH*, 23 February 1847, 'Gipps Land Expedition'. Entry for 10 November [1846].

23 *PPH*, 29 December 1846, 'The Gipps Land Expedition', Warman to Cavenagh, 24 November 1846, Eagle Point.

24 *PPH*, 21 January 1847, 'Gipps Land Expedition', Warman to unnamed correspondent, 5 January 1847. A row of asterisks halfway through the published letter suggests that some text has been edited out.

25 *Report on the Condition, Capabilities and Prospects of the Australian Aborigines*, extracts published in *SMH*, 3 September 1846. A review of the pamphlet and the final chapter was published in *GA*, 26 August 1846, 'Review'.

26 Garryowen, *The Chronicles of Early Melbourne*, Vol. II, p. 608.

27 Details on Warman contained in Sellars, Biographical notes, SLV.

28 *PPP*, 9 January 1843, 'The Late Police Case'; *PPG*, 5 January 1843, 'Wondrous Bravery'.

29 *PPG*, 24 June, 1844, 'Domestic Intelligence—Breach of the Peace'.

30 *PPG*, 7 August 1844, 'Judicial Intelligence—Supreme Court—August 2, 1844. Assessor Case—Stephen v. McCombie'.

31 *PPG*, 11 September 1844, 'Mysterious Occurrence'.

32 Deposition by C. De Villiers, sworn before C. J. Tyers at the Border Police Station, Lake King, 30 December 1846. Deposition by James Warman, sworn before W. O. Raymond Esq. J. P. and Charles J. Tyers Esq. J. P., Strathfieldsaye, Lake Wellington, 4 January 1847. Typescript copies in La Trobe Collection, SLV, MS 10065, bag 1.

33 De Villiers to Cavenagh, 1 January 1847, Eagle Point, Lake King, in *PPH*, 21 January 1847, 'Original Correspondence—The White Woman' (also in *PPP*, 22 January 1847, and *Argus*, 26 January 1847). Included De Villiers to W. Dana, 15 December 1846, Eagle Point, and De Villiers to Tyers, 23 November 1846, Eagle Point.

34 *PPH*, 21 January 1847, 'Gipps Land Expedition'.

35 Clark (ed.), *The Port Phillip Journals of George Augustus Robinson*, p. 10; Reynolds, *Frontier*, p. 62.

36 Carter, *The Road to Botany Bay*, pp. 80–1.

37 Hulme, *Colonial Encounters*, p. 3.

38 This is the first verse of the alternative version *c*. 1598 by W. Kethe, as in Daye's Psalter (1560–1) and the *Scottish Psalter* (1650). G. Cumberledge, *Songs of Praise*, Oxford University Press, London, 1950 [1926], pp. 534–5.

39 J. Bunyan, *The Pilgrim's Progress*, Oxford University Press, London, 1942 [1672], pp. 180–6.

40 Slotkin, *Regeneration through Violence*; Hughes, *American Visions*, pp. 189–194.

41 Derounian-Stodola & Levernier, *The Indian Captivity Narrative*, pp. 18–21.

42 *PPH*, 31 December 1846, 'Gipps Land Expedition', De Villiers to Cavenagh, 3 December 1846, Lake King.

43 *PPH*, 19 May 1843, 'A Trip to Gipps' Land, in April, 1843' by H. B. Morris.

44 *PPP*, 16 February 1847, 'Gipps Land Expedition'.

45 *PPP*, 18 February 1847, 'The White Woman'.

46 *PPH*, 18 February 1847, 'Ingenuity of the Natives'. This, presumably, was the item to which Brodie refers.

47 *PPH*, 25 February 1847, 'Gipps Land Expedition'. Entry for Saturday, 19th [December 1846].

48 De Villiers to the Committee, 3 December 1846, Lake King, *PPH*, 31 December 1846, 'Gipps Land Expedition'.

49 *ibid*.

50 De Villiers to the Committee, 10 February 1847, Melbourne, *PPP*, 13 February 1847, 'Gipps Land Expedition'.

51 De Villiers to Cavenagh, 3 December 1846, Lake King, *PPH*, 31 December 1846, 'Gipps Land Expedition'.

52 Carter, *Living in a New Country*, pp. 144–5.

53 *PPH*, 23 February 1847, 'Gipps Land Expedition'.

54 A Melbournite of '38, 'The Early History of Victoria, Being Reminiscences of Bygone Days', p. 495.

5 'THE DREAM-LIKE ARRANGEMENTS OF ROMANCE'

1 *PPP*, 26 January 1847, 'Burns' Festival'.

2 Hopkins, *Knights*, pp. 183–6.

3 *ILN*, 13 July 1844, p. 24.

4 Dixon, *Writing the Colonial Adventure*, p. 20.

5 *PPP*, 16 February 1847, 'Gipps Land Expedition', De Villiers to Chairman and other members of the Committee, Melbourne, 10 February 1847.

6 *PPH*, 2 March 1847, 'Gipps Land Expedition, Mr. Warman's Journal (Concluded from our last)'.

7 *PPH*, 9 February 1847, 'The White Woman'.

8 P. Beale (ed.), *Dictionary of Slang and Unconventional English*, London, 1984, p. 1340; *1811 Dictionary of the Vulgar Tongue* (unabridged ed. Northfield, Ill., 1971, [Frances Grose, London, 1785]) entry under 'Gloves', no page no; C. Hole (ed.), *Encyclopaedia of Superstitions*, Hutchinson, London, 1961, p. 171; John Gay, 'The Shepherd's Week' in G. C. Faber (ed.), *The Poetical Works of John Gay*, Russell & Russell, New York, p. 52, lines 35–9; Mary Gaunt, *Kirkham's Find*, Penguin Books Australia, Ringwood, 1988 [London, 1897], Vol. I, p. 13.

9 Scott, *Saint Valentine's Day; or, The Fair Maid of Perth*, Vol. I, pp. 102–3, 109, 119.

10 *ibid.*, Vol. I, p. 117.

11 *ILN*, 31 May 1845, p. 346.

12 Painting reproduced in E. Longford, *Wellington*, Weidenfeld & Nicolson, London, 1972, ill. 30.

13 Reproduced in Mitford, *Grace Had an English Heart*, frontispiece.

14 Peel Papers, ii. 414, cited in Lee, *Queen Victoria*, p. 109; Woodham-Smith, *Queen Victoria*, Vol. I, 1819–1861, p. 195.

15 Gernsheim, *Queen Victoria: A Biography in Word and Picture*, p. 15.

16 Anstruther, *The Knight and the Umbrella*, pp. 11, 115.

17 *Times*, 9 September 1842, 'Her Majesty's Departure for Perthshire', p. 5.

18 Scott, *Saint Valentine's Day; or, The Fair Maid of Perth*, Vol. II, p. 13.

19 The Queen was several times reported to be wearing 'a tartan shawl'. *Times*, 3 September 1842, 'Her Majesty's Arrival', p. 3; *Times*, 6 September 1842, p. 5.

20 *Times*, 10 September 1842, 'The Queen's Visit to Scotland'. p. 5.

21 Reprinted in the *Times*, 5 September 1842, 'Plan of the Royal Progress through Perthshire', p. 5.

22 Presland, *Journals of G. A. Robinson, May–August 1841*, p. 130 and fig. 56 showing 'distribution of handkerchiefs and blankets'.

23 Warman's journal was published in three instalments in *PPH*. The section in which this entry appears was published on 23 February 1847.

24 Wynne-Davies, M. (ed.), *Prentice Hall Guide to English Literature*, pp. 368–9.

25 *ILN*, 30 September 1843, p. 217.

26 Duffy, *The Erotic World of Faery*, Sphere Books, London, 1972, pp. 119, 135, 334. Brooke-Little, *Boutell's Heraldry*, p. 11.

27 Warman describes the expedition to retrieve the tree, *PPH*, 1 December 1846, 'Gipps Land Expedition'. Other reports on the tree include *PPP*, 1 December 1846, 'The Gipps' Land Expedition'; *Argus*, 1 December 1846, 'Gipps Land Expedition'; *PPH*, 4 December 1846, 'Gipps Land Expedition'; *Portland Guardian*, 8 December 1846, 'Gipps Land Expedition'.

28 *PPH*, 20 August 1846, 'Miss Lord'.

29 Anstruther, *The Knight and the Umbrella*, pp. 11, 115.

30 *ibid.* pp. 126–8.

31 Joanna Richardson, *Victoria and Albert: a study of a marriage*, J. M. Dent & Sons Ltd, London, 1977, p. 80.

32 Anstruther, *The Knight and the Umbrella*, p. 226.

33 Hopkins, *Knights*, p. 186.

34 Disraeli, *Endymion*, pp. 254–66.

35 *ibid.*, p. 262.

36 *PPP*, 4 January 1841, 'The Tournament'.

37 For a discussion of the practice of 'blackballing' by the Melbourne Club to maintain an elite membership, see De Serville, *Port Phillip Gentlemen*, p. 64.

38 *PPH*, 27 December 1844. Advertisement.

39 Fiedler, *The Return of the Vanishing American*, p. 138.

40 Brooke-Little, *Boutell's Heraldry*, p. 63. The heart appears on the Douglas arms.

41 Matthews, *The Grail*, p. 60.

42 *PPG*, 5 September 1846, letter to the editor, from X. Y. Z, Melbourne, 3 September 1846.

43 *PPH*, 19 November 1846, 'Gipps Land Expedition', De Villiers to Cavenagh, Port Albert, 28 October 1846.

44 Cowan's report, 'Proceedings of the Party under Mr. William Dana—in search of the white female said to be among the Blacks', December 1846. Letter from Tyers to La Trobe, 21 November 1846, enclosing Tyers's journal 'relative to the proceedings that have been recently adopted', OC 107/46.

45 *PPH*, 21 January 1847, 'The White Woman', De Villiers to Tyers, 23 November 1846, Eagle Point; *PPP*, 22 January 1847, 'The White Woman'; *Argus*, 26 January 1847, 'Gipps Land Expedition'.

46 Walter Scott's *Ivanhoe* featured the Black Knight.
47 *PPH*, 2 March 1847, 'Gipps Land Expedition', journal entry for Friday 15 [January 1847].
48 Col. Sec. to La Trobe, 2 February 1847, 47/72, PRO, VPRS 19/P, unit 88; Lonsdale to Col. Sec., 12 February 1847, 47/148, PRO, VPRS 2142, reel 6.
49 *PPG*, 23 January 1847, 'Doings in Gipps Land'.
50 *PPH*, 11 February 1847, 'The White Woman'.
51 *ibid.*
52 *PPP*, 13 February 1847, 'Gipps Land Expedition', De Villiers to Committee, 10 February 1847, Melbourne.
53 *PPP*, 16 February 1847, 'The White Woman—Gipps Land', letter to the editor from McLelland.
54 *PPH*, 2 July 1846, 'Original Correspondence', letter to the editor from De Villiers.
55 *PPP*, 18 February 1847, 'The White Woman'.
56 *PPH*, 18 February 1847, 'The Captive White Woman'.
57 *ibid.*, McMillan to Cavenagh, Port Albert, 6 February 1846 [should be 1847].
58 *PPG*, 20 February 1847, 'Official Correspondence—The Captive White Woman', letter to the editor from 'A Fellow Colonist', n.d.
59 *PPP*, 22 February 1847, 'The Captive White Woman'.
60 La Trobe was to remain sceptical. He advised the Colonial Secretary in April 1847 that the woman's existence was 'just barely possible'. La Trobe to Col. Sec., 15 April 1847, 47/364, PRO, VPRS 2142, reel 6, p. 102.
61 La Trobe to Tyers, 1 March 1847, 47/263, PRO, VPRS 2142, reel 4, pp. 50–2.
62 La Trobe to H. P. Dana, 9 March 1847, 47/277, PRO, VPRS 2142, reel 4, p. 59. Dana's report was subsequently submitted and forwarded by La Trobe to Sydney (La Trobe to Col. Sec., 26 April 1847, 47/390, PRO, VPRS 2142, reel 6, pp. 116–17). La Trobe was advised: 'that His Excellency regrets that He cannot consider Mr. Dana's explanation as satisfactory'. Col. Sec. to La Trobe, 11 May 1847, 47/907, PRO, VPRS 19/P, unit 92.
63 *PPG*, 10 March 1847, 'Gipps Land Expedition'.
64 *Argus*, 12 March 1847, 'Gipps Land Expedition', advertisement.
65 *PPH*, 9 March 1847, 'Gipps Land Expedition'; *Argus*, 9 March 1847, 'Gipps Land Expedition'—'Report of the Committee appointed by the Public Meeting to arrange the Gipps Land Expedition'; *Argus*, 13 April 1847, 'Gipps Land Expedition', letter to the editor, Melbourne, 10 April 1846.
66 *PPP*, 11 February 1847, 'The White Woman in Gipps Land'; *Argus*, 12 February 1847, 'Gipps Land Expedition'; *PPG*, 13 February 1847, 'Gipps Land Expedition'.
67 *PPH*, 4 November 1846 (extraordinary ed.).
68 *SMH*, 1 January 1847. Articles on exploration included 'New Year's Day' editorial; 'The Practical Value of the Recent Discoveries'; 'Exploring Expedition Under Sir Thomas Mitchell'; and 'River Boyne'.
69 On the geopolitical nature of mapping, see Huggan, *Territorial Disputes*, p. 9. See also Gibson, *South of the West*, pp. 1–18, for an examination of the 'recurrent

... preoccupation with topography on the part of Europeans who have attempted, over several centuries, to define a non-Aboriginal Australian culture'.

70 *PPG*, 11 November 1846, 'New Map of Australia Felix'; *SMH*, 4 March 1847, 'Map of Port Phillip'.

71 *PPH*, 20 May, 27 May, 3 June and 10 June 1847, 'A Review of the Map of Australia Felix'. Arden's review and Ham's map are reproduced in Arden, *A Sketch of Port Phillip*.

72 *PPP*, 10 December 1846, advertisement for Ham's map.

73 Obeyesekere, *The Apotheosis of Captain Cook*, p. 12.

74 Arden, *A Sketch of Port Phillip*, p. 17.

75 Harley, 'Maps, Knowledge and Power', in Cosgrove & Daniels (eds), *The Iconography of Landscape*, p. 292.

76 Kolodny, *The Lay of the Land*.

77 Arden, *A Sketch of Port Phillip*, p. 27.

6 SCAPEGOATS AND FIGUREHEADS

1 *PPP*, 7 April 1847, 'The White Woman in Gipps Land'.

2 *PPH*, 4 March 1847, 'The White Woman'; *Argus*, 9 March 1847, 'Gipps Land Expedition'; *PPH*, 11 March 1847, 'The Blacks'.

3 *PPH*, 9 March 1847, 'Gipps Land Expedition'; *Argus*, 9 March 1847, 'Gipps Land Expedition'.

4 *PPH*, 9 March 1847, 'The White Woman'.

5 *PPH*, 9 March 1847, 'The White Woman'; *Argus*, 9 March 1847, 'News from Gipps Land'.

6 *PPP*, 23 March 1847, 'The White Woman'.

7 *PPH*, 15 April 1847, 'The White Woman'.

8 *PPG*, 19 May 1847, 'Gipps Land'.

9 *PPP*, 7 April 1847, 'The White Woman in Gipps Land'.

10 *PPP*, 8 March 1847, 'Gipps Land Expedition'; *PPH*, 9 March 1847, 'Wrong Again'.

11 *PPH*, 20 April 1847, 'The White Woman'; *PPH*, 6 May 1847, 'The White Woman'.

12 *PPP*, 7 April 1847, 'The White Woman in Gipps Land'; *PPH*, 8 May 1847, 'The White Woman'; *Argus*, 7 May 1847, 'Gipps Land'.

13 *PPH*, 6 May 1847, 'The White Woman'.

14 For example, *PPH*, 4 May 1847, 'The White Woman'; *PPH*, 25 May 1847, 'The White Woman'; *Argus*, 2 July 1847, 'The Gipps Land Expedition'.

15 *PPH*, 25 May 1847, 'The White Woman'; *PPH*, 15 July 1847, 'The White Woman'.

16 'Journal of an expedition which started from Melbourne 6 March 1847 in search of a white woman supposed to be detained amongst the aborigines of Gippsland', SLV [hereafter Journal second expedition]. Entry for Thursday 22nd [April 1847].

17 Tyers to La Trobe, 6 April 1847, 47/701, PRO, VPRS 19/P, unit 91.

18 *Argus*, 12 February 1847, 'Gipps Land Expedition'.

19 Tyers to La Trobe, 26 April 1847, 56/47. Typescript copy in La Trobe Collection, SLV, MS 10065, bag 5.

20 De Villiers to Cavenagh, Melbourne, 15 February 1847, in *PPH*, 18 February 1847, 'Gipps Land Expedition'.

21 Tyers to La Trobe, 10 April 1847, 47/698, PRO, VPRS 19/P, unit 91.

22 Extract from Trooper Cowan's Journal, attachment to Tyers to La Trobe, 19 March 1847, 40/47. Typescript copy in La Trobe Collection, SLV, MS 10065, bag 1.

23 Journal second expedition, extract from entry for Friday 9th [April 1847].

24 *PPH*, 15 July 1847, 'The White Woman'.

25 La Trobe to Col. Sec., 9 June 1847, 47/590, PRO, VPRS 2142, reel 6, pp. 179–80.

26 *PPG*, 20 February 1847, 'The Captive White Woman', letter to the editor, from 'A Fellow Colonist'.

27 Facsimile of document in Dawson, *Australian Aborigines* (no page nos.).

28 *PPH*, 1 July 1847, 'The White Woman'. The article included an account of the expeditionists' journey to the mountains.

29 'Report of the Central Board appointed to watch over the interests of Aborigines in the Colony of Victoria', Parliamentary Paper No. 39 of 1861. Typescript copy in La Trobe Collection, SLV, MS 10065, bag 2.

30 Tyers to La Trobe, 14 June 1847, 47/1189, PRO, VPRS 19/P, unit 93.

31 H. P. Dana to La Trobe, 29 June 1847, 47/1186, PRO, VPRS 19/P, unit 93.

32 La Trobe to H. P. Dana, 30 June 1847. Typescript copy La Trobe Collection, SLV, MS 10065, bag 5.

33 La Trobe to Col. Sec., 7 July 1847, 47/742, PRO, VPRS 2142, reel 6, pp. 217–18.

34 Robinson to La Trobe, 19 July 1847, with notation by La Trobe, 47/1354, PRO, VPRS 19/P, unit 94.

35 Col. Sec. to La Trobe, 19 July 1847, 47/375, PRO, VPRS 19/P, unit 89.

36 *PPG*, 3 July 1847, 'Bungalene'; also *PPH*, 19 August 1847, 'The White Woman'.

37 H. P. Dana to La Trobe, 5 January 1848, 48/53, PRO, VPRS 19/P, unit 101; La Trobe to H. P. Dana, 14 January 1848, 48/37, PRO, VPRS 2142, reel 4.

38 Day Book of Native Police Corps, PRO, VPRS 5519, unit no. 1. After Bungelene's death, one of his wives and her two young sons were removed to the Merri Merri Creek Mission Station. In 1861, one of the children, Thomas Bungelene, came under the care of the Central Board Appointed to Watch over the Interests of Aborigines in the Colony of Victoria. His brother had by this time died. The Board considered that Thomas presented an opportunity 'of proving to the world that the Aborigines of Australia are degraded rather by their habits, than in consequence of the want of mental capacity' and sought to have him educated. The scheme was abandoned shortly afterwards and Thomas was transferred to the SS *Victoria*, to be taught the duties of a seaman. See Parliamentary Paper No. 39 of 1861. Typescript copy La Trobe Collection, MS 10065, SLV, bag 2.

39 Tyers to La Trobe, 10 April 1847, 47/698, PRO, VPRS 19/P, unit 91.

40 *PPH*, 20 April 1847, 'The White Woman'.

41 *PPH*, 29 July 1847, 'The White Woman'.

42 *Argus*, 7 May 1847, 'Gipps Land'.

43 Tyers to La Trobe, 14 June 1847, 47/1189, PRO, VPRS 19/P, unit 93.

44 *Argus*, 27 July 1847, letter to the Editor, from 'A Correspondent', n.d.

45 *Argus*, 27 July 1847, 'The White Woman'.

46 *PPG*, 10 July 1847, 'The Gipps Land Expedition'.

47 *PPH*, 12 October 1847, 'The White Woman'.

48 *PPH*, 5 November 1847 (Extraordinary ed), 'Murder of the Captive "White Woman" at Gipps Land'.

49 *PPP*, 6 November 1847, 'The White Woman'.

50 Tyers to La Trobe, 2 November 1847, 47/2171, PRO, VPRS 19/P, unit 98.

51 Cavenagh to La Trobe, 5 November 1847, 47/2061, PRO, VPRS 19/P, unit 98.

52 *PPP*, 23 November 1847, 'Odds and Ends'.

53 *PPP*, 30 November 1847, 'Gipps Land'.

54 *PPP*, 24 December 1847, 'The White Woman'.

55 *PPH*, 5 November 1847 (Extraordinary ed.), 'Murder of the Captive "White Woman" at Gipps Land'.

7   INVESTING IN A LEGEND

1 *Oban Times*, 26 April 1919, 'Pelligrina'; *J&R*, 17 December 1959, 'More than One White Woman Captured by Aborigines? Historian's Theory Substantiated by . . . Rescue at Won Wron's "White Woman's Waterhole"'.

2 Possible identities include Miss Sargent [Sargeantson] or Mrs Howie (*Argus*, 15 October 1921, 'Melbourne's Early Schools') and Miss Annie Weddon (*Gippsland Times*, 13 March 1950, 'Early Days in Gippsland: Legendary Tale Revived').

3 Bunce, *Australasiatic Reminiscences*, pp. 212–13; *ADB*, Vol. I, 1788–1850, entry on Bunce, pp. 176–7.

4 *ibid.*, p. 213.

5 *PPH*, 19 May 1843, 'A Trip to Gipps Land in April 1843', by H. B. Morris.

6 For example, Lovell-Smith, 'Out of the Hair Tent', pp. 67–76.

7 A Melbournite of '38, 'The Early History of Victoria', p. 495.

8 National Library of Australia, Canberra, lists in its catalogue under Thomas Strode, 'Annals and Reminiscences of Bygone Days—historical, statistical and social being some contributions to the early history of Port Phillip together with incidents not generally known', 1869–70, which contains the *nom de plume* 'A Melbournite of '38'. MS 19.

9 *PPG*, 27 October 1838, 'Shipping Intelligence—Arrivals'.

10 *PPH*, 10 September 1846, 'Gross Inhumanity in a Christian Government', letter from 'An Englishman', Sydney, 29 August.

11 Garryowen, *The Chronicles of Early Melbourne*, Vol. II, pp. 599–611.

12 *ibid.*, Vol. II, p. 602.

13 *ibid.*, Vol. II, p. 602.

14 *ibid.*, p. 650.

15 *ibid.*, Vol. II, p. 609.

16 *ibid.*, Vol. II, p. 611.

17 *ibid.*, Author's preface, Vol. 1, p. 1.

18 The manuscript volume was the journal kept by McLeod, a member of the second expedition, discussed in chapter 6.

19 *Argus*, 25 May 1912, 'Early Victorian Mystery: How it was Solved', by Historicus.

20 Healy, *From the Ruins of Colonialism*, p. 90.

21 Hermann, 'The Broken Honeymoon', pp. 135–8.

22 *ibid.*, p. 136.

23 *ibid.*, p. 138.

24 Cox's letter appeared in *Life Magazine*, 1 October 1913, 'The Clearing House', pp. 408–9, along with Hermann's response (Hermann was given right of reply prior to publication).

25 *Life Magazine*, 1 January 1914, 'The Clearing House', pp. 102–3.

26 Buntine, 'The White Woman in Gippsland, pp. 174–5.

27 *ibid.*, p. 175.

28 *Argus*, 30 May 1914, 'A Gippsland Tradition: The Lost White Woman—An Interesting Relic'.

29 *Oban Times*, 'A Gippsland Tradition. The Lost White Woman. An Interesting Relic'.

30 Barrett, *White Blackfellows*, pp. 176–84.

31 Daley, 'The Story of Gippsland', p. 38.

32 Harrison, 'Some Memories of Old Gippsland and its Earliest Pioneers', p. 28, and *Age*, 19 November 1926, 'The White Woman of Gippsland: An Early Settler's Version', p. 6, respectively.

33 *Argus*, 19 May 1945, 'The Sign of the Heart: A Gippsland Mystery that has never been solved', by HANS.

34 Mackirdy, *The White Slave Market*.

35 *Herald*, 2 January 1934, 'Rediscovery of Victoria: White Woman Among the Blacks', by E. M. Webb.

36 *J&R*, 31 October 1949, 'Gippsland Figures in Australia's Early History', by Arthur Bradfield.

37 *Gippsland Times*, 13 March 1950, 'Early Days in Gippsland: Legendary Tale Revived'.

38 Brookes, 'The Lost and Abandoned', *Riders of Time*, pp. 102–9. Ill. by Harold Freedman, pp. 102–3.

39 Payne, Imagining Gippsland, hons thesis, pp. 50–67.

40 *J&R*, 17 December 1959, 'More than One White Woman Captured by Aborigines? Historian's Theory Substantiated by … Rescue at Won Wron's "White Woman's Waterhole".'

41 *J&R*, 24 December 1959, 'Carrajung Lower Historian Takes Us On a Visit to Won Wron's "White Woman's Waterhole"'.

42 *J&R*, 4 January 1960, 'Diary Reveals More of our Interesting History', by W. J. Cuthill.

43 *J&R*, 13 August 1962, 'Won Wron Rescue No Fascinating Romance'.

44 *J&R*, 13 September 1962, 'Noted Historian Looks Way Back to Locate 8 White Women Held Captive By the Blacks'.

45 'Interesting Places, White Woman's Waterhole', *Yarram and District Visitors Guide*, Yarram District Tourism, December 1995, p. 32.

46 Cuthill, 'The White Woman With the Blacks in Gipps' Land', pp. 7–25.

47 Gardner, 'The Journals of De Villiers and Warman', p. 96.

48 *Age*, 31 March 1997, 'Tribal elder spells out bid for native title', p. A4.

49 *Land Matters*, no. 5, December 1998, pp. 4–5, http://www.ilc.gov.au/Newsletters/LM5.HTM.

50 Watson, *Caledonia Australis*, especially ch. 8, 'Removing Another Race'; Pepper & De Araugo, *The Kurnai of Gippsland*, especially ch. 12, 'The Hunt for the White Woman'; Elder, *Blood on the Wattle*, pp. 93–7.

51 Fels, *Good Men and True*, esp. ch. 8, 'Out in the Field—Gippsland', pp. 173–98.

52 Cited in Fels, *Good Men and True*, p. 177.

53 Fels, *Good Men and True*, p. 181.

54 *ibid.*, pp. 186–7.

55 Cannon, *Who Killed the Koories?*, pp. 210–11. See also ch. 15, 'Terror Comes to Gippsland', p. 170–7 and ch. 18, 'White Woman Captured by Gippsland Blacks', pp. 205–17.

56 For example, Adams, *The Tambo Shire Centenary History* and *From these Beginnings*.

57 For example, Porter, *Bairnsdale*; Green, *The Gippland Lakes*; Wells, *Gippsland* and *More Colourful Tales of Old Gippsland*; Wilson (ed.), *The Official History of the Avon Shire 1840–1900*.

58 Pepper & De Araugo, *The Kurnai of Gippsland*, p. 76.

59 Kolodny, *The Land Before Her*, pp. 57–61.

60 Davison, *The White Woman*, p. 57.

61 Darian-Smith, 'Capturing the White Woman of Gippsland', pp. 14–34. See also Darian-Smith, ' "Rescuing" Barbara Thompson and Other White Women: Captivity narratives on Australian Frontiers', in Darian-Smith, Gunner and Nuttall (eds), *text, theory, space*, pp. 99–114.

62 Royal Commission into British Nuclear Tests in Australia, 20 November 1985. See Vol. I, Ch. 8, pp. 273–324 for details of the 1956–57 tests at Maralinga, and Vol. II, p. 613 for recommendations that access to compensation should be extended to Aborigines and civilians exposed to radiation from the tests.

63 Sykes, 'The New White Colonialism'; Ginibi, *Don't Take Your Love to Town*; McLaren, *Sweet Water—Stolen Land*; Anderson, 'Re-claiming Tru-ger-nan-ner'.

64 Sandra McKay, 'Massacre memorials "too confrontational",' *Age*, 6 January 1996, p. 1.

65 AAP report, 'Freeman lashes out over stolen generation', *Age*, 17 July 2000; Kerry Taylor and Darrin Farrant, ' "Stolen" row intensifies UN scrutiny', *Age*, 18 July 2000.

66 David Reardon and Melissa Marino, 'Canberra denies unease over Blair', *Age*, 15 July 2000; Debra Jopson and Kerry Taylor, 'Sentence law inhuman, says

Cherie Blair to UN', *Age*, 20 July 2000; Debra Jopson, 'Amnesty backs UN call for law review', *Sydney Morning Herald*, 31 July 2000.

67 Reynolds, *Fate of a Free People*, pp. 123–31, for an account of attempts at 'conciliation' and 'reconciliation' with Van Diemen's Land Aborigines by the Executive Council in Van Diemen's Land from 1828, involving John Batman and G. A. Robinson, and the issue of land control and ownership at the heart of their 'embassy of conciliation'.

8   LITERARY AND ARTISTIC VERSIONS

1 Garryowen, *The Chronicles of Early Melbourne*, Vol. II, p. 611.

2 Ossian was the literary invention of James Macpherson.

3 Wynne-Davies (ed.), *Prentice Hall Guide to English Literature*, p. 667.

4 *PPH*, 7 September 1847, Original Poetry, 'Ode to the White Woman' by Homo.

5 Brissenden, *Virtue in Distress*, pp. 91–5.

6 Goldie, *Fear and Temptation*.

7 Said, *Orientalism*, p. 94.

8 'Oo–a–deen' appeared in the *Corio Chronicle and Western Districts Advertiser* of 2, 6 and 9 October 1847. Reproduced in Van Ikin (ed.), *Australian Science Fiction*, pp. 7–27.

9 Francis Galton, *Hereditary Genius: An Inquiry into its Laws and Consequences*, London, 1869.

10 Young, *Colonial Desire*, especially pp. 62–89.

11 Healy, 'The Lemurian Nineties', p. 316.

12 Russell, 'The Heart'. The original handwritten manuscript (MS571) is held in the National Library of Australia, Canberra. A facsimile copy (MS12795, 3561/5) and typescript copy (MS 10065, bag 4, Cuthill papers), are held in La Trobe Collection, SLV. The pagination cited is from the typescript copy, as the original MS does not have page nos.

13 *ibid.*, p. 22.

14 *ibid.*, p. 24.

15 *ibid.*, p. 22.

16 *ibid.*, p. 22.

17 *ibid.*, p. 11.

18 *ibid.*, p. 15.

19 *ibid.*, p. 17.

20 Cited in Pearce, 'The Significance of the Captivity Narrative', p. 3.

21 Russell, 'The Heart', p. 21.

22 *ibid.*, p. 36.

23 *PPH*, 14 November 1843, 'Gipps' Land'. For accounts of Barbara Thomson's experiences and rescue, see Barrett, *White Blackfellows*, pp. 161–9, and Idriess, *Isles of Despair*.

24 Two inscriptions inside the front cover trace the novella's safekeeping within Russell's family: the first, a dedication from Russell to his nephew Robert Poynder, dated September 1864; the second by J. L. Russell, dated 25 October 1910, acknowledges that the work was presented to him by Robert Poynder.

25 The selective historical details gloss over Russell's chequered career as a government surveyor. Russell Street was named after Lord John Russell, Secretary of State for the Colonies. Cannon, *Historical Records of Victoria*, Vol. 3, pp. 200–7. *ADB*, Vol. 2, pp. 409–11; Garryowen, *The Chronicles of Early Melbourne*, Vol. I, p. 15.

26 Turner, 'The Captive of Gipps Land', p. 68.

27 *ibid.*, p. 178.

28 *ibid.*, p. 182.

29 Goldie, *Fear and Temptation*, p. 59. See also JanMohamed, *Manichean Aesthetics*, pp. 31–6, for a critique of colonialist representations of Africans as children, or hyperemotional and irrational creatures.

30 A public dinner in McMillan's honor was held at Port Albert in March 1856. The text of McMillan's speech is reprinted in McCombie, *History of the Colony of Victoria from its settlement to the death of Sir Charles Hotham*, pp. 79–80.

31 Turner, 'The Captive of Gipps Land', p. 183.

32 *ibid.*, p. 183.

33 Mission stations were established in Gipps Land by the Rev. John Bulmer (Lake Tyers) in 1860 and the Rev. Hagenauer (Ramahyuck, on the Avon River) in 1863. For a detailed analysis of mission stations in Gipps Land, see Attwood, Blacks and Lohans, PhD.

34 *PPH*, 1 September 1846, 'The White Females Detained by the Blacks'.

35 A. & A. MacDonald (eds), *The Poems of Alexander MacDonald*, Inverness, 1924, p. 4.

36 For an analysis of the rise of popular evangelicalism in the Highlands in the early nineteenth century, see C. Withers, *Gaelic Scotland*, Routledge, London, 1988.

37 McLean, *Lindigo*, p. 14.

38 *ibid.*, p. 14.

39 *ibid.*, p. 26.

40 *ibid.*, p. 27.

41 *Illustrated Australian News*, 1 February 1872, 'The White Captive', p. 33.

42 *Bairnsdale Advertiser*, 31 January 1905, 'Recollections of Early Gippsland', by A. McLean.

43 Howitt, 'The Lost White Woman'.

44 In Bride (ed.), *Letters from Victorian Pioneers*, p. 207, and Bonwick, *Port Phillip Settlement*, p. 491.

45 Kolodny, *The Land Before Her*, ch. 4; Derounian-Stodola & Levernier, *The Indian Captivity Narrative, 1550–1900*, pp. 45–6.

46 Gaunt, 'The Lost White Woman', p. 209.

47 *ibid.*, p. 209.

48 *ibid.*, p. 211.

49 *ibid.*, p. 211.

50 *ibid.*, p. 213.

51 *ibid.*, p. 214.

52 *ibid.*, p. 217.

53 Dixon, *Writing the Colonial Adventure*, p. 52.

54 Gaunt, *As the Whirlwind Passeth*. See especially 'Marriage by Capture', pp. 101–15.

55 Gaunt, 'The Lost White Woman', p. 216.

56 *ibid.*, p. 217.

57 Smith, *The White Missus of Arnhem Land*.

58 'Gippsland Incident', by Sidney Nolan. Reproduced in E. Lynn, *Sidney Nolan—Australia*, facing p. 52.

59 Extract from interview with Elwyn Lynn, Sydney, 21 April 1978. Cited in Lynn, *Sidney Nolan—Australia*, p. 52.

60 *ibid.*, p. 18.

61 *Argus*, 19 May 1945, 'The Sign of the Heart: A Gippsland Mystery that has never been solved' by HANS.

62 Schaffer, *In the Wake of First Contact*, pp. 138–47.

63 Duggan, *The Ash Range*, pp. 181–4.

64 *ibid.*, p. 10.

65 *ibid.*, p. 11.

66 Joan Lindsay, *Picnic at Hanging Rock*, Penguin Books Ltd, Harmondsworth, England, and Ringwood, Victoria, 1970 [1967], pp. 38–9.

67 Richard Shears, *The Lady of the Swamp*.

68 For accounts of the Azaria Chamberlain phenomenon see John Bryson, *Evil Angels* (Ringwood, 1985) and Lindy Chamberlain, *Through My Eyes* (Port Melbourne, 1990).

69 Peter Pierce, *The Country of Lost Children*.

70 Respectively: 'Buckley's Chance and None', by playwright Adam May, performed at the Carlton Courthouse, Melbourne, late July – 6 August 1994; the exhibition 'William Buckley the Wild White Man', by English-born artist Philip Davey, at Gallery 101, Collins Street, Melbourne, 24 August – 9 September 1995, catalogue with introduction by Jan Nicholl; *Age*, 20 August 1997, 'Drawing the line', interview with Jan Senbergs by Rebecca Lancashire, Metroarts, p. C7; C. Robertson, *Buckley's Hope*, Fitzroy, 1997 [Fitzroy, 1980].

71 Schaffer, *In the Wake of First Contact*, ch. 10, 'Oppositional Voices', pp. 245–57.

72 Healy, *From the Ruins of Colonialism*, p. 165.

73 Schaffer, *In the Wake of First Contact*, argues that Eliza Fraser has been used discursively to police the boundary between coloniser and colonised.

74 *Age*, 3 November 1993, 'Malouf's Objectionable Whitewash', p. 11. Greer's view was contested or defended in a spate of articles. See *Age*, 9 November 1993, 'Grumpy, petty Greer', by Suzanne Falkiner, p. 14; *Age*, 8 November 1993, 'Malouf's vision of a spiritual inheritance', by John Allen, p. 12; *Age*, 3 February 1994, 'Frank Hardy's last blast in defence of truth', by Frank Hardy, p. 14. See also Perera, 'Unspeakable Bodies'; Otto, 'Forgetting Colonialism'.

75 Hall, *The Second Bridegroom*, p. 45.

76 Hill, *Ghosting William Buckley*, p. 143.

9   LIAM DAVISON'S NOVEL *THE WHITE WOMAN*

1 Davison, *The White Woman*, pp. 8–9.

2 *ibid.*, p. 64.

[3] Davison, *La Femme Blanche*, Editions Actes Sud, 1996.
[4] The narrator, like Thomas Hill, the 'Mountain Devil', almost drowns at the mouth of the Snowy River.
[5] For post-structuralist examinations of history making, see for example Attridge, Bennington and Young (eds.), *Post-structuralism and the question of history*, and White, *Metahistory*.
[6] Davison, *The White Woman*, p. 1.
[7] *ibid.*, p. 28.
[8] *ibid.*, pp. 2–3.
[9] *ibid.*, pp. 2–3.
[10] *ibid.*, p. 3.
[11] *ibid.*, pp. 27–8.
[12] *ibid.*, p. 6.
[13] *ibid.*, p. 5. The narrator uses the phrase 'see how' three times on pp. 4–5.
[14] *ibid.*, p. 145.
[15] *ibid.*, pp. 54–6.
[16] *ibid.*, p. 13.
[17] Curtis, *Shipwreck of the Stirling Castle*.
[18] Russell, *The Genesis of Queensland*, p. 250.
[19] Conrad, *Youth* and *Heart of Darkness*, part II, p. 126.
[20] Davison, *The White Woman*, p. 37.
[21] *ibid.*, p. 132.

Select Bibliography

ARCHIVAL SOURCES

Bairnsdale Historical Museum
Pioneer file.

Bairnsdale Library
Macalister Family file, LH box 5.

Museum Victoria
Johns, R. E., Scrapbook no. 1, Indigenous Collections.

Port Albert Maritime Museum
Buckley, P. C., Journal, MS 496.
Cox, Rev. G., papers and scrapbook
Curlewis papers.
Ewing file.
Russell, Robert, letters.
Russell, Robert, watercolours of Gipps Land 1843.
Tyers, C. J., Journal, 29 January 1844 – 31 December 1845.

Public Records Office Victoria
Day Book of Native Police Corps, Narre Narre Warren, 24 January 1845 –
    20 January 1853, VPRS 5519, unit no. 1, microfilm copy.
Superintendent, Port Phillip District: Inwards correspondence, 1839–51, VPRS
    19/P; Outward registered correspondence, local, VPRS 2142, microfilm
    copy, reel 3 (July 1843 – December 1846), reel 4 (1 January 1847 – 15 July
    1851); Outward registered correspondence, to Sydney, VPRS 2142,
    microfilm copy, reel 5 (13 November 1840 – 20 April 1844), Reel 6
    (22 April 1844 – 31 December 1847).

Sale Library
Local history collection.

State Library of Victoria
Black, Niel, 'Journal of the first few months spent in Australia, September 30
    1839 – May 8 1840', MS 11519.

Buntine, John. Letters May–July 1914, including letter from C. Armstrong and M. Murray regarding the White Woman handkerchief, and newspaper cuttings. MS 13285, box 3863/5.

Cooper Index.

Cuthill, William John. Typescript copies of newspaper articles, journals, official correspondence, fictional and historical accounts concerning the White Woman (1840–1972). MS 10065, bags 1–6.

Cuthill, William John. History of Traralgon. Boxes 219/1 and 2, and 333. [No MS number on the card but probably part of Cuthill papers, MS 10065.]

Handkerchief taken by expedition in search of the White Woman, 1846, two photoprints. MS 10720, box 286/6.

'Journal of an expedition which started from Melbourne 6 March 1847 in search of a white woman supposed to be detained amongst the aborigines of Gippsland'. H4224, box 18/11 (copy at box 32/12).

Kenyon Index.

Meyrick, H. H. Collection of twenty-eight letters to relatives in England. MS 7959, Box 101/3. H15789–15816.

Russell, Robert. Photocopy of 'The Heart', a novel, May 1849. MS 12795, box 3561/5. Original held in National Library of Australia, Manuscript Collection. MS 571.

Sellars, Ella. Biographical notes on Selina Bartlett Blake (née McLeish), James Warman and Lucinda Watson, c. 1990. MS 12866, box 3630/11.

Shillinglaw papers.

BOOKS, ARTICLES AND FILMS

Adam, Ian and Helen Tiffin (eds), *Past the Last Post: Theorising Post-Colonialism and Post-Modernism*, Harvester Wheatsheaf, Hertfordshire, 1991.

Adams, John, *The Tambo Shire Centenary History*, Tambo Shire Council, Bruthen, Victoria, 1981.

——, *From these Beginnings: History of the Shire of Alberton*, Alberton Shire Council, Yarram, Victoria, 1991.

Adams, John (ed.), *Notes on Gippsland History*, 4 vols., Port Albert Maritime Museum, Victoria, 1990.

Aitken, Richard (ed.), *Macalister Landscapes: History and Heritage in Maffra Shire*, Monash Public History Group, Kapana Press in assoc. with the Centre for Gippsland Studies, Bairnsdale, Victoria, 1994.

A Melbournite of '38, 'The Early History of Victoria, Being Reminiscences of Bygone Days', *Australian Journal*, May 1874, pp. 493–9.

Alexander, Michael, *Mrs Fraser on the Fatal Shore*, Simon and Schuster, New York, 1971.

Alexander, Sally, 'Women, Class and Sexual Differences in the 1830s and 1840s: Some Reflections on the Writing of a Feminist History', *History Workshop Journal*, Issue 17, Spring 1984, pp. 125–49.

Anderson, Ian, 'Re-claiming Tru-ger-nan-ner: De-colonising the symbol', *Art Monthly*, December/February 1993–94, no. 66, pp. 10–15.

Anstruther, Ian, *The Knight and the Umbrella: An account of the Eglinton Tournament 1839*, Geoffrey Bles Ltd, London, 1963.

Arden, George, *A Sketch of Port Phillip; Being a review of the map of Australia Felix compiled, engraved and published by Thomas Ham of Melbourne*, with intro. by Thomas A. Darragh, Garravembi Press, Thumb Creek, Australia, 1991.

——, *Recent Information Respecting Port Phillip and the Promising Province of Australia Felix, in the Great Territory of New South Wales*, by the Editor of the *Port Phillip Gazette*, Melbourne. Printed at the *Gazette* Office, Australia Felix and refurbished in London by Smith, Elder & Co, 65 Cornhill, 1841.

Arens, W., *The Man-Eating Myth: Anthropology and Anthropophagy*, Oxford University Press, New York, 1979.

Ashcroft, Bill, Gareth Griffiths and Helen Tiffin, *The Empire Writes Back: Theory and practice in post-colonial literatures*, Routledge, London, 1989.

Ashcroft, Bill, Gareth Griffiths and Helen Tiffin (eds), *The Post-Colonial Studies Reader*, Routledge, London, 1995.

Ashcroft, W. D., 'Intersecting Marginalities: Post-colonialism and Feminism', *Kunapipi*, vol. XI, no. 2, 1989, pp. 23–35.

Attridge, Derek, Geoff Bennington and Robert Young (eds), *Post-structuralism and the question of history*, Cambridge University Press, Cambridge, 1987.

Attwood, Bain M., Blacks and Lohans: A Study of Aboriginal–European Relations in Gippsland in the 19th Century, PhD thesis, La Trobe University, 1984.

Attwood, Bain and John Arnold (eds), *Power, Knowledge and Aborigines*, special ed. of *Journal of Australian Studies*, La Trobe University Press in assoc. with the National Centre for Australian Studies, Monash University, 1992.

Barker, Francis, et al. (eds), *Europe and its Others, Volume two*: Proceedings of the Essex Conference on the Sociology of Literature July 1984, University of Essex, Colchester, 1985.

Barrett, Charles, *White Blackfellows: The Strange Adventures of Europeans Who Lived among Savages*, Hallcraft Publishing Co. Pty Ltd, Melbourne, 1948.

Barthes, Roland, *S/Z*, trans. Richard Miller, Hill and Wang, New York, 1974 (orig. pub. Paris, 1970).

Bassett, Jan (ed.), *Great Explorations: An Australian Anthology*, Oxford University Press, Melbourne, 1996.

Baxter, Fred, *Snake for Supper*, Lansdowne Press, Melbourne, 1968.

Bell, Agnes Paton, *Melbourne: John Batman's Village*, Cassell Australia Ltd, Melbourne, 1965.

Bennett, Lavinia Hassell, 'Account of a Journey to Gipps Land' [1844], in William Brodribb, *Recollections of an Australian Squatter 1835–1883*, Queensberry Hill Press, Melbourne, 1976, pp. 172–94.

Berndt, R. and C. H. Berndt, *The First Australians*, A Ure Smith Publication, Halstead Press, Sydney, 1952.

——, *The World of the First Australians*, Lansdowne Press, Sydney, 1964.

Bhabha, Homi K., 'Signs Taken for Wonders: Questions of Ambivalence and Authority Under a Tree Outside Delhi, May 1817', *Critical Inquiry* 12(1), 1985, pp. 144–65.

——, 'the Other Question', *Screen*, vol. 24, no. 6, 1983, pp. 18–36.

Billis, R. V. and A. S. Kenyon, *Pastoral Pioneers of Port Phillip*, 2nd ed., Stockland Press Pty Ltd, Melbourne, 1974.

Billot, C. P., *John Batman and the founding of Melbourne*, Hyland House Publishing Pty Ltd, South Yarra, 1979.

——, *Melbourne: an annotated bibliography to 1850*, Rippleside Press, Geelong, 1970.

——, *The Life and Times of John Pascoe Fawkner*, Hyland House Publishing Pty Ltd, Melbourne, 1985.

Billot, C. P. (ed.), *Melbourne's Missing Chronicle: being the Journal of Preparations for Departure to and Proceedings at Port Phillip by John Pascoe Fawkner*, Quartet Books Australia Pty Ltd, Melbourne, 1982.

Blake, L. J., *Captain Dana and the Native Police*, Neptune Press, Newtown, Victoria, 1982.

Blake, L. J. (ed.), *Letters of Charles Joseph La Trobe*, Government Printer, Melbourne, 1975.

Bonwick, James, *Port Phillip Settlement*, Sampson Low, London, 1883.

Boys, R. D., *First Years at Port Phillip 1834–1842*, Robertson and Mullens, Melbourne, 1959.

Brady, Veronica, 'When we're said and done', review of Liam Davison's *The White Woman*, in *Australian Book Review*, no. 165, October 1994, pp. 10–11.

Branca, Patricia, 'Image and Reality: The Myth of the Idle Victorian Woman', in Mary Hartman and Lois Banner, *Clio's Consciousness Raised: New Perspectives on the History of Women*, Harper Torchbooks, New York, 1974.

Brissenden, R. F., *Virtue in Distress: Studies in the Novel of Sentiment from Richardson to Sade*, Macmillan, London, 1974.

Bride, Thomas Francis (ed.), *Letters from Victorian Pioneers*, William Heinemann Ltd, Melbourne, 1898.

Brodribb, W. A., *Recollections of an Australian Squatter 1835–1883*, this ed. by John Ferguson, Sydney, 1978 (first pub. 1883 by John Woods & Co., Sydney).

Brooke-Little, J. P., *Boutell's Heraldry*, Frederick Warne and Co. Ltd, London, 1970.

Brookes, Mabel, *Riders of Time*, Macmillan of Australia Pty Ltd, Melbourne, 1967.

Brooks, Peter, *Reading for the Plot: Design and intention in narrative*, Clarendon Press, Oxford, 1984.

Broom, Richard, *The Victorians: Arriving*, Fairfax, Syme & Weldon Associates, McMahons Point, NSW, 1984.

Broome, Lady, *Colonial Memories*, Smith Elder & Co., London, 1904.

Brown, Philip L. (ed.), *Memoirs recorded at Geelong, Victoria, Australia, by Captain Foster Fyans (1790–1870)*. Transc. from holograph MS, State Library Melbourne 1962, Geelong Advertiser Pty Ltd, Geelong, 1986.

Brown, Philip L. (ed.), *The Todd Journal*, Geelong Historical Society, 1989. This book is an ed. version of the 1835 Indented Head Journal of Andrew *alias* William Todd (John Batman's recorder), illustrator J. H. Wedge.

Bunce, Daniel, *Australasiatic Reminiscences*, J. T. Hendy, Melbourne, 1857.

Buntine, W. M., 'The White Woman in Gippsland: An Incident of the Forties', *The Victorian Historical Magazine*, vol. III, June 1914, pp. 174–7.

Burstall, Tim (director) and David Williamson (screenplay), *Eliza Fraser*, Hexagon Films, Sydney, 1976.

Butlin, N. G., *Our Original Aggression: Aboriginal Populations of Southeastern Australia 1788–1850*, George Allen & Unwin, Sydney, 1983.

Cannon, Michael (ed.), *Historical Records of Victoria*, 7 vols, Foundation Series, Victorian Government Printing Office, Melbourne. Especially vol. 2b, *Aborigines and Protectors 1838–39*, 1983; vol. 3, *The Early Development of Melbourne*, 1984; and vol. 6, *The Crown, the Land and the Squatter 1835–40*, 1991.

Cannon, Michael, *Old Melbourne Town*, Loch Haven Books, Main Ridge, Victoria, 1991.

——, *Who Killed the Koories?*, William Heinemann Australia, Melbourne, 1990.

Carr, Julie, 'Cribb'd, Cabined and Confined', in Jeanette Hoorn (ed.), *Bodytrade*, Pluto Press, Sydney, 2000.

——, 'In Search of the White Woman of Gipps Land', *Australasian Victorian Studies Annual*, 1, 1995, pp. 41–50.

——, 'Tales of the White Woman', *Meridian*, vol. 15, no. 1, May 1996, pp. 77–84.

——, 'The Great "White Woman" Controversy', *La Trobe Journal*, no. 63, Autumn 1999, pp. 37–45.

——, 'The White Blackfellow', *Island*, no. 56, Spring 1993, pp. 71–2.

——, 'Winning the Gloves', *New Literatures Review*, special edition '(un)fabric/ating empire', no. 36, Winter 2000, pp. 17–34.

——, 'The Heart of Gipps Land: envisaging settlement', *Journal of Australian Studies*, no. 65, special edition 'The Vision Splendid', forthcoming.

Carter, Paul, *Living in a New Country: History, travelling and language*, Faber and Faber, London, 1992.

——, *The Road to Botany Bay: An essay in spatial history*, Faber and Faber, London 1987.

Charlot, Monica, *Victoria: The Young Queen*, Basil Blackwell Ltd, Oxford, 1991.

Chauvel, Charles (director) in collaboration with E. V. Timms, from a story by Charles Chauvel. *Uncivilized*, Expeditional Films, National Film and Sound Archive, 1936.

Clark, Ian D., *Aboriginal Languages and Clans: An Historical Atlas of Western and Central Victoria, 1800–1900*, Monash Publications in Geography, no. 37, Monash University, Melbourne, 1990.

——, *The Port Phillip Journals of George Augustus Robinson: 8 March – 7 April 1842 and 18 March – 29 April 1843*, Monash Publications in Geography no. 34, Monash University, Melbourne, 1988.

Coetzee, J. M., *Foe*, Secker and Warburg Ltd, London, 1986.

Cohen, William B. (ed.), *European Empire Building: Nineteenth-Century Imperialism*, Forum Press, St Louis, Missouri, 1980.

Collett, Barry, *Wednesdays Closest to the Full Moon: A History of South Gippsland*, Melbourne University Press, Melbourne, 1994.

Conrad, Joseph, *Youth* and *Heart of Darkness*, J. M. Dent & Sons Ltd, London, 1965, (first pub. 1902).

Cosgrove, D. and S. Daniels (eds), *The Iconography of Landscape: Essays on the Symbolic Representation, Design and Use of Past Environments*, Cambridge University Press, Cambridge 1988.

Coutts, P. J. F., *Victorian Prehistory*, vol. 2, The Victorian Aboriginals 1800 to 1860, Victorian Archaeological Survey, Ministry for Conservation, May 1981.

Cox, Kenneth, *Angus McMillan: Pathfinder*, Olinda Public Relations Pty Ltd, Olinda, 1973.

Critchett, Jan, *A 'distant field of murder': Western District Frontiers 1834–1848*, Melbourne University Press, Melbourne, 1990.

Curr, Edward M., *Recollections of Squatting in Victoria (from 1841 to 1851)*, 2nd ed. abridged with foreword and notes by Harley W. Forster, Melbourne University Press, 1965 (first pub. George Robertson, Melbourne, 1883).

Curthoys, Ann, 'Identity Crisis: Colonialism, Nation, and Gender in Australian History', *Gender & History*, vol. 5, no. 2, Summer 1993, pp. 165–76.

Curtis, John, *Shipwreck of the Stirling Castle*, George Virtue, London, 1838.

Cuthill, W. J., 'The White Woman with the Blacks in Gipps' Land', *Victorian Historical Magazine*, vol. 31, no. 1, 1960, pp. 7–25.

Darian-Smith, Kate, Roslyn Poignant and Kay Schaffer, *Captive Lives: Australian Captivity Narratives*, Working papers in Australian Studies nos 85, 86 & 87, Sir Robert Menzies Centre for Australian Studies, Institute of Commonwealth Studies, University of London, 1993.

Darian-Smith, Kate, ' "Rescuing" Barbara Thompson and Other White Women: Captivity narratives on Australian Frontiers', in Kate Darian-Smith, Liz Gunner and Sarah Nuttall (eds), *text, theory, space*, Routledge, London, 1996, pp. 99–114.

Davidson, Jim, 'Beyond the Fatal Shore: The Mythologization of Mrs Fraser', *Meanjin*, vol. 49, no. 3, Spring 1990, pp. 449–69.

Davison, Liam, 'Landscape with Words—Writing about Landscape', *Overland*, no. 134, 1994, pp. 6–10.

——, 'My first love', *Age*, Extra Features, 20 May 1995, pp. 3, 6.

——, 'The consequences of story', *Australian Book Review*, no. 165, October 1994, p. 12.

——, *The White Woman*, University of Queensland Press, St Lucia, 1994.

——, 'William Buckley: A Man of words', review of Barry Hill's *Ghosting William Buckley*, in *Overland*, no. 134, 1994, pp. 15–17.

Dawson, James, *Australian Aborigines: The Language and Customs of Several Tribes of Aborigines in the Western District of Victoria, Australia*, facs. ed. 1981, pub. by the Australian Institute of Aboriginal Studies, Canberra (original pub. George Robertson, Melbourne, Sydney and Adelaide, 1881).

Day, David, *Claiming a Continent: A new history of Australia*, rejacketed edition HarperCollins Publishers, Sydney, 1997 (first published Angus & Robertson, Australia, 1996).

Dearborn, Mary V., *Pocahontas's Daughters: Gender and Ethnicity in American Culture*, Oxford University Press, New York, 1986.

Delafield, E. M., *Ladies and Gentlemen in Victorian Fiction*, Hogarth Press, London, 1937.

Derounian-Stodola, Kathryn Zabelle and James Arthur Levernier, *The Indian Captivity Narrative, 1550–1900*, Twayne Publishers, New York, 1993.

Derrida, Jacques, *Of Grammatology*, trans. Gayatri Chakravorty Spivak, Johns Hopkins University Press, Baltimore, 1976 (orig. pub. France, 1967).

De Serville, Paul, *Port Phillip Gentlemen*, Oxford University Press, Melbourne, 1980.

Disraeli, Benjamin, *Endymion*, Australian ed. George Robertson, Melbourne, Sydney, and Adelaide, 1881.

Dixon, Robert, *Writing the Colonial Adventure: Race, Gender and Nation in Anglo-Australian Popular Fiction, 1875–1914*, Cambridge University Press, Cambridge & Melbourne, 1995.

Dixson, Miriam, *The Real Matilda: woman and identity in Australia 1788 to the present*, 3rd ed., Penguin Books Australia Ltd, Ringwood, 1994.

Donaldson, Laura E., *Decolonizing Feminisms: Race, Gender, and Empire-Building*, University of North Carolina Press, Chapel Hill, 1992.

Duggan, Laurie, *The Ash Range*, Pan Books Australia Pty Ltd, Sydney, 1987.

Dunbar, Janet, *The Early Victorian Woman: Some aspects of her life (1837–57)*, George G. Harrap & Co. Ltd, London, 1953.

Dunderdale, George, *Book of the Bush*, facs. ed. Penguin Books Australia Ltd, Ringwood, 1973 (first pub. London, *c.* 1870).

Dwyer, Barry and Neil Buchanan, *The Rescue of Eliza Fraser*, Noosa Graphica, Noosa Heads, Qld, 1986.

Eccleston, Gregory C., *Major Mitchell's 1836 Australia Felix Expedition: A re-evaluation*, Monash Publications in Geography no. 40, Monash University, Melbourne, 1992.

Eddy, J. J., *Britain and the Australian Colonies 1818–1831: The Technique of Government*, Clarendon Press, Oxford, 1969.

Elder, Bruce, *Blood on the Wattle: Massacres and Maltreatment of Australian Aborigines since 1788*, Child & Associates Publishing Pty Ltd, Frenchs Forest, 1988.

Fanon, Franz, *Black Skins, White Masks*, Grove Press, New York, 1967.

——, *Studies in a Dying Colonialism*, trans. by Haakon Chevalier, Monthly Review Press, New York, 1965 (first pub. in France, 1959).

——, *The Wretched of the Earth*, trans. by Constance Farrington, Grove Press, New York, 1968 (first pub. in France, 1961).

Fels, Marie Hansen, *Good Men and True: The Aboriginal Police of the Port Phillip District 1837–1853*, Melbourne University Press, Melbourne, 1988.

Fiedler, Leslie, *The Return of the Vanishing American*, Stein and Day, New York, 1968.

Fison, L. & Howitt A. W., *Kamilaroi and Kurnai*, facs. ed. 1991, Australian Institute of Aboriginal and Torres Strait Islander Studies (first pub. George Robertson, Melbourne, 1880).

Frankenberg, Ruth, *white women, race matters: The Social Construction of Whiteness*, University of Minnesota Press, Minneapolis, 1993.

Friedman, Norman, *Form and Meaning in Fiction*, University of Georgia Press, Athens, USA, 1975.

Frost, Lucy, *No Place for a Nervous Lady: voices from the Australian bush*, McPhee Gribble Publishers Pty Ltd, Fitzroy, 1984.

——, *A Face in the Glass: The journal and life of Annie Baxter Dawbin*, William Heinemann, Port Melbourne, 1992.

Gale, Fay (ed.), *Women's Role in Aboriginal Society*, 3rd ed., Australian Institute of Aboriginal Studies, Canberra, 1978.

Gallagher, Catherine & Thomas Laqueur, *The Making of the Modern Body: sexuality and society in the nineteenth century*, University of California Press, Berkeley & Los Angeles, 1987.

Garden, Don, *Victoria: A History*, Thomas Nelson Australia, Melbourne, 1984.

Gardner, Peter, *Gippsland Massacres: The Destruction of the Kurnai Tribe 1800–1860*, 2nd rev. ed. Ngarak Press, Ensay, Victoria, 1993 (first pub. by Warragul Education Centre, Warragul, 1983).

——, 'Massacres of Aboriginals in Gippsland 1840–1850', *Historian*, 27, October 1975, pp. 19–24.

——, *Our Founding Murdering Father: Angus McMillan and the Kurnai tribe of Gippsland 1839–1865*, Ngarak Press, Ensay, Victoria, 1990.

——, 'The Journals of de Villiers and Warman: the expedition to recover the captive white woman', *Victorian Historical Journal*, vol. 50, 1979, pp. 89–97.

——, *Through Foreign Eyes: European Perceptions of the Kurnai Tribe of Gippsland*, Centre for Gippsland Studies, Gippsland Institute of Advanced Education, Churchill, 1988.

Garryowen [Edmund Finn], *The Chronicles of Early Melbourne 1835 to 1852 Historical, Anecdotal and Personal*, 2 vols. centennial ed., Fergusson and Mitchell, Melbourne, 1888.

Gates, Henry Louis Jr, Editor's Introduction: 'Writing "Race" and the Difference It Makes', *Critical Inquiry*, 12 (Autumn 1985), pp. 1–20.

Gaunt, Mary, 'The Lost White Woman', in *The Ends of the Earth*, T. Werner Laurie Ltd, London (u.d., 1916?), pp. 209–17.

——, *As the Whirlwind Passeth*, John Murray, London, 1923.

Gernsheim, H. and A., *Queen Victoria: A Biography in Word and Picture*, Longmans, London, 1959.

Gibson, Ross, *South of the West: Postcolonialism and the Narrative Construction of Australia*, Indiana University Press, Bloomington and Indianapolis, 1992.

Ginibi, Ruby Langford, *Don't Take Your Love to Town*, Penguin Books Australia Ltd, Ringwood, 1988.

Goldie, Terry, 'An Aboriginal Present: Canadian and Australian Literature in the 1920s', *World Literature Written in English*, vol. 23, no.1, 1984, pp. 88–96.

——, *Fear and Temptation: The Image of the Indigene in Canadian, Australian and New Zealand Literatures*, McGill–Queen's University Press, Montreal, 1989.

Grant, James and Geoffrey Serle, *The Melbourne Scene 1803–1956*, Melbourne University Press, Melbourne, 1957.

Green, Oswald, *The Gippsland Lakes*, Rigby Ltd, Melbourne, 1978.

Greig, A. W., 'Melbourne in 1839', *The Victorian Historical Magazine*, vol. XVII, no. 2, November 1938, pp. 41–51.

Griffiths, Tom, *Hunters and Collectors: The Antiquarian Imagination in Australia*, Cambridge University Press, Cambridge, New York and Melbourne, 1996.

Gross, Alan, *Charles Joseph La Trobe*, Melbourne University Press, Melbourne 1956 (reprinted 1980).

Gurner, Henry Field, *Chronicle of Port Phillip: Now the colony of Victoria from 1770 to 1840*, intro. and ed. by Hugh Anderson, Red Rooster Press, Melbourne, 1978 (first pub. George Robertson, Melbourne, 1876).

Haggard, H. Rider, *Three Adventure Novels of H. Rider Haggard: She, King Solomon's Mines, Allan Quatermain*, Dover Publications, Inc., New York, 1951.

Haggis, Jane, 'Gendering Colonialism or Colonising Gender? Recent Women's Studies Approaches to White Women and the History of British Colonialism', *Women's Studies International Forum*, vol. 13, no. 1–2, 1990, pp. 105–15.

Hancock, Marguerite (ed.) *Glimpses of Life in Victoria*, By A Resident [John Hunter, Kerr], Miegunyah Press, Melbourne University Press, 1996 (first pub. 1876).

Hall, Rodney, *The Second Bridegroom*, McPhee Gribble, Penguin Books Australia Ltd, Ringwood, 1991.

Harrison, Jessie B., *Some Memories of Old Gippsland and its Earliest Pioneers*, from the writings of Rev. William Spence Login, no publisher details (1924?).

Harvey, P. *The Earliest Located Steamship Wreck in Australia—Paddle Steamer Clonmel*, Vic. Arch. Survey Occasional Report Series No. 22, Ministry for Planning and Environment, Melbourne, November 1985.

Hassall, A. J., 'The Making of a Colonial Myth: The Mrs. Fraser Story in Patrick White's "A Fringe of Leaves": and Andre Brink's "An Instant in the Wind" ', *Ariel*, vol. 18, no. 3, July 1987, pp. 3–28.

Haydon, G. H., *Five Years' Experience in Australia Felix*, London, 1846.

Healy, Chris, *From the Ruins of Colonialism: History as Social Memory*, Cambridge University Press, Cambridge & Melbourne, 1997.

Healy, J. J., *Literature and the Aborigine in Australia*, University of Queensland Press, St Lucia, 1989.

——, 'The Lemurian Nineties', *Australian Literary Studies* 8, no. 3, May 1978, pp. 307–16.

Hendricks, Margo and Patricia Parker (eds), *Women, 'Race,' and Writing in the Early Modern Period*, Routledge, London, 1994.

Hercus, Luise Anno, *This is What Happened: historical narratives*, Australian Institute of Aboriginal Studies, Canberra, 1986.

Hermann, George, 'The Broken Honeymoon: An Extraordinary Tale of a White Woman among the Blacks', *Life Magazine*, Melbourne, 1 August 1913, pp. 135–8.

Hetherington, John, *Witness to Things Past: Stone, Brick, Wood and Men in Early Victoria*, F. W. Cheshire Pty Ltd, Melbourne, 1964.

Hill, Barry, *Ghosting William Buckley*, William Heinemann, Australia, Port Melbourne, 1993.

Hill, Ernestine, *The Great Australian Loneliness*, Robertson and Mullens Ltd, Melbourne, 1940.

Hobson, A., *Imperialism: A Study*, Ann Arbor Paperbacks, University of Michigan Press, Ann Arbor, 1965.

Hodes, Martha, *White Women, Black Men*, Yale University Press, New Haven and London, 1997.

Hodge, Bob and Vijay Mishra, *Dark Side of the Dream: Australian literature and the postcolonial mind*, Allen & Unwin, North Sydney, 1991.

Hogg, Garry, *Cannibalism and Human Sacrifice*, Robert Hale Ltd, London, 1958.

Homo, 'Ode to the White Woman', *Port Phillip Herald*, 7 September 1847.

Hopkins, Andrea, *Knights: The complete story of the age of chivalry, from historical fact to tales of romance and poetry*, Collins and Brown Ltd, London, 1990.

Howitt, A. W., *The Native Tribes of South–East Australia*, Macmillan, London, 1904.

Howitt, Mary, 'The Lost White Woman: A Pioneer's Yarn', *Australasian*, 18 December 1897, p. 1356.

Howitt, William, *Colonization and Christianity: a popular history of the treatment of the natives by the Europeans in all their colonies*, Longman, Orme, Brown, Green & Longmans, London, 1838.

Huggan, Graham, *Territorial Disputes: Maps and Mapping Strategies in Contemporary Canadian and Australian Fiction*, University of Toronto Press, Toronto, 1994.

Hughes, Robert, *American Visions: The Epic History of Art in America*, Harvill Press, London, 1997.

———, *The Fatal Shore*, Collins Harvill, London, 1987.

Hulme, Peter, *Colonial Encounters: Europe and the native Caribbean 1492–1797*, Methuen, London, 1986.

Humphreys, H. M., *Men of the Times in Australia: Victorian Series 1878*, McCarron Bird & Co., Melbourne, 1878.

Huttenback, Robert A., *Racism and Empire: White Settlers and Colored Immigrants in the British Self-Governing Colonies 1830–1910*, Cornell University Press, Ithaca, 1976.

Huxley, Julian (ed.), *T. H. Huxley's Diary of the Voyage of the HMS Rattlesnake*, ed. from the unpub. manuscript, Doubleday, Doran & Company Inc. New York, Kraus Reprint Co., 1972.

Idriess, Ion L., *Isles of Despair*, Angus and Robertson, Sydney and London, 1947.

Inglis, Amirah, *Not a White Woman Safe: sexual anxiety and politics in Port Moresby 1920–1934*, Australian National University Press, Canberra, 1974.

Jackamos, Alick and Derek Fowell, *Living Aboriginal History of Victoria: Stories in the Oral Tradition*, Museum of Victoria, University of Cambridge Press, Cambridge, 1991.

Jameson, Fredric, *The Political Unconscious: Narrative as Socially Symbolic Act*, Methuen, London, 1981.

JanMohamed, Abdul R., *Manichean Aesthetics: The Politics of Literature in Colonial Africa*, University of Massachusetts Press, Amherst, 1983.

——, 'The Economy of Manichean Allegory: The Function of Racial Difference in Colonialist Literature', *Critical Inquiry*,12(1), 1985, pp. 59–87.

Janson, Susan and Stuart Macintyre (eds), *Through White Eyes*, Allen & Unwin, Sydney, 1990.

Jayawardena, Kumari, *The White Woman's Other Burden: Western Women and South Asia During British Rule*, Routledge, New York and London, 1995.

Jeffrey, Betty, *White Coolies*, Panther Books Ltd, London, new edition 1959 (first published in Great Britain by Angus & Robertson Ltd, 1954).

Johns, Flora, *From Bundalaguah to Marlay Point* (no publication details). Copy in Bairnsdale Library.

J. R. M., 'A Lay of Lament', *Port Phillip Herald*, 29 September 1846.

Katz, Wendy R., *Rider Haggard and the Fiction of Empire: a critical study of British imperial fiction*, Cambridge University Press, Cambridge, 1987.

Kenyon, A. S., 'The Aboriginal Protectorate of Port Phillip', *Victorian Historical Magazine*, vol. 12, no. 3, March 1928.

——, 'The Port Phillip Association', *Victorian Historical Magazine*, vol. 16, no. 3, May 1937, pp. 102–14.

Kerr, William, *Melbourne Almanac and Port Phillip Directory for 1841*, facs. reprint, Lansdown Slattery & Company, Mona Vale, NSW, 1978 (originally printed at the *Herald* Office, Elizabeth Street, Melbourne, 1841).

Kestler, Frances Roe (compiled by), *The Indian Captivity Narrative: A Woman's View*, Garland Publishing Inc., New York, 1990.

Kiddle, Margaret, *Men of Yesterday: A Social History of the Western District of Victoria 1834–1890*, Melbourne University Press, Melbourne, 1967.

King, Bruce, *The New English Literatures: cultural nationalism in a changing world*, Macmillan Press Ltd, London, 1980.

Kingsley, Henry, *The Recollections of Geoffry Hamlyn*, Lloyd O'Neil Pty Ltd, Hawthorn, 1970 (first pub. 1859).

Kirkland, Mrs, 'Life in the Bush' from *Chambers's Miscellany*, 1845, in Hugh Anderson *The Flowers of the Field: A history of Ripon Shire*, Hill of Content Publishing Co. Pty Ltd, Melbourne, 1969, pp. 173–214.

Kolodny, Annette, *The Land Before Her: Fantasy and Experience of the American Frontiers, 1630–1860*, University of North Carolina Press, Chapel Hill, 1984.

——, *The Lay of the Land: Metaphor as Experience in the History of American Life and Letters*, University of North Carolina Press, Chapel Hill, 1975.

Lang, James Dunmore, *Phillipsland; or the country hitherto designated Port Phillip: Its present condition and prospects as a highly eligible field for emigration*, Thomas Constable, Edinburgh, 1847.

——, *An Historical and Statistical Account of New South Wales from the founding of the colony in 1788 to the present day*, 2 vols. 4th ed., Sampson, Low, Marston, Low & Searle, London, 1875.

Ledwell, Jane, review of Liam Davison's *The White Woman*, in *Span*, no. 39, October 1994, pp. 93–5.

Lee, Sidney, *Queen Victoria: A Biography*, Smith, Elder & Co., London, 1902.

Lemon, Andrew and Marjorie Morgan, *Poor Souls, They Perished: The Cataraqui, Australia's Worst Shipwreck*, Australian Scholarly Publishing, North Melbourne, 1986.

Lerner, Laurence, *The Literary Imagination*, The Harvester Press, Sussex, 1982.

Levi-Strauss, Claude, *Myth and Meaning*, University of Toronto Press, Canada, 1978.

——, *The Raw and the Cooked*, trans. by John & Doreen Weightman, Jonathan Cape, London, 1970.

Loney, Jack, *An Atlas History of Australian Shipwrecks*, A. H. & A. W. Reed Pty Ltd, Frenchs Forest, Sydney, 1981.

——, *Victorian Shipwrecks: All wrecks in Victorian waters and Bass Strait, including King Island and the Kent Group*, Hawthorn Press, Melbourne, 1971.

Lovell-Smith, R., 'Out of the Hair Tent: Notes further to Elizabeth Gitter's "The Power of Women's Hair in the Victorian Imagination",' *Australasian Victorian Studies Annual*, vol. I, 1995, pp. 67–76.

Lumholtz, Carl Sofus, *Among Cannibals*, Australian National University Press, Canberra, 1980 (first pub. London: J. Murray 1889).

Lynn, Elwyn, *Sidney Nolan—Australia*, Bay Books Pty Ltd, Rushcutters Bay, 1979.

McCaughey, Davis, Naomi Perkins and Angus Trumble, *Victoria's Colonial Governors 1839–1900*, Miegunyah Press, Melbourne University Press, Melbourne, 1993.

McCombie, Thomas, *History of the Colony of Victoria from its settlement to the death of Sir Charles Hotham*, Melbourne and Sydney: Sands and Kenny. London: Chapman & Hall, 1858.

——, *Arabin or the Adventures of a Colonist in New South Wales*, G. Slater, London, 1850.

McCorquodale, John, *Aborigines and the Law: A Digest*, Aboriginal Studies Press, Canberra 1987.

Mackaness, George (ed.), *George Augustus Robinson's Journey into South-Eastern Australia, 1844 with George Henry Haydon's Narrative of Part of the Same Journey*, Australian Historical Monographs, privately printed for the Author by D. S. Ford, Sydney, 1941.

Mackirdy, Mrs Archibald [Oliver Malvery] and W. N. Willis, *The White Slave Market*, Stanley Paul & Co., London, 16th ed., 1912.

McLaren, Philip, *Sweet Water—Stolen Land*, University of Queensland Press, St Lucia, 1993.

McLean, Angus, *Lindigo, the White Woman; or, The Highland Girl's Captivity Among the Australian Blacks*, H. T. Dwight, Melbourne, 1866.

McLean, Ian, *White Aborigines: Identity Politics in Australian Art*, Cambridge University Press, Cambridge, New York, Melbourne, 1998.

McNab, Robert, *The Old Whaling Days: A History of Southern New Zealand from 1830 to 1840*, Whitcombe & Tombs Limited, Christchurch, 1913.

McNicoll, Ronald, *Number 36 Collins Street: Melbourne Club 1838–1988*, Allen & Unwin/Haynes, Sydney, 1988.

——, *The Early Years of the Melbourne Club*, Hawthorn Press, Melbourne, 1976.

Maes-Jelinek, Hena, 'Fictional Breakthrough and the Unveiling of "unspeakable rites" in Patrick White's *A Fringe of Leaves* and Wilson Harris's *Yurokon*', *Kunapipi*, vol. II, no. 2, pp. 33–43.

Mahood, M. M., *The Colonial Encounter*, Rex Collings, London, 1977.

Malouf, David, *Remembering Babylon*, Random House, Australia, 1993.

Marples, Morris, *White Horses and Other Hill Figures*, Alan Sutton Publishing Ltd, Gloucestershire, 1981 (first pub. 1949).

Martin, Susan K., 'Good Girls Die; Bad Girls Don't', *Australasian Victorian Studies Annual*, vol. I, 1995, pp. 11–22.

Massola, Aldo, *Bunjil's Cave: Myths, legends and superstitions of the Aborigines of South-East Australia*, Lansdowne Press, Melbourne, 1968.

——, *Journey into Aboriginal Victoria*, Rigby, Adelaide, 1969.

——, 'The Challicum Bun-yip', *Victorian Naturalist*, vol. 74, no. 6, October 1957, pp. 76–81.

Matthews, John, *The Grail: Quest for the eternal*, Thames & Hudson, London, 1981.

Melbourne 1840–1900 "The Phenomenal City", Catalogue from a joint exhibition from the collections of the State Library of Victoria and the Melbourne City Council, State Library of Victoria, 18 July – 7 October 1984, Ruskin Press (n.d.).

Memmi, Albert, *The Colonizer and the Colonized*, trans. Howard Greenfield, Beacon Press, Boston, 1967.

Millis, Roger, *Waterloo Creek: the Australia Day massacre of 1838, George Gipps and the British Conquest of New South Wales*, McPhee Gribble, Melbourne, 1992.

Mitford, Jessica, *Grace Had an English Heart*, Viking, Penguin Books Ltd, Middlesex, 1988.

Morgan, John, *The Life and Adventures of William Buckley: Thirty-two years a wanderer amongst the aborigines of the unexplored country round Port Phillip*, Australian National University Press, Canberra, 1980.

Morgan, Patrick, *Shadow and Shine: An Anthology of Gippsland Literature*, Centre for Gippsland Studies, Gippsland Institute of Advanced Education, Churchill, 1988.

——, *The Literature of Gippsland: The Social and Historical Context of Early Writings, with Bibliography*, Centre for Gippsland Studies, Gippsland Institute of Advanced Education, Churchill, Victoria, rev. ed., 1986.

Morrison, Toni, *Playing in the Dark: whiteness and the literary imagination*, Harvard University Press, 1992.

Mouritz, J. J., *Port Phillip Directory, 1847*, first facs. reprint pub. by Library of Australian History, North Sydney, 1979 (originally printed at *Herald* office, Melbourne, 1847).

Muecke, Stephen, *Textual Spaces: Aboriginality and cultural studies*, New South Wales University Press Ltd, Kensington, 1992.

Meyers, Jeffrey, *Fiction and the Colonial Experience*, Rowman and Littlefield Inc., Totowa, NJ, 1968.

Mudrooroo [Colin Johnson], *Dr Wooreddy's Prescription for Enduring the Ending of the World*, Hyland House, Melbourne, 1983.

Namais, June, *White Captives*, University of North Carolina Press, Chapel Hill, 1993.

Narrative of the Capture, Suffering, and Miraculous Escape of Mrs Eliza Fraser, Charles S. Webb, New York, 1837.

New, William H., *Among Worlds*, Press Porcepic, Erin, Ontario, Canada, 1975.

Niall, Brenda, *Georgiana: A Biography of Georgiana McCrae, Painter, Diarist, Pioneer*, Melbourne University Press, Melbourne, 1994.

Obeyesekere, Gananath, *The Apotheosis of Captain Cook: European Mythmaking in the Pacific*, Princeton University Press, New Jersey, 1992.

'"Oo–a–deen": or, the Mysteries of the Interior Unveiled', Anonymous (1847), in Van Ikin (ed.), *Australian Science Fiction*, University of Queensland Press, St Lucia, 1982, pp. 7–27.

Otto, Peter, 'Forgetting Colonialism', review of David Malouf's *Remembering Babylon*, *Meanjin*, vol. 52, no. 3, Spring 1993, pp. 545–58.

Parry, Benita, 'Problems in Current Theories of Colonial Discourse', *Oxford Literary Review* 9 (1&2), 1987.

Pascoe, Rob, *The Manufacture of Australian History*, Oxford University Press, Melbourne, 1979.

Payne, Sharon, Imagining Gippsland: The uses of 'The White Woman of Gippsland' in claiming regional identity, Honours thesis, Department of History, La Trobe University, 1992.

Pearce, Roy Harvey, *Savagism and Civilization: A study of the Indian and the American Mind*, University of California Press, California, 1988 (rev. ed. of *The Savages of America*, 1953).

—— , 'The Significances of the Captivity Narrative', *American Literature*, vol. 19, 1947–1948 [reprinted by Kraus Reprint Ltd, Nendeln, Leichtenstein, 1966], pp. 1–20.

Pepper, Phillip, in collaboration with Tess De Araugo, *The Kurnai of Gippsland*, Hyland House Publishing Pty Ltd, South Yarra, 1985.

Perera, Suvendrini, 'Unspeakable Bodies: Representing the Aboriginal in Australian Critical Discourse', *Meridian*, vol. 13, no. 1, May 1994, pp. 15–26.

Petersen, Kirsten Holst & Anna Rutherford (eds), *A Double Colonization: colonial and post-colonial women's writing*, Dangaroo Press, Sydney, 1986.

Pierce, Peter, *The Country of Lost Children: An Australian Anxiety*, Cambridge University Press, Cambridge, New York, Melbourne, 1999.

Porter, Hal, *Bairnsdale: Portrait of an Australian Country Town*, John Ferguson Pty Ltd, St Ives, NSW, 1977.

Porteus, Stanley D., *Providence Ponds: A novel of early Australia*, reprinted 1989 by James Yeates & Sons (Printing) Pty Ltd for the Scott Family Reunion Committee, Bairnsdale.

Praed, Mrs Campbell, *Fugitive Anne*, R. F. Fenno & Co, New York, 1904.

Pratt, Mary Louise, *Imperial Eyes: Travel Writing and Transculturation*, Routledge, London & New York, 1992.

Pratt, Minnie Bruce, 'Identity: Skin Blood Heart', in *Yours in Struggle: Three Feminist Perspectives on Anti-Semitism and Racism*, Long Haul Press, New York, 1984.

Price, A. Grenfell, *White Settlers and Native Peoples: an historical study of racial contacts between English-speaking whites and Aboriginal peoples in the United States, Canada, Australia and New Zealand*, Cambridge University Press, Cambridge, 1949.

Presland, Gary (ed. and intro.), *Journals of G. A. Robinson, January 1840 – March 1840*, extracts of manuscripts held in Mitchell Library, Sydney. Records of the Victorian Archaeological Survey, 2nd ed., no. 5, July 1977.

——, *Journals of G. A. Robinson, May–August 1841*, extracts of manuscripts held in Mitchell Library, Sydney. Records of the Victorian Archaeological Survey, no. 11, October 1980.

——, *The Land of the Kulin: Discovering the Lost Landscape and the First People of Port Phillip*, McPhee Gribble/Penguin Books, Fitzroy, 1985.

——, *Aboriginal Melbourne: The lost land of the Kulin People*, McPhee Gribble Publishers, Penguin Books Australia Ltd, Ringwood, 1994.

Priestly, Susan *The Victorians: Making Their Mark*, Fairfax, Syme & Weldon Assoc., McMahon's Point, 1984.

Probyn, Fiona, 'Interview with Liam Davison, Author of *The White Woman*', *New Literatures Review*, 32, Winter 1996, pp. 59–70.

Pybus, Cassandra, 'Searching for the chimera', review of Liam Davison's *The White Woman*, *Age*, 1 October 1994, Saturday Extra Books, p. 7.

Pyke, William T., *Thirty Years among The Blacks of Australia: the life and adventures of William Buckley, the runaway convict*, George Routledge & Sons Ltd, London, 1904.

Raskin, Jonah, *The Mythology of Imperialism*, Random House, New York, 1971.

Reece, R. H. W., *Aborigines and Colonists*, Sydney University Press, Sydney, 1974.

Rees, Barbara, *The Victorian Lady*, Gordon & Cremonesi, London, 1977.

Reynolds, Henry, *Fate of a Free People: A Radical Re-examination of the Tasmanian Wars*, Penguin Books Australia Ltd, Ringwood, 1995.

——, *Frontier*, Allen and Unwin, North Sydney, 1987.

——, *The Law of the Land*, Penguin Books Australia Ltd, Ringwood, 1987.

——, *With the White People: The crucial role of Aborigines in the exploration and development of Australia*, Penguin Books Australia Ltd, Ringwood, 1990.

Richardson, John, *The Lady Squatters*, Shire of Bellarine, Drysdale, Victoria (n.d.)

Ricks, Cappy, ' "Me Um White Mary": A White Woman Held Prisoner by the Blacks of the North for 36 Years', *Australian Life Digest*, 1 June 1938, pp. 73–7.

Robertson, Craig, *Buckley's Hope*, 2nd ed., Scribe Publications, Fitzroy, 1997 [1980].

Robinson, Fergus and Barry York, *The Black Resistance: An introduction to the history of the Aborigines' struggle against British Colonialism*, Widescope International Publishers Pty Ltd, Camberwell, Vic., 1977.

Roeg, Nicolas (director and photographer) and Edward Bond (screenplay), *Walkabout*, Max L. Raab-Si Litvinoff Films Pty Ltd., Sydney, 1971.

Rogers, G. and Nelly Helyar, *Lonely Graves of the Gippsland Goldfields and Greater Gippsland*, E. Gee Printers, Bairnsdale, 1994.

Roe, Michael, *Quest for Authority in Eastern Australia 1835–1851*, Melbourne University Press, Melbourne, 1965.

Rose, Deborah Bird 'Nature and Gender in Outback Australia', *History and Anthropology*, 1992, Vol. 5, No. 3–4, pp. 403–25.

Ross, C. Stuart, *Colonization and Church Work in Victoria*, Melville, Mullen & Slade, Melbourne & London, Wise, Caffin & Co., Dunedin, 1891.

Rowcroft, Charles, *Tales of the Colonies: The Australian Crusoes; or, The Adventures of An English Settler and his Family in the Wilds of Australia*, Willis P. Hazard, Philadelphia, 1856, 6th ed., London.

Rowley, Charles D., *Outcasts in White Australia*, Penguin Books, Ringwood, 1970.

——, *Recovery: The Politics of Aboriginal Reform*, Penguin Books, Ringwood, 1986.

Rush, Desmond, The White Woman of Gippsland: Rumour and Anxiety, MA thesis, Department of History, University of Melbourne, 1994.

Russell, Henry Stuart, *The Genesis of Queensland*, facs. reprint Vintage Books, Toowoomba, 1989 (first pub. Turner & Henderson, Sydney, 1888).

Russell, Penny, *A Wish of Distinction: Colonial Gentility and Femininity*, Melbourne University Press, Melbourne, 1994.

Said, Edward, *Orientalism*, Pantheon, New York, 1978.

——, *The World, The Text, and the Critic*, Harvard University Press, Cambridge, Mass., 1983.

Samuel, Raphael (ed.), *Patriotism: The Making and Unmaking of British National Identity*, Routledge, 3 vols, London and New York, 1989.

Sanday, Peggy Reeves, *Divine Hunger: Cannibalism as a cultural system*, Cambridge University Press, Cambridge, 1986.

Sanders, Valerie, *The Private Lives of Victorian Women: autobiography in nineteenth-century England*, Harvester Wheatsheaf, Hertfordshire, 1989.

Schaffer, Kay, 'Australian Mythologies: The Eliza Fraser Story and Constructions of the Feminine in Patrick White's *A Fringe of Leaves* and Sidney Nolan's "Eliza Fraser" Paintings', *Kunapipi*, vol. XI, no. 2, 1989, pp. 1–15.

——, 'Eliza Frazer's Trial by Media', *Antipodes*, December 1991, vol. 5, no. 2, pp. 114–20.

——, *In the Wake of First Contact: The Eliza Fraser Stories*, Cambridge University Press, Cambridge, 1995.

——, 'The Eliza Fraser Story and Constructions of Gender, Race and Class in Australian Culture', *Hecate* (Special Issue), vol. 17, no. 1, 1991, pp. 136–49.

——, *Women and the Bush: Forces of Desire in the Australian Cultural Tradition*, Cambridge University Press, Melbourne, 1988.

Scott, Sir Walter, *Saint Valentine's Day; or, The Fair Maid of Perth*, parts I & II, vol. 43, Waverley Novels, Adam and Charles Black, Edinburgh, 1878.

Shaw, A. G. L., *A History of The Port Phillip District: Victoria Before Separation*, Miegunyah Press, Melbourne University Press, Melbourne, 1996.

Shaw, A. G. L. (ed.), *Gipps–La Trobe Correspondence 1839–1846*, Miegunyah Press, Melbourne University Press, Melbourne, 1989.

Shears, Richard, *The Lady of the Swamp*, Sphere Books, Thomas Nelson Australia, Melbourne, 1981.

Shoemaker, Adam, *Black Words White Page: Aboriginal Literature 1929–1988*, University of Queensland Press, St Lucia, 1989.

Slemon, Stephen and Helen Tiffin (eds), *After Europe: critical theory and post-colonial writing*, Dangaroo Press, Sydney, 1989.

Slotkin, Richard, *Regeneration through Violence: Mythology of the American Frontier, 1600–1860*, Wesleyan University Press, Middletown, Conn., 1973.

Smith, Alex, *The White Missus of Arnhem Land: A true story*, NTU Press, Northern Territory University, Darwin, 1990.

Smith-Rosenberg, Carroll, 'Captured Subjects/Savage Others: Violently Engendering the New American', *Gender and History*, vol. 5, no. 2, Summer 1993, pp. 177–95.

Smith, Sidonie, *A Poetics of Women's Autobiography: Marginality and the Fictions of Self-Representation*, Indiana University Press, 1987.

Spivak, Gayatri Chakravorty, *In Other Worlds: essays in cultural politics*, Routledge, New York & London, 1988.

——, 'Criticism, Feminism, and the Institution' and 'The Post-colonial Critic', in Sarah Harasym (ed.), *The Post-colonial Critic: Interviews, Strategies, Dialogues*, Routledge, New York & London, 1990, pp. 1–16, 67–74.

——, 'Three Women's Texts and a Critique of Imperialism', *Critical Inquiry*, 12 (Autumn 1985), pp. 243–61.

Spreadborough, Robert and Hugh Anderson, *Victorian Squatters*, Red Rooster Press, Ascot Vale, 1983.

Stone, Sharman (ed.), *Aborigines in White Australia: A documentary history of the attitudes affecting official policy and the Australian Aborigine 1697–1973*, Heinemann Educational Australia Pty Ltd, South Yarra, 1974.

Street, Brian V., *The savage in literature: representations of 'primitive' society in English fiction 1858–1920*, Routledge & Kegan Paul Ltd, London, 1975.

Strzelecki, P. E. De, *Physical Description of New South Wales and Van Diemen's Land*, Longman, Brown, Green & Longmans, London, 1845.

Sturma, Michael, 'Alien Abductions', *History Today*, January 2000, pp. 14–15.

Sullivan, Martin, *Men and Women of Port Phillip*, Hale & Iremonger, Sydney, 1985.

Sykes, Bobbi, 'The New White Colonialism', *Meanjin*, Aboriginal Issue, vol. 36, no. 4, December 1977, pp. 421–7.

Syme, Marten A., *Shipping Arrivals and Departures Victorian Ports*, vol. I, 1798–1845, Roebuck Books, Melbourne, 1984.

Tacey, David, 'Dreaming our Myths Onwards', *Island*, Issue 53, Summer 1992.

'The White Captive', *Illustrated Australian News*, 1 February 1872, p. 33.

Thomas, Glen, 'Post-Colonial Interrogations: The coloniser and the colonised in two Australian novels', *Social Alternatives*, vol. 12, no. 3, October 1993.

Thompson, Kym, 'A History of the Aboriginal People of East Gippsland'. A report prepared for the Land Conservation Council, Victoria, 1985.

Thomson, Patricia, *The Victorian Heroine: A changing ideal 1837–1873*, Greenwood Press Publishers, Conn., 1978.

Tiffin, Chris and Alan Lawson (eds), *De-Scribing Empire: Post-colonialism and Textuality*, Routledge, London, 1994.

Tiffin, Helen, 'Post-Colonial Literatures and Counter-Discourse', *Kunapipi* 9 (3), 1987.

Tonkinson, Myrna, 'Sisterhood or Aboriginal Servitude? Black Women and White women on the Australian Frontier', *Aboriginal History*, vol. 12, no. 1, 1988, pp. 27–40.

Turner, Henry Gyles, 'The Captive of Gipps Land', published anonymously in *Illustrated Journal of Australasia*, vol. II, January–June,1857, pp. 18–23, 63–73, 125–33 and 175–83.

Vargish, Thomas, *The Providential Aesthetic in Victorian Fiction*, University Press of Virginia, Charlottesville, 1985.

Walker, R. B., *The Newspaper Press in New South Wales, 1803–1920*, Sydney University Press, Sydney, 1976.

Walker, Sylvester W. [Coo-ee], *The Silver Queen*, 2nd ed., John Ouseley, London, 1908.

Watson, Don, *Caledonia Australis: Scottish highlanders on the frontier of Australia*, Collins, Sydney, 1984.

Weidenhofer, Maggie (ed.), *Colonial Ladies*, Currey O'Neil Ross Pty Ltd, South Yarra, 1985.

Withers, Charles W. J., *Gaelic Scotland: The Transformation of a Culture Region*, Routledge, London, 1988.

Wells, John, *Gippsland: people, a place and their past*, Landmark Press, Drouin, 1986.

——, *More Colourful Tales of Old Gippsland*, Rigby Publishers, Melbourne, 1980.

Westgarth, William, *Australia Felix: or A Historical and Descriptive Account of the Settlement of Port Phillip, New South Wales*, Edinburgh: Oliver and Boyd; London: Simpkin, Marshall & Co., 1848.

——, *Personal Recollections of Early Melbourne and Victoria*, George Robertson & Co., Melbourne and Sydney, 1888.

——, *Victoria; Late Australia Felix or Port Phillip District of New South Wales*, Edinburgh: Oliver & Boyd; London: Simpkin, Marshall & Co., 1853.

White, Hayden, *Metahistory*, Johns Hopkins University Press, Maryland, 1973.

——, *The Content of the Form: Narrative Discourse and Historical Representation*, The Johns Hopkins University Press, Maryland, 1987.

——, 'The Historical Text as Literary Artefact', *Clio* 3, no. 3, 1974, p. 278.

White, Hayden (ed.), *The Uses of History*, Wayne State University Press, Detroit, 1968.

White, Patrick, *A Fringe of Leaves*, Penguin Books, London, 1977.

Wiencke, Shirley W., *When the Wattles Bloom Again: The Life and Times of William Barak, Last Chief of the Yarra Yarra Tribe*, Shirley W. Wiencke, Woori Yallock, Victoria, 1984.

Wilson, John (ed.), *The Official History of the Avon Shire: 1840–1900*, Stratford, Victoria, 1951, repub. by Stratford and District Historical Society, 1991.

Wolfe, Patrick, 'On Being Woken Up: The Dreamtime in Anthropology and in Australian Settler Culture', *Comparative Studies in Society and History*, vol. 33, no. 2, April 1991.

Woodham-Smith, Cecil, *Queen Victoria: Her Life and Times*, vol. 1, 1819–1861, Hamish Hamilton, London, 1972.

Worsnop, Thomas, *The Prehistoric Arts, Manufactures, Works, Weapons, etc., of the Aborigines of Australia*, C. E. Bristow, Adelaide, 1897.

Wynne-Davies, M. (ed.), *Prentice Hall Guide to English Literature*, Bloomsbury Publishing Ltd., New York, 1990.

Young, Robert, *Colonial Desire: Hybridity in Theory, Culture and Race*, Routledge, London and New York, 1994.

Index